BATTLES OF THE
REVOLUTIONARY WAR

1775-1781

MAJOR BATTLES AND CAMPAIGNS

John S. D. Eisenhower, General Editor

MAJOR BATTLES AND CAMPAIGNS

BATTLES OF THE REVOLUTIONARY WAR

1775-1781

by W. J. Wood

Lieutenant Colonel,
United States Army (Ret.)

With an Introduction by
John S. D. Eisenhower

DA CAPO PRESS
A Member of the Perseus Books Group

Cataloging-in-Publication data for this book is available from the Library of Congress.

Second Da Capo Press edition 2003

This Da Capo Press paperback edition of *Battles of the Revolutionary War, 1775-1781* is an unabridged republication of the edition originally published in Chapel Hill, North Carolina, in 1990. It is reprinted by arrangement with Algonquin Books in Chapel Hill.

ISBN 0–306–81329–7

Published by Da Capo Press
A Member of the Perseus Books Group

http://www.dacapopress.com

Da Capo Press books are available at special discounts for bulk purchases in the U.S. by corporations, institutions, and other organizations. For more information, please contact the Special Markets Department at the Perseus Books Group, 11 Cambridge Center, Cambridge, MA 02142, or call (800) 255-1514 or (617) 252-5298, or e-mail j.mccrary@perseusbooks.com.

2 3 4 5 6 7 8 9—07 06 05

For Barbara

CONTENTS

LIST OF ILLUSTRATIONS

LIST OF MAPS AND DIAGRAMS

INTRODUCTION

by John S. D. Eisenhower

AMERICANS GENERALLY REGARD George Washington and Abraham Lincoln as the two giants of our history. And yet the degree of understanding we have accorded the two men is vastly one-sided. Lincoln we feel we know. We pace the second floor of the White House with him as, back in 1862, he anguishes over the fate of the Army of the Potomac or contemplates one of his all-too-frequent changes in the command of that army. We sit with him in Ford's Theater as John Wilkes Booth sneaks up behind him. But not so George Washington. The Father of Our Country is revered by nearly all of us, but primarily because we have been told that he should be revered. The real, living Washington, with his ups and downs, his strengths and weaknesses, has been buried in myth.

So it is with the two great wars during which each of these statesmen led our fortunes. The Civil War, like Lincoln, is vivid in our memory, kept constantly alive by hundreds of new book titles every year, by reenactments of battles at our great national parks, even by automobile license plates carrying the ever-defiant Confederate battle flag. The American Revolution, on the other hand, is largely forgotten. The "redcoats" are no longer pictured as the brutal enemies they once were in the American imagination. The period from 1775 through 1781 was fraught with confusion, upheaval, uncertainty, and incredible danger to Patriot leaders and citizens alike. But it has been lost in our consciousness.

The reasons for our so abandoning the Revolution are obvious: the passage of time, the paucity of reliable records, general indifference to our national heritage, and the timing of the invention of the photograph, which came upon the scene some fifty years after the Revolution. The reasons, actually, are not important; the *fact* of our neglect, at least to the historically minded, is important indeed.

In this book, *Major Battles and Campaigns: Battles of the Revolutionary War*, Col. W. J. Wood is making a contribution toward rectifying our ignorance of and indifference to the American Revolution. It is a worthy endeavor, and in approaching it Colonel Wood has been conscious that he is battling obstacles. Two of these are the mythology that has grown up around our Revolution and the very complicated nature of the war itself. Let me address the second problem first.

The serious reader, trying to make some sense out of the strategic course of the Revolution, is baffled by an appalling lack of pattern. A study of the war involves a plethora of battles, some large and some small, fought at great distances from each other, encompassing various sections of the United States and Canada. Usually one campaign would hold center stage at a time,* governed by the objectives of the British high command, who always retained the strategic initiative. Those objectives are not always clear to the reader. It is sometimes difficult to analyze why high-ranking British officials decided to occupy one portion or another of the United States at a given time. Why, for example, did Sir William Howe ignore the wishes of his superiors that he join Sir John Burgoyne at Albany in 1777, a move that would have altered the course of the war? The author goes into such problems with zest, and he succeeds in unraveling them with considerable success.

When it comes to the study of various individual Revolutionary battles, we find a lack of uniformity in quality, methods of operation, and competence of commanders among the armies. A British force, for example, might contain a leaven of British regulars but include as well some regiments of Hessian mercenaries, Canadian militia, and Indians—though usually not all four groups at once. An American force would vary even more because of the vast chasm in military proficiency between raw, untrained militia and the relatively well-trained Continentals. An American force might contain both these elements, although some of the most famous American successes such as Bunker Hill and Kings Mountain were fought by militia alone. Like the British, the Americans also recruited Indians as auxiliaries, though not nearly to the same extent.

The sheer number of battles fought in this erratically-conducted war makes it impossible for the author to cover every one in a single book. Colonel Wood has overcome this difficulty by abandoning at the outset any effort to follow the Revolution through as a strategic continuum. Rather, he selects certain battles to describe, purposefully omitting others. His criteria for selection includes the drama of a particular engagement,

---

*Sometimes, as with the Saratoga campaign (Burgoyne) and the Philadelphia campaign (Howe), which includes Brandywine, Germantown, and Valley Forge, they were fought simultaneously. But that circumstance was rare.

its ability to illustrate a certain military principle, and its uniqueness. None of the battles described herein exactly, or even closely, resembles any of the others. The author does, however, strive to give some continuity, some tie-in, by skillful cross-reference. He compares British tactics at Brandywine in September 1777, to those employed a year earlier on Long Island, to mention only one instance. He has successfully striven to create an overall picture by emphasizing the highlights.

As to the mythology surrounding this poorly reported war, Colonel Wood takes much of it head-on in his very thorough and educational Author's Introduction. In that indispensable section, he clearly describes the various types of soldier who fought on either side, what each had to contend with, the equipment each carried, the nature of the weapons each employed, and the tactics by which each unit attempted to derive the greatest combat effectiveness from the weapons it carried. Vital to an understanding of those tactics, of course, is an understanding of the organizations in which the troops of both sides fought.

That indispensable Author's Introduction will also give the reader an astonishing picture of the British regular, the once-maligned redcoat. That unfortunate creature was not always a soldier by choice. Sometimes he had signed up in the British army as a fugitive from some unbearable place in British society, but too often he was a victim of the indiscriminate press gangs. He was conscripted (theoretically) for life, and his lot afforded little by way of life's amenities. The British Tommy fought and marched for great distances in the unfamiliar American heat, stifled by uniforms fit only for the parade ground, a condition which the author describes masterfully. His picture calls forth our respect for the remarkable British soldier.

Besides the mythology surrounding our accepted view of the participating soldiers, Colonel Wood punctures other false concepts. One is the supposed superiority of the rifle over the musket under *all conditions*. He invites protest from super-patriots when he points out that only half of the American troops at Bunker Hill got into the fray; many of the nonparticipants were sheer skulkers. And finally he reminds us, in his chapter on Quebec, that the colonists were engaged in a full-scale war, even offensive operations, months before the Declaration of Independence.

THE AUTHOR ALSO DEALS DEFTLY with the colorful personalities who star in the drama. Of these the most remarkable treatment is accorded to the acknowledged traitor Benedict Arnold. His case is worthy of a moment's examination.

Arnold's crime of treason (and betrayal of Washington as well) was consummated by his abortive effort to sell to the British the plans for the defense of the strategic position on the Hudson River, West Point, New York. His act merits no defense; his British counterpart, Major André, was hanged when apprehended, and in the eyes of the colonists, Benedict Arnold deserved the same fate. His ignominy lasts. West Point cadets are still made well aware of the blank shield that hangs on the wall of the Old Cadet Chapel: the name of Arnold has been forever eradicated. In the American military there can be no ambivalence in condemning the traitor.

But history demands a more balanced view of a man's life, and if the student thereof is to benefit from his readings, then even the traitors, the Benedict Arnolds, deserve to have their side represented.

Colonel Wood has treated this subject with admirable evenhandedness. He does not defend Arnold or his later action. But neither does he denigrate Arnold's early contributions to the cause of American independence. He simply recounts the zeal, the self-sacrifice, the bravery, and the imagination that Arnold displayed up to and including the Saratoga campaign (1777). He tells of the two severe wounds that Arnold incurred during this time. All through this recounting, however, the author points out the character flaws that later brought on his disillusionment and treason. It is well that Arnold, by such fair treatment, receives his due.

Another great beneficiary of Colonel Wood's careful analysis is, not surprisingly, General Washington himself. Viewed strictly as a military leader, Washington is seen as he learns from his early mistakes and develops professionally. Washington's progress is not consistent, however; his brilliance at Trenton and Princeton at Christmas 1776 is followed, not preceded, by his inexplicable blundering at Brandywine nine months later. Colonel Wood gives credit to Washington for the former while not sparing the Great Cincinnatus for the latter.

The salient characteristic of Washington that shines through these pages is his great sense of balance, of his acceptance of responsibility. When Washington had completed his service to the British Crown in 1759, upon Virginia's retirement from the French and Indian War, he was, though a colonel of militia, still a brash youngster—albeit an energetic, aggressive, and experienced one. After the intervening sixteen years we see a Washington who is capable of weighing the consequences of each action and making mature, usually prudent judgments. Thus he passes up the prospect of seizing the British base at New Brunswick,

New Jersey, after his surprising victory at Princeton, great as that prize would have been. We see him assessing that decision in a message to Congress admitting the possibility of his own mistake, even the possibility that he himself had lost an opportunity to end the war. We see the commander in chief worrying about recruiting, supplying, clothing, even paying his army, matters that the Continental Congress, in a more developed country, should have been taking care of for him. Washington is impressive on the battlefield, but he is even more so when solving his everyday, grubby, but all-important administrative problems.

This book also contains splendid characterizations of many other important leaders, British and American. Among them are Prescott, Stark, Putnam, Herkimer, Greene, and Morgan on the American side. Carleton, William Howe, Burgoyne, St. Leger, and Cornwallis are featured on the British side. No photos are available, of course, but the author's word pictures do much by way of substitute.

Bill Wood has done a remarkable job in researching *Battles of the Revolutionary War.* He has developed his vast amounts of material into a readable, sometimes folksy, narrative, spiced on occasion by wry observations based on his own experiences as a lifetime soldier. Algonquin Books of Chapel Hill is proud to publish this story. Anyone who desires to attain a feel for the dramatic times that accompanied the birth of this country would do well to read it.

AUTHOR'S INTRODUCTION

THIS BOOK IS A DEPICTION and an interpretation of the way that battles and campaigns were fought during the American Revolutionary War. Because not all the battles of the Revolution are included—and because I have focused on the tactics and strategy involved in the selected examples—the book is neither a history of the American Revolution nor a chronicle of the war itself. For my purposes, the outcome of a battle and its effects on the course of the war have been secondary in its selection to its uniqueness in the comparative light of the war's other engagements and operations. Despite the wealth of historical material that has accumulated in over two hundred years, historians have developed a tendency to regard the battles of our Revolutionary War as being of questionable worth for military historians and their readers because they are "all of a piece"—too much alike. It is therefore the primary purpose of this book to refute that thesis and show, in its place, that there *were* unique battles— battles that can and should be included in the study of military history.

It would be helpful to review the character of the war itself. In the dozen years after the end of the Seven Years' War (the French and Indian War in America), Britain stood, wittingly or not, on the threshold of empire. Her American colonies were only a part of her global commitments. So far-flung were her imperial goals—from Europe to India— that the festering rebellion in North America was at first a minor irritant that grew only by degrees into what the Colonial Office could recognize as a real war.

Unfortunately for the British cause, it was that office that gave primary direction to the strategy governing military operations in the war in America, and its ineptitude from the outset caused the conduct of the war to become an operational and logistical nightmare. Separated by 3,000 miles from the theater of war and under constant attacks from its not-so-loyal opposition, His Majesty's government continued for six unhappy years to devise strategies that would win a war that the country didn't want, against an enemy whose people were—by most Englishmen's lights—Englishmen.

Against that background, British generals had to face a strategic picture that seemed to change with every campaign. Further, they were fighting in an alien environment. The British officers of all ranks were accustomed to maneuvering and fighting on the plains of Europe in campaigns and battles governed by linear tactics, following systems that came to be fashioned, in varying degree, on the models of Frederick the Great, though necessarily on a smaller scale. The British army was highly respected for its fighting qualities in Europe, and the force in America attempted to face the colonials in the same manner. But America was not Europe.

The enemy that the British faced in America, on the contrary, appeared on the battlefield in all sorts of garb, with all sorts of firearms, and was likely to take all sorts of tactical dispositions. In one engagement King George's grenadiers and fusiliers might encounter ragged militia who would flee after the first volley; on another occasion, however, the British would be faced with uniformed Continentals who stood in regular lines and exchanged volley for volley. On yet another encounter the American force might be a mixture. In consequence, the nature of the engagements of the war might vary in ways as different as the combatants themselves. The quality of American leadership also varied from battle to battle. That is why, whenever practicable, this book focuses on the American leaders, their problems—often dilemmas—and actions and reactions.

Let us consider some examples. At Bunker Hill, the rawest of American militia were led in the right places by veteran officers who knew how to handle militia from their experience in the French and Indian War. The American campaign against Quebec, also, shows desperate assaults by militia under the superb leadership of Montgomery and Arnold. It also witnesses Morgan's lapse of moral courage following his splendid display of physical courage.

Then there is the contrast between Washington at his best and at his worst. At Trenton and Princeton, Washington—dubbed "the Fox" by his opponent, Lord Cornwallis—outfoxed the British by the skillful use of intelligence and maneuver to turn the tables in such fashion as to merit the praise of Frederick the Great himself. At Brandywine, some nine months later, the same Washington mishandled both intelligence and maneuver in a way to deserve the defeat that followed.

Earlier in August of the same year (1777) the strangest of the war's battles was fought—without the participation of a single British soldier—between American militia and British Loyalists, the latter accompanied by Indian allies. The ambush, and the "turn-around" battle of Oriskany that ensued, has been called the most savage engagement of the war.

The two battles of Saratoga are examined in order to contrast the effective leadership of Arnold and Morgan with that of Horatio Gates, and show the influence of all three men on the battles.

At Kings Mountain in the South, one sees an all-out battle between two forces—both militia, and both composed entirely of Americans.

The battle at Cowpens in January of the war's final year has been included, without reservation, as a tactical gem in anybody's war. Dan Morgan, bedeviled with attacks of rheumatism and in a desperate situation, showed matchless leadership in handling a combination of militia and Continentals with such ingenuity that he inflicted losses of 85 percent on a professional enemy, in contrast with Morgan's losses of less than 1 percent.

Cowpens is followed by Nathanael Greene's brilliant strategical triumph over Cornwallis in the so-called race to the Dan, which culminated in the Battle of Guilford Courthouse. In that fiercely fought engagement Greene's poor tactics nearly robbed him of all that his superlative strategy had gained.

The book ends with the Battle of the Chesapeake Capes, which is included not because it was different from the others by virtue of being a naval battle but because of the way that de Grasse, the French admiral, turned a drawn battle into a strategical victory through a series of after-action maneuvers.

Through all the battles there runs a common thread: each one's uniqueness when viewed against others in the War of the Revolution.

WELL-MEANING EFFORTS TO THE CONTRARY, it is not possible to show a single composite portrait of the American soldier of the Revolutionary War, simply because there were two of him: the militiaman and the Continental. The former was a citizen soldier called upon to serve for limited periods of time, usually a few weeks or months, whereas the Continental was the American "regular" who had enlisted in the Continental army for three years or the duration of the war.

The militiaman belonged to a locally raised company and had a natural bent toward the traditional protection of home and community. He most often marched and fought within his home region, and would return to his fireside when, to his way of thinking, his job was done. Thus large numbers of militia often disappeared without notice—and with no feeling on the part of the deserters that they were committing an abhorrent military crime. The melting away of militia units at critical times during a campaign was the despair of Washington and his commanders, prompting them to label militia in general—usually with good cause—as less than steadfast.

The militiaman clearly lacked the discipline and training of the regular, causing him often to fail his leaders at just the wrong time—sometimes by fleeing when he found himself facing British bayonets, as at Camden or Long Island. Yet, as Mark Boatner has observed, "at Bunker Hill, Cowpens, and Guilford, the militia showed that *if commanded by experienced officers who knew their weakness* they could fight like regular soldiers" (*Encyclopedia of the American Revolution*).

The Continentals, or "regular" soldiers, were born in the mind of Washington when he found himself commanding an army of 17,000 militia at the siege of Boston in July 1775. The enlistments of his troops would all expire by the end of the year, so the new commander in chief worked relentlessly on the Continental Congress to cease depending on militia and instead place its reliance on a long-service army. "Our liberties," he wrote, "might be lost if their defense is left to any but a permanent standing army; I mean one to exist during the [duration of the] war." By September 1776 Congress authorized the raising of eighty-eight regiments of a Continental army, to be apportioned among the thirteen states—hence such terms as the "Continental Line" or the "1st Maryland Continentals" will be found in the descriptions of battles and campaigns. As for the number of regiments in the field, there was always a marked difference between what had been authorized and what was present for service. But the Continental system, with all its shortcomings, was a vast improvement over the militia system.

On rare occasions Continentals and militia fought battles on their own, but a combination of the two—regiments fighting side by side or in supporting formations—was the general rule. Later in the war, as with Daniel Morgan's little army at Cowpens in January 1781, some militia units had acquired a leavening of discharged Continentals.

The militiaman was required to report for duty, at least in the earlier years of the war, with his own firearm, usually the family flintlock musket (commonly called a firelock) or a fowling piece. Types and calibers of muskets were as varied as their owners. The weapon might be a Brown Bess (described in the section below on the British soldier) of French and Indian War vintage, a gunsmith-crafted article of local fabrication, or perhaps a contracted Committee of Safety musket. Calibers varied anywhere from .50 to .80, which necessitated all manner of bullet molds, a real headache when it came to supplying the soldiers with ammunition in the field. According to Charles L. Bolton, "The running of balls—running the lead into the molds—was a frequent duty in camp" (*The Private Soldier under Washington*).

In addition to his musket the citizen soldier had to provide either a cartridge box (a leather box containing a wooden block bored with holes to hold paper cartridges) or a powder horn and bullet pouch. Optional items might include a belt knife or hand ax and a canteen. Only a negligible few showed up with bayonets.

There was no such thing as an "issued militia uniform," though a few companies or regiments strove for uniformity with buckskin or linen hunting shirts. But the key word for militia dress was *motley,* as exemplified in Christopher Ward's description of the militia who followed Ethan Allen and Benedict Arnold in the advance on Fort Ticonderoga in 1775: "Behind them went a straggling column of men in every sort of garb—buckskin, linsey-woolsey [homespun], or what not, beaver hats, felt hats, coonskin caps, buckled shoes or moccasins—armed with firelocks, pistols, swords, knives, or simple clubs, not a bayonet among them all" (*The War of the Revolution*). Despite the varied headgear at Fort Ticonderoga, the most common was the civilian cocked hat. Another common item of clothing was the cotton or flax shirt worn beneath a jacket or coat. Below those the man wore "small clothes"—knee breeches, which were fastened below the knee, and long stockings or leggings and cowhide shoes. The militiaman would be carrying some kind of haversack suspended from a shoulder strap. His equipment would be completed with his blanket roll.

The Continental soldier's weapon was the flintlock musket, a muzzleloader some 50 to 60 inches long with a caliber varying from .69 to .75, depending on its origin. At first there was no standard model, and the Continentals were armed with whatever the Congress or states could purchase, aside from captured muskets or other guns confiscated from the Loyalists. Eventually the French Charleville musket (models of the years 1763 through 1771) could be considered standard issue; over 100,000 were shipped to America from French arsenals. Still, the basic characteristics remained unchanged. The muskets were .69 caliber with a 44½-inch barrel, an overall length of 5 feet, 2 inches, and a refined gunlock that was in fact superior to that of the British musket. The French musket was equipped with a socket bayonet about 15 inches long.

The Continental soldier was trained to load and fire his musket in a series of "times" or "motions" on command—today soldiers would call it "by the numbers." The older drill manuals like the "Norfolk Discipline" or the British "Sixty-fourth," which called for seventeen or more motions in loading, were replaced by a simplified version of Timothy Pickering's, and later by the clearer manual of von Steuben. What the soldier did, in simple terms, was to take the cartridge (a round lead bullet and a load of powder wrapped in a cylinder of paper) from his cartridge box, bite off the nonbullet end, pour a little priming powder in the pan on his gunlock, then pour the rest of the powder, followed by the bullet, and the paper as wadding, down the barrel. Next he drew his ramrod from its "pipes" below the barrel and rammed the bullet and paper firmly down against the powder charge. He then returned his ramrod, "presented his piece" (pointed it at the enemy), pulled the hammer back to full cock, and on command pulled the trigger to fire his musket.

The Continental's basic uniform consisted of his cocked hat, a cotton shirt over which he wore waistcoat and regimental coat, and below those his breeches or overalls (with gaiters, if overalls were not prescribed), stockings, and shoes of leather or hide. He wore two cross belts over his coat: one over his left shoulder to support the cartridge box at his right hip; the other over his right shoulder, carrying the bayonet in its scabbard. On campaign the soldier carried his knapsack surmounted by his rolled blanket, and a canteen on a shoulder strap. In winter, if he was lucky, he would have a greatcoat or capote (blanket coat), mittens or gloves, and a wool scarf. There were, however, far too many who were not so lucky.

The quality and quantities of uniforms varied from state to state, even for Continentals. In October 1778, however, large quantities of uniforms were supplied by the French to fill a real need. The breeches and waistcoats were white, but the coats came in two colors, brown and blue, with red facings. They were assigned to the different states by lot: North Carolina, Maryland, New Jersey, and New York drew the blue, and Virginia, Delaware, Pennsylvania, Massachusetts, and New Hampshire wore brown. As Ward explains, this was the first time that anything like uniform dress for the whole army had been made possible.

Congress was not able to supply uniforms for officers; it was difficult enough to try to keep the troops in uniform. As a result, officers' uniforms were often as motley as those of their men. When Washington assumed command during the siege of Boston, one of his first actions was to provide distinctive insignia for the officers. For general officers he prescribed "ribbands" to be worn between the coat and waistcoat. His own, at a cost of three shillings fourpence, was light blue. Major generals

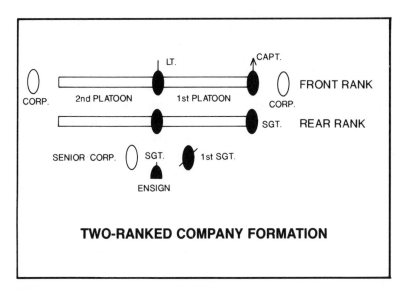

TWO-RANKED COMPANY FORMATION

were to wear purple, brigadier generals were to be pink. Field officers were to be distinguished by "red or pink cockades in their hats, captains yellow or buff; the subalterns green." Sergeants were instructed to wear a shoulder knot of red cloth on the right shoulder. Corporals would wear a green knot.*

When Congress authorized the raising of the eighty-eight Continental regiments in 1776, each state was assigned a quota in proportion to its population. Regiments in the field varied in size from about 700 men down to as few as 350, depending on how many losses they had sustained. The regiment was normally divided into two battalions, but if its total strength fell much below 350 it was thought best to reorganize the regiment into one battalion. By 1778 companies had a minimum strength of forty privates, three corporals, one ensign (the counterpart of today's second lieutenant), one lieutenant, and a captain—for a total of forty-nine; drummers and/or fifers were also authorized if available. The company's standard formation, as shown in the diagram, was based on

---

*A picture on my wall shows a 1781 New Jersey infantry officer looking very natty in a dark blue coat with yellow facings and a silver epaulet on his left shoulder; things were evidently looking better in that last year of fighting. The officer carries a spontoon (a light pike about seven feet long that was a weapon as well as a badge of rank), as did the junior officers of most infantry companies. In some instances the spontoon might be replaced with a fusil (a light musket), as was often the case with British subalterns.

von Steuben's manual: thus "a company is to be formed in two ranks,* at one pace distant, with the tallest men in the rear, and both ranks sized, with the shortest men of each in the centre. A company thus drawn up is to be divided into two . . . platoons."

The infantryman's home was his company—just as our army would have it today—and though each company had a number, it was commonly known by the name of its captain or the locale it came from: hence Captain Jones's company of the 5th Pennsylvania line, or the Danbury company, 21st Connecticut Regiment, Continental line.

No review of the American soldier would be complete without a look at the riflemen, who were not to be confused with "light infantry"—line troops armed with muskets. The rifle had been known in Europe for generations, especially in the Austrian Tyrol and Germany, where it had been developed as a hunting weapon—hence the expression "the jäger with his rifle." The short, heavy jäger rifle, though brought to America by German settlers in the early eighteenth century, was unsuited to the needs of the American frontiersman. What the hunter and Indian fighter of the backwoods needed was an accurate, long-range rifle firing a ball of relatively small caliber (he had to carry all his powder and ball; smaller lead balls taking a smaller powder charge made for more shots per pound): a rifle that was rugged, dependable, and light in weight. "The woodsmen came back from the wilderness to talk with the gunsmiths, and the gunsmiths listened" (Lagemann and Manucy, *The Long Rifle*). The eventual result was the famous "long rifle," or "Kentucky rifle," a weapon of such craftsmanship and beauty that one can still bring tears to the eyes of a collector.[†]

---

* The British continued to use their three-ranked formation as prescribed in the Manual of 1764. It might seem that three ranks would increase firepower by 50 percent over the two-rank formation. Apparently the theory did not hold up in practice. In fact, it continued to raise controversy for several generations. Marshal Saint-Cyr of the French army went so far as to declare "that one-quarter of combat losses were due to wounds inflicted by the third rank upon the first two" (Robert S. Quimby, *The Background of Napoleonic Warfare* [New York: Columbia University Press, 1957], 311). And "Napoleon, after grumbling for years about the uselessness of a third rank, finally abolished it in 1813 at Leipzig" (Brig. Gen. Vincent J. Espito and Col. John Robert Elting, *A Military History and Atlas of the Napoleonic Wars* [New York: Frederick A. Praeger, 1964]. Finally, in the British army Sir John Moore's experiments resulted in making the two-rank line acceptable for British infantry; so with Wellington in the Peninsula and for the rest of the nineteenth century the British had their famed "thin red line."

† It is given its due treatment in the chapter on Kings Mountain.

At the start of the Revolution the rifle was unknown in New England, so it was not remarkable that Congress's authorization for rifle companies was limited to two companies from Virginia, two from Maryland, and six (later increased to eight) from Pennsylvania. The riflemen were famed for their sharpshooting; their prowess never failed to amaze the New Englanders, who gawked at their feats of marksmanship when the rifle companies arrived to join the army at the siege of Boston. John Adams, in a letter to his wife in 1776, spoke of "a peculiar kind of musket, called a rifle, used by riflemen from Pennsylvania, Maryland, and Virginia."

The rifleman's dress was so practical that Washington tried unsuccessfully to adopt a similar uniform for the entire army. Its main feature was the long buckskin or linen hunting shirt, which was belted at the waist, yet was loose enough to allow freedom of movement. The shirt came about halfway to the knees, covering breeches of the same material. The garb was rounded out with leggings, and the feet were shod with moccasins or cowhide shoes. The headgear was a round wool cap with a brim. The whole outfit was as simple as it was practical.

In spite of its superior range and accuracy, the rifle had serious tactical drawbacks. It took too long to load—a trained Continental could fire three rounds with his musket while the rifleman was reloading—and it could not be fitted with a bayonet. And despite his famed marksmanship, the rifleman was found to be effective only in irregular operations which were characterized by scouting and skirmishing. Because they were without bayonets and also unable to deliver a rapid series of volleys in the face-off battles of the time, riflemen were ineffective where *volume* of fire counted above all else. Accordingly, we should dispense forever with the cherished American myth that our ancestors "licked the redcoats fair and square because the latter, with their muskets and rigid battle lines, could not stand up to the rifles of our sharpshooting forebears." The proportion of riflemen to musket-armed infantry on the rolls of the Continental army in November 1778, in fact, shows the army's authorized strength at 35,000, while the aforementioned twelve rifle companies could muster, at full strength, some 960 men—less than 3 percent of the army's total numbers.

VIEWED MORE THAN TWO HUNDRED YEARS LATER, the nature of the British enlisted man who fought in America now seems an enigma. Although he campaigned with stolidity and courage, his background would appear to have produced a man who would desert at the first opportunity. He enjoyed little public esteem. The British army in general, and its lower echelons of enlisted men in particular, were held in contempt by English society, constantly ridiculed by the press, and subject to abuse in the streets. The rank and file existed in another world from the officers, who came from the aristocracy or wealthy families who could afford to purchase their commissions. The public attitude toward the soldier can be summed up in a saying attributed to the Royal Navy (who were not such a grand lot themselves): "A messmate before a shipmate, a shipmate before a stranger, a stranger before a dog, a dog before a soldier." While there may have been a few "silly lads befooled by the glamour of the scarlet coat," the majority, in Christopher Ward's words, were unfortunates who had been impressed into service: "Boys and men made drunk by the recruiting sergeant and persuaded to take the 'king's shilling' while hardly aware of what they were doing made up a considerable part of the army." Others were criminals pardoned in exchange for enlisting. "Vagrants, smugglers, and criminals of various kinds might thus escape such legal penalties as had been adjudged them. . . . In this way every gaol served as a recruiting depot" (Edward Curtis, *The Organization of the British Army in the American Revolution*).

Coming from such discreditable backgrounds the enlisted man would seem in a position to improve his lot in the army; such, however, was seldom the case. Discipline was harsh, punishments cruel, food notoriously poor, and pay amounted to next to nothing after a private's eight pence a day had been reduced by what Edward Curtis calls "gross off-reckonings," charges for a shameful list of items, accounting for clothing, weapons repair, shaving kit, and "contributions" toward some future, nebulous medical care. Yet the British soldier not only endured but campaigned, for the most part, with a military effectiveness that served his country well.

The British army officer may likewise have served well in his own way, which was that of the professional whose family was established within or on the threshold of the upper classes. Since there were no military academies, the young officer usually got his start in the profession of arms at the tender age of fifteen, when his family purchased a commission for him in a suitable regiment. The commission was bought from the regimental commander, a colonel who had contracted with the Crown to raise and maintain a regiment. Although the purchase system had long been under attack, it continued to flourish throughout the eighteenth century. The rank of ensign in an ordinary infantry regiment went for £400, while the same grade sold for £900 in the Foot Guards. Commissions sold for correspondingly higher prices according to rank: a captaincy in an ordinary regiment cost £1,500; the same grade in the Foot Guards, £3,500. The commission, as property, belonged to the holder for life, and the only sure way to promotion was purchase of a commission of a higher grade. The unlucky exceptions were the officers whose means did not allow such advancement:

> Many of the regimental officers were none the worse soldiers for the purchase system. Realizing that their lack of wealth blocked the way to high military advancement, they came to love their calling for itself . . . they regarded the regiment as their home and grew gray in uniform. . . . While there were marked exceptions, many regimental officers displayed sympathetic consideration for the comfort and happiness of their men. The bond between them and the non-commissioned officers was often extremely close; and they came to regard the corporals and sergeants . . . with the same kindly feeling as a master does an old family servant. (Curtis, *The Organization of the British Army in the American Revolution*)

Such NCOs and soldiers would follow the officers of their regiment into any kind of danger.

The infantry regiment (or battalion for tactical purposes) had an authorized strength of 477 "of all ranks," but its average strength on campaign usually fell below 300 rank and file. The regiment was divided into ten companies, of which eight were "battalion companies," that is, ordinary line companies. There were also two "flanking companies," one of light infantry and one of grenadiers. These were the elite, called flanking companies because when deployed in standard battle formation the regiment had its most vulnerable points, the flanks, secured on the right by the grenadiers and on the left by the light infantry. Light infantrymen were selected for agility and physical endurance as well as their fighting qualities. When not in the regimental line of battle, light infantry were employed as advance guards, march flankers, outposts, reconnaissance elements, and skirmishers.

The grenadiers were expected to have the same martial qualities as light infantrymen, but in addition were chosen because they were tall men with healthy physiques. Dating back to 1677, grenadiers had the primary task of throwing hand grenades in close combat with the enemy. By 1774 the grenades had become obsolete, "but the grenadiers still remained, representing in height and strength the flower of each regiment."

It was common practice in the field to detach the flank companies from their parent regiments and form them into provisional elite battalions— what we might today call task forces. They were so employed on special missions, and were seen in action again and again in these formations when higher command deemed it necessary.

Light infantrymen were distinguished by their short red jackets and brimless caps, usually made of leather. Grenadiers wore tall bearskins faced with their regimental badges. The scarlet regimental coat was basically the same for grenadier and battalion companies, worn over a white waistcoat, and decorated with brass buttons, lace, and facings—that is, with lapels and cuffs in a distinctive regimental color that contrasted with the red coat. A white waist belt was worn under the coat, and it carried the bayonet scabbard on the left hip. There was only one cross belt, going over the left shoulder and supporting the cartridge box on the right side. The headgear of the battalion companies was the black cocked hat trimmed in white. The breeches were white and fastened tightly above the knee. Below them the soldier wore long, buttoned gaiters of black or dark brown.

Thus the uniform worn by the British soldiers in the 1770s would appear to be better suited to the parade ground than to the battlefield. Unfortunately for the soldier, it was also worn in field service, which makes it appear to be the design of madmen (or the sailors who rated the soldier below the dog), for a more impractical and uncomfortable dress for campaigning would be hard to imagine. In addition to the coat and waistcoat, the soldier had to endure a stiff collar and even stiffer stock under his chin. Everything had to be worn tightly: waist belt, breeches, coat sleeves, and gaiters. To top off the uniform, the hair had to be "clubbed," that is, tied up in a queue stiffened with tallow and white powder. In the field the infantryman carried a load of nearly sixty pounds, comprised of his musket and bayonet, sixty rounds of ammunition, knapsack with gear and rations, blanket roll, canteen, and a one-fifth share of his tent's equipage. With all this the soldier was expected to march and fight. Amazingly, he functioned well on most occasions, often under the roughest conditions.

The British infantryman was armed with the Brown Bess, a musket so called from its walnut stock. It weighed about ten pounds, was nearly four and a half feet long, and took a fourteen-inch socket bayonet, meaning that the sleeve of the bayonet was fitted on the end of the barrel and locked into place on a barrel stud. The smoothbore musket was .75 caliber, firing a three-quarter-ounce lead ball. Being smoothbore as well as oversized for the bullet, it was notoriously inaccurate, a factor which mattered little, since the soldier was trained to point his musket at enemy ranks only yards away and fire on command. A measure of the Brown Bess's accuracy: its bullet had a five-foot error at 120 yards making it hopelessly inaccurate at ranges over 100 yards.* It was loaded and fired in much the same manner as that described for the American Continental, with only minor changes in the "motions."

The Brown Bess and the Charleville musket, as well as flintlocks of any type, shared common defects, mostly due to their vulnerability to weather. A strong wind could blow the priming powder from the pan, and heavy rains could put an end to the firing in any battle. In addition, poor flints could be a real source of frustration. Colonel Lindsay of the 46th Foot was reacting typically when he complained indignantly against the authorities "for failing to supply every musket with the same black flint which every country gentleman in England carried in his fowling piece" (Curtis, *Organization of the British Army*). The American flints were consistently superior to the British, usually lasting through ten times as many firings.

Despite its shortcomings, the musket and its bayonet continued to dominate eighteenth-century tactics, having replaced the unwieldy combinations of arquebus and pike in European warfare. The British army's tactics in the Revolutionary War were, in the minds of British officers, simply a logical extension of those that had governed warfare on European battlefields for generations. In such set-piece battles, highly trained opposing infantry—in shoulder-to-shoulder lines three ranks deep—advanced at the quick step to confront each other at an *effective range* of less than a hundred yards. What took place then has been largely unappreciated by Americans, thus lending credence to the fantasy of the rifle's superiority over the musket in battle. In actuality this climax of the eighteenth-century battle was essentially a contest to deliver as many bullets as possible in the shortest time, with massed volleys. Rapidity of fire, not accuracy, was of the essence. Other factors being equal, then, the troops with superior fire discipline were bound to win the contest. A continuous fire—frequently a series of rolling platoon volleys—was exchanged at a rate of three to five rounds a minute until one side showed signs of breaking, at which time its fire slackened or its thinned ranks began to waver or disintegrate. At this time the commanders on the side

*Major George Hanger, Tarleton's second in command of the British Legion, wrote after the war that "a soldier must be very unfortunate indeed who shall be wounded by a common musket at 150 yards, provided his antagonist aims at him" (Harold L. Peterson, *Arms and Armor in Colonial America*)

that had gained fire superiority would order a bayonet charge, which almost always decided the day. This kind of intense firefight, with its requisite dependence on fire discipline, was the essence of the tactical art that American leaders and troops had to learn the hard way: They had to become so trained and disciplined that they could continue to load and fire, almost as automatons, while standing fast and taking their losses until they could make their enemy break or give way, and then follow up with the bayonet. It was not until after the winter of 1777–78, after three years of bitter experience, that the lesson began to take hold, bolstered later by the instruction of professional advisers like von Steuben.

Another operational factor that deserves emphasis was the nature of the American terrain. The battles of the Seven Years' War (1756–63) in Europe had been fought, like countless others on the Continent, on open, level ground where massed musketry could come into full play. When the British in America could fight pitched battles on such terrain, their tactical system resulted in victories such as Long Island, Brandywine, and Camden. Conversely, when rugged or heavily wooded terrain made it impossible to bring the full weight of British firepower to bear, the results were British defeats such as Freeman's Farm and Bemis Heights.

THIS BOOK IS NOT CONCERNED with stereotyped battles. On the contrary, it seeks to refute the delusion that the British army did nothing but line up in rows and advance in parade formation, while the Americans hid behind bushes and trees and potted the redcoats. On the contrary, as the battles that follow will show, the combat actions in our Revolutionary War exhibited a remarkable diversity.

BATTLES OF THE
REVOLUTIONARY WAR

1775-1781

ONE

Bunker Hill

THE BRITISH GENERALS IN BESIEGED BOSTON were fed up to the teeth with their situation. Here they were with 6,000 of King George's troops, the finest in Europe, surrounded by hordes of peasants armed with old muskets and fowling pieces. The three major generals—William Howe, Henry Clinton, and John Burgoyne—had arrived on 25 May 1775 to receive a rude introduction to the facts: scarcely five weeks before, the rebellious farmers of Massachusetts had *chased* 1,800 of General Gage's best troops all the way from Concord to Charlestown Neck, across from Boston, where they had collapsed like exhausted sheep while their officers counted their 273 casualties. The next day the colonists sealed off the city. The siege of Boston had begun.

Now, in early June, the three generals had urged on General Gage, in his dual role of governor and military commander, an operation plan designed to snatch the initiative from the rebels and break up the siege. The key to the plan's success was to be the seizure and fortification of Dorchester Heights. The heights, thus secured, would not only ensure British domination of the port and city but would provide a base from which garrison forces could attack and roll up the besieging American force from the south. By 13 June, however, the American Committee of Safety, which was overseeing affairs in Cambridge, had already received a complete report on the proposed operation, due in great part to Gentleman Johnny Burgoyne's mouth, which was at times as big as his military ambitions.

The committee's deliberations on 14–15 June were actually a council of war that focused on countermoves to defeat the British sally on Dorchester Heights. The committee resolved that "Bunker Hill in Charles-

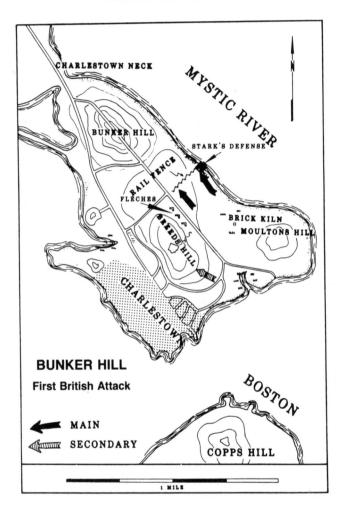

BUNKER HILL

First British Attack

← MAIN

⇐ SECONDARY

town be securely kept and defended, and also some one hill or hills on Dorchester neck be likewise secured." Since it was deemed impossible to do both, occupying Bunker Hill would serve as an immediate counter-threat to the British seizure of Dorchester Heights. So the high ground on the Charlestown peninsula would be the immediate objective for the colonists.

The map shows the peninsula, somewhat less than a mile and a half long and hardly three-quarters of a mile wide at its midsection, suspended like a bulging hornet's nest from Charlestown Neck, and bounded by two rivers: the Charles on the west and the Mystic on the east. The chief features of the peninsula, other than Charlestown itself, were its three hills and the neck. On the east lay Moulton's Hill, actually a knoll only 35 feet high. In the south center was 62-foot-high Breed's Hill. On the north was flat-topped Bunker Hill, 110 feet in height. Charlestown Neck was an isthmus, narrowing to only about ten yards at some points, and so low that at high tide it was sometimes inundated.

After taking his direction from the committee, the colonists' commander in chief, General Artemas Ward of Massachusetts, ordered the occupation of Bunker Hill to begin on the night of 16–17 June. It was to be achieved by a detachment of about a thousand men from the Massachusetts regiments of Colonels Prescott, Frye, and Bridge, along with a two-hundred-man Connecticut company commanded by Captain Thomas Knowlton. The detachment also included an "artillery train" of two four-pounders and forty-nine men, commanded by Captain Samuel Gridley. In overall command was Colonel William Prescott, a most fortunate choice to direct such an operation.

Prescott paraded his men on Cambridge Common at 6:00 P.M. on 16 June. Christopher Ward, in *The War of the Revolution*, has passed on the graphic description of an eyewitness to the formation on the common:

> To a man, they wore small clothes, coming down and fastening just below the knee, and long stockings with cowhide shoes ornamented by large buckles, while not a pair of boots graced the company. The coats and waist-coats were loose and of huge dimensions, with colors as various as the barks of oak, sumach and other trees of our hills and swamps, could make them and their shirts were all made of flax, and like every other part of the dress, were homespun. On their heads was worn a large round top and broad brimmed hat. Their arms were as various as their costume; here an old soldier carried a heavy Queen's arm, which had done service at the Conquest of Canada twenty years previous, while by his side walked a stripling boy with a Spanish fusee not half its weight or calibre, which his grandfather may have taken at the Havana, while not a few had old French pieces, that dated back to the reduction of Louisburg. Instead of the cartridge box, a large powder horn was slung under the arm, and occasionally a bayonet might be seen bristling in the ranks. Some of the swords of the officers had been made by our Province blacksmiths, perhaps from some farming utensil; they looked serviceable, but heavy and uncouth.

After their preparation, including prayers by the president of Harvard College, the Reverend Samuel Langdon, the detachment formed column and marched off about 9:00 P.M. heading eastward on the road which connected with the road running southeastward to Bunker Hill. The men and their company officers not only marched in the dark, they were equally in the dark about their destination and mission. Prescott led the way, keeping the same silence he expected of his men. At Charlestown Neck Prescott was joined by Brigadier General Israel Putnam of Connecticut, who brought wagons loaded with fascines (bundles of wood bound together) and empty hogsheads to be filled with earth and used to form the walls of a fort, and entrenching tools. After detaching Captain John Nutting's company from Prescott's regiment and sending it to Charlestown as a covering force, Prescott led the column over Bunker Hill and halted on its southeast slope.

Prescott then called the senior officers together for an informal command conference. No record was kept of what was said, but we can assume that there were lengthy and heated arguments about where to start entrenching—on Bunker Hill or on Breed's Hill. We do know that the discussion between Prescott, Putnam, and others, including Colonel Richard Gridley, the army's chief engineer, may have lasted for as long as two hours. Prescott had already pointed out that his orders were to fortify Bunker Hill, but there were arguments for taking over Breed's Hill first. Being nearer to Boston, it commanded any approach from a landing on the south end of the peninsula, and it could therefore constitute a first line of defense as a buffer to Bunker. Finally, an impatient Gridley told the group that time was wasting. The decision was then reached to fortify Breed's first, with Bunker as backup as time permitted. It was a sort of committee compromise, and as such was to lead to unexpected consequences.

Prescott led the column to Breed's Hill, where Gridley traced out the lines of a square redoubt of about 132 feet on a side, and the men began digging about midnight. These "embattled farmers" may not have been soldiers, but they were diggers, accustomed to putting their backs into it with pick and spade. And dig they must, for only four hours remained until first light, when the whole works would be revealed to the sentries on the British warships below them in Boston Harbor. Prescott kept relays working feverishly, and it may be assumed that Putnam was there urging men to dig for their lives, no doubt recalling his words to Artemas Ward at the council of war the day before: "Americans are not at all afraid for their heads, though very much afraid for their legs; if you cover them they will fight forever." Putnam stayed until about 3:00 A.M., when he decided to ride back to Ward's headquarters in Cambridge where his own battle would begin.

With the work well under way, Prescott ordered Captain Hugh Maxwell of his regiment to take a force and join Captain Nutting in Charlestown. From there they would patrol the shores of the peninsula to protect them against any British landing parties. Not content with that, Prescott later, before dawn, twice personally reconnoitered the shoreline. Under other circumstances it could have been called a romantic June night—quiet and warm under a starlit sky. Prescott and his executive, Major Brooks, could make out the forms of the British ships whose identities and anchorages they had memorized: to their far left lay the sloop *Falcon* with her fourteen guns, then the frigate *Lively* with twenty guns, off to their right lay the *Glasgow* with twenty guns, and in the distance was the ship of the line, the sixty-four-gun *Somerset.* As Prescott and Brooks moved along the silent shore they could hear across the calm harbor the routine cries of the British sentries on the ships. Assured that all was well, Prescott rounded up Maxwell and his men and returned to the redoubt. By then it was almost first light.

William Prescott was forty-nine years old, a fine New England rock of a man, still in his prime, over six feet tall and as strong of mind as he was of body. His jaw was firm and well rounded, giving his face a look of determination, and yet kindliness. He was direct of speech, though always courteous, as befitted his station of gentleman farmer. Always self-possessed, he had a natural air of command and a way of exacting respect without being domineering. His courage and coolness under fire had been first noticed by his superiors when the British had wrested Louisbourg from the French in 1745. There he had been offered a regular commission in the British army, a rare opportunity indeed for a provincial lieutenant. He had declined that offer, and at the end of King George's War had retired to his farm in Pepperell, Massachusetts. Prescott preferred that life, having been born to it in a family of wealth and prestige. He had improved upon a limited education through his love of reading. In 1775 he raised a regiment, was made its colonel, and arrived at Concord too late to fight. As we picture him now on the wall of the redoubt, with the first light of dawn breaking over the Mystic River, he looks an elegant figure in his light blue uniform, his balding head covered with a wig and crowned by a three-cornered cocked hat.

A few minutes after dawn the guns of HMS *Lively* opened fire on the

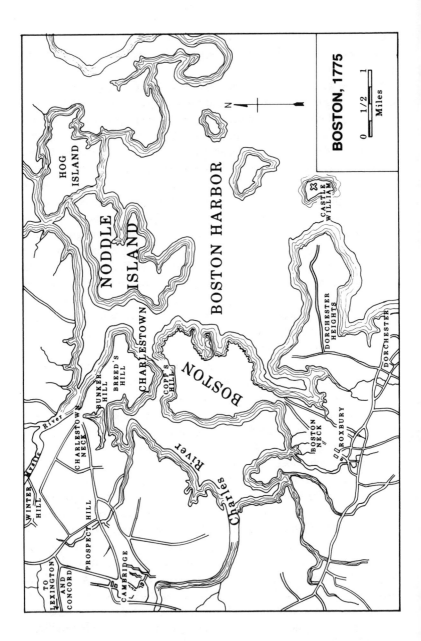

BOSTON, 1775

0   1/2   1
Miles

N

HOG ISLAND

NODDLE ISLAND

BOSTON HARBOR

CASTLE WILLIAM

DORCHESTER HEIGHTS

DORCHESTER

CHARLESTOWN

BUNKER HILL

BREED'S HILL

COPP'S HILL

BOSTON

Mystic River

CHARLESTOWN NECK

BOSTON NECK

ROXBURY

WINTER HILL

PROSPECT HILL

Charles River

TO LEXINGTON AND CONCORD

CAMBRIDGE

redoubt. After a few ranging rounds, however, the frigate's artillery fell strangely silent. Prescott took advantage of the silence to take stock of his situation. He decided to start work on a breastwork to protect the vulnerable left flank of the redoubt. He got a work detail going on a straight breastwork about 100 yards long, extending from the southeast corner of the redoubt down toward the marsh at the foot of the hill.

MEANWHILE, BRITISH GENERAL GAGE HAD CALLED a council of war that same morning of 17 June. Howe, Clinton, and Burgoyne were there, along with other senior officers. Clinton first proposed an immediate attack on the Charlestown peninsula: Howe to make a frontal holding attack from the east, while Clinton with 500 men would land on the peninsula just south of the neck and behind Prescott's redoubt to cut off the American force. The other generals opposed Clinton's plan as unsound, for it risked placing a British force between the Americans on the peninsula and those on the mainland. Howe then proposed an alternate method of attack: cut off the Breed's Hill redoubt by pinning down its defenders with a frontal attack, while an enveloping force would march up the east shore of the Mystic and attack the redoubt's left rear. Gage approved Howe's plan and ordered it put into effect that day. It was decided to wait for high tide. "High Water at two o'clock in the afternoon," Howe recorded in a letter to his brother.

Howe, as senior officer, was to lead the expeditionary force, with Brigadier General Sir Robert Pigot second in command. The force of about 1,500 infantry and twelve guns would be moved in barges, due to shove off from Boston at high noon. To be held in reserve at the Battery in the city were 700 infantry of the 47th and 63rd regiments, as well as the major elements of the 1st and 2nd battalions of marines.

The concept of such an attack was not unsound. If it had been carried out at the earliest possible moment, British landing forces would have had ample room to maneuver and possibly capture both hills. The execution, however, was fatally flawed by a six-hour delay, which gave the Americans valuable time to extend their fortifications and make additional deployments. In the actual event there was neither adequate maneuvering room nor concentration of force at the right time and place.

WHEN THE *Lively* guns opened fire, the noise awakened Connecticut General Israel Putnam, who pulled on his clothes and galloped off toward Breed's Hill. This kind of riding was to characterize Putnam's performance; to those who saw him on this day of battle, he seemed to be everywhere at once. Israel Putnam was not just a brigadier general in Connecticut's militia; he was literally a legend in his time. Old Put—he was fifty-seven in 1775—was a household name due to the legends that had grown about him. There was his killing of a great wolf in her den, and also a true story of his being about to be burned at the stake by Indians when a French officer rescued him just in time to save his hide. Then there were tales of his adventures in the Havana campaign in 1762 when he was shipwrecked on the Cuban coast; and so on. In New England myth and legend he had become a real-life Revolution-era equivalent of Baron Munchausen.

Putnam was only five feet six in height, but he was built like a great brown bear. Yet his open, jovial face and halo of unruly gray hair made him resemble not a warrior but a generous, openhearted, dyed-in-the-wool American hero. He was immensely popular. Of generalship, the planning and execution of strategy, however, he was totally ignorant. He did possess the qualities of courage, energy, and aggressiveness, but those also represented his limit. Several historians have suggested that he would have made a splendid regimental commander—and so he should have remained.*

It was fully daylight when Putnam rode up to the redoubt and conferred with William Prescott. There he learned that Prescott's men were laboring and would be doing so for hours, without resupply of food, water, and ammunition. Each man had only the powder and shot he had carried with him. Prescott was not the kind of leader to ask for relief, but Putnam could see that Breed's Hill must have resupply and reinforcements if it were to be defended. By about 5:30 he was on his way back to Cambridge.

IN CAMBRIDGE A DEMANDING PUTNAM FOUND Artemas Ward chiefly concerned over the danger to his center at Cambridge and the threat of the same attack to cut off American forces at Charlestown Neck. Ward has been criticized for not taking immediate action to throw his reserves

---

*Much argument has taken place on the question of Putnam's responsibilities as a commander on the field in the coming battle. There is nothing to be gained by jumping into such a controversy. The "army" around Boston had as yet neither a command structure nor a staff system, and if Ward had designated Putnam as his field commander, there is no record of it. Because of the army's loose organization, or lack of it, a Connecticut brigadier general would seem to have had no real authority over, say, Massachusetts or New Hampshire units. But we know enough about Putnam to be sure that he would assume on-the-spot command whenever he thought it necessary.

and meager stores into position where Putnam was demanding. But despite Putnam's pleas, the commander in chief, who was also suffering from an attack of bladder stone, was adamant about not acting until the situation became clearer to him. As John Elting saw it: "Unlike Putnam, he [Ward] was not going to immediately mount his horse and ride off in all directions." A disgusted Putnam left for Bunker Hill.

SHORTLY BEFORE 9:00 A.M. PRESCOTT HAD EXCHANGED his uniform, hat, and wig for his wide-brimmed farmer's hat and linen banyan, the light coat meant for summer wear. He had just started to climb the six-foot redoubt wall for a look around when the British ships opened up with a concerted roar. This was no mere frigate's broadside; the thundering chorus was joined by the twenty-four-pounder battery on Copp's Hill on the northeast extremity of the Boston peninsula. Prescott looked around at his farmer-militiamen and saw white faces. Fears that could grow into panic must be squelched—now. So he mounted the parapet and calmly walked along its top until the men picked up their tools and went back to work.

An hour later Prescott's senior officers were demanding some kind of relief. The men were exhausted after ten hours of constant digging, and the bombardment continued. A cannonball had smashed the last water cask; there was no food for the hungry men; and now came the news that the British troops in Boston were assembling around the waterfront, certainly to cross the harbor and attack their redoubt. Wasn't it time that fresh troops relieved them?

Their iron-souled commander refused: "The men who raised these works were the ones best able to defend them; their honor required it." Prescott did relent to the extent of dispatching Major Brooks to Cambridge to ask for supplies. Brooks asked Captain Samuel Gridley of the artillery for a horse and was refused. A disgusted Prescott sent Brooks on his way to trudge the four long miles to Cambridge on foot.

PUTNAM'S RIDE OVER BUNKER HILL MUST HAVE convinced him that entrenchment should begin at once on that position also. He rode to Breed's Hill to get the men and tools from Prescott. This, with all of Prescott's other troubles, was a little too much, and he was not bashful in protesting to Putnam that the men who left with the tools would not come back. "They shall every man return," Putnam assured him. Prescott had to give in, and Captain Bancroft, who was a witness to the scene, tells us that "an order was never obeyed with more readiness."

Not one who left ever came back. Looking about him, Prescott must have been reflecting, with understandable concern, that out of his original detachment he could now count on less than 500 men to man the redoubt and the breastwork!

AFTER GETTING THE WORK STARTED ON BUNKER HILL, Putnam rode again to Cambridge to renew his pleas for supplies and reinforcements for Prescott. During a violent session Putnam gained an ally in Richard Devens, who brought the Committee of Safety in for a vote. The vote was overwhelmingly in favor of Putnam, and a grudging General Ward yielded to the extent—mere temporizing in Putnam's view—of ordering Colonel Stark at Medford to detach 200 of his New Hampshire regiment and have them march at once for Breed's Hill.

Stark dispatched Lieutenant Colonel Isaac Wyman with the troops to reinforce Prescott. He also put the remainder of his oversized regiment on alert, and gave similar instructions to the other New Hampshire regiment under his nominal command, that of Colonel James Reed, camped near Charlestown Neck.

Being a frontier province, New Hampshire was always short of supplies. Now ammunition was Stark's chief concern. He sent a detachment to Cambridge, which rounded up a little powder, and for lead brought back strippings from the organ of the Cambridge Episcopal Church.

These New Hampshiremen were mostly frontiersmen who had known all about Indian fighting and hunting from boyhood. According to Robert Hatch, "Most of Stark's recruits were crack shots . . . they could bring down a squirrel from a high branch or stop a partridge in flight" ("New Hampshire at Bunker Hill"). The statement should be taken with a bit of salt, because the musket was still the universal New England firearm; the rifle was unknown there.

What of New Hampshire's leader? As his men saw John Stark, he was forty-six, lean, tough as frontier leather, and direct of speech. This hatchet-faced Scotch-Irish Presbyterian had been raised on the frontier as a trapper whose attendant skills included Indian fighting. Captured and held captive by Indians at the age of twenty-four, he earned the respect of senior warriors when he had to run a gauntlet of clubs, armed only with a pole. Stark *walked* through, dealing out blows himself, all the while singing out, "I'll kiss all your women" (if he said or meant more than kissing, we have to rely on the story). Later, when ordered to hoe corn, the lot of squaws and captives, Stark threw his hoe in the river, declaring, "It is the business of squaws to hoe corn and not that of warriors." The chiefs ransomed him as soon as they could. In the French and Indian War Stark rose from second lieutenant to captain in the famed Roger's Rangers. His exploits in forest forays and half dozen battles earned him a reputation to match that of Old Put. In 1759 he returned to his province to found Starksville, later renamed Dunbarton. In 1775 he raised the regiment that he now commanded, with his head-quarters in Medford.

Now Stark and his men were ready for action. He set his men to pounding the lead into crude bullets because no bullet molds were on hand. Then, at about 1:30 P.M. he led his regiment out of Medford, on Ward's order, on his way to pick up Reed's regiment near the Neck.

DURING THE NOON HOUR PRESCOTT MUST have had mixed feelings about his situation. The day of 17 June was clear and hot, with the temperature climbing toward the mid-eighties and only a light breeze, not enough to clear the dust-clouded air in the redoubt. But the redoubt was being finished off with banquettes, the firing steps essential to firing over the redoubt walls, and the breastwork would soon be completed, too.

Prescott's satisfaction was overshadowed by the condition of his men. Young Peter Brown, a company clerk in Prescott's regiment, has left us an insight: "We began to be almost beat out, being fatigued by our La-bour, having no Sleep the night before, very little to eat, no drink but rum, but what we hazarded our lives to get, we grew faint, Thirsty, hun-gry and weary."

Prescott's worries were not confined to shortages of food and water. Three hours before, the British cannonade had resumed with a sort of harassing fire. At first the incoming shells had not cowed the men work-ing outside the walls, but their initial casualty created a crisis. Young Asa Pollard of Billerica had his head blown off by a cannonball, to the horror of his comrades. When Prescott answered their pleas of what to do, with a curt "bury him," they clustered around the body to hear prayers from a self-appointed chaplain. After two attempts to get them back to work, Prescott threw up his hands and let them finish their rites.

Then there was the matter of the artillery: there were no solid firing platforms and no embrasures made in the walls—and no tools to make them. Prescott finally ordered Captain Gridley—Colonel Gridley's son and a captain by virtue of that relationship alone—to move his two guns out near the breastwork where, in Peter Brown's words, Gridley "swang his hat three times to the enemy." Thereafter Gridley displaced his bat-tery to Bunker Hill.

Shortly after noon Prescott's previous worries were dwarfed by the impact of a renewed bombardment that made the morning's seem like mere artillery practice. It soon reached the highest intensity of the day. *Falcon* and *Lively* blasted the ground around Moulton's Point and east of Charlestown, the mighty *Somerset's* sixty-four-gun broadsides were joined by two floating batteries and the twenty-four-pounders on Copp's Hill, while *Glasgow, Symmetry,* and two gunboats kept fire sweeping across the Neck. The ships' broadsides could bring to bear forty guns at a time. The colonials were fearful: was all this artillery preparation a signal that the British were about to launch an amphibious landing?

The answer soon came. Before the weary eyes of the militiamen—and thousands of citizens who crowded the rooftops of Boston and the hillsides above the Charles and the Mystic—a double column of landing barges, fourteen in each, appeared rounding the north end of Boston, headed for Moulton's Point. In its martial splendor and military might, the spectacle seemed to embody the threat that the Old World was posing to the hopes of the colonies. The midday sun sparkling on the waters of the harbor was reflected back from the glittering steel of hundreds of bayonets and musket barrels, made even brighter by the scarlet ranks massed in the boats.

Prescott may have been as impressed as the others, but there can be no doubt that his no-nonsense eye was estimating the size of the force in the boats: perhaps somewhere between one and two thousand infantry, with several fieldpieces in the leading boats. And he knew how the brave martial display could quickly disintegrate into the reality of combat, producing results like the headless corpse of Asa Pollard, buried down there in the ditch of the redoubt.

SIR WILLIAM HOWE'S LEADING ELEMENTS began landing around Moulton's Point about 1:00 P.M. While his troops were marching to deploy in the classic British order of three lines, Howe took time to study the terrain and the enemy. His professional sensibilities were jarred at his first look. The colonials' position had been greatly improved since early morning. The single redoubt had been extended eastward, thus cutting down Howe's room for maneuver, although there was still enough space for an envelopment on the east side toward the Mystic. And the breastwork was not the only change: he could see a mass of men milling around on Bunker Hill, probably some sort of reserve force. As Howe watched, a long column began coming down the forward slope of Bunker Hill, heading toward the Breed's Hill redoubt.

Howe saw the potential danger of getting his present force, now form-ing on Moulton's Hill, caught between the two hills while making an en-velopment of Breed's. He realized that he would need more troops (his reserve waiting at the battery), and he gave orders to return the barges to bring up the reserve. At the same time he began pushing forward two covering forces from his present position. Four light infantry com-panies were deployed in the low ground in front of his main body, while General Robert Pigot was ordered to move to the left (west) with the battalion companies of the 38th and 43rd regiments (sixteen companies) to an area below the southern extremity of Breed's Hill. Howe's last order then was to let the men fall out in place and break out their rations for the noon meal.

PRESCOTT HAD WATCHED THE BRITISH INFANTRY companies land and form into massed lines, and by 1:30 P.M. he saw clearly the threat to his left (north) flank. Between the end of his breastwork and the Mystic there was a wide gap, only partially protected by the marsh on that side. Already, British light infantry companies were moving down the forward slope of Moulton's Hill to come into skirmish lines. Prescott at once ordered Captain Knowlton to take his Connecticut company, along with Captain Callender's two fieldpieces, and oppose them.

Prescott had good reason to trust Knowlton. Like Stark, Knowlton had been an Indian fighter, having gone off to fight the redskins and the French as a boy of fifteen. He had been a lieutenant at seventeen with a reputation for courage and leadership. He was now thirty-five and, like Stark, tough and lean. He was making his decision as he marched, having observed the British deployments while standing alongside Pres-cott. Knowlton's eye settled on a rail fence running parallel to Prescott's breastwork and about 300 yards to its rear, extending to the bank of the Mystic. He ordered his men to stack arms and begin tearing out the rails of nearby fences, which he then used to fill the gaps in his chosen fence, whose rails rested on posts set in a stone base. The men then stuffed loose hay between the rails to give it the appearance of a solid breast-work. It proved good enough to fool General Howe, who later described it as a breastwork "which effectively secured those behind it from Mus-ketry." Knowlton did not yet know it, but he had prepared a defensive position whose tactical importance would equal that of Prescott's re-doubt. Yet while Knowlton was checking out his fields of fire across the meadows to his front, Captain Callender, following Gridley's precedent, quietly decamped with his guns for Bunker Hill.

Since he had left Prescott around 11:00 A.M., Israel Putnam was learning the hard way the frustration that came to a Connecticut general who sought to hurry forward Massachusetts troops and officers not legally under his command. He had raged back and forth between the Neck and Bunker Hill, even riding across the Neck under fire as an example, but the chaotic mass of intermingled regiments was too much for him, especially when he couldn't get their officers to lead them. The occasional ships' cannon shot, really a slow interdiction fire, was all it took to cow the green militia.

Putnam's temper didn't improve when he bumped into Captain Callender and his two guns heading across Bunker Hill. When the general asked why he was retreating, he got an evasive answer from Callender, a mumbled reply about being low on ammunition. An irate Putnam checked the side boxes on the gun carriages to find them nearly full. When Putnam ordered him to make a 180-degree turn toward Breed's Hill, Callender refused. But Putnam's pistol muzzle at his head quickly convinced Callender that indeed Breed's was a logical destination.

Putnam, however, was rewarded when he looked down the forward slope of Bunker Hill to see in the distance a most pleasant sight: Connecticut men under a resourceful leader building that rail-fence breastwork smack in the path of any British force attempting to flank Prescott's position. He also encountered Stark's Lieutenant Colonel Wyman and directed him toward Knowlton's position.

IN CAMBRIDGE NEWS OF THE BRITISH LANDING had moved Ward to order forward all the forces he could muster. The area north of the Neck became a madhouse of activity as nine Massachusetts regiments were ordered forward, thereby increasing the mass of confused companies who were blocking the road onto the Neck. Stark led his regiment through the congestion like the bow of a ship breasting the waves. He had sent forward Major Andrew McClary to open a path, and this six-foot-six frontiersman took pleasure in the task. "If Massachusetts didn't need to use the road just then, would they please move over and let New Hampshire through?" The Massachusetts troops stepped aside.

Captain Henry Dearborn, marching alongside Stark, nervously "suggested the propriety of quickening the march of the regiment, so it might sooner be relieved of the galling crossfire." In Dearborn's words, "He fixed his eyes upon me, and observed with great composure: 'Dearborn, one fresh man in action is worth ten fatigued ones' and continued to advance in the same cool and collected manner." When Stark passed

Putnam on the forward crest of Bunker, he was met with an order—a request?—from the latter to detach enough men to finish entrenching the hill. Stark ignored him. Surveying Knowlton's position and finding it much undermanned, he paused only long enough to make some brief remarks to his men, then led them on to the rail fence.

After taking command of the fence line and assigning his officers the tasks required to bolster the position, Stark went down to survey the end of the fence line at the bank of the Mystic. Looking down the steep eight-foot bank, he saw a beach made narrow by the same high tide that had carried the British boats to Moulton's Point. Recognizing at once that the beach could still support a column of British infantry moving to envelop the left flank of the rail-fence position, he immediately detailed enough men to haul stones from the riverbank and nearby fences to build a waist-high breastwork in prolongation of the rail fence.

Stark's final act in organizing the position was based on his experience with Roger's Rangers and the battles of the French and Indian War. He knew that the disciplined British infantry could take the shock of a defender's first volley and close with the bayonet before the defenders could reload—a matter of fifteen to thirty seconds. Stark therefore formed the whole of his command into three ranks, with strict orders that each rank would fire only on order, then step back to reload, thus leaving the enemy no respite between volleys. Stark was well aware that his volley system would eventually degenerate into firing by individuals, but he hoped he could count on pouring enough volleys into the British to smash their leading ranks to pieces before that occurred. To make his point clear he paced out fifty yards to the front, drove a stake into the ground, and gave orders that no man was to fire until the British front rank reached the stake. Stark was ready.

PRESCOTT, VIEWING THE BRITISH DEPLOYMENTS, now picked up a red-coated column moving from the landing beach to take up position nearer Charlestown. Ever since he had detached Knowlton to cover his left, he had grown equally concerned about his right. He sent Lieutenant Colonel John Robinson with 150 men to strengthen the defense in Charlestown, in order to secure the redoubt on its right (west) side. Robinson's departure left Prescott with about 150 men in the fort and 300 to 500 at the breastwork.

Other developments demanded Prescott's attention. Some time after Robinson had gone, Prescott noticed the smoke of arching trajectories left by shells from the British ships and the Copp's Hill battery. Such "tracers" were made by red-hot shot and carcasses, a type of shell filled with combustibles and pierced with holes. In minutes fires were breaking out in Charlestown houses, and soon the whole town was ablaze. Still, Prescott's men in the doomed town would be able to scamper away and take cover in barns or behind stone walls, from which they could continue to delay any British flanking attack.

To his left Prescott could see that the three small flèches—V-shaped, hastily made breastworks pointing toward the enemy like arrows, hence their French name—were being occupied by colonial reinforcements. Later he was to learn that the flèches had been ordered constructed by Colonel Gridley and were manned by Massachusetts men from the regiments of Colonels Doolittle, Brewer, and Nixon.

By 3:00 P.M. the panorama of the coming battle was unfolding under Prescott's eyes. To his left rear, the rail fence—he couldn't see the beach below the river bank—and the flèches were lined with the ranks of waiting American troops. In front of the flèches and Stark's fence, the sweep of the meadows was broken only by the rectangles of fenced-in fields and an occasional shade tree. To Prescott's immediate left, newly arrived reinforcements were being posted along the breastwork while the "older" men were taking their ease on the grass behind it; it was the only rest they were to get after their morning's labor. Others were sorting out their ammunition for a final inspection. The militiamen nearest Prescott had emptied their pouches and pockets of bullets, which they were counting into their broad-brimmed hats, estimating how long their powder charges would last.

From Prescott's vantage point the whole of the American positions, excepting, of course, Stark's beach, could be discerned. From left to right there was first the rail fence, then—between the fence and the redoubt—the flèches, next the redoubt crowning Breed's Hill, and finally the scattered elements between the redoubt and the shores of the Charles River on the right.

Now the British movements to his left front caught Prescott's eye. The light infantry north of Moulton's Hill was reforming into a single, long, scarlet column and was marching off toward the Mystic. Other columns were marching from Moulton's Hill toward the Brick Kiln and deploying into line on the slopes being cleared by the light infantry. Directly in front of Prescott, battalion columns had moved up from the landing beach and were fanning out into precise three-deep lines. This force was obviously forming for an attack on the redoubt, probably to begin in concert with the lines massing north of the Brick Kiln.

In the background the leaping flames in Charlestown were giving off clouds of dark smoke that were drifting slowly eastward before a light summer breeze. Over it all the rolling roar of the British guns continued to drown out all other sounds. Now they were joined by the British battery of six-pounders that had gone into firing position on the edge of the marsh near the Brick Kiln. Its fire was apparently being directed against the rail fence and flèches, with no discernible effect.

In the redoubt and along the breastwork the men were silent, engrossed like their commander in the spectacle that was closing in on them. And like Stark's men, Prescott's were ready.

HOWE'S RESERVE LANDED NEAR PIGOT'S FORCE south of Breed's Hill and immediately marched up to reinforce the waiting forces. While awaiting his reserves Howe had formulated his plan of attack. In contrast to the unimaginative and simple frontal assault that has so often been pictured, Howe's plan was to attack in two wings. Pigot, on the left, would pin down Prescott's men in the redoubt while distracting them from Howe's main attack, and Howe would personally lead the other wing to envelop and encircle the American left. In his scheme of maneuver Howe was to attack the rail fence with the grenadier companies* in the first line, followed by the battalion companies of the 5th and 52nd regiments in the second line. But the key to his attack lay with the eleven light infantry companies he was drawing off to his right to form an assault column, which would move rapidly along the beach to envelop the Americans at the rail fence and then, in conjunction with his frontally attacking force, move to outflank the Americans on Breed's Hill. Howe's attack was to be preceded by an artillery preparation from the ships, directed at the redoubt and breastwork, and supplemented by his field artillery pieces, which were pushed forward to fire on the American positions.

Howe's overall plan shows the tactical skill that he would employ time after time to defeat Washington on the battlefield. However, he was not yet aware that the Americans in the redoubt and the rail fence—Howe and his officers could not see Stark's men on the beach—were backed up by a few key American officers with combat experience who knew how to make every bullet count, even though those bullets were fired by the greenest of militia.

---

*This is an example of the common practice of detaching "flanking companies" to form elite forces with special missions.

JOHN STARK HAD WATCHED THE BRITISH BATTERY open up, and the few round shot that had come his way had whistled overhead. After a few rounds the battery ceased firing, leaving Stark to wonder at the sudden lull.* Without waiting to puzzle over such things, however, he strode on down to the beach to take post behind his three-ranked line. Now the Americans, muskets primed and hammers at half-cock, could only wait for the redcoats to appear.

Some few minutes before the enemy came in sight, Stark and his New Hampshiremen heard the rattle of marching drums. There was an eerie pause as the men heard the sound but did not see a single soldier. Suddenly there they were, a close-ordered column of fours coming around a curve of beach. There were officers in the lead and alongside the column, and Stark could see the rhythmic swing of their sword arms, moving in time with marching beat. Now he could make out the short leather caps of the soldiers, and he realized that they were light infantry.

Stark had already given his order to "fire at the top of their gaiters or the waistcoat," and it was being obeyed, for he could see the barrels of the front-rank muskets lowered as his men took aim. The British officers under the Americans' aiming eyes were shouting commands, and the files of the column fanned out to deploy into line. All movements were being made at the double in disciplined silence. Commands rang out again, and the forward company came on, muskets leveled at charge bayonet. To Americans, who were seeing them for the first time over their leveled musket barrels, the steel hedge of bayonets was a fearsome sight.

When the scarlet jackets surged past his stake in the sand—curiously, Stark noted the stake being knocked over by a charging infantryman—he shouted his command. "Fire!" The volley crashed out like the firing of one great musket, every trigger pulled in the same instant.

Stark's eyes strained to see through the drifting haze of white smoke. In seconds he could make out the sight: whole ranks of light infantry had been leveled as though a giant hand had swept them down to the sand. Here and there wounded men were trying to rise between heaps of bodies. Yet British discipline held fast, and a second company came thrusting its way through the remnants of the first, officers shouting the men on, eager to exploit the precious seconds it would take those farmers to reload.

These professionals were about to get the shock of their lives. When

---

*The battery had been supplied with twelve-pound balls instead of six-pound, so the battery did indeed cease firing after their few six-pound shot had been expended.

the new company was still bounding over the dead and wounded, Stark gave his second rank the command to fire. Their scythe of fire cut down the second company with the same slaughter that had wiped out the first. The cries of the wounded rose again after the stunned silence that followed the first volley.

Both British charges had been designed to depend on the bayonet, and a third was deploying to repeat the attempt at bayonet point. Stark, peering through the clearing smoke, watched the scattered survivors, often as few as one man in ten, falling back, to be passed over by the surging rush of a third company coming on with the same dash as its predecessors. And with Stark's third volley the result was a repeat of the same slaughter. This time, however, the British officers made no attempt to rally platoons or companies; nowhere were there enough men standing to form one line. The repeated sheets of fire were more than even British infantry could stand.

Now Stark's men were firing at will, the better shots picking off rank and file whenever their aim found them. Restraining a few hotheads who wanted to pursue their rapidly withdrawing enemy to get in another shot, Stark and his officers herded them back into ranks, and he went forward to count the dead. The redcoat light infantry had carried off their wounded, leaving only the dead. There were ninety-six in all, lying "like sheep in a fold."

ABOVE THE BEACH, IN THE FIELDS THAT STRETCHED for a quarter mile beyond the rail fence, the other British attack was developing. The defenders' flimsy breastwork was manned by the men of Connecticut, New Hampshire, and Massachusetts, perhaps 1,500 in all. They had listened to the crashing volleys down on the beach; now it was their turn to take on a British attack.

This attack was not a charging rush like that of the light infantry. The long red lines were struggling forward in the afternoon heat, carrying the weight of a musket, sixty rounds of cartridges, three days' rations, and rolled blanket—fifty pounds of marching order. Then too, their tight wool uniforms were anything but comfortable under the hot sun.

To the waiting militia their enemy seemed to be taking his own good time in advancing, as if to build on the Americans' suspense. Actually, the British were having a time of it, being forced to clamber over or knock down fences and then wade through knee-deep grass, keeping their ranks dressed all the while. Veterans like Knowlton could see now that the leading three-rank line consisted entirely of grenadiers, their tall black bearskins fronted by regimental badges flashing in the sun. When the leading grenadiers realigned ranks, Captain Dearborn recalled that they did it "with the precision and firmness of troops on parade, and opened a brisk but regular fire by platoons."

It was the "fire by platoons" that got the grenadiers into trouble. As they opened fire they were met with a heavy return fire that tumbled dozens of dead and wounded into the grass. The American firing began, in spite of their officers' cautioning, by a few eager souls like Lieutenant Dana of Knowlton's company, who fired, as he said, "with a view to draw the enemy's fire." (One wonders what John Stark was to say about this lame excuse, a palpable effort to cover up nervousness.) The grenadiers returned fire, though it may be doubted that it was as regular as Dearborn recalled it. In any case, most of the bullets of the British volleys whistled over American heads.

When the militia was brought to order by veteran officers such as Knowlton, fire was held as the British advanced again. To the New England farmers and village youths the scarlet wall of towering grenadiers was an incredible sight. What would it take to stop these massed ranks marching forward again with such precision?

The answer came when the grenadiers reached another fence only yards from the muskets leveled over the fence rails. Following a brief hesitation, the British began knocking down rails in their haste to get over the obstacle. Israel Putnam, waiting with sword in hand—once again where he figured he was needed most—saw that it was the right moment and bellowed "Fire!" This time a controlled volley crashed out, and the length of the rail fence was a solid sheet of yellow flame. Grenadiers were not knocked over singly; instead, great gaps were torn in their ranks, leaving the shaken survivors to fall back from the terrible fire.

The slaughter continued. To the incredulous Americans, the black-cocked hats and single white cross belts of battalion companies repeatedly appeared one after the other through the haze of powder smoke. It was the second, supporting line of the attack. The jumbled mass presented targets that the greenest militiaman couldn't miss. The supporting battalions had come forward too fast, and were now intermingled with the shattered remnants of grenadier companies. Flushed with success, Connecticut farm boys and New Hampshire hunters were calling out eagerly to each other as they selected targets at will.

The disordered mass fell back of its own accord, despite the commands and pleas of the British officers. Heaps and rows of wounded and dying were left behind. In the colonial lines, officers were restoring order and getting men back into place. The veterans among the Americans knew that this local victory might mean only the beginning of prolonged combat, so an exhilarated Putnam remounted and rode back to Bunker Hill to hasten up reinforcements.

IT WAS ALMOST 3:30 P.M. WHEN PRESCOTT saw the next attack coming, this time against Breed's Hill. When the long red lines came into view on the south slopes, he recognized the cocked hats of battalion companies. To his right front a mixed force was appearing. Some units wore the round caps of light infantry, other companies were in the bearskins of the grenadiers, and still others were clearly battalion companies. In the redoubt and behind the breastwork, Prescott's men were feeling the same stomach-clenching fear that the men at the rail fence had felt. The rattle of the drums and the high-pitched shrill of the fifes were coming nearer. In the intervals between battalions could be seen the twin colors, king's and regimental, carried high by ensigns. To the men crouching on the firing steps or braced against the breastwork it seemed unbelievable that this splendid sight could actually be coming against *them*. But it was.

On shouted command the scarlet ranks snapped to a halt and came to order arms. From the British right, platoon volleys cracked out, obscuring the ranks with their white smoke. Again the fire was too high, most of it passing overhead. Prescott couldn't believe his eyes: what were the British up to, firing at distances of seventy to eighty yards? He had no time to think about it; nervous militiamen were beginning to fire back. Lieutenant Colonel Robinson mounted the parapet and ran along its top, kicking up any musket barrels he found being aimed.

New commands rang out, and the British ranks advanced up the hill. Prescott waited until they had closed within forty yards before he gave the order to fire. In the British front ranks the scene Stark's unbelieving eyes had witnessed earlier was repeated: shattered ranks and falling casualties. This time, however, British officers remained in control and conducted a reasonably orderly withdrawal.

Prescott ordered a cease-fire. Enough precious ammunition had been fired away, and the enemy was getting out of musket range. Had this attack been a feint, a secondary effort? It was too early to know, but one thing was certain: this attack—so easily beaten back—would not be the last.

HOWE HAD LED THE ATTACKING LINES FORWARD against the rail fence. There he had personally witnessed the slaughter from the muskets of the militia, who had not only held their ground but had delivered such a deadly, sustained fire that his best troops could not stand against it. As he walked back, sword in hand, an aide was giving him the report of the disastrous failure of the attack of the light companies on the beach. His attempt at envelopment had failed as disastrously as the frontal attack he had led forward. Consequently his whole main attack had collapsed.

Still, plenty of time remained to reorganize and renew the offensive. Within a quarter of an hour, Howe had given his order and a new attack was under way. This time the light infantry companies, withdrawn from the beach and redeployed, would make a secondary effort against the rail fence while Howe and Pigot would make a new main attack against the redoubt, attacking simultaneously from the east and south.

STARK WALKED HIS LINE, CHECKING AMMUNITION and voicing words of encouragement where he thought it needed. The men, "blooded" now, were almost eager for a renewed attack. In less than half an hour the British obliged them. This time, as the deployed lines moved forward, they seemed to be having less trouble with the fences. Soon Stark realized why the enemy could come ahead so rapidly; the leather caps of the faster-moving, less-encumbered light infantry came into sight—perhaps the companies that had been at the rear of the column on the beach. Farther off and to his right, Stark could see columns of grenadiers and line companies moving obliquely across his front, apparently advancing on the flèches. For the moment he could ignore them; he would have his hands full with the attack coming at his fence. But he had full confidence in his men, and they had all been encouraged by the arrival of Captain Trevett's two artillery pieces, now in position at the right end of the fence.

The lines of light infantry had crossed the fence 150 yards away and were coming on at a steady pace. New Hampshire and Connecticut men waited in silence, front-rank muskets resting on fence rails, second and third ranks standing with muskets at "poise firelock." Then, to Stark's surprise, the British suddenly halted and opened fire. It was too good to believe: a fixed target within easy musket range of no more than sixty yards. He shouted the command to fire.

For an incredible quarter hour the British infantry stood fast, firing and reloading in an attempt to exchange fire with the Americans. This was no even exchange, though. Volley after volley flamed over the rail fence, taking a more fearsome toll than that inflicted upon the first attack. When Stark could see through the smoke, the sight was shocking,

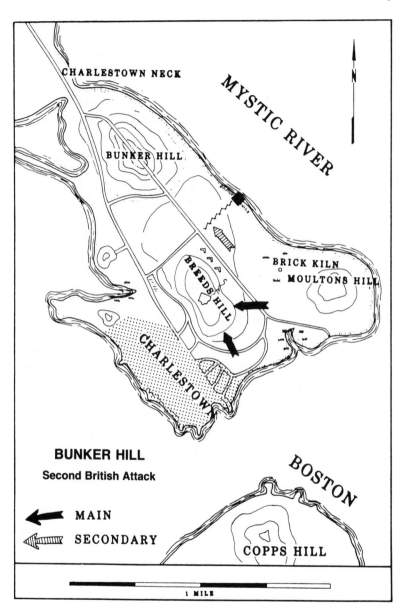

CHARLESTOWN NECK

MYSTIC RIVER

BUNKER HILL

BRICK KILN

MOULTONS HILL

BREEDS HILL

CHARLESTOWN

BUNKER HILL

Second British Attack

◄■■ MAIN

◄▥▥ SECONDARY

BOSTON

COPPS HILL

1 MILE

even to him. Here and there a brave file still stood, firing with mechanical precision, but the huge gaps between those few files astounded Stark. Where companies had stood in solid ranks, as few as eight or nine men were left standing in some, in others, four or five.

It was more than any infantry could bear. Where Trevett's guns had blasted holes in British ranks, the job had been finished by hundreds of muskets. Now those red-coated infantrymen who could were hastily falling back out of range, and Stark saw what appeared to be a high-ranking British officer walking, sword in hand, among the retreating men. The second attack, as anyone could see, had been smashed, not only in front of Stark's position but also in front of the flèches, where windrows of British dead and wounded attested to the fact.

PRESCOTT HAD BEEN ABLE TO SNATCH a few minutes to observe the disastrous repulse of the attacks against the rail fence and the flèches before a renewed attack against his hill was mounted. To his front the British battalions marching up the slopes appeared to be the same as before. On Prescott's right, however, it was a different story: the formations coming from that quarter seemed to have been heavily reinforced.

Prescott had been at his toughest in cautioning officers and men to hold their fire, and as these attacks came up the hill, his words had been effective. The men were confidently silent, and not a musket had yet been aimed. He waited "till the enemy advanced within thirty yards, when we gave them such a hot fire that they were obliged to retire nearly one hundred and fifty yards before they could rally." That hot fire had covered the green grass of the hillsides with scores of red coats. There were a few American casualties, among them Sergeant Benjamin Prescott, who took a British bullet in the shoulder. He managed to hide his wound from his father, who was passing down the line below the banquette praising his men for their stout defense.

When his officers reported their ammunition count to Prescott, however, it was anything but encouraging. Many men would be able to fire only three or four more shots. Prescott ordered the cannon cartridges from the guns abandoned by the artillery to be slit open and the powder distributed, at best a token resupply. And there had been no resupply of anything from Cambridge: no food, water, or ammunition.

While the second British attack was being fought off, Putnam rode back to Bunker Hill, where he had stationed units of Massachusetts militia for the purposes of continuing the entrenching or to be prepared to move forward to reinforce the troops on Breed's Hill or the rail fence. When he reached the top of the hill, Putnam's plans and hopes were both dashed in one glance. Instead of troops busily digging or standing by in formations ready to march, he saw a disordered mass of milling men moving around the top of the hill or down the reverse slope in groups apparently out of control. He learned later that most of the mob was made up of stragglers or fugitives from units that had moved on forward. The arrival of these men had so disorganized the troops already on the hill that their officers, through incompetence or inexperience, had given up any attempts at rallying and reorganizing their units. What Putnam was seeing has been described by Captain John Chester, who had marched his Connecticut company past Bunker Hill: "There was not a company in any kind of order. They [stragglers, fugitives, skulkers] were scattered, some behind rocks and hay-cocks, and thirty men, perhaps, behind an apple tree . . . frequently twenty men round a wounded man retreating, when not more than three or four could touch him with advantage. Others were retreating, seemingly without any excuse."

Putnam rode through the chaotic scene down to Charlestown Neck, where he found the roads choked with the same kind of uncontrolled and intermingled companies that Stark had marched through on his way forward. Putnam again tried to show the shirkers, by example, how ineffective the British ships' fire really was. After riding back and forth across the Neck, he called on men to follow him—all without success.

Frustrated, Putnam raged back to Bunker Hill, where he again tried to rally officers and men so that they could be marched on toward Breed's Hill. After finding fat Colonel Gerrish lying on the ground with no idea of how to assemble his regiment, Putnam cut loose with tongue and sword: "He entreated them, threatened them, and some of the most cowardly he knocked down with his sword, but all in vain"—all except Gerrish's adjutant, Christian Febiger, who rallied a group of the more resolute and led them forward. Some more of this kind Putnam directed to the flèches where he thought help was most needed. But those were only a fraction of the mass which continued to skulk on Bunker Hill.

HOWE HAD TO WATCH THE FAILURE OF HIS second attack. The American fire in all parts of the field had been sustained with the same ferocity as before, and the casualty toll had continued to climb alarmingly.

Clinton had arrived during the second British attack and had taken it on himself to rally two regiments that had fallen back toward the beach south of the redoubt. More welcome to Howe, however, were the newly arrived 63rd Regiment and the flank companies of the 2nd Marine Battalion, a reinforcement of 400 men.

Over the protest of some of his senior officers, Howe now doggedly prepared for an all-out assault of the redoubt, with only a token attack against the rail fence. This time Howe, Pigot, and Clinton would lead forward everything else in a bayonet attack on the redoubt. And this time Howe's field artillery would be relied on to move into a forward position where it could deliver enfilading fire on the breastwork's defenders, thus eliminating the threat from that quarter. The infantry men were ordered to lay aside all their impedimenta—knapsacks, blanket rolls, everything but muskets, bayonets, and ammunition. The Americans were to be driven from their position, whatever the cost.

Sometime after 4:00 P.M., as Prescott watched the British regroup for a third attack, he saw deployments to his front and both flanks, to the northeast and southwest. It was evident that Breed's Hill was going to be attacked this time by a giant pincers which would close in from front and flanks.

From behind his rail fence, John Stark watched more light infantry moving forward in an approach march. This time, however, their companies did not mass for a frontal assault, but deployed into a thin skirmish line at a discreet 200 yards. If it did materialize, this attack could be a holding attack meant to keep Stark's men tied down to their position. As before, however, Stark was seeing more than light infantry to his front. Again, moving obliquely in the distance, were lines of battalion companies headed toward the flèches and the left flank of Prescott's breastwork. And there was a new threat in the same direction. A British six-pounder battery had been manhandled into a new firing position, where it broke its hour-and-a-half silence by opening fire against Prescott's breastwork. As the battery opened up, the light infantry advanced another fifty yards and began an ineffective skirmishing fire against the rail fence. Stark knew how to play the game: he directed officers to select a few good marksmen to pick off what British they could at long range.

PRESCOTT AND HIS OFFICERS WERE MAKING SURE that every man was on the firing step and spaced to man all three walls of the redoubt. Then it was time for Prescott to keep his eye on the advancing enemy. They came forward at charge bayonet, and Prescott knew that there would be no halting to fire—this was to be a bayonet assault. He let the front ranks

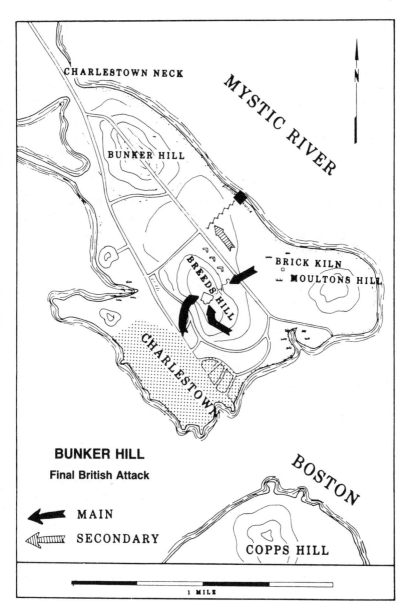

CHARLESTOWN NECK

MYSTIC RIVER

BUNKER HILL

BRICK KILN
MOULTONS HILL

BREEDS HILL

CHARLESTOWN

BUNKER HILL

Final British Attack

MAIN

SECONDARY

BOSTON

COPPS HILL

1 MILE

come within a sweat-wringing twenty yards before he gave the command to fire.

As before, the shattered front ranks staggered back. Again Prescott's men mounted the firing step and fired another volley which brought the British ranks to a halt. But in a matter of seconds everything was changing. The six-pounder battery began firing sheaves of grapeshot, which swept through the rear of the breastwork with devastating effect. The enfilading blasts of grapeshot blew men into flying chunks of flesh, and the screams of the wounded could be heard above the guns. It was more than the Americans could endure; some fled to the rear, others took shelter in the redoubt.

Prescott saw his control slipping away like floodwater rushing through a burst dam. His men were firing their last desperate rounds, and as their ammunition ran out, their fire died away—as someone recalled—"like a candle sputtering out." Now the British second line had reached the ditch and was fighting its way up the outer wall. While the grenadiers were fighting to scale the walls, Prescott got a frantic message that the British had taken the breastwork. The only recourse now was to order a retreat through the opening in the rear of the redoubt.

Prescott's last look at the wall revealed British officers, swords in hand, clambering over the parapet. A Marine major stood on the south wall, waving his sword at his men behind him. A last shot from Peter Salem, a black soldier, knocked the major backward from the wall.* Now British soldiers were dropping into the redoubt from three sides. Prescott and his exhausted men were fighting like devils, with musket butts, rocks, even their hands. Thirty of them died under British bayonets, among them the gallant Major General Joseph Warren of the Continental Congress, who had come to fight as a volunteer. Another of the dead was the already wounded Benjamin Prescott, cut in two by a cannon ball.

The last minutes in the redoubt were like hell itself. The blinding, choking dust that rose from the melee made it difficult to tell friend from foe, and the Americans could scarcely make their way through the rear opening. No shots were fired by the British coming over the wall; the mingled mass of fighting men was too dense for that. Prescott was one of the last through the opening, parrying British bayonet thrusts with his sword. Later, he found that his coat had been pierced in half a dozen places by bayonets.

---

*This was Major Pitcairn, who had led the British Detachment against the Minutemen on Lexington Common.

Once into the open behind the redoubt, the escaping Americans, fleeing toward Bunker Hill, were spared by a stroke of fortune. The British soldiers who dashed around the redoubt to seal off the rear faced each other across a sort of gauntlet; they couldn't fire for fear of hitting each other. That impasse lasted just long enough for the Americans to flee down the reverse slope of Breed's Hill. But now fortune deserted them; the British closed ranks and opened fire, causing more casualties among the fugitives than the Americans had suffered in the redoubt. There was nothing that Prescott could do now. Things were too far gone, and he had to make his way alone to Bunker Hill.

STARK PLAYED OUT THE GAME TO THE END. When it was clear that Breed's Hill and the flèches had fallen, he could see how untenable the rail-fence line had become. If he continued to hold his position, it would soon be outflanked at its right end by a continuation of the present British advance. Reluctantly he gave the order to withdraw, but from then on he made it a dogged fight, dropping back from fence to fence, all the while directing fire to delay the British and to cover—where he could— the Americans falling back from the flèches. Later, even General Burgoyne had to report that Stark's "retreat was no flight; it was even covered with bravery and military skill." But this was happening as his men were firing their last rounds of ammunition.

Stark has been criticized for failing to make a counterattack against the exposed British right flank. The censure is unjustified. Stark's regiments, even companies, had become so intermixed that the control needed to reorganize and maneuver under fire would have been impossible to exercise. To maneuver Connecticut, New Hampshire, and Massachusetts troops from a defensive posture into counterattacking formations would have been an impossible task. Moreover, there were very few bayonets, no reserves to support a counterattack, and Captain Dearborn tells us that "by this time our ammunition was exhausted. A few men only had a charge left."

In withdrawing, Stark took with him Captain Trevett's single remaining fieldpiece, the only gun saved out of the whole battle. There is little doubt that Stark's fighting retreat saved a large part of the American army on the peninsula.

AS SO OFTEN HAPPENS TO A DEFEATED FORCE trying to escape pursuit, the Americans took their greatest losses between Breed's Hill and Bunker Hill, especially on the slopes of the latter. Putnam had to abandon any hope of rallying fugitives to fight from his half-finished entrenchments. The panicked men continued to pass by him as he sat on his horse like a tiny island in a surging flood. His entreaties and curses were equally unheard. The only fighting units—elements of the regiments of Little and Gardner and some unidentified companies—had already gone forward and were fighting, like Stark and his men, to cover the retreat. When those last men passed Putnam, even he had given up, and so he rode back to find a new position to stop the British. It is said that Prescott and Putnam came face to face near the Neck. Prescott's first words were to question Putnam, asking why he had not gotten reinforcements to Breed's Hill. "I could not drive the dogs," Putnam replied. Prescott snapped back, "If you could not *drive* them up, you might had *led* them up."

While the American rear guards covered the rush of men across the Charlestown Neck, the British halted on the reverse slope of Bunker Hill. General Howe had halted the pursuit, convinced that he lacked enough fresh troops to follow up his costly victory.

In any event, Prescott went on to confront Artemas Ward in Cambridge, where, as the story goes, he demanded permission "to re-take the Heights that night or perish in the attempt, if the Commander-in-Chief would give him three regiments with bayonets and sufficient ammunition." It is hardly surprising that Ward refused.

Putnam made his way to Winter Hill, northwest of Charlestown Neck, where he did succeed in rallying enough units to work them all night, "and by morning had built an entrenchment . . . a hundred feet square." But the Battle of Bunker Hill ended when the British halted on that hill sometime between five and six o'clock in the afternoon.

IT WAS A COSTLY BATTLE. THE TOTAL NUMBER of Americans on the Charlestown peninsula has been estimated at 3,000, but it appears that only half that number were ever actually engaged in combat. American casualties were 140 killed, 271 wounded, and 30 captured, for a total of 441. Thus, if one considers the American force to have numbered 3,000, their combat loss was nearly 15 percent. Conversely, if one considers only the 1,500 Americans actually engaged with the enemy, their combat loss amounted to 30 percent.

By comparison, in cold military terms the losses of the British were grim indeed. Out of Howe's force of 2,500, the casualties totaled 1,150, or about 45 percent. Officer casualties were particularly high, and the losses within many grenadier and light infantry companies ran as high as a staggering 80 percent. That troops could take such losses and return to the attack says all that is needed about British courage and discipline.

The capability of colonial militiamen to have made such an astounding defense against British regulars has been pointed out again and again in histories—probably deservedly so—but such stout resistance would not have been possible without the leadership shown by (in order of their apparent contribution to the outcome of events) Prescott, Stark, Putnam, and Knowlton. All four had learned the military trade in the hard school of the French and Indian War, and their experience paid off handsomely in their handling of their men at Bunker Hill.

Yet that leadership, as we have seen, could extend no further than any one leader's battle: Prescott's at the redoubt, Stark's at the beach and rail fence, and Putnam's in his presence everywhere. The phenomenon of three battles in one was due to an inescapable fact—the lack of a higher command structure. Stating such a fact, however, does not mean laying blame on anyone involved in the battle. That no chain of command existed between Ward and Putnam or between Putnam and others was merely a fact of life at the time, a fact that disappeared with the appointment of Washington as commander in chief and the establishment of a Continental army.

When we look back across two centuries and more than two hundred July Fourths, we tend to think of Bunker Hill as the accepted symbol of patriotic fortitude and triumph of our forefathers over their oppressors. It was not so to the people in the colonies, especially in New England. The prevailing public feeling at the time was that the battle was not only a defeat but a military misadventure that should never have been undertaken. Even from a purely military viewpoint it was unnecessary and unjustified. And so Prescott, Stark, Putnam, and company were not exactly hailed as heroes in June 1775.

Soon, however, things began to be seen in a kindlier light, and then came the realization that, "by God, those British regulars were not invincible, and if we had been better organized we'd have licked 'em fair and square!" This complete turnabout in popular opinion led to the idea that patriotism was all that was required to make militia into freedom fighters who could win the war. The facts have been recognized by two British military historians. Sir John Fortescue, in his *History of the British Army*, said that "it [Bunker Hill] not only elated the Americans . . . but encouraged them to blind and fatal trust in undisciplined troops, which went near to bring ruin to their cause." Later, J. F. C. Fuller had this to say in

Decisive Battles of the U.S.A.: "It convinced the rebels that a regular military establishment was unnecessary, and so added enormously to Washington's difficulties."

Those difficulties will appear and reappear in some of the battle scenes that follow, and it is worthy of note that they were by no means confined to George Washington's command.

TWO

Quebec

IN 1775, FIVE YEARS BEFORE KARL VON CLAUSEWITZ was born, the Second Continental Congress was already applying the Prussian's dictum that war is only a continuation of national policy by other means. Early in that session the Congress made two commitments that were to change the colonies' form of resistance from rebellion to all-out war. The first was to appoint a committee to draw up the organization of a Continental army. Then, on 15 June, George Washington was named "to command all the Continental forces, raised or to be raised, for the defense of American liberty." At the same time it appointed Washington general in chief of the army, Congress appointed other officers. Four were named major generals: Artemas Ward, Israel Putnam, Charles Lee, and Philip Schuyler.

Washington assumed command of the army when he arrived at Boston on 3 July. By then the action at Bunker Hill had established in everyone's mind the idea that pitched battles were to be the realities of the future, so Washington set about preparing the army for that type of warfare. That meant instilling discipline, an uphill fight in the face of the conviction so endemic to New Englanders that any man was as good as another. This concept, inspiring as it may have been in a town meeting, had an opposite effect on Washington's efforts to build a force that would stand up in battle. Organizing a disciplined army occupied Washington's attention for a long time after his arrival.

Long before the French and Indian War (1754–63), one word had always spelled trouble for the more northern settlements of New England—Canada. From there, for generations, had come the war parties, led or encouraged by the French, that had savaged the frontier and the interior with tomahawk and torch. The treaty of 1763 brought peace, but relief for the colonies was short-lived. The Quebec Act of 1774 that recognized the rights of the Canadian French had an alarming effect on Virginia, Connecticut, and Massachusetts, because a provision of the act extended Canada's boundaries to the Ohio River, thus giving back to Canadians lands already being settled by Americans in regions like the Ohio Valley.

In 1775 the Continental Congress sought a peaceful solution to the threat of British-occupied Canada. On 29 May it appealed in a letter "to the oppressed Inhabitants of Canada" to join "with us in the defense of our common liberty." Like many such ideal solutions, this one didn't work. The Canadians turned a deaf ear. There were those in Congress, however, who felt that if the Canadians were of a mind to stay loyal to Britain, they might be more responsive to things like invasion and occupation. For the moment cooler heads prevailed, and on 1 June Congress went so far as to resolve that "no expedition or incursion ought to be undertaken . . . against or into Canada." The impasse was not to last.

Earlier, on 10 May 1775, Ethan Allen and eighty-three of his Green Mountain Boys, accompanied by a Massachusetts-commissioned colonel named Benedict Arnold, "stormed" half-ruined Fort Ticonderoga on Lake Champlain, forcing its commander to surrender its half-invalid garrison to Allen "in the name of the great Jehovah and the Continental Congress!"* Congress did nothing at first to follow up the success. Though Arnold and Allen had their personal differences, both were convinced that Canada was vulnerable to invasion. Arnold made a written report to that effect on 13 June, and ten days later Allen, on the floor of Congress in Philadelphia, presumably agreed. In any case, Congress revised its policy toward Canada on 27 June. General Philip Schuyler was directed "to take possession of St. Johns, Montreal, and . . . other parts of the country."

Schuyler's orders sounded more like permission—"if General Schuyler finds it practicable, and that it will not be too disagreeable to the Canadians"—and were in keeping with the lack of a strategy for invasion. Though Congress did not produce a grand strategic plan, it did develop, in piecemeal fashion, two expeditions, each with a logical objective: in the west it was Montreal, in the east Quebec. By taking these two objectives and defeating the weak and scattered British forces, the "four-

---

*What was actually said is unknown, but Allen thoughtfully added those ringing words in an account published four years later.

teenth colony" could be brought to terms. It was not an unsound strategy, and it could have succeeded. That it did not may be attributed
mainly to three factors: unexpectedly rough terrain, the forces of nature,
and the abilities of General Guy Carleton, governor of Canada and commander of the British forces.

After much delay in preparations, the expedition in the west began on
25 August 1775 when Brigadier General Richard Montgomery, in place
of the ailing Schuyler, advanced northward up Lake Champlain. At age
thirty-seven Montgomery was a leader possessed of the essential qualities that Schuyler lacked: aggressiveness, decisiveness, personal magnetism, physical and moral courage, and the strength to endure the hardships of a wilderness campaign. He had been born the son of a baronet in
Ireland, had been educated at Trinity College, Dublin, and at seventeen
had taken up a military career. He had fought with the British army at
Louisbourg in 1753, and under Geoffrey Amherst at Ticonderoga, Crown
Point, and Montreal. In 1772 he resigned his commission, moved his
home to America, settled down as a gentleman farmer near Kings Bridge,
New York, and married Janet Livingston, daughter of a prominent New
York family. In June 1775 he accepted a commission as a brigadier gen-
eral in the Continental army, left his young wife on her estate, and went
to join Schuyler.

From the outset Montgomery might well have concluded that the luck
of the Irish had abandoned him. The expedition consisted of about
1,700 Connecticut and New York militia, untrained, undisciplined, and
likely to flee upon hearing the word "ambush"—as they had done on one
occasion already. By 16 September, however, Montgomery had reas-
serted control and headed for Fort Saint Johns, his first objective. This
small outpost, together with Chambly, ten miles to the north, commanded the Richelieu River and thus the approaches between Lake
Champlain and Sorel on the Saint Lawrence. In spite of its strategic importance, Saint Johns (Saint Jean in French) had been only a frontier
outpost with a couple of brick buildings and a storehouse until British
General Carleton had reinforced the garrison to a total of 725 regulars
and militia and ordered the commander, Major Charles Preston, to con-
struct two redoubts, which made it a formidable fort.

Montgomery moved his makeshift flotilla of a schooner, a sloop, and a
collection of "gondolas, bateaux, row-galleys, pirauguas, and canoes"
northward past Ile Aux Noix, and disembarked his force to take Saint
Johns. He sent out detachments to cut the road to Montreal, twenty-five
miles to the north, and to forage.

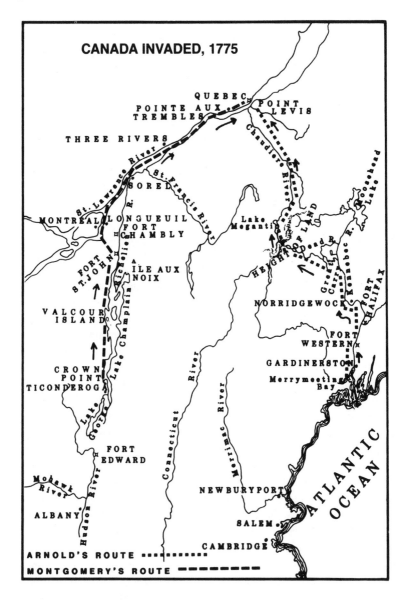

CANADA INVADED, 1775

When Montgomery had assessed the situation, it was clear that his motley force, now reduced by sickness to 1,100 effectives, could not take Saint Johns by assault. He therefore began to entrench, emplacing his two guns and some small mortars. The conditions for the besiegers were difficult. The ground everywhere was swampy and entrenchments quickly filled with knee-deep water. It was early October, and the cold rains were becoming intolerable. In a letter Montgomery wrote that "we have been like half-drowned rats crawling through a swamp." Supplies, both food and ammunition, were running out. To make things worse, the British in their fort were holding out steadfastly in spite of incoming artillery rounds.

For General Guy Carleton, the reinforcement and fortification of Saint Johns had been his first priority. Earlier, however, he had discovered to his dismay that his French subjects were more neutral than loyal. He had counted on the Quebec Act (which he had sponsored) to win over the French Canadians, but in 1775 he had found them generally unwilling to enlist in the British forces. Moreover, Carleton had sent all but 800 of his regulars to Boston. In June 1775, realizing his precarious position, he declared martial law and began to mobilize all the British and Scots he could muster. He was a competent general as well as an excellent administrator. After strengthening Saint Johns, he personally took over in Montreal and began to rally what forces he could in the west.

By 18 October, when things were looking bleak for the Americans, a near-miracle occurred. The night before, two American bateaux mounting nine-pounder guns had sneaked past the defenses of Chambly and had reported to Montgomery. Montgomery therefore decided to take Chambly, the weaker garrison, first. With their guns in position, Montgomery's detachment of 50 Americans and 300 Canadian allies was able to surround the fort at Chambly. After a few artillery rounds had penetrated the walls, the British commander surrendered. Among the stores captured were six tons of powder, 6,500 musket cartridges, and 125 muskets. Of no less importance were eighty barrels of flour and 272 barrels of foodstuffs.

The captured stores enabled Montgomery to lift the spirits of his men enough to make the maneuver he needed to push the siege of Saint Johns itself. On 25 October he got a battery of twelve-pounders and lighter artillery into position on a hill that dominated the fort. The British commander, Major Preston, continued to hold out for a while, but Canadian prisoners, released by Montgomery, convinced him that his situation was hopeless. Preston surrendered Saint Johns on 2 November, having held out for fifty-five days. The garrison laid down its arms, and officers and men were paroled; the Canadians went home, and the British regulars were sent to a port where they could sail for England.

Three days later, Montgomery took up his slow march to Montreal, where Carleton awaited him with a tiny force of 150 regulars and militia. On 11 November Montgomery began to surround Montreal by landing a detachment north of it. On the same day Carleton, recognizing the town to be indefensible, set sail down the Saint Lawrence, carrying with him all that he could of the military stores. He almost failed to make it. Near Sorel, adverse winds and American shore batteries brought his little flotilla to bay, and Carleton's ship, the brigantine *Gaspée,* had to surrender. Carleton escaped in civilian clothes with two of his officers. Montreal was surrendered to Montgomery by its citizens on 13 November.

IN LATE SUMMER OF 1775 NEWLY APPOINTED General Washington had come to realize that the western expedition to take Montreal was only half a strategy: Quebec would still command the Saint Lawrence River, gateway to Montreal and inner Canada. Moreover, so he reasoned, an invasion in the east against Quebec, if timed in coordination with that of Montgomery against Montreal, would force Carleton to fight on two fronts, with all the embarrassment that went with it.

Washington soon became convinced that the most promising invasion route was a waterway, specifically up the Kennebec River, thence to the Chaudiére River, which emptied into the Saint Lawrence not far from Quebec. Much of the route had been mapped and described in his journal by Captain John Montresor, a British army engineer, in 1761. Montesor's map turned out to be incomplete, however, and the consequences of relying on it would later prove nearly disastrous. Nevertheless Washington had no alternative, for in 1775 huge areas of the Maine and Canadian wilderness were not mapped at all. Washington was aware of the hazards of the expedition, but he had confidence in the commander he had selected, Benedict Arnold, to whom he offered a commission as a colonel in the Continental army and the command of the eastern expedition to take Quebec. Arnold jumped at the opportunity.

Who was this Benedict Arnold who caught Washington's eye at the right time? In the first place he was a born leader. One of his soldiers voiced what all believed: "He was our fighting general [at Saratoga]. . . . It was 'Come on boys!' twarn't 'Go boys.' He was as brave a man as ever lived." He had an eye for sizing up a tactical situation, and he was as skillful in planning as he was bold in executing his plans. He was strong-willed, a quality which made him resolute in adversity. In sum, he showed most of the soldierly virtues, and it was mainly the fatal flaws of excessive ambition, hypersensitivity, and love of glory that would eventually bring him to ruin.

In 1775 Arnold, from a well-to-do Connecticut family, was thirty-four years old. He had gone adventuring in the French and Indian War. Later, he settled down in business after selling the family property. As a merchant he had sailed his own ships to the West Indies and Canada, and he later sold horses in Montreal and Quebec. At the outbreak of rebellion he was prosperous, "the possessor of an elegant house, storehouses, wharves, and vessels. . . . Rather a short man, he seemed, but stocky and athletic, and very quick in his movements. Raven-black hair, a high, hot complexion, a long, keen nose, a domineering chin, persuasive, smiling lips, haughty brows, and the boldest eyes man ever saw, completed him" (Justin Smith, *Our Struggle for the Fourteenth Colony*). Completed him indeed! Benedict Arnold was not a man easily overlooked. Small wonder that the man and his reputation had come to Washington's attention.

In August Arnold had already been dealing with Reuben Colburn, a Kennebec boatbuilder, to have two hundred bateaux built. On 3 September Washington approved an order for the boats and stores of provisions, and two days later the organization of the expedition was announced in army orders. The detachment was to consist of two battalions of five companies each, the men to be volunteers who should be "active woodsmen well acquainted with batteaus." That specification was never filled; with the exception of riflemen, the volunteers assigned were from New England regiments which they had joined from their farms. The detachment also included three companies of riflemen: Captain Daniel Morgan's company of Virginians and two companies from Pennsylvania under Captains Matthew Smith and William Hendricks, 250 riflemen in all. The total strength of Arnold's force came to about 1,100, counting miscellaneous troops, which included 6 "unattached volunteers," one of whom was nineteen-year-old Aaron Burr.

One leader among the riflemen had already achieved a reputation for bravery and ability: Captain Dan Morgan, a dyed-in-the-wool product of the frontier wars. Over six feet tall, broad-shouldered, with a solidly muscled body, he was renowned for his strength (exerted in his youth in scores of tavern brawls) and woodcraft, learned the hard way from the Indians. He had been a wagoner in Braddock's expedition, and the story of his laying out a British officer with his fist for striking him with his sword was a well-known frontier tale. Flogged by the British for that military offense, he bore a bitter hatred for them. The "Old Wagoner," as Morgan was called, was a natural leader, and his grasp of tactics was phenomenal. He was admired by his men—he could lick any one of them—and they would follow him anywhere. He was further noted for his blunt speech and quick temper, both of which covered a kindly nature and a rough-hewn sense of humor.

When Arnold reached Gardinerston on 22 September, he found to his dismay that the two hundred bateaux—flat-bottomed boats with flared sides and tapered ends, propelled by oars or paddles in deep water and pushed by poles in rough or shallow water—had been hastily made of green lumber. They would be heavy and clumsy craft for portaging, and difficult to handle in white water. But Arnold was stuck with them, and even had to order twenty more. On 25 September the expedition left Fort Western—today's Augusta, Maine. Arnold divided his force into four divisions. The first division was composed of the three companies of riflemen commanded by Captain Morgan. Morgan's riflemen were preceded by two scouting parties, led by Lieutenants Steele and Church. The other three divisions followed Morgan's between 26 and 28 September, departing in numerical order. Arnold went ahead of the main body, and he seems to have been ubiquitous, showing up anywhere his command presence was needed.* Thereafter matters developed as follows:

30 September 1775: After passing Fort Halifax the divisions had to make their first portage around Ticonic Falls, shoulder carrying a hundred tons of boats and supplies.

3 October: Main body had to pass through a "chute" of vertical rock banks to get past Showhegan Falls. Bateaux had to be pushed and carried through.

4–8 October: After the passage of the Bombazee Rips (rapids) the divisions faced the dreaded Norridgewock Falls with its three "pitches" each separated by a half mile. The bateaux began to give

---

*One should not think of Arnold's expedition as advancing in one coherent column. The divisions (and companies within them) moved subject to a kind of "accordion action," the head of one division bumping into the tail of its predecessor, then falling back and out of contact, and, on occasion, one division even passing another. Thus, the journal-like dates which follow should be regarded as approximate because they apply to the bulk of the expedition, and not to a particular division. In this "composite journal," which must depend on a chronological order, I have tried to condense the more significant events into narrative form.

out. Seams were wrenched open and water poured through the cracks. Colburn and his artificers came up, and "the seams had a fresh calking, and the bottoms were repaired as well as possible." The provisions casks had also been split open and washed through with water. "The salt had been washed out of the dried fish . . . and all of it had spoiled. The casks of dried peas and biscuit had burst and been lost . . . while the salt beef, cured in hot weather, proved unfit for use."

9–10 October: Curritunk Falls—cold rains set in.

11–17 October: The Great Carry Place, with its three ponds and four portages. The Kennebec River was left behind. Fierce winds and snow squalls. Ponds choked with roots, forests filled with bogs, men up to their knees. Lieutenants Steele and Church reported in. Steele's last five men staggered in, starving wretches at life's end. The divisions reached Bog Brook, which flows into Dead River.

19–24 October: Thirty miles on the Dead River. Unaccountably Greene's division (commanded by Lt. Col. Christopher Greene, a distant kinsman of Nathanael Green) passed Morgan's riflemen, who stole their food. On 21–22 October a hurricane-spawned rainstorm turned the river into a raging flood. Whole country under water. Many bateaux lost. A conference was held to determine if march should continue; Arnold's eloquence and show of determined courage made them decide to go on.

25 October: Enos's fourth division elected to turn back, and would not yield its flour to Greene's starving men, who were subsisting on candles mixed in flour gruel. Expedition was reduced to seven hundred men out of original eleven hundred. [Enos was later court-martialed for desertion.]

25–28 October: Height of Land, "prodigious high mountains," the divide where streams flow north to the Saint Lawrence, south to the Kennebec. South of Lake Megantic, Arnold's men were betrayed by Montresor's map, which didn't show Rush Lake, Spider Lake, or False Mouths of Seven-Mile Stream (Arnold River). They tried to skirt the two lakes and wandered among swamps until they almost perished.

1–3 November: Starving men ate soap, hair grease, boiled moccasins, shot pouches, a company commander's dog. Men staggered on, supported by their muskets. On 3 November a miracle: a herd of cattle arrived, driven by men dispatched by Arnold, who had gone ahead to scour the country. The cattle were manhandled to slaughter, roasted, torn to bits, and eaten "as a hungry dog would tear a haunch of meat."

4 November: Reached Sartigan, the wilderness left behind them. Arnold's provisions, left there for them, gobbled up so fast that men became ill, and three died.

5 November: Left the Chaudiére below Saint Mary, headed for Point Levis, across the Saint Lawrence from Quebec.

On 9 November 1775 Canadians at the Saint Lawrence were astounded to see a ragtag column of six hundred survivors hobbling toward the river, "ghosts with firelocks on their shoulders." As they streamed from the woods they at first spread alarm, though that soon turned into admiration when Canadians learned of the conditions of the heroic march.

Arnold's march has been compared to Xenophon's march to the sea and Hannibal's crossing the Alps. Yet what did this band of heroes find to greet them after enduring such incredible hardships? An indefatigable Arnold was busily rounding up boats, canoes, and scaling ladders so that they could cross the Saint Lawrence—under the very guns of the frigate *Lizard,* the sloop-of-war *Hunter,* and four other armed craft—and storm the walls of Quebec!

HECTOR CRAMAHÉ, CARLETON'S LIEUTENANT GOVERNOR and governor of Quebec City, had seen to it that the Point Levis shores of the Saint Lawrence across from Quebec had been swept clean of any boats the Americans might use to cross the river. But Arnold, as usual, was equal to the emergency. His scrounging parties, with the help of friendly Indians, soon assembled a mixed flotilla of about forty canoes and dugouts. By 10 November he was ready to make a night crossing, his only chance to get by the British warships in the river. A heavy gale came up, however, which made the river impassable for Arnold's light craft, and he had to wait until 9:00 P.M. on the thirteenth for the storm to subside. Then Arnold ferried his men over in shifts, slipping silently past the anchored British ships to land in Wolfe's Cove, where in 1759 the British General James Wolfe had landed in his successful operation against Quebec. Arnold got all his force across except for 150 men who remained on the Point Levis side until the next night.

Having led his men way up to the Plains of Abraham on the road Wolfe had used sixteen years before, Arnold halted them a mile and a half from the city's walls. There they took shelter until daylight. Unknown to Ar-

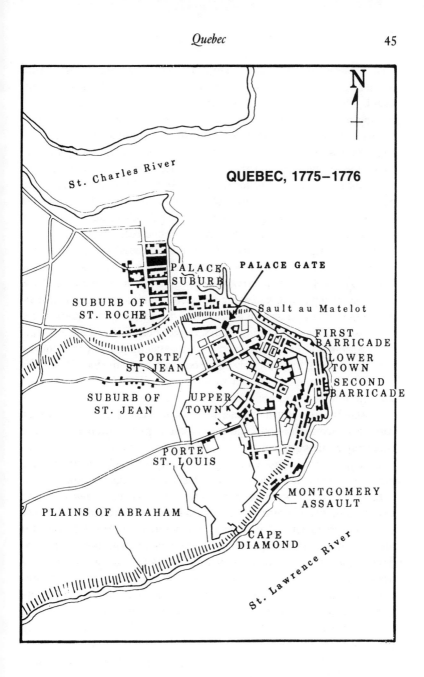

N

QUEBEC, 1775–1776

St. Charles River

PALACE SUBURB

PALACE GATE

Sault au Matelot

SUBURB OF ST. ROCHE

FIRST BARRICADE

LOWER TOWN

SECOND BARRICADE

PORTE ST. JEAN

SUBURB OF ST. JEAN

UPPER TOWN

PORTE ST. LOUIS

MONTGOMERY ASSAULT

PLAINS OF ABRAHAM

CAPE DIAMOND

St. Lawrence River

nold, however, the firebrand Allan MacLean had brought eighty of his Royal Highland Emigrants to Quebec and had taken over military command. The garrison was an improvised force of about 1,200 men, including militia and sailors and marines from the ships. The city MacLean had to defend has been described as rising grandly from a majestic river, the vast rock towers high and broad. On the north were plains between the promontory and the Saint Charles River, which flowed into the Saint Lawrence east of town. Along the Saint Lawrence, slopes tapered off from the rocky sides to the river, affording passage to the Lower Town, which was guarded by double palisades and, behind them, a blockhouse. On the south side Cape Diamond rose 300 feet above the river. In the Lower Town itself there were wooden barriers blocking the Sault au Matelot, a narrow street which led to steep passages to the Upper Town. The latter dominated the greater part of the city. It was protected by a 30-foot wall along its whole western and northern sides. There were six bastions with artillery and three main gates: on the north the Palace, in the center Saint John's, in the south Saint Louis.

To Arnold and his ragged men the fortress city must have seemed a Gibraltar indeed, but with only about 600 men to do the job, Arnold did not hesitate to summon the city to surrender. Allan MacLean, however, was unimpressed, and both Arnold's first and second messengers were greeted with an eighteen-pound round shot, the first "splattering the American envoy with dirt," the second passing just over his head in "a very straight direction."

Other grim facts faced Arnold. He had no artillery, only five cartridges per man remained, and over 100 muskets were unserviceable. In the light of the situation, he settled for a blockade of the city on its west side. On 18 November the Americans got word that MacLean was planning a sortie with 800 men. A council of war then concluded that even the blockade was no longer practicable. The next day Arnold began withdrawing his whole force to Pointe aux Trembles (Aspen Point) twenty miles upriver, where the men could find shelter. On the same day that the Americans disappeared from the Plains of Abraham (19 November), Guy Carleton entered Quebec to salvoes of saluting cannon.

Two weeks passed before Brigadier General Richard Montgomery, the overall force commander, arrived at Pointe aux Trembles. At nine o'clock on the night of 2 December a boat put out in the dark from the schooner that had just arrived from Montreal. Arnold waited to turn over command to the respected Montgomery. In formal manner he stood in front of a double-ranked honor guard lined up in the foot-deep snow.

The flickering light from torches reflected from the snow and lit up the rocky beach. When the bow of the boat rasped across the rocks, commands rang out and Arnold's detachment snapped to attention and presented arms. Arnold saluted and Montgomery, stepping ashore, returned the salute.

What Arnold's men saw of their new commander—most of them on the following day—they liked. "Noticeably pock-marked, but well-limbed, tall and handsome, with an air and manner that designated the real soldier," recorded John Joseph Henry in his journal. Montgomery has been further described as having "a bright, magnetic face, and winning manner." There is no doubt, too, that his air of command, while not inviting familiarity, was pleasant yet forceful. What is more, Montgomery returned the men's approbation. In a letter to Schuyler (still in overall command of American forces in Canada) he wrote, "I find Colonel Arnold's corps an exceeding fine one, inured to fatigue . . . there is a style among them much superior to what I have used to see in this campaign."

Montgomery had brought with him more than a pleasant manner. In several other craft following his schooner were over 300 men and a supply of ammunition, clothing, and provisions, as well as much-needed artillery. No doubt the greatest morale builder for Arnold's ragged, half-shod men was the clothing. Montgomery had captured all the winter uniforms of the 7th and 26th British regiments—long white overcoats, heavy leggings, moccasins, and cloth caps with fur tails. With the initial distribution of the clothing Montgomery made a short but effective speech, which was answered with huzzahs.

Montgomery and Arnold wasted no time in returning to Quebec with their reorganized forces. They took up the siege, with Arnold's positions on the north in the Saint Roche suburbs that had been burned by Mac-Lean as part of his defensive preparations, while Montgomery held the plains between Saint Roche and Cape Diamond. Montgomery then sent a personal letter to Carleton with the standard demand for surrender, this time using a woman as a messenger, with instructions to hand it to no other than the governor himself. But even she failed. He called for a drummer and commanded, "Take that pair of tongs and throw it into the fire." This done, he sent the woman back to Montgomery.

Ten days later Montgomery tried again, with the same result. Montgomery, however, was not relying on surrender demands; he was busy getting his artillery batteries into position. On the night of 10 December his biggest battery was set up 700 yards from the walls. The frozen ground prohibited entrenching, so gabions were filled with snow, then soaked with water, which froze them into solid walls. But Montgomery's six- and twelve-pounder guns and howitzers were too light to have an effect on the walls; no more, a Quebecois commented, "than peas would have against a plank."

Montgomery sat down to evaluate his situation. His conclusions were anything but pleasing. Since he lacked siege artillery, there was no way to breach Quebec's walls for an assault. He couldn't dig siege trenches and parallels in the frozen ground. Arnold's men's enlistments were up at the end of December, and with the departure of the New England troops would go the bulk of his force. No resupply of ammunition was forthcoming from the colonies, and his Continental paper money was worthless in Canada. Moreover, he couldn't wait for spring, because it would bring the thaws that would break up the ice in the Saint Lawrence, a sure herald of the coming of British reinforcements.

The realistic Montgomery had long been aware that he could never take Quebec by siege. As early as 4 November he had written Schuyler of his intention to attack the Lower Town. So Montgomery the professional had no trouble in deciding to take Quebec by storm. The other Montgomery, the leader of a motley militia army, was having trouble securing popular approval (that old New England convention) to attack. Many New Englanders held back because of differences between their leaders, mainly between Arnold and Major John Brown. Montgomery took the situation in hand by addressing the men at parade to such obvious effect that their patriotism overcame their reluctance to join in the proposed attack.

Montgomery and Arnold now had to wait for a dark night and snow if his small force, now less than a thousand men, were to succeed in storming the city. The night of 27 December was overcast and snow began to fall. But while the Americans were moving to assembly areas the sky cleared and the moon came out. Montgomery had to call off the attack, and after the weather reports he got more bad news. A Rhode Island sergeant, Stephen Singleton, had deserted and doubtless had carried the plan of attack to the British.

Montgomery revised the methods of attack but retained as the main objective the Lower Town. He added two feints against Quebec's western walls. His new plan called for two converging attacks on the Lower Town. Arnold would mount a northern attack from the suburbs of Saint Roche, smash through the barriers at the north end of the Lower Town, and link up with Montgomery in or near the street called Sault au Matelot. Montgomery's attack would move along the shoreline of the Saint Lawrence from Wolfe's Cove, pass Cape Diamond, break into the Lower Town, and head toward the Sault au Matelot. When the converging forces had linked up, they would make a combined attack to take the Upper Town. The two feints were to be made against Saint John's gate (Porte Saint Jean) and the Cape Diamond bastion. After the new plan had been confided to senior officers, Montgomery had to continue waiting for his black night with a snowstorm. That night was not long in coming.

INSIDE THE FORTRESS CITY, CARLETON WAS well aware that the Lower Town was Quebec's most vulnerable section. He blocked the Sault au Matelot with two formidable log barricades covered by cannon. To protect the Lower Town in the south he erected palisades along the Saint Lawrence shoreline. The inner one was covered by a battery of four three-pounder cannons positioned in a blockhouse made from an old brewery. That little battery was fated to have an effect on the coming battle out of all proportion to its size. Carleton had assigned his forces defensive positions along the walls and inner defenses, using to best advantage his 1,800 men.

Saturday morning, 30 December, was clear and cold, but in the afternoon the sky darkened and a rising wind brought the first snowflakes. By nightfall it was blowing a thick snow that increased with the darkness, drifting to two and three feet. The snowfall was the common signal the American units had been waiting for. At 2:00 A.M. on the last day of the year they began moving to their assembly areas.

In the suburbs of Saint Roche, Benedict Arnold stood in a shed under lantern light, peering over Captain Oswald's shoulder while he checked off the units as their captains reported in. In the south Richard Montgomery had finished a letter to his wife Janet: "I wish it were well over with all my heart, and I sigh for home like a New Englander." For a moment this man who loved farm life was back on his land at Kings Bridge. Then the soldier took over; General Montgomery shrugged on his greatcoat and went out in the storm to take command of his 300 men assembling on the Plains of Abraham.

Montgomery caught sight of the brief flare of the rockets fired by Captain Jacob Brown to signal the launching of his feint attack against the Cape Diamond bastion. He led the way down the steep, snow-heaped path that descended from the plains down to Wolfe's Cove, followed by his three aides: Macpherson, Cheeseman, and Burr. Behind them came Colonel Donald Campbell, the second in command. The storm had become a blizzard whose wind carried the clanging of alarm bells in the city; the rockets had signaled the alarm to the defenders.

The descent of the mile-long path had been harrowing enough in the howling darkness, but the next two miles along the shoreline were even worse. The frozen river had piled up massive heaps of ice slabs that forced the single file of men to detour up against the rocky cliff sides at every turn. The men carrying the clumsy scaling ladders had the hardest time of all because they had to push or pull their ladders over the sharp slabs of ice or around the snow-covered rocks on the steep slopes. And all the way the wind drove the snow into eyes that were straining to find a way in the black night. Under great difficulties, Montgomery passed Cape Diamond; farther on, near a limit called the Prés de Ville, he could see through the driving snow the palisade of the outer barrier.

The carpenters with the advance party quickly hacked and sawed down four posts of the undefended palisade. The general was the first through the opening, followed by his aides. Keeping left against the cliff slope, Montgomery came around a curve to the second palisade. He took a saw from a carpenter and cut through the first two posts himself. Followed by only fifty men, he slipped through the opening and slowly made his way up the narrow street. He reached a point where, peering through the falling snow, he could make out the dim outline of a two-story building about a hundred paces ahead. No guards or sentries were visible. Had they fled along with the defenders of the palisades? He waved his storming party forward, drew his sword, and strode ahead for about fifty paces. Then he broke into a run, the others at his heels. A blinding yellow flash burst from the front of the blockhouse, and a burst of grapeshot killed Montgomery instantly, shot through the head. He lay on his back in the snow, one arm still extended, a dozen men dead behind his body. The storming party had been wiped out; only Aaron Burr and a couple of others had escaped unhurt.

That ended the attack. Colonel Campbell called a council of officers who, it was said, "justified his receding from the attack." The column turned around, leaving the bodies of Montgomery and the others. It retraced its grim path through the storm back to the Plains of Abraham. No word of Montgomery's death and the retreat reached Arnold or any of his men until after the battle.

At Saint Roche, Arnold checked off his units, finding only Captain Dearborn's company unaccounted for. Unwilling to wait any longer, Arnold left orders for Dearborn to catch up, and, clutching a musket, he led his column off in single file at 4:00 A.M. His advance guard consisted of twenty-five men; following them came Captain John Lamb with forty artillerymen dragging a six-pounder gun on a sled. Next came the three rifle companies led, respectively, by Captain Morgan, Lieutenant Steele, and Captain Hendricks. The main body consisted of the New England musketmen, followed by a mixed bag of some forty Canadians and Indians. Arnold's plan was to attack the first barricade with Lamb's cannon, then to send the riflemen to flank the barricade on both sides.

Unknown to Arnold, the feint against Saint John's gate conducted by Colonel Livingston's poorly motivated Canadians was a fiasco: the men had fled as soon as their fire had been returned by the gate's defenders. Farther south, Captain Brown's men did better. They stood their ground, maintaining a rolling fire against the Cape Diamond bastion. As it turned out, however, the feints fooled no one, least of all Carleton.

Arnold's 600 men trotted along, keeping parallel to the north wall, and were able to pass the Palace gate and a two-gun battery undetected. However, where the advance party came abreast of a row of buildings beyond the battery, a fierce fire of musketry broke out from the walls above them, causing some casualties. There was no way to return the fire, so Arnold pushed on, taking no time to attend to casualties. "Let the dead bury the dead" had been the watchword from the start. So the column simply ran the gauntlet for 600 yards under the galling fire.

When the column reached the quay along the river, it had to thread its way through a network of hawser cables stretching from houses and bollards out to moored ships. After passing those obstacles, Arnold and the advance party entered a narrow street where they were met with "a smart discharge of musketry." The riflemen took cover against the housefronts and returned the fire. This was the first barricade, which, unknown to them, was only lightly defended.

Arnold, with his usual dash, was everywhere, stopping the useless fusillade against the barrier and organizing the assault to take the barricade. Since Captain Lamb's cannon had been abandoned back in a snowdrift, Arnold decided to lead a frontal assault himself. As he was shouting his commands for men to follow him, he felt a rasp of pain that stopped him in his tracks. A ricocheting bullet had struck his left leg below the knee, torn along the leg bone, and lodged in his Achilles tendon. Though he tried to prop himself up on his musket and shout the men forward, his men, seeing him wounded, held back. As Arnold was being carried to the rear, Morgan came up. Though he was a captain, the field officers turned over the command to him. Later he was to acknowledge modestly that their acclaim "reflected credit on their judgement."

Morgan shouted for a ladder to assault the barrier just as a two-gun battery opened up on him. The first two volleys were ineffective. Morgan led his men up the first ladder. He was almost over the barricade when a blast from the defenders' muskets hit the ladder and blew him backward. A bullet went through his cap, another grazed his cheek, and his beard was singed by powder grains. Morgan was back on his feet in a flash; he clambered up the ladder again and flung himself over the top of the barricade. He tumbled to the ground, rolled under the muzzle of a British cannon to dodge the bayonets, and was saved only by Lieutenant Heth and Cadet Porterfield, who had swarmed over the wall behind him. The defenders ran into a house and Morgan followed, dashing around to the rear door. He declared them surrounded and took the surrender of their Captain McCloud.

Morgan and his riflemen pressed on and entered the Sault au Matelot. About two hundred yards down the narrow street they could see the second barricade and the cannon platform behind it. Incredibly, the sally port was open. While the Americans were still staring, they heard shouts of "Vive la liberté!" from windows and doorways; the Quebecois in the street were demonstrably friendly. With the citizens sympathetic and the barricade undefended, the way to the Lower Town was open.

Morgan then made his first mistake. In front of the undefended barricade, in the first faint light of day, with the wind whipping snow in their faces, he called a council of war. He was for going on, but his officers counseled against a further advance. Later he would recall, "Here I was overruled by sound judgment and good reasoning." For one thing, his orders specified that he was to wait for Montgomery. Further, he couldn't take his 150 prisoners along. They outnumbered his riflemen, and if he released them they could fall back to the first barricade and cut off his retreat. Both Montgomery and the main body must be close behind, and when they all joined forces they could take the Upper Town. So Morgan hesitated and gave in. "I gave up my own opinion, and lost the town"— how simply put, and what a simple truth! He had afforded Carleton, now aware of Montgomery's disaster, time to dispatch Colonel Caldwell to stop the Americans at the second barricade.

Morgan went back to find the main body. He found Lieutenant Colonel Greene and Major Meigs with 200 men; all of them had been lost in side streets and byways when their guides had failed them. Morgan led them forward to the second barricade, and *now*, belatedly, decided to advance through the obstacle to the Lower Town. Meanwhile, one of Colonel Caldwell's officers was massing a detachment behind the second barricade and preparing to sally out and pin down the Americans. That officer, Lieutenant Anderson, debouched from the gate and called on the Americans to surrender. Morgan snatched up a rifle and shot him through the head. After a pause, the fiercest firefight of the battle broke out. As Morgan's men exchanged fusillades with the Canadians, others packed down mounds of snow on which they could set their ladders. Morgan and his best leaders—Hendricks, Steele, Humphreys, Heth, Greene, and Lamb among them—tried to scale the barrier but were blasted back by a hail of grapeshot and bullets.

Riflemen broke into the lower story of a stone house from which their fire could reach the defenders. The Canadian Colonel Caldwell saw the tactical importance of the house and ordered a detachment to use a captured ladder to get into the upper story before the Americans. The Canadians got inside the second floor and drove the Americans from the house with their bayonets. Other riflemen, firing from windows down the street, drove the gunners from their firing platform. The Canadian musket fire now increased in such intensity that the American toll of casualties rose. The American officers, even Morgan, could no longer exhort their men to come out of the houses and renew the attack.

Morgan ordered the men around him to take cover in the houses while he conferred again with his senior officers. Morgan argued for continuing the fight, but there was an unhesitating consensus for an immediate retreat. Yet even then their fate was being sealed. Carleton, informed that Colonel Caldwell's Canadians were holding back the Americans, had ordered Captain Laws with 200 men and two fieldpieces to move down from the Palace gate and cut off the American rear from the direction of Sault au Matelot. Although the overzealous Laws charged ahead of his men and became an American prisoner, the rest of his men soon arrived. At a final hasty conference, Morgan urged the commanders to try to cut their way out through Laws's men, but a majority insisted on holding out in the hope of being relieved by Montgomery.

By this time—sometime after 9:00 A.M.—Laws's gunners had gotten a nine-pounder in position where it could sweep the street or batter down house walls. While the American officers continued to argue, men began to give up, holding their musket butts out of doors and windows in sign of surrender. Finally Lieutenant Colonel Greene, stepping in, made a formal offer of surrender, and it was accepted. Americans were routed out of houses to be lined up and marched away as prisoners.

But not Dan Morgan. He set his back against a housefront, and with tears of rage and frustration streaming down his face, defied his enemies.

Canadians were calling on him to hand over his sword or be shot, while his men were shouting at him, begging him to give up before he was killed. The scene ended when Morgan spotted a man in black among the crowd of onlookers. When Morgan was assured that the man was a priest, he bellowed, "Then I give my sword to you. But not a scoundrel of these cowards shall take it out of my hands."

THE THREE-HOUR BATTLE FOR THE SAULT AU MATELOT was over. With its end went all hope of taking Quebec by storm. The American losses were 60 killed or wounded and 426 captured. Among the prisoners were Captain Dearborn's entire company, which had been cut off while trying to catch up to Arnold's column and forced to surrender. Carleton's losses were insignificant: 5 killed and 13 wounded out of his garrison of 1,800.

When one reflects on the failure to take Quebec by storm, it is tempting to play the game of "what if." What if the gallant Montgomery had not been struck down? What if Arnold had not suffered the wound that removed him from command? What if Morgan had shown the moral courage to match his physical courage in the moment that called for bold decision? It may seem reasonable to hypothesize that a reversal of any of those three misfortunes might have made Canada a fourteenth colony. But after all, the hard reality is that the attack on Quebec turned out to be what Wellington was to say of Waterloo: "the nearest run thing you ever saw in your life." And that is how Quebec must remain in history—a near thing.

What followed in the months after the failure at Quebec is a dismal tale. An indomitable Arnold held out, trying to keep up the semblance of a siege until he could get the reinforcements he pleaded for. When the reinforcements eventually came, it was the old story of too little too late, never enough at any time to enable Arnold and the commanders who succeeded him to mount an effective offensive. The three generals who followed Arnold in command—Wooster, Thomas, and Sullivan—ranged in performance from mediocre to unfortunate. Then the arrival of General Burgoyne at Quebec in early May 1776 brought Carleton's forces up to 13,000 men. The American effectives in Canada never numbered over 5,000 at any time, although a total of 8,000 men had been committed at various stages throughout the invasion.

Finally, after further severe reverses, the demoralized remnants of the American army straggled into Crown Point in mid-July 1776. Just ten months after the first expedition had left there to conquer Canada, the invasion of Canada was over.

THREE

Trenton and Princeton

IF HISTORIANS WERE TO SEEK a redeeming feature in the latter phases of the invasions of Canada, it might be found in the backhanded effect they had on Washington's operations after he ended the siege of Boston in March 1776. Despite their string of defeats, the American forces in Canada continued to be the magnet that drew British reinforcements down the valley of the Saint Lawrence—reinforcements that otherwise would have gone earlier to General Sir William Howe at Halifax, Nova Scotia, and later would be used at New York. For it was to Nova Scotia that Howe had—through the courtesy of his brother, Admiral Viscount Richard ("Black Dick") Howe—shipped his army after he evacuated Boston on Saint Patrick's Day 1776.

Washington had not hesitated in moving his army from Boston to New York. His recognition of the latter's strategic significance was clearly expressed in a letter to Brigadier General Alexander, temporarily in command of American forces in the New York area: "For should they [the British] get that Town . . . they can stop the Intercourse between the northern and southern Colonies, upon which depends the Safety of America." Washington was also keenly aware of two other great advantages that would be Howe's if he were to take and hold New York City. The British would have a direct link to Canada if they were able to command the Hudson River. More important, they would have the seaport base they needed to launch offensives against the middle colonies to the south or against New England to the north.

In early June 1776 Howe was finally ready to take New York, and a month later he had assembled an army of 25,000 on Staten Island after his brother the admiral had employed 130 warships and transports to

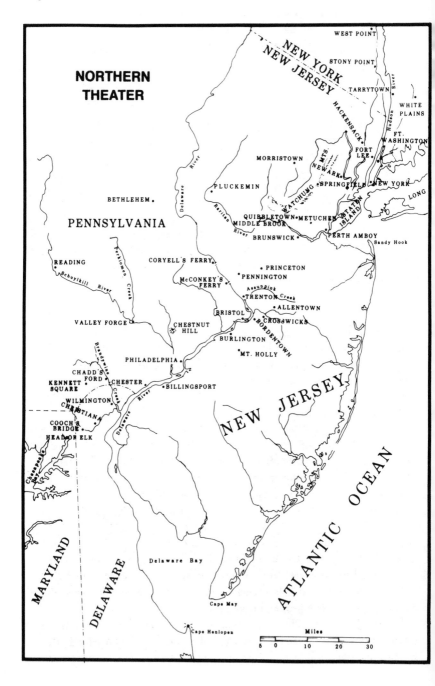

NORTHERN THEATER

move the army from Nova Scotia. Washington could muster a force of 18,000, most of which he had positioned on or near Brooklyn Heights on Long Island.

Howe started crossing from Staten Island to Long Island on 22 August. On the twenty-seventh the Battle of Long Island resulted in such a drubbing for Washington that his army was almost captured and his cause almost lost. Washington and his commanders had performed like ungifted amateurs while Howe had displayed real professionalism, executing a classic turning movement around the American left flank that rolled up their line and annihilated a large part of it.

Washington, however, was not going to give up Manhattan without another fight. He occupied Harlem Heights, and upriver had Fort Washington constructed on the east bank of the Hudson, as well as Fort Lee across from it on the west bank. But his army, now less than 15,000, was being bled white by desertions and expiring enlistments.

In mid-September Howe began a series of chess moves to capture the enemy's queen, Washington's army, while checkmating his king, New York City. Howe's first major move was a strategic envelopment which forced Washington to abandon Harlem Heights and at the same time isolated Fort Washington. At White Plains on 28 October Howe again used his favorite gambit to envelop Washington's flank, defeating his army but not routing it. Washington withdrew northward to North Castle. Again Howe did not move to exploit success, and again he missed his chance to destroy Washington's army. Instead, Howe turned southward and on 16 November captured isolated Fort Washington, along with 3,000 prisoners with all their weapons and supplies, a jolting loss to the Americans. Four days later Fort Lee fell to Howe's forces; this time, however, the garrison escaped, though it had to abandon all the matériel in the fort.

Washington's so-called retreat across the Jerseys became a retrograde into a series of accumulating crises. By the time Washington's army had reached the point where the Delaware formed a long nose of Pennsylvania protruding into New Jersey, it could count less than 5,000 half-clad, half-shod effectives to oppose Howe's 10,000 well-fed, well-equipped British and Hessians, who were poised to take Philadelphia, the colonial capital and largest city. The inhabitants, seeing the danger, had in large numbers shut up shop and fled to the countryside. In New Jersey the Howe brothers, general and admiral, had assumed the role of peacemakers and had issued a proclamation offering pardon to all who would come forward and reaffirm under oath their allegiance to King George. The New Jersey folks jumped at the chance, and in such numbers that Washington was disgusted enough to write: "Instead of turning out to defend the country and offering aid to our Army, they are making their submissions as fast as they can."

It was these defections and the other accumulating woes that prompted Tom Paine to write that famed pamphlet *The Crisis*, which began, "These are the times that try men's souls: The summer soldier and the sunshine patriot will, in this crisis, shrink from the service of his country; but he that stands it Now, deserves the love and thanks of every man and woman." Paine knew at first hand what he was saying; he had joined up and carried a musket in the retreat to the Delaware. His published pamphlet caught on at once with stouter-hearted Americans, and it was read aloud in towns and villages as well as to groups of soldiers around the camp fires. Its effect was to stiffen the determination of those who would listen.

BY 7 DECEMBER WASHINGTON HAD SUCCEEDED in getting his ever-diminishing army across the Delaware and redeploying it on a dangerously extended front behind the river, extending roughly from Coryell's Ferry on the north to the ferry near Bordentown, New Jersey, in the center, and from there to the vicinity of Bristol, Pennsylvania. In all there were nine ferries to be guarded by a tiny army of only 4,300 men, but its commander had wisely ordered the seizure or destruction of all the boats to be found along a seventy-five-mile stretch of the Delaware.

Howe's field commander, General Lord Cornwallis, had pushed his advance guard to the outskirts of Trenton in time for its leaders to see the last of the Americans crossing to the Pennsylvania shore. Nevertheless, Cornwallis's operations now ground to a halt. On 13 December, a day the English historian Trevelyan said that Americans "might well have marked . . . with a white stone in their calendar," Howe decided that "the Approach of Winter putting a stop to any further Progress, the Troops will immediately march into Quarters and hold themselves in readiness to assemble on the shortest Notice." Initially Howe envisaged establishing a line of deployment halfway down New Jersey between Newark and Brunswick. Cornwallis was bolder and recommended manning forward posts at Pennington, Trenton, and Bordentown with a base of operations at Brunswick. Howe concurred and the British occupied those posts. Such a bold and far-flung deployment could be reckless, in view of the danger of exposing the forward posts to isolation and subse-

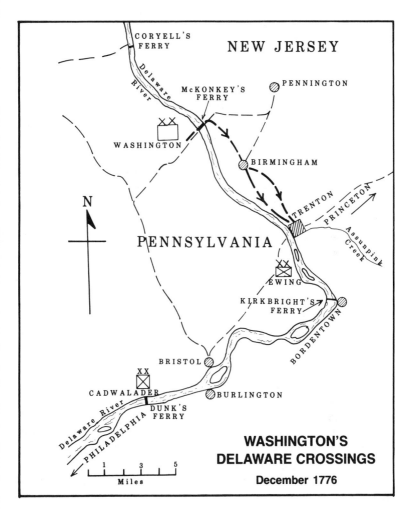

WASHINGTON'S DELAWARE CROSSINGS

December 1776

quent attack as well as to the cutting of their lines of communication to Brunswick. Yet Howe and Cornwallis obviously felt nothing but contempt for an enemy who, they believed, was not only incapable of mounting a winter offensive but who would, in all probability, not be able to survive the winter as a force to be reckoned with. Come spring, the British commanders could reassemble their forces and lean forward to pluck the apple of Philadelphia from the colonial tree.

Not the least of the anxieties that hung over George Washington at this juncture was the knowledge that by 31 December, only three weeks in the future, expiring enlistments would reduce his army to a mere 1,400 men. Adding to that knowledge was a host of logistical headaches that would have driven a lesser leader to write a letter of resignation: unpaid soldiers without the essential tents, adequate food, clothing, and blankets, let alone the requirements for winter operations.

There is sufficient evidence that Washington had begun to think boldly as early as 14 December, when he confided in three letters that if he received the reinforcements he anticipated,* he could hope to undertake effective and audacious attacks on one or more of the British forward posts. His anticipations were rewarded; by Christmas, reinforcements brought his army's strength close to 6,000. He must, he knew, employ that strength before the dreaded date of 31 December.

Additional evidence shows that by 23 December Washington's concepts had crystallized. Excerpts from his letter to Colonel Joseph Reed on that date make it clear; Washington wrote "to inform you that Christmas day at night, one hour before day, is the time fixed upon for our attempt on *Trenton* . . . necessity, dire necessity, will, nay must, justify my attack. . . . [in postscript] For if we are successful, which Heaven grant, and the circumstances favour, we may push on." The last phrase indicated an intention to pursue the offensive in New Jersey, beyond the Delaware.

Finally, on Christmas Eve, a plan discussed at a command conference attended by Generals Greene, Stirling, Roche de Fermoy, St. Clair, and Sullivan gained Washington's approval. Also present were several colonels, most notably John Glover, who commanded the "amphibious regiment" from Marblehead, Massachusetts, the hardy soldier-sailors who had rescued Washington's army after the disaster on Long Island.

The main terrain objective was the town of Trenton. The real objective was the destruction or capture of a Hessian force consisting of three regiments in the town, with cavalry and artillery detachments, 1,400 strong, all under the command of the Hessian Colonel Johann Gottlieb Rall.

Washington's plan called for three separate, coordinated river crossings which, when effected, would result in the two of the three provisional divisions (organized as such solely for the operation) of the army converging on Trenton to seal off the town and capture or destroy its

---

*General John Sullivan's 2,000, the remainder of General Charles Lee's 5,000 after desertion and expired enlistments (Lee, to the good fortune of the American cause, had been captured by British cavalry on 13 December), also General Horatio Gates's 500 plus 1,000 Philadelphia Associators (gentlemen volunteers) under Colonel John Cadwalader.

garrison. Looking from south to north, the division on the south—1,900 men and two artillery companies commanded by temporarily appointed Brigadier General John Cadwalader—was to cross the river near Bristol and mount a diversionary attack against the Hessian Colonel von Donop's garrison at Bordentown. As Donop held the overall command of the Hessian and British forces of about 3,000 men posted at Trenton and Bordentown, it was essential that his attention be diverted from the main attack on Trenton.

The center division under Brigadier General James Ewing—700 Pennsylvania and New Jersey militia—had the mission of crossing at Trenton Ferry to seize the bridge over Assunpink Creek at the south end of Trenton, then taking up position along the south bank of the creek to seal off any enemy attempt at escape in that direction.

The north, and main, attack force was to be commanded by Washington in person. It was to be divided into two columns, commanded by Nathanael Greene and John Sullivan. The force totaled 2,400 men selected from seven brigades of the army, and it would cross the river at McKonkey's Ferry, nine miles north of Trenton. This main body was heavy in artillery, with eighteen pieces in six batteries under the overall command of Colonel Henry Knox.

Washington's concept of the offensive further envisaged that after taking Trenton, the three divisions of the army would concentrate near Trenton and, reunited under Washington's command, resume the offensive against the British at Princeton and—here one can imagine Washington's eyes turned heavenward—even Brunswick! Such a breathtakingly bold continuation of the offensive would, of course, have to depend upon a successful strike against Trenton.

BY 2:00 P.M. ON CHRISTMAS DAY THE UNITS of Washington's main division began to form up in their assembly areas in the little valley west of McKonkey's Ferry. It was a clear, wintry afternoon, with the thermometer hovering around thirty degrees, and a brisk northeast wind was making officers and men clap their hands and stamp their feet to keep them warm. Companies were kept at attention only for the few minutes it took the officers to make sure that each man was carrying his required load of three days' cooked rations, forty rounds of ammunition, bayonet, and blanket.

By 3:00 P.M. brigades had formed into column and were marching toward their assigned crossing sites, where Colonel Glover and his Marblehead men were readying their Durham boats to take on their loads.

Enough of these sturdy craft had been assembled from the Delaware's shores to transport the columns in shifts. The boats varied in length from forty to sixty feet, with a beam of eight feet, and could carry a crew of four and a load of 30,000 pounds while drawing less than two feet of water. They had strong keels, were pointed at each end, and had removable steering sweeps so that the boats could load, unload, and move either forward or backward. They were also equipped with a mast and sail, as well as footboards along the gunwales where two crewmen on each side could walk while propelling the boat with their push poles. While the Durham boats may have looked awkward to Colonel Glover's seamen, they were ideal for the task at hand because they could carry full loads of men and even the horses and cannon of the artillery.

By 4:30 P.M. the sun had begun to set, and in minutes it was dark enough for the embarkation to begin. The Pennsylvanians in Stirling's brigade were making odds that the feel of snow in the air was a sure harbinger of a snowstorm before the night was over. The embarkation began with the advance guard of Stephen's brigade loading onto the first boats. Behind them artillerymen moved forward the four guns and their horse teams, which were intended to march with the head of both Greene's and Sullivan's columns. In all there would be nine artillery pieces with each column. Colonel Henry Knox's bullhorn bellow could be heard above the wind and the rattling of rolling gun carriages, assuring everyone within a quarter mile of the crossing site that the artillery would have first priority in entering the boats.

The artillery's high priority was not secured merely through Knox's powerful voice; it was the result of careful planning based on Knox's recommendation and Washington's approval. Jac Weller's perceptive study of the artillery's role in the campaign points out that the fact that the

> entire crossing of the Delaware was subordinated to the passage of the field artillery to about 2,100 [*sic*] infantry is an almost unheard of proportion. The usual ratio was two or three pieces per thousand foot-soldiers. . . . [This unusual proportion at Trenton was based on two factors; first,] the artillery was considered to be the wet-weather weapon. . . . It was difficult to load a musket in really wet weather and get it to fire. The gunners, on the other hand, could plug up the vents and muzzles of their pieces and keep the inside of the weapon entirely dry. . . . The second factor [was that] . . . Continental gunners had a high morale throughout their entire organization. . . . Washington and his generals knew this and planned

accordingly. ("Guns of Destiny: Field Artillery in the Trenton-Princeton Campaign")

With the artillery in place in the boats, Greene's column loaded and shoved off in sections. Stephen's brigade led. The second section was composed of Mercer's brigade. Next came Stirling's brigade, which was to constitute the reserve in Greene's column. Although the almanac called for a full moon, it was fully obscured by a heavy cloud layer, leaving the whole crossing to be carried out in complete darkness.*

A historical weather study by David M. Ludlum assures one that "there was no lack of ice of some kind: solid shore ice, floating cakes in midstream, and a glaze tending to form on the most exposed surfaces of boats and objects along the river" ("The Weather of Independence: Trenton and Princeton"). Nor was floating ice the end of the troubles besetting the crewmen and the soldiers in the boats. To make things worse, the storm soon turned from snow to sleet and hail driven by a bitterly cold wind. The storm brought equal misery to all ranks from general to private. Captain Thomas Rodney recalled in this diary that "it was as severe a night as ever I saw . . . [a] storm of wind, hail, rain, and snow." These miserable conditions were to last intermittently throughout the night and the following day. As a probable consolation to Washington and his commanders, it justified the commander in chief's foresight in relying on the artillery to provide wet-weather fire support.

Washington's plan called for his entire command to cross by midnight, thus allowing for a five-hour night march to reach Trenton and deploy into battle formation before first light. But the storm and river conditions had ripped that timetable to soggy pieces. It was after 3:00 A.M. when the last soldiers were landed on the New Jersey shore, and another hour before Greene's and Sullivan's columns were formed in marching order and started on the road toward Trenton. Only then was Washington finally able to leave the riverside and join Greene. The diary of an officer on Washington's staff gives us this glimpse of his commander overseeing the last of the troop landings: "He stands on the bank of the stream, wrapped in his cloak, superintending the landing of his troops. He is

---

*That the operation proceeded throughout a pitch-black night makes it somewhat difficult to appreciate Emanuel Leutze's famous painting of *Washington Crossing the Delaware*, especially with Washington standing fully erect gazing shoreward. Surely George must have taken his seat with the others, most certainly when the floating blocks of ice were banging against the sides of the boat.

calm and collected, but very determined. The storm is [again] changing to sleet and cuts like a knife."

Washington's calmness and determination were obviously on the face that he showed to his officers and soldiers. What was not revealed to them will never be known, but certainly part of his secret self was bearing the strain of knowing that he must attack Trenton in broad daylight, with the probable loss of the surprise he had so counted on in his plan for a night attack. Add to that stress the awareness that he had received no word from either Ewing or Cadwalader, both of whom should have crossed the river before Washington's force, and one begins to appreciate Washington's moral courage in maintaining such composure.

On the nine-mile march to Trenton the mental stress being borne by the commander in chief was matched by the physical misery of the men, who continued to be battered by the shifting blasts of snow, sleet, and freezing rain. Their only meager compensation was that the northeast wind was bringing the storm's effects against their backs instead of their faces. The rutted road made treacherous footing for the men without shoes. Most of that wretched lot had bound their feet with rags, and it was these unfortunates who were leaving the bloody tracks in the snow that have been mentioned so often in schoolbooks.

Washington halted the column at the hamlet of Birmingham, where the road forked into two roads to Trenton. He let the troops fall out just long enough for a breakfast of hard rations. When the officers gave the word to fall in again, sergeants were kept busy rousing men from the roadside where they had fallen asleep over their cold meal.

The force now split into the two designated columns. Greene's men took the left-hand fork, the Pennington Road, which led into Trenton at its north end. The column was made up of the brigades of Stephen, Mercer, Stirling, Roche de Fermoy, the Philadelphia troop of light horse, and the nine artillery pieces in the batteries of Captains Forrest, Hamilton, and Bauman. Washington rode with Greene in the northern column.

The other column, under Major General Sullivan, took the right-hand fork, following the River Road to come into Trenton from the south, in order to cut that end of the town off from the river. Sullivan's force was composed of the brigades of St. Clair, Glover, and Sargent.

The two roads were nearly equal in length, between four and five miles long. Washington, looking across the snow-covered fields, watched the van of Sullivan's column trudging off in the distance. From now on, the chances for a coordinated attack would have to depend on unfolding events as the two columns closed in on the Hessian outposts around the town. His commanders knew the Hessians' locations, but how well manned were the enemy positions? And how alert?

COLONEL JOHANN GOTTLIEB RALL COMMANDED the three infantry regiments that made up the Trenton garrison: his own regiment plus those of Knyphausen and von Lossberg. There was also a detachment of jägers—infantry armed with short, heavy rifles—a company of artillery with six three-pounder brass fieldpieces, and twenty British dragoons, in all about 1,400 men. Rall had been given the honor of commanding the forward detachment of von Donop's sector, which stretched from Trenton to Burlington.

Johann Rall was a stiff professional with an undisguised contempt for the American rebels. He had received the surrender of the garrison of Fort Washington hardly six weeks before this Christmas Day, watching the Americans marching without arms between the two Hessian lines of the Regiments Rall and Lossberg. He spoke no English and had no intention of learning the language. He was a hard drinker and a hard charger in battle, and that was as far as his talents went. He had no interest in fortifying his garrison—"if the Americans come we'll give them the bayonet"—and seldom bothered to visit outposts. Instead, he inspected companies in ranks, and his chief joy was to listen to the band play as it marched around the house of Abraham Hunt, where Rall had set up headquarters. The cannon were paraded with the band, as Lieutenant Andreas Wiederhold recorded, "instead of being out at the head of the streets where they could be of use." It would seem that the attitude and personality of Johann Rall were among the good breaks that came Washington's way at Trenton.

In keeping with Rall's personal style of celebrating Christmas, his troops (with the exception of his own regiment, which had "the duty" for Christmas Day) were allowed to relax—to drink and sing hearty German songs while gathered around the *Tannenbaum* they had cut and trimmed for the occasion. Only one incident had almost marred the celebration. While playing cards with a Tory merchant, Rall had heard firing about 7:00 P.M. on the north side of town. He marched several companies of Regiment Rall to the roads at the head of the town, where he was informed that some thirty or so rebels had shot up an outguard, wounding six of the Regiment Lossberg.* The rebels had vanished, and Rall's pa-

---

*The adventuring Americans' identity remains a mystery. It seems that they were not an authorized patrol, and they may have been militia or farmers out on a "ram-

trols, having gone two miles, returned without seeing a rebel. At this time Major von Dechow urged Rall to send out another series of patrols as far as the ferry landings, but Rall felt no need of such precautions and ordered the troops to stand down. All returned to their quarters while Rall went on to Abraham Hunt's, where he joined the party playing cards and guzzling Christmas cheer. By 10:00 P.M. Rall had dismissed his adjutant, Lieutenant Jacob Piel, with no further orders for the night. This standing down seems to have created a détente which gave the Hessian commander and his men all the more reason to relax and enjoy themselves.

One other incident—seemingly trivial—also failed to alert Rall to impending danger. A Tory farmer from Bucks County knocked at the Hunt house door, telling the servant he had an urgent message for Colonel Rall. The servant told the farmer that the colonel was busy and would see no visitors. The Tory wrote out a note and asked that it be given to Rall at once. The man, his duty done, disappeared into the night. The scribbled message told Rall that the whole American army had crossed the river and was marching on Trenton. Rall didn't bother to read it; he slipped it in his pocket and picked up his cards to go on with his game.

Lieutenant Andreas Wiederhold was no admirer of Colonel Rall's, so it was small wonder that he didn't share his commander's complacency. He had strengthened his oupost at the Richard Howell house on the Pennington Road north of Trenton, bringing up nine more men on Christmas night. At about 7:45 A.M. of the twenty-sixth Wiederhold decided to stretch his legs and take a look outside. What he saw pulled him up short. Two hundred yards away, about sixty men were coming at the house on the double. Already his sentinels were running toward the house—to their command post—shouting: "Der Feind! Heraus! Heraus!" (The enemy! Turn out! Turn out!).

What Wiederhold was seeing was a part of Stephen's brigade, the advance guard for Greene's division, which had orders to advance with all speed into the town, overrunning any outguards in the way. At the same time the regiments of Mercer's brigade were swinging around to the south in order to support Stephen's attack by outflanking any resistance they met.

The American tactics were working as planned. Wiederhold's guard got off a volley before it had to fall back across the fields to its left rear, toward King Street. Realizing that he was in danger of being cut off by

---

page" in the spirit of raising a bit of hell with the Hessians, who were universally despised as looters and pillagers.

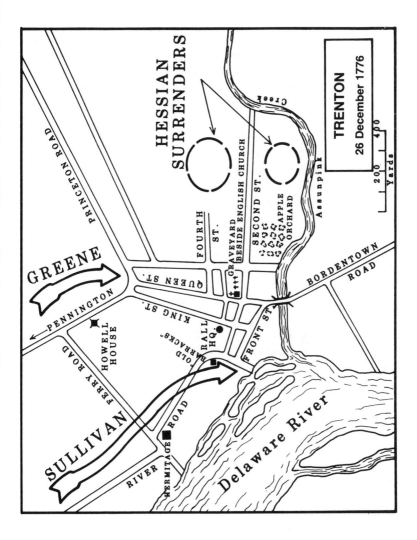

Mercer's men, Wiederhold led a rush rearward to fall back on Captain von Alterbockum's company, which was forming up to block the Pennington Road. Hardly had Wiederhold's panting men lined up on the captain's left flank, however, when Alterbockum realized that a delaying action was out of the question and ordered a withdrawal, the Americans hard on his heels, firing as they came. When Alterbockum's company reached the north end of the town, he had it fall back down King Street, while Wiederhold's men, joined by Captain Bruback and a guard detachment of the Regiment Rall, split away to retire down Queen Street, taking advantage of the cover between houses as they withdrew.

In the south, Sullivan had sensibly held up his advance guard long enough to ensure that Greene's division had time enough to drive in the enemy's outposts in the north. Then Sullivan's advance guard struck out against the Hessian outguard occupying the Hermitage, the home of Philemon Dickinson on the River Road. Like Lieutenant Wiederhold, Lieutenant von Grothausen saw that he must take action at once. He took a sergeant and twelve of his detachment of fifty jägers and started off on the double toward the firing on the Pennington Road. Grothausen had gone hardly three hundred yards when he looked over his left shoulder to see a column of Americans heading toward the Hermitage. It was too late to get back to the rest of his jägers at the house, so Grothausen doubled back toward the river at the south end of town, joined en route by a corporal and the rest of the jäger detachment, which had left everything but their muskets and cross belts at the Hermitage. Grothausen tried to make a stand near the old barracks, but after one futile volley the jägers had to run for their lives or face capture. Some succeeded in fording Assunpink Creek south of King Street, while the bulk of the fleeing light infantry escaped across the Queen Street Bridge, which the Americans had not yet reached.

Lieutenant Jacob Piel, Rall's adjutant, was the first officer in the town to hear the firing on the Pennington Road. He ran from his quarters, next door to Rall's headquarters, turned out the guard there, and started them up King Street to reinforce the outposts. That done, he beat on the front door of Rall's house until the colonel stuck his night-capped and no doubt hung-over head out of an upper window.

"What is the matter?" Rall called down.

"Haven't you heard the firing?" Piel shouted back.

"I will be out in a minute," and Rall was as good as his word. When he stepped out of the house, American musketry and artillery had already begun rattling down King Street. Rall mounted his horse and ordered his own regiment to form up near the lower end of King Street. When Lieutenant Colonel Scheffer asked, by messenger, when to deploy the Regiment Lossberg, Rall ordered it to parade in the graveyard behind the English Church and prepare to advance up Queen Street. He then directed the Regiment Knyphausen to stand by as a reserve on Second Street, east of King Street.

THE INITIAL PHASE OF WASHINGTON'S ENCIRCLING attack on Trenton had been carried out without a hitch, no mean accomplishment for a co-ordinated eighteenth-century operation. The outposts had been driven in, and there were Americans in position on three sides of the town.

While the Hessian regiments were being rousted out, the next phase of Washington's battle plan got under way. Two brigades of Greene's division took off to their left, bypassing the upper end of town to deploy between the Princeton Road with their left flank extended toward Assunpink Creek, thus cutting off any Hessian attempt to break out of Trenton to the northeast. At the same time his third brigade was turning to the south, extending its right flank to link up with the left brigade of Sullivan's division to complete the encirclement of the town.

The resulting gap between Stephen and Mercer was quickly filled by Stirling's brigade and its artillery, which was moving straight ahead around its objective, the juncture of King and Queen streets at the upper end of town. Henry Knox came into his own, leading forward his artillery into firing positions at the head of the two streets. Captain Forrest's battery of two six-pounder guns and two howitzers had been marching near the head of Greene's column and thus was practically on the edge of its designated firing position at the head of Queen Street. Captain Alexander Hamilton's battery of two six-pounder guns had unlimbered about 200 yards north of town, and in no time its battery commander was urging his cannoneers forward with drag ropes to come into position and open fire down King Street. After Henry Knox had called off the range, the ruddy-faced Hamilton could be heard shouting his fire commands, and the first ranging rounds boomed out.

Not far away, Washington, trailed by his staff and an escort of Philadelphia Light Horse, took up his position on the higher ground where he could observe the movements of his troops and the enemy. Visibility, however, was not yet good enough for the commander in chief to see the far end of town and the bridge over the Assunpink. Hence he could see nothing of Sullivan's actions and would still be anxiously trying to determine whether Ewing had crossed the river and taken the bridge. Closer in, though, he could see Mercer's men beginning to break into houses on King Street or slip between them to find places to get a shot at the Hessians.

When Hamilton's and Forrest's guns opened fire, the Hessian commander directed his regiment, supported by companies of the Regiment Lossberg, to advance up King Street and clear it. Led by Lieutenant Colonel Brethauer, the Hessian ranks marched behind the colors of Regiment Rall, snatched from the colonel's quarters just in time to join the formation. No sooner had the Hessians stepped off, however, when the round-shot from Hamilton's battery tore through their ranks. At the same time Mercer's men, firing from the cover of houses and fences, took their toll on the enemy's left. The Hessians halted and got off two volleys. As Brethauer gave the command to fire, his horse was shot and sent him tumbling. The combined fires of American artillery and musketry were too much. The battalions of Regiment Rall broke, and the flood of fleeing men tore through the supporting Lossbergs' ranks, breaking up their formation.

The two Hessian three-pounder guns coming to the support of their infantry on King Street were just as roughly handled. When Rall had ordered his regiment forward he had called out to Lieutenant Engelhardt, who was standing by his two guns in front of the house where the guard reserve had been quartered: "My God, Lieutenant. . . . Push your cannon ahead!"

Since the guns were already hitched to their horse teams, Engelhardt took off up the street at the head of his little battery. They had hardly gone fifty yards when the shot from Hamilton's guns smashed into them. Engelhardt made a gallant effort to get into firing position and return the fire. He did get off six rounds from each gun, but at a devastating cost. In a matter of minutes he had lost half of his men, and five horses were down with fatal wounds. The artillerymen left standing dropped their rammer staffs and cartridge bags and ran for cover behind the houses.

Henry Knox, at the head of King Street on Princeton Road, saw the Hessian guns being knocked out of action. He ran over to Colonel George Weedon, whose Virginia regiment of Stirling's brigade had deployed along the road ready to attack into the town.

"Can some of your men take those guns?" Knox asked. Without replying, Weedon ordered Captain William Washington forward. Washington took off on a run, followed by Lieutenant James Monroe, Sergeant Joseph White, and a half-dozen men. Keeping close to the houses and running for all they were worth, they swarmed over the guns and tried to turn them on the Hessians down the street. In that brief flurry of action both officers were wounded—Washington in both hands and Monroe in the shoulder. The capture of the cannon was followed at once by Weedon's men charging down King Street.

Over at the head of Queen Street, Forrest's battery was sweeping the street with deadly effect. One of his two howitzers went out of action with a broken axle, but the other three cannon did their share in breaking up Hessian attempts to advance, as well as silencing two more Hessian guns after they had fired only four times.

While those Hessian guns were being silenced, Stirling's men were attacking southward down both Queen and King streets. Meanwhile, what was happening to Sullivan's column in its attack from the River Road into the south end of the town?

After the advance elements of St. Clair's brigade had driven the Hessian jägers from the Hermitage and the old barracks, most of the jägers had fled across Assunpink Creek. Following Captain John Flahaven's New Jersey Continentals came Colonel John Stark, of Bunker Hill fame, with his regiment of New Hampshiremen. Stark, being Stark, didn't wait for the niceties of orders and deployments. He led a thundering charge from the right—formerly the head—of St. Clair's brigade straight ahead toward the Regiment Knyphausen, which was now deployed facing south, and Major Dechow's battalion of the Lossbergs. In Major Wilkingon's account, "the dauntless Stark dealt death wherever he found resistance, and broke down all opposition before him."

Not to be outdone, Sullivan personally led a column of Sargent's and Glover's men past the old barracks, then double-quicked up Front Street toward Queen Street, intending to cut off any Hessian attempt at escape over the Assunpink bridge. In this he was not completely successful, since most of the jägers and a good many fugitives from Regiment Rall had already gotten away via the bridge, preceded by a detachment of twenty British dragoons who had not waited to hear more than the opening shots of the battle before decamping.

IN FOLLOWING THE AMERICAN FORCES IN THEIR movements and actions, as well as the Hessian attempts to defend and counterattack, one should not lose sight of two major factors that determined the character of the battle from start to finish: the continuing storm, and the transformation from a coordinated American attack to a "soldier's battle," Ludlum's

"The Weather of Independence" concludes that the storms most prevalent at this time of winter were "bringing first snow, then ice pellets [sleet], and finally rain, often with alternate periods of each, or a mixture of all three." From other records it can be ascertained that those "alternate periods of each" made conditions miserable for both sides throughout the battle. From the Americans' viewpoint, even though the Continentals and militia had taken the precaution to cover their flintlock muskets with rags and to keep them under blankets or coats on the march, there was no way of protecting the firing pans, flints, and touchholes once the musket had to be exposed for firing. Consequently, no sooner did an infantryman go into action than this weapon was rendered useless except for the bayonet. The Hessians did have dry flintlocks when they charged out of the buildings in which they were quartered, but after firing a round or two they fell victim to the same weather that plagued their enemies. Christopher Ward has summed it all up: "The flints would not strike a spark; the priming charges would not flash; the touchholes were clogged with wet powder. . . . Those that got into the houses dried their gunlocks and could fire toward the end of the battle" (*The War of the Revolution*).

It was artillery, which could keep its necessaries dry enough to continue functioning, that ruled the battle of the main streets. What went on around the houses, in the alleys and side streets, and behind fences and walls was another matter. Once Greene's and Sullivan's battalions were committed to action inside the town, the situation resembled the pouring of water into a cauldron of molten lead. The resultant eruptions became battles of single men or small groups, moving and firing when they could at whatever enemy they encountered. Over it all, the sleet beat down through the pall of smoke that continued to hang over the town. It was an affair, then, of bayonet and sword. Adding to the confusion of weather and smoke was the noise of battle: the booming of the cannon, the shouts of men charging with the bayonet, and the commands of officers who had to shout their loudest to be heard. It was this last factor, the regaining of control by the leaders, that eventually brought order out of chaos.

On the Hessian side, Rall's officers had managed a rally toward the south end of the town, along the River Road at Front Street. They pleaded with their commander to renew the attack. Rall was in a daze, seemingly unable to make a decision. Major von Hanstein made a final plea to the brigade commander: "If you will not let us press forward up this street [Queen Street], then we must retreat to the bridge; otherwise the whole affair will end disastrously." Rall then agreed to a renewed counterattack. The two regiments, Rall and Lossberg, were brought into line facing northward toward King and Queen streets, the lines were dressed, and the colors brought to the front of the color companies.

"Forward march!" Rall commanded, "and attack them with the bayonet." The two regiments, Rall on the left, Lossberg on the right, marched forward under the direct command of Lieutenant Colonel Scheffer. As they moved out, the band joined them, striking up a martial air. Then, with colors drooping in the freezing rain and band playing, Scheffer guided the formation into Queen Street.

There the brave show came to a quick and bloody end. In a matter of minutes the Americans, firing from the houses and alleys, found ready targets in the packed ranks of Hessians, who were further exposed to the blazing guns of Forrest's battery firing down Queen Street. The demoralized Germans floundered about in spite of their officers' attempts to restore ordered formations. Then more Americans, needing no urging from their officers, came pushing in through the alleys from King Street, striking the enemy mass on its left flank.

Rall's adjutant, the loyal and ever-present Lieutenant Piel, tried to convince his commander that there was still a chance to withdraw through the escape route over the Assunpink bridge. Rall agreed, and ordered Piel to reconnoiter and make sure the route was open. Piel made it as far as the corner of Queen and Second streets, from where he found that the Americans were in control of the bridge. He turned back to Rall, to find the colonel shouting to his milling soldiers, "Alles was meine Grenadiere sind, vorwärts!" (All who are my grenadiers, forward!).

It was too late. Captain Joseph Moulder's battery of three four-pounders, attached to Sullivan's division, began to blast into Queen Street from a hastily occupied position near Second Street. The Americans were closing in from Rall's left and rear, and there was no longer a chance to withdraw southward. Rall gave the order to move eastward to reassemble in the apple orchard at the southeast corner of town. No sooner had he given the order than he was struck by two bullets in his side. He fell from his horse and was helped by two soldiers to the Methodist Church on Queen Street.

When the three remaining field officers finally got the remnants of the two regiments through the side streets to the orchard, they held a hasty council. It was agreed to make a breakout attempt from the orchard toward the Brunswick Road. But when they tried to execute their plan, they found the way blocked by Stephen's and Fermoy's brigades of Greene's division, supported by Forrest's and Bauman's batteries. The Hessian field officers thereupon surrendered to General Stirling.

In the meantime, Sullivan's division was dealing out the same kind of bashing to the Regiment Knyphausen and its attached battalion of Lossbergs. The brigades of St. Clair and Sargent surrounded a fleeing mob of fugitives from the three Hessian regiments that were trying to reach the Assunpink bridge and captured the lot. The Regiment Knyphausen tried to counterattack but was driven back. Major Dechow, commanding the last of the Lossbergs, was severely wounded and had to surrender. The beaten Germans tried to retreat to the bridge but found it held in strength by the Americans; then they turned away to try to cross the creek by a ford, but they found none that was passable. They then turned to follow the creek eastward; some did get across, only to find themselves looking into the muskets of St. Clair's men on the far side. In the end, the Regiment Knyphausen, complete with screaming camp followers, colors, and field music, was surrendered to General St. Clair. It was nearly nine o'clock. The Battle of Trenton was over.

IN SPITE OF THE ESCAPE OF SOME 400 or 500 of the enemy during the battle, Washington's bag of men and matériel was truly impressive: over 900 men and officers, all their muskets and accoutrements, their six pieces of artillery complete, ammunition and supply wagons, fifteen sets of colors, and all the instruments of the band that had played so bravely up to the end. The American losses: one officer and one private!

Yet even these totals, much as they meant to the quartermasters, were insignificant compared to the moral effects on the British and American causes. Howe was so shocked by the news—imagine these costly European professionals not only beaten but captured by a ragtag army that had been struggling to stay alive—that he sent posthaste for Cornwallis, who was about to board ship for England. The earl must return at once to resume command in New Jersey. In the same breath, Howe ordered reinforcements forward toward the stricken area. It would seem that this General Washington, who had been earlier dubbed "the Fox" by Cornwallis, did have a fearsome bite!

The news of Trenton was greeted with elation throughout the colonies. Washington emerged from the depths of crisis to the stature of hero. The man who had taken such a series of drubbings, from Long Island to Forts Lee and Washington, was restored to popular favor, all his defeats set aside. On 27 December Congress, still safely ensconced in

Baltimore, resolved to give Washington dictatorial powers for the next six months: to raise all kinds of troops, to appoint all officers up to brigadier general, to take "whatever he may want for the use of the army."

THE VICTORIOUS GENERAL HIMSELF WAS FEELING anything but heroic there in Trenton in mid-morning of his day of triumph. It was obvious that neither Ewing nor Cadwalader had crossed the river, let alone accomplished their missions. Washington learned later that Ewing had flatly turned back from a river crossing, judging the conditions impossible for such a venture. Cadwalader had at least tried by crossing more than 600 men at Dunk's Ferry, but he withdrew them when he thought it impossible to get his artillery across the river. Thus Washington was left with his worn-out men and his bag of prisoners and matériel to fend for himself.

At a conference of senior officers, Washington soon realized that the original plan to drive on to Princeton and New Brunswick was out of the question. Without Ewing's and Cadwalader's aggregate force of 2,600, and with only his exhausted 2,400, Washington was not only unable to pursue the offensive, but his present position would soon be untenable in view of approaching British reinforcements and the problem of trying to fight them with his back to the river. It was clear that the only course of action left was to recross the river and reorganize his forces around their cantonments on the Pennsylvania side. Washington summed it up in a letter to General Heath on 27 December: "I thought it most prudent to return the same evening [26 December], with my prisoners and the artillery we had taken."

Shortly after noon the dreary march began back to the boats at McKonkey's Ferry. The winter storm continued to beat upon the cold and weary men with the same snow and sleet that they had endured in the early morning hours. The river crossing was even harder than the first time; it was so cold that three men froze to death in the boats. It was dark before the last boats had landed their men in Pennsylvania, and most of the units didn't make it back to their camps until the next morning, falling asleep as soon as they reached their huts. They had marched, most of them, as far as fifty miles and had fought a brutal action. The morning reports of 27 December showed over a thousand men unfit for duty—over 40 percent ineffectives. And those worn-out men would have been anything but comfortable had they known what their commander in chief was planning for their immediate future.

For the next two days, after recrossing the Delaware on 26 December, it was business as usual for Washington: "business as usual" meaning that every bit of good news—e.g., the reception of the news of his Trenton coup—would be evened by a jolt of bad. He knew all too well that the effectives in his army numbered only about 1,500, and that the enlistments of most of his Continentals would expire on 31 December.

Washington met those challenges with typical Washingtonian courage. He offered a bounty of $10 to every man who would extend for six weeks, thereby pledging the public credit, with no authority other than his own word, since his military treasury was completely defunct. A hurried letter begged Robert Morris, the financier of the revolution in Philadelphia: "If it be possible to give us assistance do it; borrow money when it can be done. . . . No time, my dear sir, is to be lost." Morris raised $50,000 in paper money, which he sent, and on the morning of 1 January 1777 canvas bags from Morris arrived containing all the hard money he could scrape up: "410 Spanish milled dollars . . . 2 English crowns, 72 French crowns, 1,072 English shillings."

Making separate and largely successful pleas to the Continentals, Washington, Knox, and Mifflin succeeded in getting all but the most feeble and sick to stay on. Things began to look up enough for Washington to start his army back across the river, and by 30 December he had reassembled it in Trenton, where he awaited the expected reinforcements. General Mifflin had miraculously raised nearly 1,600 men in and around Philadelphia, and these troops were now moving on Trenton via Bordentown. In addition, Cadwalader's militia were marching from Allentown and Crosswicks. When these reinforcements were concentrated at Trenton, Washington would have 5,000 men he could count on for the resumption of his offensive in New Jersey. The commander in chief had never abandoned his concept of taking Princeton as the big step toward the capture of the British base at Brunswick.

The background picture, however, was not all rosy. Of the 5,000 troops that Washington was concentrating in Trenton, a great part of the militia was made up of untrained farmers and villagers who had no knowledge of combat. They must have been in good physical shape and even well clothed for winter, but that was the only bright aspect. On the other hand, the Continentals, while battle-hardened and dependable, had been labeled a "flock of animated scarecrows." Against this brittle instrument of Washington's, Cornwallis was already moving southward a force of 8,000 professionals—well fed, completely equipped, disciplined, and combat ready.

Washington's combat intelligence, reliable as usual, had made him aware of Cornwallis's movements across New Jersey, and his chief concern became the security of his forces concentrating at Trenton. It was evident that Cornwallis had as his main objective the American army in Trenton. On New Year's Day 1777 the earl was preparing to advance with a force of nearly 7,000, with twenty-eight pieces of artillery, under his personal command. As a rear guard he left the 4th Brigade under Lieutenant Colonel Mawhood at Princeton; it was a force of about 1,200, composed of three infantry regiments: the 17th, 40th, and 55th. The main baggage train was to return to Brunswick.

To counter this formidable array, Washington on New Year's Day dispatched a covering force under the French General Roche de Fermoy made up of Fermoy's own brigade, Colonel Hand's Pennsylvania riflemen, Colonel Hausegger's German Regiment, Colonel Scott's Virginia Continentals, and the two-gun battery of Captain Forrest. Fermoy's mission was to execute a delaying action as the British moved southward toward Trenton, beginning with an initial position at Five-Mile Run, a little over a mile south of Maidenhead (now Lawrenceville). He was to delay on successive positions, causing the British to deploy as often as possible and thereby disclosing the strength of Cornwallis's main body.

This covering force, and the American army in general, got an unexpected break in the weather beginning on New Year's Eve. Southerly winds brought on a temporary thaw that melted the snow and softened the ground. When Cornwallis's men began their march on 2 January, the hard-frozen roads were turned into quagmires. The British artillery, despite the cracking of the drivers' whips over the horses and the pushing and shoving of the gun crews, became bogged down time after time. Realizing the difficulties, Cornwallis had his force move in three columns. He also detached General Leslie's 2nd Brigade of about 1,500 men at Maidenhead, while he pushed ahead with the remaining 5,500 men.

At about 10:00 A.M. the British advance guard elements encountered the American outposts north of Five-Mile Run. At this point General de Fermoy saw fit to return to Trenton "in a questionable manner"— whether he was drunk or just befuddled is not certain. With his departure the covering force got a good break in the form of Colonel Edward Hand of the Pennsylvania riflemen. This Irish-born, thirty-two-year-old former British soldier, who had resigned an ensign's commission in 1772 to try his hand at medicine, was the stuff of which natural leaders are made. Under his masterly control the Pennsylvania rifles took their deadly toll of British infantrymen long before the British Brown Bess could open fire. Hand also saw to it that the muskets of his other units came into play as the British deployed.

Fighting from all kinds of cover, the Americans forced the British to deploy again and again before scampering away through woods or across fields. After having to fall back from Five-Mile Run, Hand took up his next position along Shabbakonk Creek, where the initial skirmishing turned into an all-out brawl. The fire of Hand's men caused so many casualties that the British mistook the skirmish line for the American main battle position. After they had destroyed the bridge across the creek, the Americans continued to lay down such a fire that the British artillery blasted the tree lines for half an hour while two Hessian battalions waited in deployed order to assault the creek's defenders. When the British finally advanced, Hand's force had melted away unseen to take up a new position behind a ravine known as Stockton's Hollow, about a half mile north of Trenton. There the Americans, with the continuing support of Forrest's guns, forced the British to deploy units once more, under cover of a new artillery cannonade. When the enemy's fire and impending attack became too much of a threat to his position, Hand reluctantly withdrew into Trenton. By now it was 4:00 P.M., and he had carried out superbly the mission of the covering force, but he was not finished by any means. Firing from behind and within the same houses from which they had battled Rall's Hessians just a week before, Hand's men continued to hold back the British advance guard of 1,500 men. Finally the covering force units were safely withdrawn across Assunpink Creek, where American batteries on the south side took the British under fire and stopped them in their tracks. Washington was indeed indebted to Edward Hand for buying the time he so badly needed to organize his incoming reinforcements and deploy them in their defensive positions behind Assunpink Creek. The commander in chief's debt was repaid, at least in part, when Congress acted on his recommendation and made Hand a brigadier general some two months later.

While Hand was holding up the British advance, Washington and his generals had made good use of the hard-bought time to occupy a defensive line on the ridge just south of the Assunpink. Entrenchments were well under way after the brigades took up their positions: Mercer's on the left, Cadwalader's in the center, and St. Clair's on the right. Behind this front line was another line forming a reserve.

Hand's men had done their work so well that it was not until sunset (close on 5:00 P.M.) that the renewed British advance struck at the Assunpink Creek bridge while Hessian units tried to cross at a ford. The overall British attack could be described as halfhearted at best. It became almost an affair of artillery, from the American standpoint, as the batteries laid down such a heavy fire that the enemy was easily repulsed. Musketry followed, as well as the British artillery return fire. The affair, sometimes called the Second Battle of Trenton, hardly seems worthy of such a title, though there were casualties on both sides.

DARKNESS HAD SET IN BY THE TIME Cornwallis arrived in Trenton with his main body. Since the advance guard had already collided with the American main battle position, Cornwallis took counsel with his staff in regard to a night attack. His quartermaster general, Sir William Erskine, called for an immediate strike, concluding with, "If Washington is the general I take him to be, his army will not be found there in the morning." General Grant disagreed—the rebels were securely dug in, there were no boats for an assault, and the British troops were exhausted after their long, difficult march. An early-morning attack could turn the rebel right flank with their backs to the Delaware. Other officers offered many of the same points. Cornwallis himself was dubious about trying to find and turn the American right flank in the dark, while the alternate course of action, a frontal attack against an entrenched enemy, seemed equally risky. In the end Cornwallis decided that he already had Washington in a trap that could easily be sprung in tomorrow's daylight, and so closed the council of war with: "We've got the old fox safe now. We'll go over and bag him in the morning."

Withdrawing to the north side of Trenton, the British set up camp for the night. Their sentinels and patrols took note of the numerous and unusually bright camp fires along the rebel lines on the ridge beyond the Assunpink, and anyone who came within a hundred yards or so of rebel outposts could hear the clinking of entrenching tools as the rebels continued to dig in.

As darkness wore on, the men who were awake in both British and American lines began to feel the wind swinging in from the northwest, bringing the temperatures down to the freezing point. Before midnight the mercury began a steady decline, until by daylight (sunrise was at 7:23 A.M. on 3 January) the cold could be measured in the low twenties.

Peering through the morning mists that were beginning to dissipate after first light, British sentries and patrols could see the American lines. Not a rebel was to be seen. When the senior commanders were alerted and had gathered around Cornwallis, their field glasses confirmed the reports of the patrols. Cornwallis's fox had made his getaway, stealthily slipping out of that cul-de-sac. Just how, in the name of all that was unholy, had he managed it? And where had he gone?

In the early evening of 2 January Washington had summoned his own council of war and had decided to have the army slip away that night. They would pass around Cornwallis's left flank, bypass the British force at Maidenhead, strike the British rear guard at Princeton, and—if all went well—push on to capture the enemy's baggage, stores, and treasure at Brunswick.

While the details of the plan were being worked out, Washington was taking note of a second fortunate break in the weather. The southerly winds and warm rains that had hindered Cornwallis's advance were being succeeded by northwesterly winds and falling temperatures that would assure the freezing of the ground's surface. His army and its cannon could march with confidence on its objectives.

A sketch map showing the disposition of British forces in Princeton, as well as the road network in and around the town, had been passed to Colonel Cadwalader by an American spy. Now it served to strengthen Washington's plans, especially through the potential use of a route along the back (eastern) and more vulnerable side of the town.

Advice as to routes out of the Assunpink positions was essential to the American success. Local farmers were summoned, and guides were selected from them. All ranks were alerted to the necessity to form ranks and march quietly. The wheels of the cannon carriages were wrapped in rags and ropes, which would further serve to give traction for moving the guns over frozen roads. The baggage train of 150 wagons, accompanied by three heavy guns which couldn't keep up with tactical marches, were marched quietly away, bound for Burlington. By midnight the last preparations had been completed.

Once the plans had been approved, they were put into execution. A party of 400 men was detailed to carry out the simulation of an army warmed by its camp fires and putting out work details on its entrenchments. Some of the party gathered fence rails to keep the campfires burning brightly, while others banged away with pick and spade to simulate continued digging in. Some also made noises like clumsy patrols near the bridge and along the creek. Their work would cease just before daylight, when they too would slip away and follow the army's march.

At 1:00 A.M. on 3 January the eastward march began, with no one under the grade of brigadier general knowing where the army was headed or what it was supposed to do when it got there. Light infantry, backed up by the Red Feather Company of Philadelphia, made up the van, followed by Mercer's brigade. Then came the artillery, followed by St. Clair's brigade, which was accompanied by Washington and his staff. After St. Clair came the rest of the army, and its rear was closed by Captain Henry with three companies of Philadelphia militia.

By 2:00 A.M. the army was clearing the front of the British lines, and its van was crossing the little tributary that flowed into the Assunpink. The chosen "road" was really a woodsman's path hacked through thick woods, and the countless stumps made the going miserable for the infantry, who stumbled over them in the darkness, as well as for the cursing artillerymen whose guns and limbers got hung up on them.

The strung-out column passed the log huts of the hamlet called Sandtown, taking the road to Quaker Bridge. Somewhere along that way, panic broke out among Captain Henry's militia: they were being surrounded by Hessians! The companies broke and fled toward Bordentown—to the southeast. The rest of the army trudged along, oblivious to the racket in the rear. They were long since clear of the British at Trenton, marching in the pitch blackness under only a few dim stars. By the time the first light appeared in the east, the advance guard was already crossing Stony Brook, about two miles west of Princeton. One of Washington's aides recalled that "the morning was bright, serene, and extremely cold [around 23°F], with a hoar frost which spangled every object." The roads and fields were bare, with no snow, only the hoarfrost glittering under the early winter sun.

At Stony Brook the column divided according to plan. Brigadier General Hugh Mercer took the fork to the left in order to carry out the first part of his mission: to tear down the bridge at Stony Brook near Worth's Mill, thus delaying any interference should any of Cornwallis's units in Trenton come up in pursuit of the Americans. When General Sullivan's command—the army's main body—crossed Stony Brook, it took the right fork, to march up the Back Road and enter Princeton from its least-defended side on the east.

Something was also stirring at dawn on the British side. Cornwallis had left a rear guard of three infantry regiments—the 17th, 40th, and 55th—at Princeton under Lieutenant Colonel Mawhood. That gentleman, following his orders, marched out at dawn on 3 January intending to join General Leslie at Maidenhead, via the Post (Princeton-Trenton) Road, leaving the 40th Regiment to guard the baggage and stores left in Princeton. It was a quietly confident Mawhood who mounted his brown pony in Princeton and whistled for his two spaniels, who trotted along after his horse. His column was preceded by a troop of the 16th Light Dragoons, followed by the 17th Regiment and part of the 55th. Shortly before 8:00 A.M. a couple of Mawhood's troopers, having crossed the Stony Brook Bridge, were topping the small hill that the Post Road crossed just west of the bridge at Worth's Mill when they caught sight of the glitter of the sun on steel and moving figures coming from the southwest, up the road that paralleled Stony Brook. After a second look, a trooper took off to inform Mawhood that rebel troops were approaching. When Mawhood had seen things for himself, he was faced with immediate decisions. His primary responsibility was for the safety of the 40th and all those supplies and the wagon train back in Princeton. A rider was dispatched to alert the commander of the 40th to the possible approach of a rebel force. Mawhood's next decision was a tough one to make. Should he carry on, carrying out his mission to the letter—that is, moving to join General Leslie at Maidenhead? Should he send a detachment southward to block the rebels approaching Stony Brook Bridge? Or should he countermarch his command and attack the threat with his whole force?

Mawhood's personal reconnaissance had convinced him that it was part of the rebel army making for Princeton. By blocking the rebel force—perhaps a strong force; he could not yet be sure—he would protect Princeton and Brunswick as well as develop what was still a hazy situation. Accordingly, he turned the head of his column to reverse its march, recross the bridge, and retrace its route toward Princeton. His next action has been open to controversy. Historians have generally accepted that Mawhood then directed his column—preceded by some dragoons—back across Stony Brook Bridge and toward the orchard of William Clark, which lay about 1,000 yards to the east on a southerly slope of a large hill mass, the summit of which came to be known as Mercer Heights. T. J. Wertenbaker ("The Battle of Princeton"), however, has contended logically that Mawhood's appreciation of the terrain decided him to seize the high ground of Mercer Heights itself, the most critical terrain feature of the area. Consequently, Mawhood pushed ahead a part of the 55th, which had been bringing up the rear of his column, to occupy Mercer Heights until he could join it there with his main body.

As his scouts and van approached Stony Brook Bridge, Mercer became aware of the movements of Mawhood's main body only when it was recrossing the bridge. Evidently he then decided to head off Mawhood's eastbound column. The sensible action was to turn his column to the

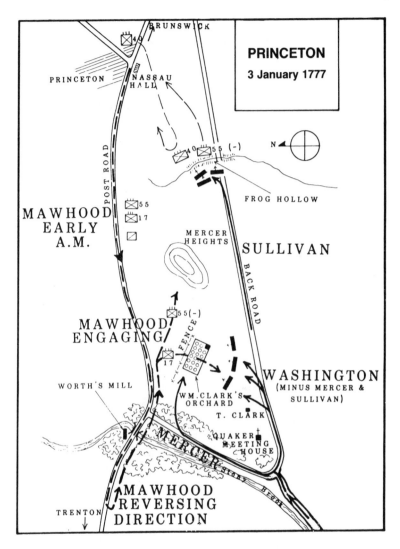

right and seize the heights to his right, some sixty feet above the little valley of Stony Brook. He so ordered the new direction of his column, and as its head was ascending the hill, a sergeant saw a horseman looking toward them. They were discovered.

When Mercer reached the top of the hill, he could observe Sullivan's division marching northward along the Back Road to Princeton and

Mawhood's column of British coming up from the west. Seeing this, and at the same time deducing the intent of the British commander, Mercer turned his column northeastward to screen Sullivan's flank from an attack by Mawhood, which meant that his van would be passing through William Clark's orchard.

Mawhood was marching back along the Post Road. When he came to a leftward jog in the road, he found it more practicable to leave the road and head eastward across the fields for Mercer Heights. While on this new leg of his march, Mawhood saw Mercer's men approaching the orchard and hastened Captain Truwin's cavalry troop forward to take up position to hit the rebel column in flank. Truwin's dragoons dismounted and—as yet unseen by the marching Americans—deployed along the north side of the orchard, taking cover along a ditch and a fence that ran along that side.

Truwin's men began the battle when they opened fire on the Americans. Although surprised, Mercer kept his head and turned his advance units to the left to return the fire with a volley. The British cavalrymen withdrew as the Americans advanced, yielding the fence line to the Americans. At first the Americans had the best of it, driving back the enemy and inflicting casualties, but things took a new turn when Mawhood came up with his 17th Regiment, which he quickly deployed into line, with his two fieldpieces going into action on the right of his line. Both forces were now fully deployed and exchanging volleys—at ranges, it is said, of as close as forty yards. The Americans got off three volleys before their fire slackened. This was one of those times when disciplined British musketry—all training and weapons designed to deliver maximum firepower at short range—came into its own. In addition, the two British cannons, firing canister at forty yards, took their toll of American casualties.

When Mawhood saw his enemy begin to waver, he seized his opportunity and ordered a bayonet charge. The British line came on at charge bayonet, and the infantrymen were carried away by battle fury, screaming to get at their enemy in close combat. Mercer's men broke and fled. Many became vulnerable when they had to scale another fence on the orchard's south side. Mercer was among them, his horse having taken a bullet in the foreleg. He was struck down by a musket butt, knocked to this knees, and though he tried to defend himself with his sword, was bayoneted seven times and left for dead. For a time Mawhood's men were out of control. They pulled a lieutenant from his refuge under a farm cart where, in spite of his broken leg, he was repeatedly bayoneted. Lieutenant Yeates, already wounded, suffered thirteen bayonet wounds.

Captain Fleming was shot dead while trying to rally his Virginians. Colonel Haslet of the Delaware Continentals was killed while trying to form a new line below the Clark farmyard.* The British also captured the two guns of Captain Neil's battery after the captain had died defending them. The guns were then turned on the American fugitives.

Mawhood finally got his men reassembled and formed into line again, this time south of the orchard, with most of his line behind a fence. He now had four guns, including the two captured pieces, which he positioned to the right rear of his line. Here he waited, ready to take on a renewed attack.

Meanwhile, Sullivan's division, after taking the road to Princeton, had advanced up the Back Road until his column's head was abreast of those companies of the British 55th that had just reached Mercer Heights. Having no way of knowing what strength the British had on the heights—Sullivan could see some redcoats in front of the trees on the summit but couldn't tell how many units were hidden by the trees—he halted to keep them under observation. For a while there was an impasse. Faced with this large force of Americans marching on Princeton, the British commander of the 55th could not leave the heights to go to Mawhood's aid. Nor could Sullivan continue his march with an enemy of unknown strength on his flank, one who also was in possession of the critical terrain, Mercer Heights. So neither British nor American commander could break away to join the fight that had begun in William Clark's orchard.

WHILE SULLIVAN WAS MARCHING UP the Back Road, the gap in the American column created by the splitting off of Mercer's men had widened to about a thousand yards. At the south end of that gap was the head of Cadwalader's column of militia. Following Cadwalader was Hand's regiment of riflemen, with Hitchcock's brigade of New England Continentals bringing up the rear. With these American dispositions in column (at the time Mercer's men were being chased by the bayonets of Mawhood's 17th Regiment) one can appreciate the problem facing the next American leader, Cadwalader, as he led his men over the crest of the low hill south of William Clark's farm. He had swung leftward and marched—in that good old phrase—"to the sound of the guns," only to

---

*Haslet was soldiering on his own, his regiment having been discharged on 31 December 1776. In his pocket was found an order sending him home on recruiting duty, an order he had chosen to ignore.

find, coming up the hill straight at him, a mob of Mercer's panicked men in full flight from the fury of British bayonets. Beyond the mob of fugitives Cadwalader could see Mawhood's reformed line, and in its front about fifty light infantry deployed as skirmishers. Cadwalader wasted no time in sending Captain George Henry with 100 men to turn the left flank of the British skirmishers. At the same time Captain Moulder's battery of two guns went into position on the top of the hill to his left. The combined fire of Henry's men and Moulder's guns soon drove the British light infantry back to the cover of Mawhood's main line.

Then Cadwalader made a fatal mistake. Instead of deploying his column of militia into line *behind* the crest where they would be screened from sight of the enemy, he led them over the hill into view of the British. Riding in front of his column, he ordered his detachments to peel off alternately right and left to come into line of battle. Such an exercise in minor tactics would have been difficult enough for even seasoned Continentals in that situation. For half-trained militia the result was a fiasco of milling men being shoved about by their sergeants and officers until some semblance of a line was formed *while* it advanced on the enemy. When that ragged line came within fifty yards of Mawhood's waiting regulars, the storm of musket balls and canister it met head-on was too much. The disordered militia companies broke and turned tail. A hundred yards or so to the rear Cadwalader managed to rally several companies, but after they had gotten off a couple of volleys, they too disintegrated as a fighting force. In no time Cadwalader's command had followed the example of Mercer's men. The whole mob was making a run for the safety of the woods about a hundred and fifty yards to the southwest.

At this critical point Mawhood was doubtless tempted to order his entire command to charge his broken enemy and turn the resultant flood onto any American units behind it, to sweep them all away in what would become a smashing victory. One thing changed Mawhood's mind. A young American captain, Joseph Moulder, commanding his two four-pounders, stood his ground on the hill and kept up a continuous rolling fire of canister into the British, which discouraged any idea of a frontal attack. For a time Moulder was all on his own, banging away without support, until 150 Pennsylvania infantry came up and took cover behind stacks and buildings around the Thomas Clark farmyard, off to Moulder's left. Some of them failed to stay, but enough remained to keep up a fire that convinced the British that Moulder's guns were now supported by several infantry units.

George Washington had been marching behind Sullivan's division when he heard the firing to his left. As the rattle of musketry and the booming of cannon grew in volume, the commander in chief realized that something more than a skirmish was going on. In Richard M. Ketchum's description, "a tall man on a white horse could be seen galloping toward the scene of battle with half a dozen aides and orderlies strung out behind him, and behind them came the veteran Virginia Continentals and Hand's riflemen at a dead run" (*The Winter Soldiers*). While Hand's riflemen were forming into line, Washington rode straightaway to aid Greene and Cadwalader in rallying the fugitives of Mercer's and Cadwalader's commands. As soon as order was restored in that area, Washington could turn his attention to Daniel Hitchcock's brigade of Continentals, which was coming up on the double.

Washington directed Hitchcock to form a line to the right of Cadwalader's men, who were getting back into line. The gallant Hitchcock (only ten days were left to him before he was to die of tuberculosis) lined his veterans up in parade order: Massachusetts under Henshaw on the left, the three Rhode Island regiments in the center, and Nixon's New Hampshiremen on the right. Washington saw to it then that Hand's riflemen fell in on the right of Hitchcock's brigade, and soon an American line of battle stretched from the front of Moulder's battery all across the hillside to the north, where Hand's regiment could outflank the left of the British line. Washington gave the signal for the advance, posting himself in the right front of Cadwalader's line, and from there he led the concerted attack of the whole American line.

As the big man on the white horse came within easy musket range of the British line, there was a climactic instant when everything hung in the balance. The British infantrymen looking over the barrels of their muskets were astounded to see the rebel commander right in their field of fire.

When he was thirty yards from the enemy, Washington gave the command to fire. For seconds the smoke from Americans and British volleys hid Washington from sight. Colonel John Fitzgerald of his staff covered his eyes so that he would not see his commander blasted from the saddle. Yet when the smoke began to clear, there was Washington standing in his stirrups, calmly waving his men forward.

For moments the Pennsylvania militia hesitated. Then Hitchcock's firm line, marching forward in perfect order, paused to fire their first volley, and advanced again. On the far right, Hand's riflemen were swinging around in a scythelike curve to threaten Mawhood's left flank. Over the roar of musketry Moulder's guns continued to thunder their volleys of grape and round shot, cutting wide swaths in the British ranks. The alternate fire and advance of Hitchcock's brigade brought it within charging distance, and finally the militia, following Washington, joined in the surge of the closing-in assault.

The British continued to fire by volley. Mawhood even tried shifting part of his line leftward to counter the threat of Hitchcock's and Hand's envelopment. The united assault of the whole American line, however, was too much for the British. They fell back, by platoons at first, still trying to cover their artillery, until the inspired Americans swept the British soldiers out of their formations and overran the artillery, capturing all four guns. Pockets of British infantry were fighting to escape the inevitable encircling of Hitchcock's and Hand's men. Finally, when all was hopeless, British soldiers had their turn in breaking and running. Mawhood, rallying a group of his toughest and most disciplined men, made a final, gallant effort. He led this small body in a desperate bayonet assault that broke through the encirclement to the rear, where most of the group escaped across Stony Brook Bridge. Others scattered in all directions, some toward Maidenhead, some toward Princeton; some others were pursued for miles up Stony Brook and toward Pennington. A few dragoons tried to make a stand on the hill west of Worth's Mill, but they too were swept away by the ruthless American pursuit.

The pièce de résistance in the whole affair was the American commander in chief shouting, "It's a fine fox chase, boys!" while leading the pursuit. (One pauses to wonder whether Washington was unconsciously voicing thought to the several references Cornwallis had made to bagging a fox.) Followed by the Philadelphia Light Horse, he gloried in the chase until finally his blood cooled, the general again took over, and he turned his escort back in the direction of Princeton.

As for the standoff between General Sullivan and the British 55th Regiment at Mercer Heights, part of Mawhood's orders to the commander of the 55th had included going to the support of the 40th in Princeton should the situation so dictate. So the 55th marched on, and when it came to a stream crossing on the Back Road, a place known as Frog Hollow, there was the 40th deployed in line on the north side of the hollow! The commander of the 55th immediately took up position, extending the line of the 40th to its left. There the regiment and a half stood, prepared for battle.

Sullivan followed on the heels of the 55th and, once that unit had crossed Frog Hollow to deploy alongside the 40th, sent two regiments to attack the British left. Hardly had the Americans gotten within good musket range—sixty yards from the British line—when, for reasons still not clear,* the redcoats panicked and streamed away in flight into Princeton. With both enemy regiments in pell-mell flight, Sullivan was once more at their heels. Some of the mob escaped by fleeing toward Brunswick; the rest, seeing they were about to be overtaken, took refuge in Nassau Hall. They had plenty of room, the building being the largest in the colonies at the time. They knocked the glass out of windows and prepared for a last-ditch defense.

The ensuing defense was a perfect trump to follow the "defense" of Frog Hollow. Captains Alexander Hamilton and Joseph Moulder moved their artillery into firing position. Hamilton's first shot went through a window of the prayer hall, neatly beheading a portrait of King George II on the opposite wall. A second-round shot ricocheted off the building. These messages were followed by an assault on the front door led by Captain James Moore of Princeton, whose house had been looted by the British. Seeing that Captains Hamilton and Moore really meant business, the defenders waved a white flag from one of the windows. The surrendered prisoners, numbering 194, were described by American Sergeant R. as "a haughty, crabbed set of men." Such was the finale of the Battle of Princeton.

IN HIS REPORT TO LORD GERMAIN, Sir William Howe listed the British losses at 276. Not surprisingly, his totals did not match those of Washington, who estimated his enemy's losses at between 500 and 600, a figure which had to include 300 prisoners. One indisputable fact did remain: Cornwallis's fine 4th Brigade had been annihilated, at a cost to the Americans of 30 soldiers and 14 officers. Among the American dead were the irreplaceable Hugh Mercer, who died nine days later of his wounds, and Colonel John Haslet, also a promising combat veteran.

After Washington had halted the various pursuits and saw to it that the army was reassembling, he held a council of war on horseback. It was the consensus of his senior officers that the strike at Brunswick would have to be given up and that the army should march at once toward Morris-

---

*It is probable that the 40th and the 55th had been demoralized by Mawhood's defeat, and thinking that the whole American army would turn on them in flank or rear, they took off in the safest direction.

town, where a base was already being set up. With perhaps the greatest reluctance at any time during his military career, Washington had to concur. Two days later he wrote to Congress:

> My original plan when I set out from Trenton was to have pushed onto Brunswick, but the harassed state of our own Troops (many of them having had no rest for two nights and a day) and the danger of losing the advantage we had gained by aiming at too much, Induced me, by the advice of my Officers, to relinquish in the attempt but in my judgement Six or eight hundred fresh Troops upon a forced March would have destroyed all their Stores and Magazines: taken (as we have since learnt) their Military Chest containing 70,000 pounds and put an end to the war.

Consequently the army moved out of Princeton, and none too soon. Cornwallis, after overcoming his stupefaction at finding Washington's army missing (perhaps with some lingering doubts about chasing foxes), heard the sounds of the guns up Princeton way. He lost no time in driving his sweating brigades up the Maidenhead-Princeton Road until they came to the bridge over Stony Brook at Worth's Mill. Here American Major John Kelly was trying to finish demolishing the bridge. Undeterred by British cannon fire, Kelly was tearing up the last of the planks when a round shot hit the end of the one on which he stood, tossing him into the freezing water. He swam to shore while the rest of his demolition crew escaped. Kelly's clothes quickly froze in the winter air, slowing him down so that British infantrymen took him prisoner. The bridge, however, was for a time unusable, and Cornwallis's men had to find a nearby ford through which they passed in waist-deep water.

The British advance guard then made its way so rapidly that some of its officers caught sight of the American rear guard leaving the north end of Princeton. The British pursuit, however, never did catch up to Washington's rear guard—except in one case, when the redoubtable Captain Moulder, attached to the rear guard, blasted away with canister at his pursuers, bringing them to a halt. It was such a close thing that Moulder, having sent his horses on because he feared their capture, was dragging off his guns with man-powered drag ropes. At this point some Philadelphia cavalrymen came to his rescue and held up the British until Moulder got his guns hitched up to his horse teams.

At Rocky Hill Washington turned his column up the left-hand road, following the Millstone River Road northward. When Cornwallis reached the same fork, he took the right-hand road to Brunswick. Meanwhile,

Washington's men went on to camp around Somerset Courthouse, where the last of the rear guard closed in around 11:00 P.M. The next day the army reached Pluckemin, where it rested and absorbed about a thousand stragglers. Finally, on 6 January, the army was going into camp at Morristown. In the meantime, other American forces took Elizabeth Town and Hackensack, leaving the British only their strongholds in Brunswick and Amboy.

Washington had swept the British almost out of New Jersey in a winter campaign that had been carried out in spite of Sir Billy Howe's proclaimed cessation of hostilities.

FOUR

Brandywine

FROM JANUARY TO MAY 1777, following his victories at Trenton and Princeton, Washington occupied a defensive base at Morristown, sometimes raiding British posts in New Jersey and New York. During the same period, from January to May, Sir William Howe was occupying winter quarters in New York City, leaving major outposts at Amboy and Brunswick, New Jersey.

Washington's five months in Morristown were critical and frustrating ones. By mid-March his army had shrunk to a mere 3,000 effectives, two-thirds of them militia whose enlistments would be up by the end of the month, while in ironic contrast he was authorized by Congress to enlist up to 75,000 men—a ridiculous paper figure. At about that time two shiploads of French weapons and ammunition arrived, with enough muskets, powder, and gun flints to equip 22,000 men. Where was the commander in chief to get the men to make proper use of such bounty? By late spring, after constant entreaties to Congress and his own ceaseless recruiting efforts, he had succeeded in building his army's strength to slightly less than 9,000 men. Of these, some 6,000 were ready to take the field at the first bugle call.

After some small and indecisive maneuvering between Washington's and Howe's armies in June 1777, the British general reassembled his army on Staten Island. His plan now was to get at the Americans from below Philadelphia; 15,000 troops would embark on 260 ships for the long voyage that would, eventually, take his forces southward past the Delaware Capes and up Chesapeake Bay. The British armada sailed past Sandy Hook on 23 July under the command, of course, of Admiral Lord Richard Howe.

Washington learned of the fleet's sailing the following day, and now faced a dilemma. Just where was Howe bound? Would he join the expedition that Burgoyne was initiating from Canada, moving southward by way of Lake Champlain? Or was Howe's real objective Philadelphia, via either the Delaware River or Chesapeake Bay? Charleston in South Carolina could not be ruled out, and neither could a British return to Boston. Where should Washington go?

On 29 July Washington decided to move his army toward Philadelphia, only to discover that after six days at sea the Howe brothers' fleet had not yet been sighted off the Delaware Capes. But two days later his anxiety was eased by definite word that the British fleet had indeed been observed off the Delaware Capes on 30 July. Washington again ordered his columns toward Philadelphia. Not until 22 August, however, did he receive a reliable express that Howe's fleet was in Chesapeake Bay, "high up in the North East part of it." By Sunday, 24 August, Washington was marching at the head of the long column of his army as it paraded through Philadelphia in a manner designed to encourage the Patriots and to impress those of doubtful persuasion—and the members of Congress. John Adams, after watching the parade, wrote his wife: "They marched twelve deep [in ranks twelve men wide?], and yet took up above two hours in passing by." Their number had been reported as high as 16,000 though a figure of 11,000 seems more realistic in light of the total forces that ended up at the Brandywine.

On Monday, 25 August, British troops began disembarking from the Chesapeake near Head of Elk (in the vicinity of present-day Elkton, Maryland). In the first of five serials, loaded on flat-bottomed landing craft, were two regiments of Hessian and Anspach jägers. The four companies of American militia who had been posted to oppose them soon fled, and the rest of Howe's army—less the cavalry and its horses—completed the landings throughout the day.

Two days later, Washington, accompanied by staff aides and Generals Greene and Lafayette, rode out of the encampment near Wilmington on a personal reconnaissance. From the summit of a hill Washington could make out the tents of a huge encampment, but his scouting of the terrain in the area was ended abruptly by a fierce and prolonged thunderstorm.

The same thunderstorm pinned down Howe's sodden regiments. The British troops were still aching from over a month's confinement aboard their transports and were in need of a rest and a chance to stretch out, even if in rain-soaked tents. Moreover, the surviving cavalry and artillery horses were in shockingly bad shape; over 300 dead or dying horses had been thrown overboard during the voyage.

Howe finally got moving on 28 August, marching in two corps over separate routes. Cornwallis marched on Elkton, and the Hessian Lieutenant General Knyphausen crossed the Elk River and camped at Cecil Courthouse. Both corps remained encamped for the next five days while selected units foraged the countryside. The troops were starving for fresh meat, and horses were needed to replace the 300 lost on the voyage, as well as those unfit for service. The foraging parties rounded up hundreds of cattle and sheep, and one party even brought in a herd of over 200 horses and mules.

Washington, fully occupied with concentrating his Continentals and levies of militia, was powerless to prevent this ravaging of the countryside. He managed, however, to send out a covering force under Brigadier General William Maxwell to keep Howe's forward elements under observation, with the additional order to be "constantly near the Enemy and to give them every possible annoyance." In all, Maxwell's force totaled 720 soldiers, officers, and noncommissioned officers.

On 2 September Washington relayed a warning to Maxwell that British preparations were under way to resume the advance toward Philadelphia. Maxwell wasted no time in preparing a reception for the enemy's advance guard. He redeployed his light infantrymen in ambush positions, mainly along the road northeast of Elkton.

About nine o'clock on the morning of the third, the advance guard of Cornwallis's column—Hessian and Anspach jägers under Lieutenant Colonel von Wurmb—was feeling its way up Maxwell's road. Their caution notwithstanding, a sudden volley from the woods dropped the jägers at the point. Von Wurmb deployed his advance party and called for support from the British light infantry following the van. Thus began the Battle of Cooch's Bridge, a lively skirmish marking the first real engagement of the campaign.

Maxwell succeeded in having his men deliver several stinging fires from a series of delaying positions, but von Wurmb kept up his attempts to outflank the Americans, and eventually the skirmish became a running fight which degenerated into flight by Maxwell's men. The disorganized Americans ended their retreat at Washington's outposts along White Clay Creek, about four miles north of Cooch's Bridge. On 6 September, following a command conference, Washington decided to reconcentrate his forces north of Red Clay Creek astride the main road to Philadelphia.

Maxwell was deployed again as a covering force, this time along White Clay Creek. Learning that Howe's fighting units were storing their tents and baggage in their assembly area, Washington ordered all of his own army's baggage and equipment, save what men could carry on the march, to be dumped north of the Brandywine.

On 8 September Howe was moving to the northeast, apparently toward Kennett Square on the northern road (now U.S. 1) to Philadelphia. To counter this threat to his right flank, Washington withdrew his army to Chadd's Ford on the Brandywine the next day and deployed it along the east side of that stream.

So on 9 September both armies were maneuvering toward a fight. The British had already achieved an advantage. They had been exploiting their reconnaissance capabilities to the full; the Americans had not. Washington was thus relatively ignorant of many critical terrain features in the area where the action was pending, and was even unsure of the movements of Howe's main advance.

THE BRANDYWINE,* IN DOUGLAS SOUTHALL FREEMAN'S description, "flows from Northwest to Southeast into the Delaware [River] on a course parallel to that of the Schuylkill and at a distance of fifteen to twenty miles from that stream. . . . The area between the two streams consequently included the direct approaches to the Quaker City from Head of Elk" (*George Washington*). The creek behind which Washington had elected to defend had two main tributaries, the West and East branches. Howe's chief engineer described the countryside as "a succession of large hills, rather sudden with narrow vales." Though much of the country was farmland at the time of the battle, a great many of the steeper slopes of the hills bordering the valley were densely wooded.

The hills and the forests along the stream helped make the Brandywine, if properly defended, a major tactical obstacle. The creek itself varied in width from 50 to 150 yards, and its varying depth was sufficient to require troops to use the fords. There were seven of these fords that might be used to cross an army. The most important was *Chadd's Ford* on Washington's left, where the main road from Kennett Square to Philadelphia crossed the Brandywine. Then, proceeding northward were *Brinton's Ford, Jones's* (or *Painter's*) *Ford,* and *Wistar's Ford.* North of the

---

*The Brandywine has been variously referred to as a creek, river, or even rivulet. Ward calls it a river; Freeman and Boatner call it a creek. I lean toward the latter since the stream is so labeled on topographical maps.

junction of the East and West Branches, *Trimble's Ford* crossed the West Branch. *Buffington's* and *Jeffrie's* crossed the East.

All these fords were easily accessible to an advancing enemy and feasible for the crossing of artillery. Therefore the American commander in chief needed to guard all of them, or at least keep them under observation. A glance at the map will show that the road network, especially the parts using the fords, was fairly extensive.

ON THE MORNING OF 9 SEPTEMBER Washington began deploying his forces east of the Brandywine. He entrusted his left flank at Pyle's Ford (south of Chadd's Ford) to General Armstrong with 1,000 Pennsylvania militia. Greene's division, with Wayne's brigade attached, held the center at Chadd's Ford, supported by the bulk of the army's artillery. Work began immediately on earthworks, with first priority going to the artillery's protection.

Washington placed the entire right wing under Sullivan's command. He was to be responsible for defending a large sector, the entire Brandywine north of Chadd's Ford. The wing was composed of three divisions, each with two brigades. On the south was Sullivan's own division, in the center was Stephen's division, and on the extreme right was Stirling's division.

Maxwell, with 800 light infantry, was assigned to cover the approaches to the army's center. He deployed his companies on high ground west of Chadd's Ford, centering them on the main road leading to Elkton, the direction from which Washington expected Howe to attack.

On the afternoon of 10 September General Sullivan reported to Washington's headquarters, expressing concern about the vulnerability of the army's right flank. Specifically he asked whether any fords existed above those under his care. In answer he was informed that the local people, familiar with the creek, had assured him that there were none within twelve miles. Washington also informed Sullivan that "all the Light Horse of the Army," meaning Colonel Theodorick Bland's 1st Dragoons, were being shifted to the right to "watch the enemy there." But that one regiment was weak, understrength, and poorly commanded, a weak reed to lean on.

When Washington's army had paraded through Philadelphia, John Adams's description mentioned "four regiments of light-horse, Bland's, Baylor's, Sheldon's and Moylan's." Charles Francis Adams put it this way: "With an overpowering hostile force creeping around the army's right wing, the question naturally suggests itself, where were Bland's,

Baylor's, Sheldon's, and Moylan's four regiments of light-horse? Of them and their movements no mention is made" (*Studies, Military and Diplomatic, 1775–1865*). That absence would turn out to be a critical factor that crucially influenced the outcome of the battle.*

During the night of 10–11 September a light rain fell over the Brandywine valley, and a dense fog covered the countryside at dawn on the eleventh. While the fog was inhibiting visibility, Washington heard that an enemy column was headed his way from Kennett Square. He sent Maxwell to intercept it. Scotch Willie Maxwell proceeded to advance his companies a couple of miles to Kennett Meeting House (now Old Kennett Meetinghouse on the present U.S. 1) and posted them under cover of a graveyard wall and some woods, sending forward a small mounted patrol. The patrol went about a mile down the road to Welch's Tavern, whereupon the troopers dismounted and, in the finest of cavalry traditions, deployed along the bar of the tavern. About 9:00 A.M. a trooper looked up from his drink and saw, through a window, the green jackets and black-plumed caps of Tory scouts, Wemyss's Queen's Rangers, and across the road the jackets of Major Ferguson's riflemen. The patrol dashed out through the back door and retreated on foot, leaving their horses to the British. Before leaving they did manage to fire off one ragged volley. Unfortunately it caused only one casualty, wounding one of the patrol's own horses.

After this fiasco the British advance guard increased its pace on the road toward Chadd's Ford, followed by 5,000 British and Hessian soldiers, all under the command of the Hessian General Knyphausen. Knyphausen's corps was made up of three brigades. Two were British, under Major General Grant; one, under Stern, consisted of three Hessian regiments. With them went a train of heavy artillery. Two separate battalions of the 71st Highlanders protected Knyphausen's flanks, and half of the 16th Dragoon Regiment preceded the column.

It was now the turn of the advance party of Captain Wemyss's rangers and Major Ferguson's riflemen to be surprised as it approached Kennett Meetinghouse. Maxwell's men, firing from cover, stopped the British advance in its tracks, forcing it to deploy. The superior British numbers

---

*A final look at the American security forces shows that Sullivan did send out the following security detachments: the Delaware regiment to Jones's (Painter's) Ford, a battalion of Colonel Hazen's regiment to Wistar's Ford, and another to Buffington's. Additionally, Major James Spear, with a detachment of Pennsylvania militia, was outposting the area just north of the "forks," the point where the East and West branches join to form the Brandywine proper.

forced Maxwell to retire from position after position, almost to the Brandywine, where he was reinforced by the Virginia regiments of Porterfield and Waggoner. Finally Maxwell was outflanked, and the Americans were forced to fall back across Chadd's Ford, bearing marvelous tales of the frightful slaughter they had inflicted on the enemy. The British and the Hessians closed to the creek unopposed.

The line that Knyphausen deployed along the Brandywine consisted of the four British and two Hessian regiments on the immediate heights. Donop's reinforced Hessians were posted astride the road, while four more British regiments were pushed forward down to the edges of the flats along the creek. By 10:30 A.M. Knyphausen was in position to launch a coordinated attack between Brinton's and Chadd's fords.

Meanwhile, Washington and Greene waited at army headquarters in the house of the Quaker Benjamin Ring, about a mile east of Chadd's Ford. Throughout the morning the obvious question was uppermost in the minds of the commander and the staff: Since the British were, to all appearances, poised to attack, where and when would it come?

IF WASHINGTON AND GREENE HAD BEEN calmly awaiting a frontal attack across the Brandywine, their confidence was about to be jolted. About 11:00 A.M. word arrived from Colonel Hazen at Jones's Ford that an enemy column had been sighted marching northward on the Great Valley Road toward the Brandywine (the road, as such, has no modern counterpart, but in 1777 it ran roughly parallel to and west of the Brandywine).*

Washington's reaction was immediate and prudent. He sent orders to Colonel Bland to pay "vigilant attention to the movements of the enemy." Since the enemy was reported to have gone up to a ford seven or eight miles above Chadd's Ford, Bland was to send up a reliable officer immediately to find out the truth.

Following closely on Colonel Hazen's report came another message, this time from Lieutenant Colonel Ross of the 8th Pennsylvania, who had been reconnoitering along the Great Valley Road:

*Hazen's report is the first of at least six items of combat intelligence that Washington would have to evaluate. Because a number of authorities have mentioned these pieces of intelligence in varying and often confusing ways, I have assembled them in chronological order in Table 1. In my evaluation of the intelligence picture I found it possible to estimate the times of origin or receipt of certain messages through an analysis of distance, terrain, and mounted messenger rates of movement. The times so estimated are marked with asterisks on the table.

Great Valley Road
11 o'clock A.M.

Dear General,

A large body of the enemy, from every account five thousand, with sixteen or eighteen field-pieces, marched along this road just now. . . . We are close in their rear with about seventy men, and gave them three rounds within a small distance. . . .

Yours,

James Ross, Lieutenant-Colonel

Washington's reactions to the two reports, as well as his subsequent orders, can be summed up as follows:

1. Howe had exposed his army to defeat in detail, by dividing his forces in half, virtually on the battlefield;
2. Washington would attack and destroy the enemy facing Chadd's Ford, employing the divisions of Sullivan and Greene. The British right flank would simultaneously be enveloped by Armstrong on the south;
3. The American right flank would be protected by the divisions of Stephen and Stirling, which must move at once from their positions along Brandywine Creek to the vicinity of the hamlet of Birmingham, where they could block any British attempt at a flank attack from the direction of the Brandywine Forks.

Accordingly, Stephen's and Stirling's divisions were soon moving in march column toward Birmingham, and the forward elements of Greene's command at Chadd's Ford were beginning to cross the Brandywine. Everything seemed set for a series of brilliant moves that might have given Howe a significant defeat, had they been successfully executed.

But they were not executed at all. Washington canceled them before they were fully under way. At 1:30 P.M. he had received a message from Sullivan saying that Hazen's earlier message, which he had transmitted, "must be wrong." A militiaman who had just come in from Martin's Tavern (present-day Marshallton) to Welch's Tavern had heard nothing of the enemy above the forks of the Brandywine. Sullivan was checking further.

Washington apparently accepted Sullivan's evaluation at full and face value. He countermanded Greene's orders and pulled back his advance elements from across the creek—and did the same with Sullivan's division. He also sent orders to Stephen and Stirling to halt in place. Maxwell, however, was ordered across the creek to feel out the enemy's positions while Greene's troops were pulling back.

But Washington's shaken confidence that Howe would attack him frontally across the Brandywine at Chadd's Ford was soon further disturbed by a development from a new and most unmilitary quarter. A horseman, hatless, coatless, and bare-legged, galloped up to Sullivan's command post, demanding to see Sullivan. The farmer turned out to be Squire Thomas Cheyney, a known Patriot in this Tory-ridden part of Pennsylvania. For some reason Sullivan refused to see him, but he did allow him to go on to Washington's headquarters. There he managed to see Washington and to blurt out his alarming news. The farmer had, since early morning, been doing some scouting of his own, when suddenly, while riding across the crest of a hill, he had confronted an advancing British column. He had been fired at but had escaped unhurt. The British were across the Brandywine and coming down on Washington's right. Washington and his army would soon be surrounded! An incredulous Washington still was not persuaded. Nor was the staff. Cheyney raged at them: "I'd have you know I have this day's work as much at heart as e'er a blood of ye!"

Outside the headquarters house, Cheyney tried once again to convince Washington. He drew in the dust a crude map, using his finger: there were the fords and the roads and the place where he had encountered the British. Washington was still unconvinced. A purple-faced Cheyney was driven to shouting "You're mistaken, General. My life for it you're mistaken. By hell! It's so. Put me under guard 'til you find out it's so!"

A wavering Washington was preparing to mount up and go to see things for himself when a courier from Sullivan rode up to Washington with two dispatches, both sent by Sullivan. One, from Colonel Bland to Sullivan, had been sent at 1:15 P.M., and it reported that "a party of the enemy" had been discovered on the heights about half a mile to the north of the Birmingham Meetinghouse. Sullivan, in passing on this message to Washington, added even more alarming news. As of 2:00 P.M., he reported the enemy "to the rear of my right about two miles, coming down, about two brigades of them"—a fairly accurate assessment, as events proved. Bland had seen "a dust cloud rising for above an hour," Sullivan said.

Finally all doubt was blown away. Hazen, Ross, and Squire Cheyney had been right. Howe had succeeded in pulling off the same, exact turning movement that had outflanked and defeated Washington's army at

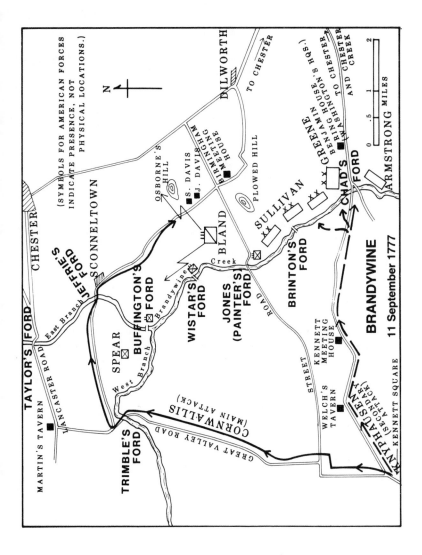

BRANDYWINE
11 September 1777

(SYMBOLS FOR AMERICAN FORCES
INDICATE PRESENCE, NOT
PHYSICAL LOCATIONS.)

TABLE 1. Brandywine Intelligence Picture
Chronology and Actions

TIME MESSAGE ORIGINATED	SOURCE AND LOCATION	TIME MESSAGE RECEIVED
10:50 A.M.*	Col. Hazen at Jones's (Painter's) Ford	11:00 A.M.
11:00 A.M.	Lt. Col. Ross on or near Great Valley Road	11:25 A.M.*
1:25 P.M.*	Gen. Sullivan at Brinton's Ford	1:30 P.M.*
	An excited Squire Cheyney at Washington's headquarters	
1:15 P.M.	Col. Bland, location unknown at this time	2:10 P.M.*

*Estimated time derived from an analysis of the terrain, distances, and possible mounted messenger rates of movement.

ESSENTIALS OF MESSAGE	ACTION TAKEN
Large body of British marching northward on Great Valley Road	1. Washington orders Col. Bland to send an officer and party to "find out the truth." 2. Washington orders divisions of Stephen and Stirling to move toward Birmingham.
5,000 British with 16–18 cannon marching on road toward Trimble's, Taylor's, or Jeffrie's fords.	1. Washington prepares to attack Howe across Brandywine with divisions of Sullivan and Greene. 2. Armstrong ordered to envelop British right flank from Pyle's Ford. 3. Maxwell to probe enemy across Brandywine. 4. Stephen and Stirling to move on Birmingham to protect American right flank.
"One of the militia [Maj. Spear] told me he had gone from Martin's to Welch's Tavern and had seen no enemy and heard nothing of enemy above forks of the Brandywine." So Col. Hazen's information must be wrong.	1. Washington cancels all orders for an attack across the Brandywine. 2. Instead, prepares to defend against an attack from the west (frontal attack). 3. Washington also orders Stephen and Stirling to halt in place.
British army is on the east side of the Brandywine and moving southward. Washington's army will be surrounded if he does not act at once.	Washington is incredulous and perhaps confused by Cheyney's report. He does, however, consider verifying Cheyney's information—in person if necessary.
To Gen. Sullivan: I have discovered a "party of the enemy" in vicinity of Birmingham (near houses of the widows Davis).	Gen. Sullivan encloses this message of Col. Bland's with his own to Washington, cited below.

TABLE I. *(Continued)*

TIME MESSAGE ORIGINATED	SOURCE AND LOCATION	TIME MESSAGE RECEIVED
2:00 P.M.	Gen. Sullivan at Brinton's Ford	2:10 P.M.*

*Estimated time derived from an analysis of the terrain, distances, and possible mounted messenger rates of movement.

Long Island hardly a year ago! To make things worse, Howe's outflanking column, as well as his forces in position west of the Brandywine, had gone about their business undisturbed by American action.

What had *really* been happening while Washington and his staff had been occupied with their on-again, off-again preoccupations at headquarters?

At 4:00 A.M. that day Cornwallis had marched out of Kennett Square with the main striking force of Howe's army, about 7,500 men, consisting of the 3rd and 4th infantry brigades, reinforced by the 1st and 2nd battalions of the British grenadiers, the guards, three squadrons of dragoons (two mounted, one dismounted), and Hessian troops. Cornwallis had marched to a road junction west of Welch's Tavern and there had turned his column left, (north), coming on to the Great Valley Road. Marching north on that road (as observed by Hazen's and Ross's reconnaissance parties), his column had crossed the West Branch at Trimble's Ford and turned eastward for two miles to cross the East Branch at

ESSENTIALS OF MESSAGE	ACTION TAKEN
To Gen. Washington: Col. Bland has just sent me word that the enemy, estimated to be at least two brigades in strength, is in my right rear and advancing. Col. Bland also observed dust cloud rising for about an hour.	Washington concludes that the reports of Hazen and Ross had been accurate. He gives orders for the following actions: 1. Sullivan to resume command of the right wing and move it, in its entirety, to Birmingham, in which vicinity he will oppose the British threat to the army's right and rear; 2. Wayne's brigade, reinforced by Maxwell, supported by artillery, to defend against an attack across the Brandywine; 3. Greene's division to constitute the army reserve, prepared to support either Wayne or Sullivan, on order.

Jeffrie's Ford. From there, Cornwallis had headed south through Sconneltown toward Osborne's Hill, where Colonel Bland had observed "a party of the enemy." At about 2:30 P.M. Cornwallis's column had closed up on its advance guard, and the troops were allowed to fall out for a rest, after marching for some fifteen miles through the muggy heat. Now, there they were, 7,500 strong, poised to strike the American right rear.

In the meantime, Knyphausen had marched his column of 5,000 from Kennett Square to Chadd's Ford, where his artillery began "early to cannonade the Enemy on the opposite side, thereby to take up his attention and make him presume an attack was then intended with the whole Army, whilst the other Column should be performing the *détour.*" As Major André described the plan, Knyphausen was to cross the ford and "push their advantage" when he learned that Cornwallis had become engaged.

Washington had no time to indulge in the bitter regret of a lost opportunity. Now that the fog of war was clearing away, he needed to take immediate measures to save the situation—and the army. He gave Sullivan command of the three divisions of the right wing once more and directed him to take position so as to face northward to counter the British threat from Osborne's Hill. He stripped the Chadd's Ford positions of all troops except Wayne's Pennsylvania brigade, reinforced by Maxwell's light infantry. Greene's division would make up the army reserve, prepared to go to the aid of Sullivan or Wayne, on order. The commander in chief would remain at headquarters until the situation was clarified.

When Colonel Hazen had learned of Cornwallis's march from Trimble's Ford to Jeffrie's Ford, he prudently began withdrawing his force behind the Brandywine, using Buffington's and Wistar's fords. At Jones's Ford the Delaware regiment joined his column. On his way south to rejoin the main body of the army, Hazen encountered Sullivan, who was leading a brigade of his own division up the road on the east side of the Brandywine.

As the two leaders stopped long enough to exchange information, Sullivan explained that he was marching to link up with Stephen's and Stirling's divisions, which should, by now, be going into position near Birmingham (Birmingham Meetinghouse). Sullivan's leading brigade, under the French General de Borré, had gone ahead. Suddenly the conversation was interrupted by an enemy force that appeared about 200 yards from Sullivan's advance guard. Quickly Sullivan decided that this was not the field on which he desired to fight, so he commanded "column right" to his advance guard, directing it toward Birmingham. (As it turned out, he had probably seen a flanking detachment thrown out to protect Cornwallis's column). Hazen's regiment and the Delawares remained with Sullivan's command.

Sullivan began deploying his division to face northward on the high ground, assuming that he was lining up on the left flank of Stephen's and Stirling's divisions. He soon discovered, however, that he was far to the left of the other two divisions of his wing, which were already drawn up to his right and rear 500 yards away. To correct the error he directed Hazen's regiments to file off to the right to cover the gap, while he galloped over to confer with Stephen and Stirling. Stephen and Stirling recommended that Sullivan's division should drop back on line with the other two and "that the whole Should incline further to the right," to guard against being outflanked on the right by the oncoming British. Sullivan approved and rode back to move his own division.

The inclining further to the right proved to be a lot more awkward, and dangerous, than foreseen, but eventually the American main battle position took shape, curving around the northern slope of a hill about 500 yards southwest of Birmingham on defensive terrain, known as Plowed Hill. Cornwallis, observing the American dispositions, even remarked that "the damn rebels form well." And so they had. Sullivan's wing was now in position, with his own division on the left, Stirling's in the center, and Stephen's on the right. The extreme right flank was extended a little beyond Stephen's right by de Borré's brigade of three Maryland regiments. Four fieldpieces of the artillery were already in supporting position.

AT 3:30 P.M. THE BRITISH FORMATIONS began marching across the valley which lay between the American battle position and Osborne's Hill. They came on in parade-ground order, the scarlet of the British uniforms and the blue of the Hessians showing brightly in the afternoon sun. The solid, compact columns were topped with rows of glittering bayonets, all part of the eighteenth-century martial display designed to strike awe into the enemy.

Cornwallis had formed his corps into three battle divisions. On the British left was the light infantry and the Hessian and Anspach jägers, on the right were the guards, and in the center the grenadiers, their bands playing "The British Grenadiers"—

> Some talk of Alexander
> > And some of Hercules;
> Of Hector and Lysander,
> > And such great names as these!
>
> But of all the world's great heroes
> > There's none than can compare,
> With a tow-row-row-row-row-row,
> > To the British Grenadier!

In support of the first line were the Hessian grenadiers and the British 4th Brigade. The reserve, under Major General Grey, was made up of the 3rd Brigade.

The battle began when the British left began to reach Street Road, which ran east-west up the middle of the valley. The jägers, shaken by a blast of fire from an American outpost in an orchard, closed up and came on as the British light infantry joined in. Soon de Borré's brigade crumbled under the assault, broke, and fled into the woods behind, leaving

Stephen's right flank wide open. As this occurred, the guards and grena-
diers marched up the hill on the right at charge bayonet, their officers
disdaining to offer a volley, and smashed into Sullivan's division. These
American units, still in varying stages of disorder, couldn't face up to the
British bayonets. They also broke and fell back, streaming away in flight.
All the efforts of Sullivan and his officers to rally and reform the line
were in vain. Sullivan was in the middle of it all, later writing that "no
Sooner did I form one party than that which I had before formed would
Run off." Soon the American defense consisted of Stephen's and Stir-
ling's divisions, along with Hazen's regiment. Those units were left to
take on the whole of the British attack.

BY 4:30 P.M. WASHINGTON HAD BEGUN to hear the sound he had been
dreading—the rising and falling thunder of battle from the direction of
Birmingham. Knyphausen heard it at the same time and opened up his
artillery to support his attack across the Brandywine. The booming of
Knyphausen's guns told Washington that he would soon have to fight on
two fronts. Yet, with his customary calm, he "occupied himself by telling
Colonel Harrison, an aide-de-camp, what to say in the second of the
promised dispatches of the day to the president of Congress: "At half
after four o'clock, the enemy attacked General Sullivan at the ford next
above this, and the action has been very violent ever since. It still con-
tinues. A very severe cannonade has began [*sic*] here too, and I suppose
we shall have a very hot evening" (Freeman, *George Washington*).

Washington had a new decision to make: Should the reserve—Greene's
command—stand to bolster Wayne's defense of Chadd's Ford, or should
it be moved to the support of Sullivan's wing? Washington quickly decided to send Greene to support Sullivan. The move might retrieve the
situation in the battle; at worst it would serve to keep open a retreat to
Philadelphia.

Soon, new orders were given. Wayne and Maxwell, supported by
Proctor's artillery, would defend Chadd's Ford on the east bank of the
Brandywine. Greene must move with all speed to reinforce Sullivan and,
if possible, stabilize the situation near Birmingham; if that were not possible, then he must cover the retreat of the army. Washington also decided to join Sullivan on the right, but as he didn't know a direct route,
he deputized an old countryman, Joseph Brown, to lead him. The old
fellow took off across country with Washington, it is said, goading him
from a trot to a gallop with a constant "Push along, old man! Push along,
old man!"

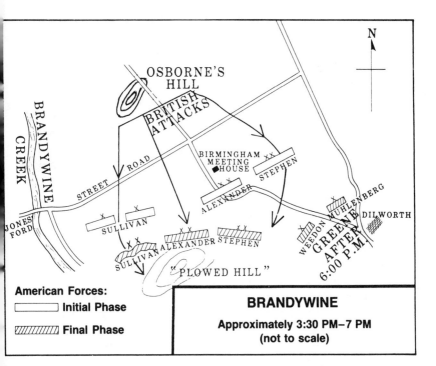

American Forces:

▭ Initial Phase

▨ Final Phase

BRANDYWINE

Approximately 3:30 PM–7 PM
(not to scale)

Washington's staff strung out behind the two. One rider, however, was to beat them all to the battle. Young Lafayette had started out on his own, too eager for action to wait on formalities.

WASHINGTON ARRIVED ON THE FIELD at Birmingham about 5:30 P.M. Quickly he took in the situation on the American left. Sullivan's divisional units had fallen back and then broken, and there was neither the time nor the opportunity for Washington to rally and lead the broken units in person, as he had at Princeton. His efforts to rally the rearmost until officers could reorganize them had no decisive results. Lafayette, seeking to emulate his chief, got a bullet in the leg for his trouble, and for a while was out of the action.

Meanwhile, Greene's command was getting under way. Weedon's brigade was in the lead, followed by Muhlenberg's brigade, both making forced marches. Weedon's men covered four miles in forty-five minutes, a rate of over five miles an hour.

The situation along the entire American right was becoming grim.

Now 3,000 Americans were trying to hold against a determined enemy who outnumbered them two and a half to one. Although the British and Hessians were fatigued from their fifteen-mile march through the sweltering heat, there was plenty of fight left in them. For over an hour and a half the fighting raged around Plowed Hill and the slopes of nearby hills. An American commander later characterized the fighting: "Cannon balls flew thick and many and small arms soared like the rolling of a drum." He himself was wounded, but his men beat back the British "until most officers and half the men were casualties."

Cornwallis concentrated his heaviest pressure against the American right, trying to get his leftmost units to drive on to the town of Dilworth, which, if taken, could seal off the American right wing—even the whole army—while opening the road to Philadelphia to the British. Yet he enjoyed more immediate success against the American left, where Sullivan's division was crumbling away under the attacks of British and Hessian troops. A terrain feature may have saved Sullivan's troops from immediate destruction when the British guards and Hessian grenadiers became entangled in some thick woods so that their tactical organization broke down; they were not reorganized and advancing again until late in the battle.

By the time the leading battalions of Weedon's brigade (Greene's division) arrived on the field at the "quickest step," the situation could no longer be restored. The ever-growing flood of fleeing men on the American left was too wide and deep to rally. Greene's units could only open gaps in their ranks to let the fugitives get through to the rear. Eventually Weedon's men went over to a dogged defense, then a delaying action from position to position. This they managed, keeping up such an effective fire that they never lost their disciplined formations.

AT CHADD'S FORD, KNYPHAUSEN CROSSED the Brandywine supported by an artillery preparation with his six twelve-pounders, four howitzers, and the light artillery. His spearhead was the 1st Battalion of the 71st Highlanders, followed by the Queen's Rangers and the British 4th Regiment, with Knyphausen leading them in person. The attack was finally on, after hours of carrying out the mission of making the Americans "presume an attack was intended with the whole army." It must have seemed to Wayne's and Maxwell's men that they were fighting all of Howe's army. The British and Hessians, fresh and ready for the fight, managed to ford the Brandywine and climb the opposite bank. The attacking troops in the lead paused only long enough to realign their formations, then pushed on with such élan that they captured an American artillery battery of four pieces near the Brandywine.

Even so, Wayne's and Maxwell's tenacious defense lasted for two and a half hours—from 4:30 P.M. until darkness at 7:00 P.M. Major Baurmeister, a Hessian professional, described the American defense in its final phases: "Our regiments gained one height after another as the enemy withdrew. They withstood one more rather severe attack from behind some houses and ditches in front of their left wing. Finally, we saw the entire enemy line and four guns which fired frequently, drawn up on another height in front of a dense forest, their right wing on the Chester road."

What Baurmeister saw "finally" was not Wayne's and Maxwell's troops but Muhlenberg's brigade occupying their last defensive position, taken to cover the pell-mell flight of the remainder of the American right wing. Eventually Greene was able to hold off the British and Hessians from both directions in the falling light of day. Then he could pull back his still-intact division under cover of darkness. Sometime around 7:00 P.M., as night was setting in, the right of Cornwallis's command made contact with the troops of Knyphausen's left.

The Americans, however, were to have one last word, albeit a short and nasty one. Two battalions of the British grenadiers were given the mission of following the American retreat beyond Dilworth, far enough to take and occupy several houses east of the village. The grenadiers' officers, overconfident in their conviction that the Americans were still in full flight, marched the battalions without the cover of security elements. When their leading company came within fifty yards of the nearest houses, they were fired on from an ambush set up by Maxwell's men. The fire was so hot that the grenadiers were halted in their tracks while their officers sent for support. The Americans withdrew before supporting troops arrived.

Elsewhere in the American retreat on the road to Chester, chaos was compounded by darkness. Any unity of organization had disappeared in the dark, and the "army" was reduced to a mob of thousands of stumbling fugitives all along the road and in the surrounding fields, every man seeking only to follow someone in front of him. Confusion, however, did not turn into panic. The mass of men surged on for twelve miles until the head reached a roadblock at the bridge across Chester Creek. There the wounded Lafayette, his thigh bound up in a bandage, had organized a straggler control point, and the flight was halted. Eventually Washington and Greene, who had maintained his division unbroken, arrived and restored order.

By midnight Washington was so exhausted that he was able only to tumble into bed with a parting order to his staff, "Congress must be written to, gentlemen, and one of you must do it, for I am too sleepy."

THERE IS NO ACCURATE RECORD OF American casualties—Washington did not set down any figures. Howe's casualty toll came to 583, which included 89 killed, 488 wounded, and 6 missing. Howe's estimates of his enemy's casualties, always subject to question due to his penchant for exaggeration, were 300 killed, 600 wounded, and 400 captured.

Surprisingly, the defeated Americans took their defeat not as a disaster but simply as a setback. The reaction, prevailing throughout the army, has been expressed in Captain Enoch Anderson's record: "Come boys, we shall do better another time."

Looking at Brandywine from a purely strategical perspective, one cannot take issue with Washington's selection of a defensive position along Brandywine Creek, in the light of his mission to protect the colonial capital. Howe's objective was made unmistakably clear once he had landed his army at Head of Elk and moved northward. Accordingly, Washington needed a suitable position for the tactical defensive, and as Douglas Freeman has remarked, "the position taken by the Americans at Chadd's Ford appeared to be about as good as any available nearby *for an army that wished to be free to maneuver and to avoid or to accept the enemy's attack*" (*George Washington*, italics mine). The position, however, was a good one only as long as the American commander could maneuver or fight on his own terms. Washington relinquished that choice when he allowed himself to be pinned down by Knyphausen's advance toward an apparent frontal attack at Chadd's Ford. Yet even that attack could have been parried had the American right flank been adequately secured. In the actual event, however, that flank was never safeguarded or even effectively screened. Why did Washington and his generals seem to accept, with confidence, the idea that Howe would employ his main force in a frontal attack? Why had they apparently forgotten the bitter lesson of Long Island, in what Christopher Ward has aptly called "an exactly similar situation"?

The mystery surrounding Washington's apparent paucity of cavalry before and during the battle has already been noted. When one is forced to accept the fact that Washington had only Colonel Bland's regiment of dragoons to screen both his front and right flank, it is only reasonable to focus attention on the scanty information that Washington received—and how it was evaluated.

Table 1 shows not only the chronological order in which the intelligence was obtained; it further points out the reactions to the reports in the form of tactical actions that were taken. First, then, consider Colonel Hazen's report. It triggered two highly significant actions: Washington's orders to Colonel Bland "to find out the truth," then his orders to alert Stephen's and Stirling's divisions to move toward Birmingham.

Next came Lieutenant Colonel Ross's report, which confirmed Colonel Hazen's: at least 5,000 British with sixteen or eighteen cannon were marching northward on the Great Valley Road toward Trimble's and Jeffrie's fords. Washington's reactions seem almost explosive, his decisions momentous. Convinced now that Howe had divided his army, Washington decided to attack with everything except the divisions of Stephen and Stirling, which would move on to Birmingham to secure the right flank. Then came Sullivan's bombshell, the report that was to change everything. Washington's acceptance of Sullivan's negation of Hazen's information—and, by implication, Ross's—is nothing less than astounding. A deeper examination of Sullivan's message reveals that "some of the militia who came in this morning from a tavern called Martin's on the forks of the Brandywine"* was, in actuality, Major James Spear of the Pennsylvania militia. It is evident that Major Spear had proceeded from Martin's Tavern (note location on map) to Welch's Tavern, a distance of some seven to ten miles, depending on the roads or cross-country route taken. If Spear had been on or near the Great Valley Road (the most direct route between Martin's and Welch's), he could hardly have missed seeing Cornwallis's 7,500-man column. Therefore the time Spear was en route becomes a critical factor. If he had made his reconnaissance on 10 September, the day before Cornwallis marched, he could have reported truly that there was no enemy "in that Quarters." On the other hand, if Spear had made his reconnaissance on the eleventh in *early morning,* he might have turned back too soon to have seen even the advance guard of Cornwallis's column. Yet neither Sullivan nor Washington "appears to have asked the essential question: At what hour did Spear make his reconnaissance?" (Freeman, *George Washington*). In-

---

* Another item may have been a cause of misinterpretation: Martin's Tavern was not *on* the forks of the Brandywine; it was actually about three miles northwest of the forks.

stead, the attack across the Brandywine was called off, and the divisions of Stephen and Alexander were halted in place.

In retrospect, it was probably fortunate that the attack *was* canceled. Sir John Fortescue described what could have happened had the attack been executed: "For Knyphausen was an able commander, his troops were far superior to Washington's in training and discipline, and by Howe's forethought he had been supplied with plenty of guns, so that he could certainly have held his own until Cornwallis came up in the enemy's rear and destroyed the Americans utterly" (*A History of the British Army*). The terrain certainly did not favor such an attack. The advancing troop formations doubtless would have been fragmented, and in the face of Knyphausen's determined defense, disaster could have resulted.

Although John Sullivan appears as the principal culprit in the uncanny repetition of his Long Island errors, it was Washington who must shoulder the blame—which, in his customary fashion, he did. The general who performed so brilliantly at Trenton and Princeton, handling operations and intelligence in such fashion as to draw praise from Frederick the Great, was somehow not the same commander at the Brandywine.

Left: Prescott on the Parapet at Bunker Hill.—*from Henry Cabot Lodge,* The Story of the Revolution *(1898)*
Bottom: The Battle of Bunker Hill.—*U.S. Army Center of Military History*

Portaging the Batteaux around Skowhegan Falls.—*from* Century Magazine *(1903)*

General Putnam's Escape at Horse Neck.—*from Benson J. Lossing,* Pictorial Field-Book of the American Revolution *(1850–52)*

Colonel John Stark.—*from John Spargo, The Stars and Stripes in 1777 (1928)*

General Richard Montgomery.—*from* The National Portrait Gallery of Distinguished Americans *(1834)*

Sir Guy Carleton.—*from* Century Magazine *(1902)*

Colonel Benedict Arnold.—*from John Codman II*, Arnold's Expedition to Quebec *(1902)*

Embarkation of Montgomery's Troops at Crown Point.—*from* Century Magazine *(1902)*

The famous Leutze portrait of "Washington Crossing the Delaware." That the general would have been sitting down in the boat, rather than standing, is quite likely.—*from Robert B. Towns,* Battles of America by Sea and Land *(1878)*

Washington leads the attack at Princeton.—*from Robert B. Towns*, Battles of America by Sea and Land *(1878)*

Lafayette wounded at the Brandywine.—*from Robert B. Towns*, Battles of America by Sea and Land *(1878)*

Hugh Mercer.—*from John Goolrick,* Life of General Hugh Mercer

William von Knyphausen.—*from Howard M. Jenkins,* Pennsylvania Colonial and Federal *(1906)*

Colonel Johann Gottlieb Rall.—*from William S. Stryker,* The Battles of Trenton and Princeton *(1898)*

General John Sullivan.—*from William Cullen Bryant et al.,* Scribner's Popular History of the United States *(1896)*

Battle of the Brandywine.—*from* Scribner's New Monthly Magazine *(1898)*

Battle of Oriskany. Herkimer, with wounded leg, is shown directing the fighting.—*from* Harper's Weekly *(1879)*

Right: Colonel Barry St. Leger, portrait by Thomas Gainsborough.—*from* Art Journal *(1902)*

Bottom left: General Horatio Gates, portrait by Robert Edge Pine.—*from Henry William Elson,* History of the United States *(1906)*

Bottom right: Joseph Brant (Thayendanegea).—*from John Fiske,* The American Revolution *(1891)*

FIVE

Oriskany

BRIGADIER GENERAL NICHOLAS HERKIMER had watched his four Tryon County militia regiments take what seemed an interminable time to shuffle into an awkward column, preparatory to moving out of Fort Dayton, and the diminutive, swarthy New York militia general, age forty-nine, was feeling testy that Monday morning, 4 August 1777. Moreover, it seemed as if he himself was the only officer aware of the urgency to move this 800-man force to the aid of the small American garrison at Fort Stanwix, a good two-day's march to the west. The enemy, in fact, could already be laying siege to it. As the train of creaking oxcarts lumbered to its place in the column, Herkimer mounted his old white horse and rode toward the head of the column. This obscure New York militia general was destined to play a critical role in an operation that would affect the outcome of the American Revolution in the northern theater.

The operation in which Herkimer's militia was about to take part had been initiated by Major General John Burgoyne's offensive, launched out of Canada in mid-June of that year. Burgoyne's plan was based on a two-pronged operation that was designed to secure control of the Hudson River and split the northern colonies by preventing the movement of American troops and supplies either to north or south while assuring future British freedom of movement toward New England or, conversely, toward the Middle Atlantic colonies. Hence Burgoyne's primary objective was Albany, New York, where the main column of his offensive was headed in late June. The other column, under Lieutenant Colonel Barry St. Leger, was to move by way of the Saint Lawrence River to Oswego on Lake Ontario, and with the assistance of Iroquois Indians and Tories, capture Fort Stanwix and move down the Mohawk Valley to Albany, where he would link up with Burgoyne.

———

ON 5 JULY BURGOYNE'S MAIN FORCE HAD captured Fort Ticonderoga, and by 29 July British advance elements had reached Fort Edward and Fort George. At this point, however, the expedition of Barry St. Leger is the focus of our attention.*

St. Leger's operation is usually referred to as a diversionary effort. It was intended to be more than that; it was intended to serve political ends as well as military. The Mohawk River valley formed the central terrain feature of what was then Tryon County,† whose expanse extended almost from Schenectady to the west and northwest as far as Canada and Lake Ontario. Its inhabitants came from a half-dozen regions of western Europe—English, Irish, Scotch-Irish, Germans, Netherlands Dutch, and Highland Scots.

The area was a hotbed of Toryism centered on a Tory stronghold—Sir William Johnson's Johnson Hall. Sir William had acquired vast holdings in and around the Mohawk Valley, and his growing influence with the Indians, particularly the Iroquois, made his name familiar to Indians and settlers as far away as Ohio and Florida. He had died on the eve of the Revolution in 1774, leaving his son-in-law, Colonel Guy Johnson, as superintendent of Indian affairs, and his son, Sir John Johnson, as his heir and titular head of the family.

Guy Johnson had performed his inherited task well and had kept many Indians loyal to the Crown. But shortly after the Council of Oswego (1775), after persuading most of the Six Nations to confirm their alliance with the British, he had left for Canada, taking with him the Indian chief Joseph Brant. Sir John Johnson later followed him. It was the wish to restore this Tory hegemony—and to take vengeance upon the colonists—that persuaded the Tories of the region to band together under John Johnson to serve with St. Leger.

St. Leger was a soldier with over twenty years of active service, whose leadership qualities had been demonstrated in the French and Indian War under Abercromby, Wolfe, and Amherst. In 1777 he was forty years of age, holding the permanent grade of lieutenant colonel in the 34th

---

*Burgoyne's plans and operations are covered in chapter 6.

† Tryon County no longer exists; its territory has been divided among ten counties: Herkimer, Montgomery, Otsego, Fulton, Oneida, Oswego, Jefferson, Lewis, Hamilton, and St. Lawrence.

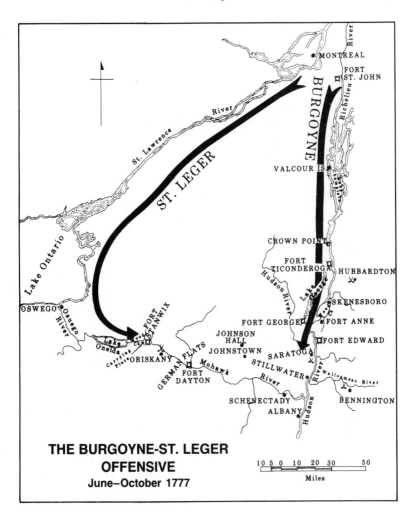

**THE BURGOYNE-ST. LEGER
OFFENSIVE
June–October 1777**

Foot. Upon his assignment to command this expedition he was appointed temporary brigadier general.

His expeditionary force was an assortment of British regulars, Hessian jägers, Royal Artillerymen, Tory rangers, Tory light infantry, Canadian irregulars (including axmen), and about a thousand Indians under Joseph Brant:

Detachment from 34th Foot	100
Detachment from 8th Foot	100
Detachment, Hesse-Hanau Jägers	100
Sir John Johnson's Royal Greens	133
Col. John Butler's Loyalist Rangers	127
Canadian militia (including axmen)	535
Artillery crews for two six-pounders, two three-pounders, and four mortars	40
Joseph Brant's Indians	1,000
Total rank and file	2,135

The force totaled over 2,000 men when it was finally assembled at Oswego, the rendezvous where St. Leger was joined by Brant on 25 July. On the following day he commenced his march toward Fort Stanwix. Although the fort had been built to guard the western passages to and from the Mohawk Valley, St. Leger believed it to be a crumbling and easily reducible ruin.

Nearly half of St. Leger's force—1,000 men out of 2,135—were Indians under the leadership of Chief Joseph Brant. Brant could be a figure cast in a heroic mold or a monster in half-human form, depending on the viewpoint of Indian and Briton or that of the Patriot settler exposed to frontier warfare. Son of a Mohawk warrior and an Indian mother, he became known as Brant when his mother remarried after his father's death, but to the Iroquois he was always Thayendanegea, their warrior-leader. Brant was no ordinary savage. After serving under Sir William Johnson in his Lake George campaign, he had studied English at Lebanon, Connecticut, and had later led Iroquois warriors loyal to the British in Pontiac's Rebellion. As Guy Johnson's secretary, Brant had been presented at court in London and was so socially celebrated that his portrait was painted by Romney. After his return to America he led tribesmen during the British-Canadian victory over the Americans at The Cedars in May 1776. In July 1777 he joined St. Leger at Oswego, ready to march with the British leader on Fort Stanwix.

Fort Stanwix, erected in 1758 during the French and Indian War, was strategically located to command not only the Mohawk River but also the portages linking the river with the waterways flowing into Lake Ontario. As long as it was adequately garrisoned, it clearly dominated the Mohawk Valley, but by 1777 it had been long abandoned. In April of that year it was occupied once more by twenty-eight-year-old Colonel Peter Gansevoort and his 550 New York Continentals. Though he declared the fort "indefensible and untenable," Gansevoort set his regiment to work against time to restore the fort. He and his capable second in command, Lieutenant Colonel Marinus Willett, pushed the men until the works might withstand attack or siege, just in the nick of time to take on St. Leger's advancing army.

But though Fort Stanwix was being prepared for battle, news from Canada, magnified by the constant threat of Indian raids, brought about "a general paralysis" among the people of the valley. In that atmosphere they turned to Nicholas Herkimer. Accordingly, on 17 July 1777 Herkimer distributed copies of a ringing proclamation calling on "every male person, being in health, from 16 to 60 years of age, to repair immediately, with arms and accoutrements, to the place to be appointed in my orders." From there they would "march to oppose the enemy with vigor, as true patriots, for the just defense of their country." The proclamation produced the desired effect. The Patriot settlers placed their trust in Honnikol—as his German Flats neighbors called their neighbor. They were ready to rally at his call.

ST. LEGER'S FORCE WAS SKILLFULLY DEPLOYED on the march. Brant's Indians moved as a screening force, covering advance elements of the main body as well as both flanks of the force. The main body was composed of the rest of the Tory units and the British regulars marching in two parallel detachments. As a whole, the force managed a march rate of ten miles a day, no mean accomplishment in such rough wilderness terrain.

On 3 August St. Leger arrived outside Fort Stanwix and attempted to bluff the garrison into surrender. First, he assembled his whole force to pass in review—at a safe distance—under the eyes of the garrison, a display as colorful as it was arrogant. The scarlet of the British 8th and 34th regiments contrasted with the blue of the German regulars, who were followed by the green of the Tory units. The nonuniformed Indians, in war paint and shouting their battle cries, completed the review. Instead of being awed by the whooping savages, the American soldiers were forcefully reminded of the fate that would be theirs if they fell into the hands of Indian torturers, not to mention what would happen to the settlers of the valley the fort's garrison was there to protect. Two days later St. Leger sent a written threat to Gansevoort threatening dire consequences for his resistance. Gansevoort returned the document with his refusal to surrender.

He soon recognized that the restored fortifications could not be taken by storm, and St. Leger then disposed his army for a siege. The besieg-

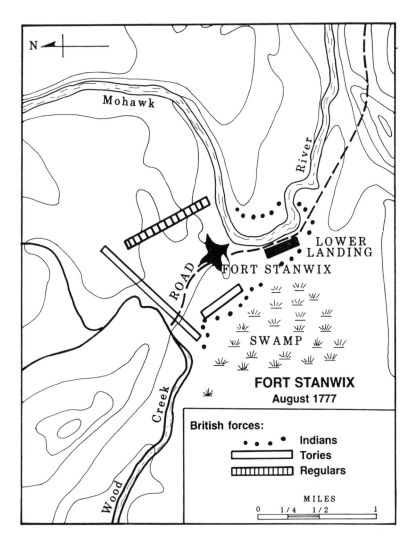

ing forces took up three main positions, roughly making up the sides of a triangle. The regulars occupied the position north of the fort; Tories, Canadians, and Indians stretched along the so-called Lower Landing to positions west of the fort. Finally, Indians were also posted on the east bank of the Mohawk across from the Lower Landing.

With the fort thus surrounded on three sides, St. Leger's force occupied itself clearing a passage for his supply and artillery bateaux and exchanging sniper fire with the garrison through 4 and 5 August.

On the evening of the fifth St. Leger received a message that was to change his plans for continuing the siege. Joseph Brant's sister Molly, who had remained behind, had dispatched a runner to inform St. Leger that an American column was on its way to relieve Gansevoort. By the time that St. Leger received the message, the Americans could be within a few miles of the fort.

HAVING LEFT FORT DAYTON IN GERMAN FLATS on the morning of 4 August, Herkimer's column of 800 Tryon County militia encamped that evening near Starring Creek, about twelve miles to the west. On the following day Herkimer's column crossed to the south bank of the Mohawk and later halted on the night of 5–6 August to encamp along the road to Fort Stanwix, in the vicinity of present-day Whitesboro. The head of the column was about eight miles from the fort, between Sauquoit and Oriskany creeks.

On the march, the temper of Herkimer's men had been changing rapidly from mild resolve to grim determination. Their regimental commanders, Colonels Jacob Klock, Ebenezer Cox, Peter Bellinger, and Richard Visscher, had fanned these fires. Now, at nightfall on the fifth, with their campfires making islands of yellow light against the blackness of the hemlocks and beeches, they were spoiling for a fight.

Herkimer, despite his reputation for a phlegmatic temperament, was worried. There were too many unknowns to ponder. Particularly he was concerned about what both Gansevoort and St. Leger knew, and what their reactions would be when they received word of his column's strength and whereabouts. Would St. Leger dispatch a force to intercept him? Would Gansevoort launch a sortie against St. Leger to distract the British commander from intercepting the relief column?

Herkimer dispatched Captain John Demooth and several men to find their way through to the fort and tell Gansevoort to acknowledge Demooth's message (and his willingness to make a sortie) by the firing of three cannon shots.

Herkimer's concern was eased somewhat by the arrival of sixty friendly Oneidas under Chiefs Honyerry and Cornelius, who agreed to employ their warriors as scouts on the march to Fort Stanwix. But the danger of ambush remained. Herkimer's problem was exacerbated by the rashness of his senior officers. In a council of war the next morning the four regimental commanders, their bright blue and buff uniform coats contrasting with the brown of Herkimer's, urged immediate action. Colonel Ebenezer Cox, in fact, set the tenor by abruptly demanding marching orders from Honnikol before the little brigadier had time to make a formal opening of the council. Herkimer replied by recounting his dispatching of Captain Demooth and his men during the night, as well as his request of Gansevoort for a sortie to be acknowledged by three cannon shots. It was still early morning and there had been no cannon shots. After all, Demooth had to be given reasonable time to get through to the fort.

The explanation, while sensible, didn't suffice to keep the colonels quiet. Though Herkimer, a veteran of the French and Indian War, probably reminded the council of Braddock's ambush and defeat less than a generation before, the argument went on for almost an hour. Meanwhile, a gaping throng of militiamen left their breakfast cooking fires to crowd around and listen to the fascinating sounds of growing discord among the higher-ups.

The challenges to Herkimer's caution eventually became taunts of disloyalty and even of cowardice. Though reminded pointedly that at least one member of his family was marching with St. Leger's Tories—a low blow—Herkimer managed to sit quietly, smoking his pipe and listening for cannon shots that never came.

Finally he gave way. He knocked out his pipe, reminded his accusers that "burning, as they now seemed[,] to meet the enemy . . . [they would] run at his first appearance," and dismissed the council by mounting his horse and giving the order to march on. His words "were no sooner heard than the troops gave a shout, and moved, or, rather, rushed forward."

Thus the march began, four itchy regiments led—with the exception of Herkimer—by impetuous men who had cast aside what little they knew about forest warfare. They marched in double column, a file in each rut: Cox leading off, followed by Jacob Klock, then Peter Bellinger, and finally Richard Visscher. The Oneidas were out somewhere to the front, out of contact, as were the company of rangers who were supposed to have been acting as scouts and flank guards.

About 9:00 A.M. the head of the column, with Herkimer and Cox riding in the lead, was approaching the wide and deep ravine made by the little stream that would become known as Battle Brook. Without hesitating, Cox put his horse down the steep eastern side of the ravine, crossed the corduroy causeway, and led the way up the more gentle slope on the western side.

WHILE HERKIMER'S MEN WERE STILL PREPARING to halt for the night of 5–6 August, St. Leger had received Molly Brant's timely message and had decided to take the action he later described in his report: "I did not think it prudent to wait for them [Herkimer's men], and thereby subject myself to be attacked by a sally from the garrison in the rear, while the reinforcement employed me in front. I therefore determined to attack them on the march, either openly or covertly, as circumstances should offer."

As it turned out, the circumstances did offer an ideal opportunity for an ambush, the most reliable tactic that St. Leger's provincial officers could use to employ the Indians to best advantage. So St. Leger dispatched a detachment of the Royal Greens, Tory rangers, and perhaps half of the Indians (about 400) under Sir John Johnson.* (The British regulars were noticeably missing.) The total strength of the force came to about 500.

The ambush site was an excellent choice, and the deployment of the Tories and Indians was equally well adapted to the terrain. The spot selected was about six miles east of Fort Stanwix, where the military road on which Herkimer's column was marching crossed a deep ravine about 700 feet wide and 50 feet deep. The summer rains had made the ravine passable only on the log causeway. The forest of beech, birch, maple, and hemlock provided a dark shade for the thick undergrowth which came within a few feet of the road. To make the picture complete, according to Hoffman Nickerson, "when the middle of the advancing column was down in the ravine [it would be impossible] for either the van or the rear to see what was going on" (*The Turning Point of the Revolution*).

The deployment of the ambushing force was as practical as it was classical. Its form might be seen as the sleeve of an inverted bayonet scabbard. The top—the closed end—was astride the road on the west side of the ravine; there the Tory troops provided the blocking force whose opening fires would smash the head of Herkimer's column and thus bring the whole to a halt. The Indians were disposed along the sides of the sleeve to attack the flanks of the column and, of equal importance, to close around the end of the rear guard and thus complete an encircle-

---

*There are conflicting reports concerning the commander; I have relied on St. Leger's report, which states that Johnson took command of the force.

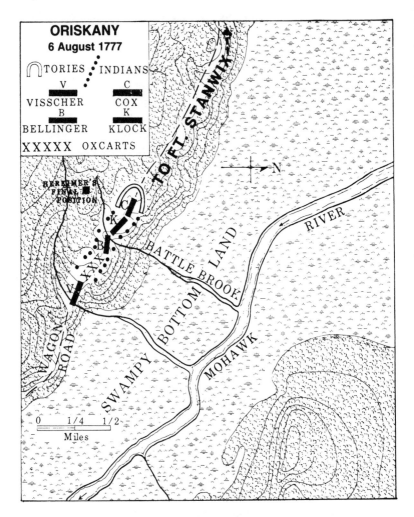

ment so that the fire of the entire ambushing forces converged on their entrapped enemy. To open the action, the bottom end of the sleeve was left open to allow the advancing column to enter and proceed until its head would be abruptly halted by the first volley.

HERKIMER, COX, AND THE WHOLE COLUMN marched unhesitatingly into the trap. (What may have happened to the security elements supposedly protecting the column remains an unknown factor.) Tories and Indians lying hidden in the undergrowth listened to the militiamen of Cox's regiment as they stumbled across the causeway and filed up the western slope of the ravine. The August heat was growing in intensity under the interlaced branches and thick leaves of the trees. Many of the farmer-soldiers fell out of the column to get a hasty drink from the shallow brook while dipping the cool water in their hats to splash over their flushed faces.

While the first oxcarts were getting closer to the causeway, Ebenezer Cox had crossed the little spur that made up the west side of the ravine and was riding toward the shallower depression beyond it. As his horse started up the slope, he heard the shrill blasts of a silver whistle sounding three times. They were the last sounds Cox ever heard. The volley from the Tory muskets crashed out of the brush, tearing into the militia's vanguard with fearful effect and dashing Cox from the saddle, dead before he hit the ground.

A few yards behind Cox, Herkimer heard an even greater roar of firing to his rear. Could it be that his whole column was already falling victim to this ambush? He had wheeled and started toward the rear when a bullet felled his horse. At the same time Herkimer took a bullet in his leg, shattering the bone beneath the knee. The Indians on the east side of the ambush broke from their cover, unable to resist the hope of scalps to be taken and oxen to be slaughtered. They swept forward, whooping their war cries, brandishing tomahawks, spears, and scalping knives to fall upon the wagon train and the rear guard. Their headlong rush became a torrent of war-painted bodies that poured around the oxcarts and directed itself upon the terror-stricken rear guard. The best of the Tory eyewitnesses, Colonel John Butler, saw not only the premature attack but its results:

> The causeway was already hopelessly choked with their unwieldy wagons, when the eagerness of some drunken Indians precipitated the attack and saved the rearguard from the fate that overtook the rest of the column. The first deliberate volley that burst upon them from a distance of a very few yards was terribly destructive. Elated by the sight, and maddened by the smell of blood and gunpowder, many of the Indians rushed from their coverts to complete the victory with spear and hatchet. The rearguard promptly ran away in a wild panic.

Despite what Butler wrote, the rear guard did not save itself. Except for a few units such as Captain Gardenier's, Colonel Visscher's regiment took off at a dead run, pursued by whooping Indians. The flight became a massacre. Skeletons were later found as far back as the mouth of Oriskany Creek, over two miles from the battlefield.

A look into the ravine after the smoke of the initial volleys had settled must have been like a glimpse into hell itself. Unwounded men had fallen to the ground as though struck by the same blasts of fire that had killed or wounded men all around them. After the first shock, however, militiamen knelt or propped muskets across the bodies of the dead to return the fire. At first, they could only fire back at flashes from the underbrush or even at the yells of their enemies when they moved behind cover. Soon a ragged line formed, extending from the head of the shattered wagon train, along the road up the slope from the causeway, and ending where Cox's surviving men hugged the dirt to form an inadvertent spearhead facing the Tories at the west end of the ambush.

It was not an organized movement; it was instinctive action alone that made these frontier Americans seek cover and comradeship as they tried to fight back. They rallied along the road, and the line eventually became a series of small circles of men taking cover behind trees. The tight little circles gradually moved up the slope until they formed a rough semicircle on the higher ground between the two ravines. Fighting back was the only way to survive. Retreat into the hell of the ravine would mean certain death by musket or tomahawk.

The ambush was now becoming a pitched battle. Pressure on the main body was relieved by the departure of the mass of Indians, who were intent on pursuing the rear guard. Herkimer's men were therefore able to fall back fighting. One must admire the toughness of seemingly undisciplined frontier militia to rally on their own until their officers could bring order out of chaos.

From the outset, leadership came right from the top. When Herkimer was pulled away from his dead horse, he was carried to high ground. There he ordered his saddle brought up and placed against a large beech tree somewhere near the center of his encircled command. Seated on his saddle, with his wounded leg stretched out before him, he maintained control. To set an example, he coolly took out his pipe, lit it, and continued to puff away as he gave his orders. One of those orders, which was to prove a decisive factor, pertained to individual tactics. Herkimer observed that an Indian would wait until an American had fired, then dash in for the kill with the tomahawk before his victim could reload his musket. He ordered the men to be paired off behind trees so that one would be ready to fire while his partner was reloading. The simple tactic paid off demonstrably; the Indians' dashes declined markedly.

The slackening of the Indians' fire, however, did little at first to reduce the fierceness of the hand-to-hand fighting that occurred where enemies closed in personal combat. Bayonets and clubbing muskets took their toll again and again as former neighbors, Tories and Patriots, found themselves face to face. In about an hour, however, this deadly combat was brought to an abrupt halt. By 11:00 A.M. black thunderheads had arrived overhead, and soon peals of thunder and lightning flashes swept across the forest, followed by a torrential downpour. The rain prevented keeping priming dry enough for firing, and the guns fell silent as suddenly as the firing had begun.

The rain continued to beat down for another hour. Herkimer and his officers took advantage of the summer storm to tighten up their perimeter. Then a strange distraction appeared. A solid column of men in oddly colored uniforms—at a distance they appeared to be wearing gray-buff jackets and an odd assortment of hats—came marching down the road from the direction of Fort Stanwix, aligned like regular troops. A ragged cheer went up from Herkimer's men: they must be a battalion of Continentals making a sortie from the fort!

As the column drew nearer, Captain Jacob Gardenier (whose company of Visscher's rear-guard regiment had stayed to fight with the main body) took a second look, and barked out to his men: "They're Tories, open fire!" The men heard him, but none obeyed. One militiaman even dashed forward to greet a "friend" in the front rank and was immediately yanked into the formation and made prisoner. Gardenier sprang forward, spontoon in hand, to lead a charge against this new enemy. And enemies they were indeed—a detachment of the Royal Greens under Major Stephen Watts, the young brother-in-law of Sir John Johnson. The Tories had turned their green jackets inside out in an almost successful trick to deceive the militiamen into holding their fire.

Gardenier plunged into the Tory formation, thrusting about him with his spontoon until he had freed the prisoner. Three of his nearest enemies recovered enough to attack Gardenier with their bayonets, pinning him to the ground by a bayonet in the calf of each leg. The third Tory thrust his bayonet against his chest, but the rugged Gardenier, a blacksmith, parried it with his bare hand, pulled his attacker down on top of him, and held him as a shield. One of Gardenier's men jumped in to help his captain and managed to clear enough room for him to regain his feet. Gardenier, by now berserk in his battle fury, jumped up, grabbed his spontoon, and plunged it into the man he had been holding. The wounded Tory was recognized by some of the militia as Lieutenant Angus Mac-

Donald, one of the despised Highlanders who had served as one of Sir John Johnson's close subordinates.

In spite of the deadly scuffle going on right in front of them, the militiamen still hesitated, but only until the enraged Gardenier was back among them, roaring out his command to fire. This time the militia obeyed, and thirty of the Royal Greens went down at the first volley. Then began the most savage fighting of the fiercest frontier battle of the war. The pitch of ferocity that mounted in both sides has been told best by the novelist Walter D. Edmonds, who lived and did his research in the Mohawk Valley: "Men fired and flung their muskets down and went for each other with their hands. The American flanks turned in, leaving the Indians where they were. The woods were filled suddenly with men swaying together, clubbing rifle barrels, swinging hatchets, yelling like the Indians themselves. There were no shots. Even the yelling stopped after the first joining of the lines, and men begun to go down" (*Drums along the Mohawk*).

Such bloodthirstiness could not sustain itself, and finally unwounded men began to pull back to reform the lines they had left before the bloodbath. They left between them heaps of the dead, some still clutching hatchet or musket, others lying faceup where they had fallen. For a while there was intermittent sniping, but it seemed mostly to come from the muskets of the white men. The Indians had fallen strangely silent. The restless lull in the firing was broken by new sounds, at first thought to be another rainstorm. But it was soon recognized for what it was: the booming of a cannon shot, followed by a second and a third. Demooth had gotten through to the fort and there was going to be a sortie!

In the meantime, Indian runners had brought word to their fellow warriors that their camps had been attacked by the Americans in the fort and were being ransacked. It was too much for Brant's Indians. They had never intended, and had never been trained, to fight a pitched battle. Where were the British? The Iroquois had lost many warriors—and for what? There were no dead to be looted or scalps to be taken here under the deadly fire of American muskets. So, in spite of the pleas of Butler and his officers, Brant made the decision to slip away back to the camps where his warriors might still retrieve some necessities for survival. The mournful cry "oonah, oonah" sounded back and forth through the forest, and the militiamen realized that the Indians were retreating, disappearing silently through the underbrush. They were soon followed by the Tories, who needed no convincing that without their Indian allies they would be outnumbered by Herkimer's men, who still thirsted for revenge.

The woods were soon emptied of the enemy, all except three Iroquois who, not as easily discouraged as their brothers, had remained hidden until they could loot and scalp when the militiamen left. They were discovered, and in a last desperate rush made for Herkimer himself. The three were shot down as they dashed in, one falling almost at the general's feet.

It was all over, all except the tragic counting of the living, the dead, and the wounded. There was no accounting for the missing. The exhausted survivors had neither the strength nor the time to search for them. They came to pick up Honnikol, who was still seated with his back to his tree, still smoking his pipe and nursing his wounded leg with its red bandanna bandage. But first they had to hear his decision. It was not easy, yet it was obvious: The militia were in no condition to take on the redcoats at the fort; there were fifty wounded to be carried, and only a hundred or more left who could march. Herkimer ordered the march to begin homeward, and a detachment was sent ahead to arrange for boats to come up the Mohawk and pick up the wounded at the nearest ford.

The actual losses on both sides were never accurately totaled. A reasonable estimate has it that of the 800 militiamen who had set out from Fort Dayton on 4 August, "all but 150 of Herkimer's men had been killed, wounded or captured—counting out those of the rearguard who fled" (Scott, *Fort Stanwix and Oriskany*). As for the Tory and Indian losses, probably 150 had fallen.

The sortie that Gansevoort had ordered, a somewhat limited effort, was made by Willett with 250 men and a fieldpiece. It was they who had attacked the Tory and Indian camps and systematically looted them, carrying off twenty-one wagon loads of everything movable—weapons, ammunition, blankets, clothing, and all sorts of supplies. Willett was careful to strip the Indian camps of all cooking utensils, packs, and blankets, an act which went far to stir a seething discontent between the Indians and their British masters. Willett withdrew before a British counterstroke could cut him off from the fort, getting all of his loaded-down wagons through the gate without the loss of a single man.

Three days later, Willett performed another feat. He crept out of the fort at 1:00 A.M. and made his hazardous and painful way through swamps and wilderness to General Schuyler at Stillwater. The general was brought up to date on the siege of Stanwix and the results of Oriskany. As Schuyler believed that St. Leger was making a methodical siege of the fort, he selected Benedict Arnold to lead an expedition to relieve it. Arnold, a major general, had eagerly volunteered to do the job, which would ordinarily have gone to a brigadier general.

Arnold left with several hundred volunteers from New York and Massachusetts regiments. By the time he had left Fort Dayton, he had picked up enough reinforcements to bring his total to about 950. Since St. Leger reportedly had about 1,700, even the intrepid Arnold had to pause and consider the odds. As he pondered, a subordinate came up with a stratagem that Arnold heartily approved. A Mohawk Valley German named Hon Yost Schuyler was respected and honored by the Indians, though considered a halfwit by the whites. At the time Schuyler was under sentence of death for trying to raise recruits for the British, so Arnold's offer of a pardon was appealing. Hon Yost was to go to the Indians with St. Leger and spread stories of Arnold advancing to attack them with an army of thousands.

Hon Yost was a cunning rascal when he wanted to be. He propped up his coat and shot it through several times. Then, with an Oneida as his accomplice, he entered a camp near Stanwix, going in alone at first, to relate a marvelous tale of his escape from Fort Dayton, exhibiting the holes in his coat as evidence. The Indians were dismayed to hear of thousands of Americans led by Arnold, the most feared name on the frontier.

Hon Yost was finally brought before St. Leger, in whose presence he added to his story by relating how he had managed to escape on his very way to the gallows. In the meantime the Oneida had passed among the camps to warn his brother Iroquois of their imminent danger: Arnold's force had now grown to 3,000 men, all sworn to follow their legendary leader in a campaign of revenge and massacre.

St. Leger's Indians, already disgusted with Oriskany and its aftermath, were quick to pack up what few belongings they had left and rally around for an immediate departure. The efforts of St. Leger and his officers to placate them and persuade them to stay were words lost on the wind. As the Indians gathered to leave, they became more disorderly. They began to loot the tents of officers and soldiers, making off with clothing and personal belongings, and seizing liquor and drinking it on the spot. St. Leger reported the rioters as "more formidable than the enemy."

Without his Indians, St. Leger now had to give in to pressures to leave, and his whole force took off for the boats at Wood Creek, taking only what they could carry on their backs. They left behind them tents as well as most of St. Leger's artillery and stores.

Arnold arrived at Fort Stanwix on the evening of 23 August, saluted by the cheers of the garrison and a salvo of artillery. The next morning he dispatched a detachment to pursue St. Leger. Its advance elements reached Lake Oneida in time to watch the enemy's boats disappear down the lake. Arnold left Stanwix with a garrison of 700 men, and marched with the other 1,200 to rejoin the main army at Saratoga.

THE QUESTION OF WHETHER ORISKANY WAS a victory or defeat for the Patriots cannot be answered by looking down the narrow vista provided by the battlefield. In one sense Oriskany was a defeat, simply because the battle prevented Herkimer from accomplishing his mission of relieving Fort Stanwix. Even more seriously, Tryon County had been dealt a severe blow because its staggering casualties left the Mohawk Valley virtually defenseless in terms of its own militia protecting it. In another sense, the battle was a victory for Herkimer and his cause. Not only had his militia fought its way out of an ambush, it had beaten the enemy on the field of battle, and at battle's end remained masters of the battlefield.

In the long run, the consequences of Oriskany made possible the eventual relief of Fort Stanwix on 23 August. Moreover, the battle was a strategic success, for St. Leger had been forced to retreat all the way back to his starting point in Canada. Now there would be no one to don the dress uniforms of St. Leger's officers that were being carried in Burgoyne's baggage train, and no one would be coming out of the west to join and reinforce Burgoyne in his fateful advance southward.

SIX

Saratoga: Freeman's Farm and Bemis Heights

AT SOME POINT IN HIS STUDIES THE STUDENT of military history begins to perceive great events as climaxes to a series of ironies. Burgoyne's campaign, launched from Canada in June 1777, aptly fits that perception. Conceived in intrigue and activated by ambitions, it was in the end left to its fate by an incompetent strategist in London who was far removed from the realities of warfare in North America. The ironies were brought to a climax by two generals who, on a world stage, would perform as second-rate commanders.

Before witnessing the twin battles that climaxed the campaign, we should take a glance at the conception of Burgoyne's "Thoughts for Conducting the War from the Side of Canada," and the strategic planning that King George eventually approved. First, however, a brief look at the three British characters who were essential to the drama from its first act until the final curtain.

George Bernard Shaw, in his play *The Devil's Disciple*, introduces Lieutenant General John Burgoyne as "a man of fashion, gallant enough to have made a distinguished marriage by an elopement, witty enough to write successful comedies, aristocratically-connected enough to have had opportunities of high military distinction"—and, Shaw could have added, a parliamentary career to match.

The future general came from an old Lancashire family whose lands were deeded by John of Gaunt (c. 1387) and could claim a baronetcy conferred by Charles I. By the time of Burgoyne's birth in 1722, his father, a "former army captain, rake, and gambler," was deeply in debt, and he probably did well to send his son John to Westminster School at age ten. Five years later John entered the army through the purchase of a cornet's commission in the Horse Guards, and was able to become "aristocratically-connected" through his old school chum, the only son and heir of the eleventh earl of Derby, head of the rich and powerful Stanleys.

By 1759 Lieutenant Colonel Burgoyne was commissioned by the king to raise one of two new regiments of light cavalry, his being the 16th Light Dragoons. The new regimental commander became known as Gentleman Johnny to his soldiers when he began to implement innovative ideas that were far ahead of his time. His instructions to his officers demonstrated his determination to treat his men as human beings: "There are two systems which . . . divide the disciplinarians: the one [Prussian] is that of *training men like spaniels, by the stick;* the other, after the French, of *substituting the point of honour in the place of severity.* . . . I apprehend a just medium between the two extremes." His "just medium" paid off so well that the 16th Dragoons became known as Burgoyne's Horse, a showpiece for British cavalry.

Burgoyne took his regiment to Portugal in 1762, becoming somewhat of a hero following his bold actions at Valencia d'Alcantara and Villa Velha. The following year he returned to London as one of high society's darlings. With a permanent commission as colonel of the 16th assuring him £3,000 a year for life, and the substantial inheritance that was now his wife's, he could devote full time to politics. The influence of the Stanleys and his own energetic politicking soon got him a seat in Parliament, where he was received as a hero and voted the thanks of the House for his military achievements.

Yet the restless soldier-politician found ways to exercise other talents. He became, in James Lunt's view "a clubbable man," a fashionable man-about-town with an untiring fascination for the gaming table and the theater (*John Burgoyne of Saratoga*). In 1774 his first successful play, *Maid of Oaks*, was so well received that it caught David Garrick's eye, which was enough to have it performed at Drury Lane the following year.

In that same year Burgoyne, having been commissioned a major general in 1772, went back to soldiering, this time as the junior of the three major generals, Howe, Clinton, and himself, who traveled aboard His Majesty's frigate *Cerberus*, destination Boston Harbor. After some five months acting as "fifth wheel of the Boston Coach," Burgoyne managed a return trip to London. He returned to America in May 1777 with the reinforcements to Quebec that spelled ruin to the American cause in Canada, but he still had to play the role of second in command to Carleton, the governor and commander in chief in Canada. So again he went back to London. Having escaped the frigid Canadian winter, he warmed his cause with his pen, this time in his paper presenting "My Thoughts for Conducting the War from the Side of Canada." The king warmed to the proposed expeditionary plan in general, and so indicated his approval to Lord North, the prime minister. The key figure, however, in transforming concepts into operational directives was Lord George Germain, the secretary of state for colonies from 1775 to 1782, whose department controlled the operations of all His Majesty's forces in colonies.

Germain (1716–1785) was known as Lord George Sackville until 1770 when, under the terms of a will, he agreed to become Lord Germain. In 1745 Sackville had led a regiment against the French at Fontenoy, where he was wounded and captured. Thereafter his rise was rapid: he was a major general by 1755, and two years later a lieutenant general. In 1759 he managed to end a military career of outstanding promise by his baffling conduct at Minden (1 August 1759), where he refused to obey an order to unleash his cavalry against the wavering French center. The immediate result of Sackville's behavior was that the French commander made an orderly withdrawal and saved his army. The ultimate result was that a British court-martial judged him guilty of disobedience and "unfit to serve his Majesty in any military capacity whatsoever." King George II's reaction to Sackville's performance was to wish him court-martialed and shot for cowardice, a wish that was never carried out. The eventual effects on Sackville's political career may seem as incredible as his actions at Minden. In the public mind, Sackville was a victim of governmental and military bureaucracy. Soon after he entered politics he allied himself with Lord North. Eventually, and with apparent ease, he succeeded Lord Dartmouth as secretary of state for colonies in November 1775.

The king's approval of Burgoyne's proposed offensive led eventually to Germain's letter to General Carleton on 26 March 1777, in essence calling for Carleton to hold about 3,000 troops in Canada while Burgoyne with some 7,000 would move southward on Lake Champlain, capture Fort Ticonderoga, and continue the advance to take Albany. A secondary effort and diversion, a force of 2,000 under St. Leger, would descend the Mohawk Valley to link up with Burgoyne at Albany. The operational instructions of the letter concluded with the statement that Burgoyne and St. Leger *"must never lose view of their intended junctions with Sir William Howe as their principal objects"* (italics mine).

At this point it might seem that the "intended junctions" with Howe had been made clear by the planners to the operators. Howe had previously written two letters to Germain (December 1776 and 20 January 1777) in which he pointed out that *the direction of his main effort in 1777 was the capture of Philadelphia*. When Germain answered both of Howe's letters in a single one on 3 March 1777, he approved of Howe's objective and called his plans "solid and decisive." In Hoffman Nickerson's words, "As far as this 3 March letter from Germain was concerned, Burgoyne and the Canada army might have been on the moon" (*The Turning Point of the Revolution*).

Germain's final mistake was his failure to send a direct order to Howe to cooperate by dispatching forces up the Hudson to Albany. One of Germain's under secretaries had in fact remarked on the oversight, and had been directed to send a copy of the Carleton letter to Howe. A little later, Germain realized that sending such a copy was not enough, and he directed that an order to Howe be drafted to remedy the deficiency. Germain's secretaries, however, were no better than their chief; Howe's orders were somehow mislaid and forgotten by them, too.

If this series of fumbles were not enough to subvert an operation, there remains the question of the character of Sir William Howe, last of the three principals of the drama. He was of royal blood, though on the wrong side of the blanket, since his mother had been a mistress of George I. His first military successes came in the French and Indian War, where he commanded the 58th Foot under Amherst at Louisbourg. In 1759 he became famous for leading the storming party of Wolfe's light infantry up the cliffs to the Plains of Abraham, where Wolfe won the decisive battle of the war. Like many officers of his time, he had already entered Parliament—in his case by assuming the seat of his oldest brother, George, who had been killed in the attack on Ticonderoga. George had been popular with the Americans, who so admired him that the citizens of Massachusetts had subscribed to a monument to his honor in Westminster Abbey. William shared his brother's sympathy for the Americans, a feeling which was to trouble him when he was ordered to America in May 1775.

In 1777, at age forty-five, Howe's was a fine six-foot-tall figure, with heavy, dark features and gracious manners to match an amiability that made him popular with both sexes. In the main he was a clear-sighted strategist and a skilled tactician, yet his tendency toward indolence, both professional and personal, too often tended to negate his victories on the battlefield. His physical courage (witness his presence on the field at Bunker Hill) was unfortunately not matched by his moral courage, at least in those cases where his apparent hesitation caused him to fail to follow up his battlefield successes. Time after time he had beaten Washington, only to let him escape with his army and renew the war. This, then, was the man on whom Burgoyne and Germain would rely, at various times and in varying ways, for cooperation with the invasion army from Canada, a man who had his own strategy, which did not envision Burgoyne's operations to be of overriding importance.

Burgoyne arrived at Quebec on 6 May, just after the ice in the Saint Lawrence had broken up, to find that Carleton had succeeded so well in preparing his troops and their logistical support for the campaign that operations could begin by 13 June. Burgoyne's expeditionary force was organized as shown in Table 2, its two main divisions being a British right wing under Major General Phillips and a German left wing under Major General Baron von Riedesel.

The artillery totaled an imposing 138 pieces. Burgoyne's actual field train, however, would be made up of 42 pieces; the remaining 96 cannon were either mounted in lake-going vessels, left at Saint Johns, or dropped off at Forts Ticonderoga and George after they had been captured. The cannon of the artillery train were to be divided equally between the two wings. There were about 250 British Royal Artillerymen, 78 German artillerymen from the Hesse-Hanau artillery company, and some 150 matrosses—infantry soldiers serving as cannoneers.

The only cavalry with the army (dismounted out of necessity) was composed of 250 Brunswick Dragoons who were designated as army reserve. A more ludicrous reserve for a wilderness operation could hardly have been conjured up. The dragoons wore thigh-high cavalry jackboots, weighing six pounds apiece and equipped with giant spurs admirably suited for getting entangled in forest undergrowth. Above the boots were leather breeches, wide gauntlets, stiff tunics, and high cocked hats with long plumes. And to make the dragoons really immobile, each carried a heavy carbine and trailed a long broadsword. The German infantrymen were better off, though they had to get by with worn uniforms and shoes.

Taken all in all, Burgoyne's regular troops were hardened, disciplined men and a formidable fighting force. Their officers were all professionals, and the generals were competent veterans. General Phillips, the second in command, was a fine artilleryman and a noted strategist. Baron von Riedesel, the major general commanding the left wing, was a twenty-year veteran with a splendid record of campaigning under the duke of Brunswick in the Seven Years' War. He was noted for his tact, good judgment, and coolness in the heat of battle. At thirty-eight he was

TABLE 2. Organization of Burgoyne's Expedition to Albany

RIGHT WING (British): Major General Phillips

Advance corps: Brigadier General Fraser
 24th Foot; flank companies of 29th, 31st, 34th foot*

1st Brigade: Brigadier General Powell
 9th, 47th, 53rd regiments of foot

2nd Brigade: Brigadier General Hamilton
 20th, 21st, 62nd regiments of foot

250 Loyalist scouts (Canadian and American)

 Total: 3,724 rank and file

LEFT WING (German): Major General von Riedesel

Advance corps: Lt. Col. Breymann
 Grenadier battalion; light infantry detachment: Jägers and British marksmen

1st Brigade: Brigadier Specht
 Regiments Riedesel, Specht, Rhetz

2nd Brigade: Brigadier Gall
 Regiments Prince Frederick, Hesse-Hanau

400 Indian scouts

 Total: 3,016 rank and file

ARTILLERY: 42 guns, one-half with each wing

ARMY RESERVE: Brunswick Dragoons (250)

 Total strength (not including Loyalists and Indians): 7,213 rank and file

---

*The "battalion companies" of these regiments remained in Canada.

in his prime—strong and in good health. He was accompanied by his blue-eyed baroness and their three children. Both baron and baroness have left valuable personal histories of their experiences in America.

Burgoyne was less fortunate in assembling his anticipated forces of irregulars. Instead of the 2,000 Canadian militia counted on, only 150 joined up, most of them Frenchmen who had fought for Montcalm under the French flag. Of the 2,000 Indians expected to join the expedition, only about 400 showed up for duty as scouts and guides. Last, only 100 Tories enlisted, but Burgoyne was counting on the Tory population in New York and other provinces rallying to his cause as his army moved to "liberate" them. This was the typical illusion that British forces held throughout the war, an illusion that was consistently frustrated.

Burgoyne was faced with another shortfall, one that was to cost him dearly on wilderness marches: an inadequately furnished land transport. It was a major logistical problem that neither Carleton nor Burgoyne had solved. There were not only insufficient horses to move the artillery, but the baggage train also lacked its required allotment. Then too, the train had to be made up of 500 light Canadian two-horse carts, hastily built out of green lumber, transports which would not stand up under the rough usage of forest warfare.

IN SPITE OF ITS DEFICIENCIES, BURGOYNE'S EXPEDITION was launched with pomp and ceremony. Carleton arrived at Saint Johns to bid farewell to the officers at a formal dinner. The next day, 13 June, the royal standard of Britain was raised on board the *Thunderer*, the flagship of Burgoyne's flotilla, as it was saluted by all ships' guns and those of Saint Johns; then Britain's martial might moved out toward Lake Champlain. The ships—twenty-eight gunboats and columns of bateaux loaded with troops and supplies—made a colorful spectacle moving across the water to the accompaniment of rolling drums and martial music.

This "most compleat and splendid regatta" arrived at Crown Point on 27 June, and on 1 July had reembarked for Ticonderoga. From 2 to 4 July Burgoyne invested the "Gibraltar of America" and the defenses on Mount Independence. The whole issue was decided when Major General Arthur St. Clair, commanding the American defense, looked up at Sugar Loaf Mountain to observe British artillerymen moving two twelve-pounder guns into firing position on the mountaintop. Since Sugar Loaf clearly dominated the defensive works of Fort Ticonderoga, St. Clair held a hasty council of war, which was unanimous in voting for an immediate withdrawal that night under cover of darkness. The withdrawal plan provided for a retreat in two echelons. It was decided that all the invalided personnel, along with as much of the artillery and stores as could be loaded that night, would be taken on the available vessels (200 bateaux and small craft plus the five ships remaining out of the Valcour Island flotilla) southward down the lake to Skenesboro. St. Clair's main force would move southward by land, starting down from the Mount Independence side, thence to Hubbardton, and from there down to Castleton, a rough forty-five-mile march.

St. Clair's plan for a hasty retrograde movement was a practicable one, but it was ruined by the bungling of his subordinate commanders. Brigadier General Roche de Fermoy evacuated Mount Independence prematurely, setting his own headquarters ablaze in doing so. Four gunners were left to man the fieldpieces, which had been sited to defend the bridge from Ticonderoga to the east side of the waterway. When British General Fraser's point men sneaked up on the battery, they found all four passed out around a breached cask of Madeira. St. Clair meanwhile took off for Hubbardton, pursued by Fraser with his force of light infantry and grenadiers. Fraser in turn was followed by Riedesel with the Regiment Riedesel and Breymann's light troops and grenadiers.

THE OVERALL BRITISH PURSUIT WAS well planned. While Fraser and Riedesel chased after St. Clair, Burgoyne sent General Phillips with a division loaded on boats to go southward down the lake after the fleeing American flotilla. Burgoyne followed Phillips with several frigates and the fastest of his gunboats.

The next commander to fail St. Clair was Colonel Seth Warner, a former Green Mountain Boy who was unaccustomed to discipline. St. Clair ordered him to remain at Hubbardton with his 150 men to cover the main body's six-mile march to Castleton. Warner was told to wait for Colonel Turbott Francis's rear guard to join him. The combined forces, acting as a strengthened rear guard, were then to fall back without delay to join St. Clair at Castleton. The twenty-four-mile march through the wilderness, following a rough wagon track, had been tough going, especially as the July heat pressed down through the thick forest, and when the two forces joined at Hubbardton the men had been near exhaustion. Disregarding St. Clair's orders, the two colonels decided to bed down for the night. Warner, however, failed to provide security outposts. In the meantime, Fraser and Riedesel pushed their troops without letup until they were able to bivouac just out of contact with the Americans while their Indians scouted out the American camps. Marching out quietly on the early morning of 7 July, the British commander deployed his 750 men and attacked at first light.

The surprise assault caught Hale's New Hampshiremen in the act of cooking their breakfast and brought on the vicious two-hour battle of Hubbardton. Although Hale's men fled in panic, the regiments of Warner and Francis were thrown into some kind of a firing line whose first volley killed or wounded twenty-one of the enemy. The British advantage of surprise was soon negated by the forested terrain, which favored the Americans fighting in open order, taking cover behind trees and in the thick underbrush. The battle raged over a front half a mile long.

Fraser first tried outflanking the American left by taking the hill that commanded that end of their line. The Americans fell back while refusing that flank, and Francis tried to reverse things on the American right, where Fraser's force had been thinned out. Now the British were getting the worst of it as Francis's attack continued to make headway, due mostly to the British lack of experience in forest warfare. Just when things were beginning to look disastrous for the British, however, they were saved by Riedesel, who had rushed his men toward the sound of the fighting. The German general threw his jägers into an attack against the American right, with bands playing and the Germans singing a battle hymn, a neat touch which must have astounded the American militiamen. For a few minutes the Americans held, but Colonel Francis was killed and they saw themselves being outflanked. They then began to fall back. The relieved Fraser renewed his attack, this time with the bayonet, against Warner's Vermonters. Seeing the other two regiments disintegrating, Warner gave an order, succinct and sensible under the conditions: "Scatter and meet me at Manchester."

It had been a bitterly fought little action, ending in a clear British victory. The American losses were 324 out of a force of about 600 after the flight of Hale's regiment; twelve guns were captured by the British. Fraser's and Riedesel's losses came to 35 killed and 148 wounded.

When St. Clair at Castleton heard the sounds of the battle, he sent orders to two militia regiments encamped about two miles from Hubbardton to reinforce Warner. They deemed such an action inappropriate, and instead retreated to Castleton.

While St. Clair was taking his reverses during his retreat by land, Colonel Pierce Long of New Hampshire, with somewhere between four and five hundred able-bodied men, was charged with getting the supplies and some artillery from Ticonderoga to Skenesboro. Long was counting on the massive boom and bridge at Ticonderoga to hold up the British while he made his way up the lake with his makeshift flotilla. With a few well-directed shots, however, Burgoyne's gunboats smashed the links in the great chain, after which his sappers cut through enough bridge piles to allow the ships and gunboats through. When Long got to Fort Anne, after burning all that he could not salvage of the stores from Ticonderoga, Lieutenant Colonel Hill with the British 9th Regiment was right on his tail. In a skirmish the Americans were deceived into believing that Indians and British reinforcements were closing in, and they took off for Fort Edward.

If St. Clair were to save the main body of his army, he had no choice now. He made a circuitous march around Skenesboro and arrived on 12 July at Fort Edward.

THUS FAR BURGOYNE'S SOUTHWARD MARCH had been a triumphal parade. He had taken Ticonderoga, the first of his major objectives, with little effort. His pursuing forces had been successful in accomplishing their missions at Hubbardton and Skenesboro and had driven his enemies back on Fort Edward. Now he was faced with a decision of which of the two available routes he should use to advance on Fort Edward. He could fall back on Ticonderoga, get his shipping across and into Lake George, and from the upper end of that lake he could use a passable road to move ten miles overland to the Hudson River. In his "Thoughts" paper he had also considered an alternate route up Wood Creek from Skenesboro and Fort Anne, and from there marching another sixteen miles by a wilderness trail to Fort Edward. Although he had stated that the water route by Lake George would be "the most expeditious and commodious" route to Albany—his final objective—he decided nevertheless to take the overland route, a decision which he later defended by saying "a retrograde motion [falling back from Skenesboro and Hubbardton to Ticonderoga] is apt to make upon the minds both of enemies and friends [an impression of weakness]."

The terrain into which Burgoyne's army was now committed was a military nightmare. The "roads" were no more than crude trails hacked out of dense forests and running every which way, without plan or reason. The undergrowth was dense and broken only by countless fallen trees. The main route from Skenesboro to Fort Edward generally followed the valley of Wood Creek. In Christopher Ward's account: "It crossed no fewer than forty deep ravines over which high and long bridges had been built. There were also numerous swamps and bogs" (*The War of the Revolution*).

Such terrain was a godsend to a general who sought to delay an enemy while building up forces to fight him. General Philip Schuyler, commanding the Northern Department, was ready to make the most of the natural obstructions in the way of the advancing British. He sent out a thousand axmen to fell trees across the route and Wood Creek. They rolled boulders down the hills into the creek to make it impassable to boats. Some of the woodsmen destroyed bridges, while others dug ditches that drained rainfall into newly created quagmires.

Schuyler instituted a scorched-earth operation in which farmers were coerced into driving away their cattle and hiding their foodstuffs. They were even persuaded to burn their grainfields so that the British would have to advance across a wasteland when they were not struggling through the impasses of the forest.

From the British viewpoint, Burgoyne was as determined as Schuyler was obstinate. He sent sappers, soldiers, and Canadian woodsmen by the hundreds ahead of the army to clear the trails, drain the swamps, and rebuild the bridges—in short, to undo all that Schuyler's men had done. They even constructed a causeway two miles long to pass the artillery and wagons. They made headway, but by 25 July Burgoyne's main body had advanced only to Fort Anne. Four days later he was finally approaching Fort Edward. It had taken twenty-one days to move twenty-three miles!

WHILE BURGOYNE'S COLUMNS WERE CREEPING through the wilderness, Schuyler's delaying actions bought him the time and the reinforcements he so badly needed. By 12 July he was joined by St. Clair with his main force, and Colonel Long had brought his detachment from Skenesboro. When Brigadier General John Nixon came in with his 600 Continentals, Schuyler's strength at Fort Edward came to 4,500, of which 2,900 were Continentals and 1,600 were militia. But Schuyler was not about to defend so dilapidated a fort. Fort Edward's condition was so bad, indeed, that he had told Washington how he had jumped his horse over its ruined walls. Consequently, he left a small rear guard at Fort Edward and withdrew down the Hudson to Saratoga, and on 3 August back to Stillwater, twelve miles farther south.

During the period of his retreat three events occurred that were to have a significant effect on Schuyler and the northern army. The first was the arrival of Major General Benedict Arnold at Schuyler's headquarters on 24 July. The second was Schuyler's decision to dispatch Arnold, some three weeks later, with 950 volunteers to relieve Fort Stanwix, already recounted. The third incident, on 27 July, was the murder and scalping of Miss Jane McCrae, which would have far-reaching effects on both armies and their commanders.

Despite Schuyler's wisdom in delaying Burgoyne and dispatching St. Leger on his way back to Canada, on 3 August he was relieved of command of the northern army. His replacement was Major General Horatio Gates. This congressional action spelled the culmination of months of vicious factional fighting, during which the New England troops spread stories that both Schuyler and St. Clair were traitors. And even the ridiculous story of the "silver balls"* gained credence among many of the Yankees.

Gates arrived to assume command on 19 August and was received graciously by Schuyler, who put himself at Gates's disposal, beginning with detailed briefings to familiarize the new commander with all aspects of the situation. Two generals more opposite in background and manner would be hard to conceive. Horatio Gates's lower-class beginnings haunted him all his life and made him what Hoffman Nickerson has called "a snob of the first water." He became adept at screening an abrasive personality behind a veneer of pleasantness that could be charming when occasion demanded. He entered the British army at an early age and was promoted rapidly for one of so humble an origin. A captain at twenty-seven, he served in Braddock's disastrous campaign. Wounded in the ambush of Braddock's forces by the French and Indians in the Battle of the Monongahela, he was carried to safety by an enlisted man, whom he neglected to thank. In 1765 he was retired on half pay and went to settle in Virginia, where he renewed his friendship of Braddock days with Washington, and in 1775 offered his services to the colonials' cause. Washington recognized Gates's administrative ability and nominated him for the grade of brigadier general, to serve as his own adjutant general. In that job he was an unquestioned success.

On the other side of the coin, an incident in December 1776, when Washington needed reinforcements to attack the Hessians at Trenton, shows Gates in another light. Gates had been ordered south with several regiments to join Washington, who was planning to include him as the commander of his right wing. Gates, however, sent an aide to Washington with a letter that begged off the duty on the grounds of an illness that—so it would seem—could be cured only by his going away for a rest in Philadelphia. Instead he appears to have followed Congress to Baltimore, where it had fled in fear of Howe's advancing army, and there he was miraculously cured, after pointing out his capabilities for command of the northern army, where he had recently been serving as a subordinate commander.

---

*Burgoyne had supposedly bought off both generals by firing silver balls into Fort Ticonderoga which St. Clair sent to Schuyler as payment for their joint treason!

Lest Gates be painted with the same kind of brush that later blackened Arnold, it should be remembered that he had qualities that round out a more favorable portrait. His biographer, Samuel White Patterson, found that "intellectually, Horatio Gates was easily abreast of his fellow officers and the superior of most of them." Allan Nevins noted that "the Gates who emerges from these vivacious pages [Patterson's *Horatio Gates*] is a singularly attractive figure—warm-hearted, generous, magnanimous even; a faithful husband, a devoted father, a loyal friend, an earnest citizen of his adopted country, a zealous democrat." At age fifty, when he took command before Saratoga, he must have appeared capable: "As Charles Willson Peale portrayed him [Independence Hall, Philadelphia], he had a youthful appearance, though his hair was graying and rather thin above his long, well-modeled face. His shoulders were a bit stooped. His aquiline nose was set between an engaging pair of eyes, clear and penetrating at times, but generally kindly. . . . He appears to have been slightly above medium height, his whole body well proportioned" (Patterson, *Horatio Gates*).

At the time that Gates took over the northern army on 19 July its strength was about 4,500. It was encamped on the west side of the Hudson, where the river is joined by the Mohawk. Arnold was with Gates, as was Major General Benjamin Lincoln, who had arrived with Arnold on 24 July. Lincoln was sent to Vermont with about 500 militia to raise a force to threaten Burgoyne's communications with Canada.

BY THE TIME GATES ARRIVED AT THE CAMP at the mouth of the Mohawk, Burgoyne's troubles, which had begun with his three weeks in the wilderness, had been multiplying. His thrown-together supply transport could not be depended on for the indefinite shuttling of supplies over miles of wilderness roads, and shortages were already being felt. Meanwhile a letter from Howe on 17 July had made it clear that he would soon be going all-out in his campaign against Philadelphia, and so would certainly not be coming up the Hudson. Still, Burgoyne's orders were to proceed to Albany, and he had no intention of failing to carry out those orders.

There were other concerns. Burgoyne had already listened to Riedesel's plea for an expedition to sweep the country for horses for his dismounted dragoons. Now, at Fort Edward, Riedesel reinforced his proposal with detailed plans for the expedition, which would entail much more than mere horse hunting. The orders told the commander of the raid—for in truth that was what the plan really called for—that his mission was "to try the affections of the people, to disconcert the councils of the enemy, to mount Riedesel's dragoons, to compleat Peter's corps [of Tories] and to obtain large supplies of cattle, horses, and carriages." In addition, it was specified that the commander could take hostages for the delivery of the above and further take prisoner "all persons acting in committees, or any officers acting under the directions of Congress, whether civil or military."

The commander designated for the raid was the most unlikely choice imaginable, especially in the light of trying to win "the affections of the people." The German officer, Lieutenant Colonel Baum, couldn't speak one word of English. His mission included sweeping a sizable area extending as far east as the Connecticut River and bounded by Manchester on the north and Bennington on the south. Baum's force consisted of 170 of the dismounted dragoons, 100 German jägers and grenadiers, Hessian artillerymen with two three-pounders, and 300 Tories, Canadians, and Indians. The only British contingent was Captain Fraser's company of 50 light infantry. Overweighted with officers, musicians, and batmen, the force totaled about 800.

The planning for the raid was haphazard at best. The scope of the mission was out of all reason when one considers the vast area to be covered and the lack of intelligence regarding the potential of the enemy within it. Moreover, the indispensable characteristic of a raiding force—its mobility—seems to have been completely ignored. When one envisions the Brunswick dragoons stumbling along rutted roads and over stony New England fields to the accompaniment of clattering broadswords and a German band, the whole affair would have seemed comic opera, were it not for its bloody outcome.

The forces that would bring the foray to its end were already gathering. In response to a call for help from badly strapped Vermont, the New Hampshire General Court (the state legislature) had called on John Stark of Bunker Hill and Trenton fame to raise a brigade of militia which he would command. Stark had resigned his commission in disgust after being passed over for brigadier general by Congress in 1777 and retired to his New Hampshire farm. He answered the call. "Yes, he would take command of the proposed new brigade, but on one condition; it was to be a New Hampshire brigade pure and simple, independent of the Congress and the Continental Army, accountable only to the General Court of the state" (Ward, *The War of the Revolution*).

Within a week after his commissioning on 17 July, Stark had raised almost 1,500 men. By the thirtieth he had organized a brigade—no uniforms, and armed only with family firearms—to march to Manchester for a rendezvous with Colonel Seth Warner's Vermonters, who had obeyed Warner's final order at Hubbardton to "scatter and meet me at Manchester." After a week's interlude in which he disobeyed an order from Schuyler, relayed through General Lincoln, to join his forces, Stark moved his brigade to Bennington, where Colonel Gregg and a few militia were guarding a supply depot important to the Americans.

In the meantime, Burgoyne had dispatched Baum from Fort Miller on 11 August with a last-minute change in objective from Manchester to Bennington. Burgoyne had put stock in a Tory officer's report that the Bennington depot was not only stocked with supplies and livestock, but guarded by no more than 300 or 400 raw militia. As Hoffman Nickerson notes: "To Burgoyne such a windfall would be a godsend. Could Baum return bringing with him any considerable stock of provisions, Burgoyne saw himself in Albany at once" (*The Turning Point of the Revolution*).

As Baum marched south, his Indians were causing no end of trouble. They had run amuck over the countryside, slaughtering cattle and destroying farm property to such a degree that the frightened farmers had fled with horses and cattle, negating Baum's mission to round them up. When Stark heard of these depredations, he sent Colonel Gregg with 200 men to stop the Indians. Baum's advance guard encountered Gregg's men at Sancoick's Mill on 14 August. After firing a volley, Gregg's men withdrew, destroying a bridge to delay Baum's pursuit.

Stark sent an order to Seth Warner at Manchester to join him, then moved his brigade to a position about four miles northwest of Bennington. Meanwhile, Baum was advancing up the Walloomsac River valley, after sending a message to Burgoyne reporting that Bennington was guarded by 1,800 militia, not 400. On the night of 14–15 August Baum had his men building breastworks on a round-topped hill west of the river. There, in the so-called dragoon redoubt, he posted some 200 men, including half of Captain Fraser's "marksmen," and one three-pounder. On the enemy (east) side of the river he stationed 150 Tories, who threw up hasty breastworks. Some Canadians and Tories occupied two log cabins on either side of the crossing. The other half of Fraser's company and another 50 Germans, with the second three-pounder, were posted west of the crossing. To their rear, and southwest of the dragoon redoubt, were stationed another 50 German infantry and a few Tories, their mission to protect the rear. The Indians' camp, minus some scouts and pickets, was set up about a quarter mile west of the dragoon redoubt. In Christopher Ward's summation: "Having thus scattered his men as effectively as possible all over the landscape—some of the little detachments

more than a half-mile from the others—Baum awaited Stark's move."
He also sent a second message to Burgoyne asking for reinforcements.

Burgoyne passed the request on to Riedesel, asking him to send Lieutenant Colonel Breymann with most of his advance corps to Baum. By 8:00 A.M. of August 15 Breymann was on his way with 642 men and two six-pounders, but he was soon slowed down by heavy rains which quickly turned the roads into muddy wallows. The combination of rain, mud, and rigid German march formations allowed Breymann to complete only eight miles by nightfall, seventeen miles short of Baum's location.

Because of the heavy rains, the American move did not begin until noon on 16 August. Two bodies of Stark's shirt-sleeved farmers were launched in an uncoordinated movement against deliberately prepared defensive positions which had no means of mutual support, to be followed by a central frontal attack by Stark's main body. With 200 New Hampshiremen, Colonel Moses Nichols was sent to make the four-mile northern circuit around the mountain to the northeast of the dragoon redoubt and attack from the north. Colonel Samuel Herrick with 300 Bennington militia and Vermont Rangers was dispatched to make a similar envelopment from the south. A small initial frontal attack was to be made by Colonels David Hobart and Thomas Stickney with 200 men against the enemy positions south of the crossing while a diversionary demonstration by 100 men was being made against Baum's main position. The central, main attack would be made by Stark with some 1,200 men, to jump off at the sounds of musketry from Nichols's and Herrick's attacks.

Incredibly, the whole American operation ticked away with clocklike precision. From his post in the dragoon redoubt, Baum had an excellent field of view that led him to draw two erroneous conclusions from his observations. He mistook the movements of armed parties leaving Stark's camps for the beginnings of a general retreat. Later, when he and his men observed small bodies of men in civilian clothes, albeit bearing muskets or fowling pieces, approaching his rear and flank, he took them for Tories coming to join him or seeking refuge within his fieldworks. The German commander not only allowed Nichols's and Herrick's men to slip into attack positions, but he pulled in some outposts so as not to drive off the approaching "friends." By 3:00 P.M. Nichols's men opened fire, with Herrick's attack getting off at about the same time. Hobart and Stickney then went forward with a neat little double envelopment of their own against the Tory redoubt, and John Stark mounted his horse to lead the main attack and—no account of the Battle of Bennington would be complete without it—made his famous cry, "We'll beat them before night, or Molly Stark will be a widow."

In no time the Tory redoubt was overrun. When its defenders had fled across the river, the Canadians and Indians swiftly departed. Only the dragoons and Fraser's men held out stubbornly in the dragoon redoubt. A fierce firefight lasting for two hours ensued, which the battle-wise Stark later called "the hottest I ever saw in my life." Just as the ammunition in the defenders' pouches began to run out, the ammunition wagon caught fire and the last reserves blew up. Baum's dragoons drew their great swords and started to slash their way through their attackers. The Germans were actually hacking their way out to the road—the Americans had no bayonets to oppose them—when Baum fell mortally wounded. The fight went out of the dragoons, and they surrendered en masse. It was nearly 5:00 P.M., and what could be called the First Battle of Bennington was over.

MEANWHILE, HEINRICH BREYMANN'S column, advancing from Sancoick's Mill at about 4:30 P.M., was about to bring on the second battle. In spite of the fatigue that beset his troops after their tiring day's march, Breymann had his chance to turn defeat into victory because Stark's forces were scattered all over the countryside chasing fugitives, looting, and rounding up prisoners. Breymann advanced stolidly, beating off skirmishers who fired from the hillsides at his main column. What saved Stark was Warner's arrival with his 300 men. Stark managed to rally a good number of his men, then he and Warner joined forces to face Breymann's oncoming attack. The German first tried to outflank the American right, but was outflanked in turn by some 150 of Warner's men. The rest of Warner's command extended a line with Stark's men, and a new and equally hot fight began, lasting until daylight began to fail. By then Breymann's ammunition, like Baum's, had begun to run low, and the German ordered a retreat. The Americans continued to close in, and retreat turned into rout. Breymann's drums beat out the demand for a parley, a signal not comprehensible to raw American militia, who continued firing. Increasing numbers of Germans threw down their muskets, while others just ran. Wounded in the leg and with five bullet holes in his coat, Breymann rallied a rear guard and led it personally to cover the retreat of his main body. He got away with about two-thirds of his force after Stark had to call off the pursuit because of nightfall. Stark summed it up: "Had day lasted an hour longer, we should have taken the whole body of them."

The German and Tory losses for the day's fighting came to 207 killed and wounded and some 700 captured; of Baum's dragoons, only nine got back to base. The material losses were also severe: hundreds of muskets and jäger rifles, four ammunition wagons, 250 swords, and four cannon. The Americans claimed to have suffered only 30 killed and 40 wounded out of forces totaling about 2,000.

Even the loss of nearly 1,000 men, however, pales in comparison to Burgoyne's failure to capture the critical supplies he had so counted on, as well as the impact on British spirits and capabilities. The most immediate need now was to feed the army. Lieutenant Hadden's journal quotes from a general order in which Burgoyne explained the need and his plans to meet it. Baum's expedition had failed to return with the anticipated food stocks "as might have enabled the Army to proceed without waiting the arrival of the Magazines. That attempt having failed of success thro. the chances of War, the Troops must necessarily halt some days, for bringing forward the Transport of Provisions." Accordingly, Burgoyne's army encamped at Fort Miller, about four miles above Saratoga. While he waited to build up his supplies, his woes accumulated. Two factors combined to disaffect his Indian allies. After the unfortunate Jane Mc-Crae incident, Burgoyne had been forced to oversee and restrict the movements of his Indians to a much greater degree. Being deprived of their operational independence didn't sit well with them. The news of Bennington, brought firsthand by the braves who had fled the field, caused them to decide to head for home, and in a few days Burgoyne's Indian allies dwindled from over 400 to fewer than 80.

Burgoyne was also disenchanted with the Tories. The illusion that they were only waiting for a chance to fight against the rebels had been shattered. In a letter to Germain after Bennington, Fonblanque quoted Burgoyne as saying, "I have about 400 [Tories] (but not half of them armed) who may be depended upon. The rest are trimmers merely actuated by [self] interest."

The final blow to Burgoyne's plans was struck on 23 August, a week after Bennington, when St. Leger made his unseemly departure from Fort Stanwix along with some 350 regulars, 300 good Tory soldiers, and hundreds of Indians, a force that would have made up most of Burgoyne's recent losses. Now all of that was gone, along with any hope of bringing in Tryon County and adjacent regions to the British cause.

WHILE BURGOYNE WAS COUNTING HIS TROUBLES, Horatio Gates was receiving reinforcements. By the first week of September Arnold had brought in 1,200 men, after leaving a garrison of 700 at Fort Stanwix. In the same week another reinforcement, dispatched by Washington before Brandywine, reported to Gates. Although relatively small in numbers—331 plus 36 on the sick list—it was a mighty addition: Colonel Daniel Morgan's corps of Virginia, Pennsylvania, and Maryland riflemen. Gates not only welcomed Morgan but also decided to strengthen the corps by placing under Morgan's command Major Henry Dearborn, the veteran of Bunker Hill and Quebec, with 250 hand-picked light infantry armed with muskets and bayonets. Gates's army was thus vitalized with an elite corps of light infantry.

By 9 September Gates's strength had reached 7,000 rank and file, and he was looking for better ground on which to oppose Burgoyne's advance. The open farmland around the mouth of the Mohawk was terrain more suitable for Burgoyne's regulars than an American army heavy in militia and reinforced with riflemen—light infantry who could do their best fighting in woods and undergrowth. Gates also wanted fortifiable terrain, and so by 12 September he moved the army to an area called Bemis Heights, where Arnold and the Polish engineer Kosciuszko had marked out the lines. The position was an ideal one for defense. A plateau with steep bluffs rising some 200 to 300 feet above the Hudson, Bemis Heights dominated the narrow defile of the river on its west side, and with the heavily wooded terrain surrounding the bluffs, blocked the way to Albany. The dense forests were broken only by a few clearings and deep ravines formed by streams flowing into the Hudson. The greatest of these obstacles were Mill Creek and the Great Ravine to the north.

South of Mill Creek and its southernmost tributary were the lines of the American entrenchments. The overall plot of the fieldworks resembled a three-sided square with the rear end open. When completed, the works consisted of trenches and breastworks of logs and earth running for about three-quarters of a mile along each side of the open square, with an artillery redoubt centered in each of the three sides. At the northeast angle Farmer Neilson's barn had been fortified and was dubbed Fort Neilson. The overall defensive position had one drawback. Not far from its western side was a greater height which, if occupied by the enemy, could command the American position. That height had not yet been occupied by any of Gates's units before the British advance on 19 September. It was to draw the keen attention of Generals Burgoyne and Fraser later in their scheme of maneuver.

IN SPITE OF LEARNING THAT HOWE HAD SAILED from New York for Philadelphia, Burgoyne had not wavered from his objective of taking Albany as soon as he had been provisioned and supplied for the march. And march he did, following his decision to cross the Hudson River and move down its west side. Albany was on the west side of the river; moreover, the farther he continued down the east side, the more difficult a crossing would be. So on 13 September, resupplied and strengthened by the arrival of 300 regulars and more artillery, Burgoyne started crossing the Hudson on a bridge of boats. The transit was completed on the fourteenth, and the boat bridge was dismantled on the following day. By 17 September he had marched southward and encamped around Sword's Farm, north of Gates's position. Although separated from his enemy by only about four miles, Burgoyne's intelligence was so poor that he was still not sure of Gates's dispositions. His failure to be kept informed can be laid to the scarcity of Indian scouts, whose numbers had declined to fifty. Hence Burgoyne's first real knowledge of an American reconnaissance of *his* force came when an American patrol surprised a British foraging party in the act of digging potatoes on an abandoned farm. The patrol killed and wounded several British soldiers and camp followers and captured twenty prisoners. The incident jolted Burgoyne into pushing his limited intelligence means, and soon he became certain of Gates's positions and had some idea of his enemy's strength.

HORATIO GATES'S FORCES WERE DEPLOYED about a center with two wings. The center, under Brigadier General Ebenezer Learned, was made up of Learned's own brigade of Continentals plus Colonel Livingston's New York regiment and the Massachusetts Continental regiments of Colonels Bailey, Jackson, and Wesson. The right wing, heavy in artillery, was composed of Continentals under Brigadier Generals Glover and Patterson, together with those of Colonel Nixon. This wing's positions dominated the ground sloping down to the river; it remained under Gates's own command.

The left wing, under Major General Benedict Arnold, included the New Hampshire Continental regiments of Colonels Cilley, Hale, and Scammel. Next there were New Yorkers under Colonels Van Cortlandt

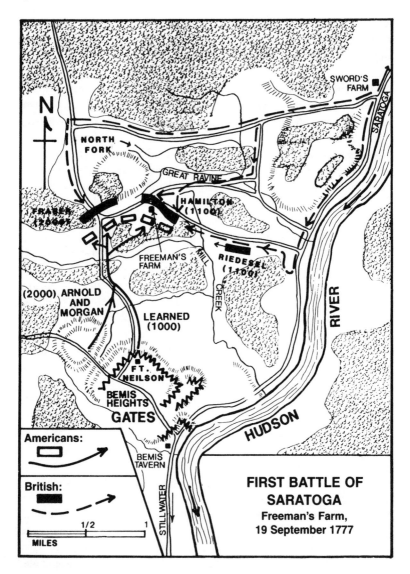

FIRST BATTLE OF
SARATOGA
Freeman's Farm,
19 September 1777

and Livingston, then Connecticut militia under Colonels Lattimer and
Cook. Last, but certainly not least, was Colonel Daniel Morgan's corps
of riflemen and Major Henry Dearborn's light infantry.

His organization for combat established and his troops deployed accordingly, Gates was content to await Burgoyne's next move. His intel-

ligence was incomparably better than Burgoyne's, so much so that the major movements of British forces were quickly known to him. In Samuel W. Patterson's account, "Wisdom favored General Gates' decision to bide his time. He was strongly entrenched. His troops were disposed to advantage—their morale never better. He kept a watchful eye and a listening ear at his headquarters . . . at the foot of a hill near the battlefield" (*Horatio Gates*). In this case, "near" was about two miles from the upcoming battle.

On Thursday, 18 September, Burgoyne had completed his plans for the next day's operation. Whether as a reconnaissance in force or as a three-pronged attack, Burgoyne planned and executed an advance upon his enemy's position with almost three quarters of his effective strength (4,200 out of 6,000) deployed in three columns.

At both the battles of Freeman's Farm (19 September) and Bemis Heights (7 October), the major terrain feature was an extensive forest with only a few small openings that had been cleared for active or abandoned farms. The thick woods precluded European-type maneuvering in close order, or the effective use of artillery. They favored the skirmishing in which riflemen and light infantry were most effective. Of equal importance, the vast extent of the woods and the scarcity of roads made control and coordination of large troop movements next to impossible. Despite this, Burgoyne's attack on 19 September was made in three widely separated columns, in terrain that ruled against timely mutual support.

The British order of battle was based upon a center and two wings. The left wing was commanded by Riedesel, who was accompanied by General Phillips. The wing's strength came to 1,100, composed mainly of the three Brunswick infantry regiments, followed by Captain Pausch's six six-pounders and two three-pounders of the Hesse-Hanau artillery. Six companies of the British 47th guarded the bateaux with the army's stores. Riedesel's mission was to move south along the river road and attack the American right.

The center force, 1,100 men under Hamilton, was made up of all the battalion companies of the 9th, 20th, 21st, and 62nd British regiments. Their artillery support, under Captain Jones, included three six-pounders and three three-pounders. Burgoyne chose to accompany this force, which was to make a frontal attack in the center.

The right wing, under General Fraser, had the mission of enveloping the American left by seizing the high ground to the west of the fort. From there he could dominate the American fortifications with his artillery while it supported his assault against them. If successful, he could drive the Americans back against the river and envelop their rear. Fraser had a brigade of artillery for the job: four six-pounders and four three-pounders. The infantry of his wing included the light infantry companies of ten British regiments, plus the grenadier companies of the same ten regiments. In addition Fraser had the battalion companies of the British 24th, as well as Lieutenant Colonel Breymann's Brunswick riflemen. Because Fraser commanded the advance corps, his wing also included 50 Indians, about 150 Tories, 80 Canadians, and 50 British marksmen.

THE EARLY MORNING OF THE NINETEENTH WAS cool and foggy, but by 11:00 A.M. the sun had broken through and it had become a fine September day. At about the same time the booming of a signal gun started the columns in motion. Riedesel's wing actually marched in two parallel columns: the pioneers, the baggage train, and some infantry used the road along the river, while the other column marched through the wide meadows between the road and the hills. Both columns had to move in fits and starts because the road column was frequently halted by destroyed bridges. When that happened, the dark-blue columns would dress their ranks before being allowed to rest in the wet grass. The pioneers had to be protected in their work, however, so grunting detachments moved up the hillsides until the high ground was secured. By about 1:00 P.M. the heads of Riedesel's columns had slowly advanced southward until they were at a point about a mile and a half to the east of Freeman's Farm.

While Riedesel's Brunswickers were crawling southward, Fraser was making good time marching to the west. His scarlet column swung out on the road from Sword's Farm, heading due west until it had passed the head of the Great Ravine, continuing on for another mile and a half until it reached a T-junction with the road running south toward Bemis Heights. Fraser made a column left at the junction, marched south, then halted on some high ground about a half mile west of Freeman's Farm. There he waited, apparently for action in the center or word from Burgoyne.

Hamilton's column in the center followed in the tracks of Fraser's column for a little over a mile, then moved left—southward—on a road that eventually turned westward to cross the bottom of the Great Ravine over a bridge that was, miraculously, still intact. Burgoyne, since he was with Hamilton and in overall command, halted the force at noon on the other side of the ravine to give Fraser time to get into position.

THE MOVEMENTS OF THE SCARLET COLUMNS snaking through the woods and over the rough roads were observed by the American scouts and patrols throughout the morning. All this was reported to Gates, who continued to sit tight: not a battle order was forthcoming.

This inertia was unbearable to the impetuous Arnold, who, perhaps more keenly aware than anyone of the impending danger, pleaded with Gates to take action, if not on all fronts then at least against the threat to the army's left flank or left front. His arguments for action were not only forceful but logical. If Burgoyne was allowed to get a force with artillery on the height to the west of the American position, he could attack after an artillery preparation, and if he were successful in penetrating the defensive lines, he could drive the defenders into the Hudson. On the other hand, if Burgoyne were to be attacked *now*, the battle would be carried to him where, entangled in the woods, his troops could not maneuver, nor would his artillery be effective. There the Americans, with superior firepower, would be at their best. According to Charles B. Todd, "Arnold begged, stormed, and entreated, but still he could get no orders. At length Gates consented to let Dearborn's infantry and Morgan's riflemen go in" (*The Real Benedict Arnold*). It seems that Gates also agreed to let Arnold support Morgan with other units of his wing if the situation called for it.

ONCE IN POSITION, FRASER SENT A DETACHMENT of Tories, Canadians, and Indians to set up outposts in the area just south of Freeman's Farm. The detachment seems to have been haphazardly commanded. About 12:30 P.M., after the mixed force—or "picket"—arrived at Freeman's cabin, the men were lying or strolling about in the open. A few minutes later the far edge of the woods suddenly was ablaze with the fire of Morgan's rifles. In the crash of that volley every officer was struck down by a rifle bullet, as were many of the men around them. Those left standing took off in panic.

Morgan's riflemen, after advancing to the attack in disciplined silence, could be restrained no longer. They broke away from their firing line in a mad rush to pursue and slaughter the survivors. Hearing the firing and seeing the fleeing men pass his position, the Tory Major Forbes led his own detachment forward in an organized counterattack, and Morgan's men, caught off guard with their units dispersed, were taken aback in their turn and driven helter-skelter to the rear. Following in his accustomed place behind the center of his line, Morgan was dumbfounded as his men fled past him. His surprise turned to instant rage as his notorious temper overcame him. Soon he cooled down and began to rally his men and reform a fighting line at the south end of the clearing.

Morgan had Dearborn extend the line to the left (westward), which, as Morgan quickly realized, was not far enough to cover the British front opposing it. The problem was soon solved, however, when the resourceful Arnold hurried up units to Morgan's support. The New Hampshire Continentals of Cilley's and Scammel's regiments dashed up into line to the left of Morgan's men. This reinforcement wasted no time in attacking the British right in an attempt to outflank it but was repulsed by "a tremendous fire." As Major Henry Dearborn recorded the action in his journal: "I ran to his [Major Cilley's] assistance with the Light Infantry, But he was Obliged to Retreet Before I Came up.—Colonel Scammel's and Hale's Regiments then Came to our Assistance it was now about 2 O'clock P.M. when a very Heavy fire Commenced on both sides." The Battle of Freeman's Farm was on.

Burgoyne and Hamilton had already arrived at the clearing (about 350 yards long from west to east, some twenty acres in all) at Freeman's, and Hamilton positioned his artillery in the center of the edge of the woods on the north side. He deployed his infantry regiments in line beside and behind the guns.

When Arnold sized up the situation, he saw that a wide gap still existed between Fraser's force and Burgoyne's center at Freeman's Farm. Quickly he decided to attack the British center and then, if he could muster enough combat power, separate the two enemy forces and smash each in turn. He started forming his attack line as fast as he could rush up his regiments.

Arnold's regiments then went forward to strike Hamilton's center and left flank. Now began the fiercest fighting of the battle, lasting for about four hours. An American penetration of Hamilton's position created a gap in the British line which forced the individual units to fight, at times, in three directions—in front and to each flank. Fraser sent eight British companies, reinforced by riflemen, to support Hamilton; it was Fraser's only move to intervene in the main battle raging off to his left.

The American assaults failed to break through and around Hamilton's right, and the battle became an exchange of frontal attacks and counterattacks which surged back and forth, south to north, north to south, across the clearing of Freeman's Farm. The fire on both sides was so continuous and intense that British officers who had seen the greatest battles of the Seven Years' War declared that they had never experienced so hot a fire.

Although the American rifle and musket fire was superior—riflemen climbed into trees and picked off British officers and artillerymen throughout the action—their attacks were beaten back by British bayonets. When the British counterattacked, they in turn were beaten back by the fierce fire of the Americans. The British artillery pieces were taken and retaken. The American infantry's fire drove the British back into the woods behind their guns, but the Americans could not turn the captured cannon on their enemy because the gunners carried their linstocks away when they fled. When General Phillips, the veteran artillerist, rode up after leaving Riedesel's wing, he found only one artillery officer alive and unwounded, while thirty-six out of forty-eight—75 percent—of the enlisted artillerymen were casualties. Phillips sent for artillery replacements from Riedesel, who responded at once with four of Captain Pausch's guns.

Phillips's actions were not confined to the artillery. The British 62nd Regiment in the center was taking punishment far greater than the other three regiments of Burgoyne's center. When it was thrown at the Americans in a bayonet attack, it drove deep beyond supporting distance and lost twenty-five men as prisoners. Phillips then led a supporting attack in person, which freed the 62nd and allowed it to rally and reform. Before the day was over, the 62nd suffered losses of 83 percent. The other regiments of the center took casualties of 44 percent.

On the American side, Arnold was getting desperate. His whole command had been committed to the battle, yet he had not been able to deliver the decisive blow that would break through between the British center and right wing. He called for reinforcements. None came in time to decide the action in Arnold's favor. Too late in the day Gates finally released Learned's brigade. Instead of supporting Arnold at Freeman's Farm where he was so urgently needed, however, Learned made a half-hearted attack on Fraser's wing and was driven off.

During the critical period before Learned had been sent into battle, another general was acting to intervene decisively. Riedesel, having heard the sounds of continuous firing and sensing Hamilton's perilous situation, decided to risk the loss of the vital supply train and bateaux at the river by taking part of his wing to the aid of Burgoyne's center. He led off with two companies of the Regiment Rhetz, followed by the entire Regiment Riedesel and Captain Pausch with two six-pounders. Just as he had done so brilliantly at Hubbardton, the fat German general plunged forward to save the day for the British. He urged the two Rhetz companies forward on a trail through the forest for the mile and a half between him and Freeman's Farm, until he arrived at the top of a hill where he could see the clearing. What he saw made him all the more eager to get into action. The long, solid line of three British regiments had been reduced to small groups "surrounded by heaps of dead and wounded," and yet the unwounded were still firing. Riedesel saw that every minute counted, and he attacked with his leading companies without waiting for his own regiment to come up. With his men shouting and drums beating, he fell on the American right flank that had rested on the North Branch of the Great Ravine.

Riedesel's piecemeal attack caught the Americans by surprise and drove them back into the woods. The attack was soon supported by Captain Pausch's two guns, which had been manhandled through the forest and up the slopes until they could be gotten into firing position. German jägers, aided by British soldiers and even officers, helped man the drag-ropes to get the guns up. Pausch opened fire with grapeshot, which quickly decided things in that quarter. Regiment Riedesel came panting up and fired its first volley. Burgoyne then launched the whole force—Germans, British, whatever was available—in a last desperate attack. The Americans resisted at first, then began withdrawing. It was growing dark, and American hopes of smashing the British faded with the end of the day.

The British still held the field—but at what cost! The losses of the infantry regiments of the center and their supporting artillery have already been mentioned. The overall loss to Burgoyne's army was 600 killed, wounded, or prisoners. Of the 600, 350 came from the three British regiments in the center. American losses, out of forces outnumbering the British by two to one, were 65 killed, 218 wounded, and 36 missing.

Burgoyne paid the full penalty for dispersing his combat power in difficult terrain. Only Riedesel's willingness to take a calculated risk saved Burgoyne's center from destruction. In contrast, Fraser's refusal to send substantial aid to Hamilton at a critical time remains a mystery. On the American side, Gates's indecisiveness lost the opportunity to smash his enemy on this first day of battle. As things add up, Arnold deserves credit not only for bringing on the battle but for leadership in directing the employment of American forces throughout the fighting.

If Burgoyne had acted to continue the attack on the exhausted Americans the next day, 20 September, things may well have gone his way. The American units were in dire need of reorganization. Actually Burgoyne wanted to go ahead the next day, but Fraser was of a different mind. He insisted that his light infantry and grenadiers needed a day's rest before continuing an attack. In view of the relative inactivity of his wing when compared with the terrific punishment taken by the regiments of the center, it seems a strange argument. Yet Burgoyne listened, then finally agreed to hold up operations. On the twenty-first, Burgoyne's army was ready to fall in and advance to the attack, but its commander was busily going over a dispatch just received from Sir Henry Clinton, commanding in New York. The letter, dated 12 September, informed Burgoyne that Clinton was going to "make a push" northward against the American forts along the river. Gates might therefore be forced to weaken his forces on Bemis Heights in order to send a significant number southward, thus enabling Burgoyne to advance again at the right time.

So Burgoyne called off the attack and ordered his units to dig in along the same general lines they had occupied, while awaiting the results of Clinton's operations. It was a fatal decision, because in so doing Burgoyne gave up his last chance at maneuvering against his enemy or retreating back to Ticonderoga. He was pinned down, with his supplies running out and his army weakened by desertions and sickness.

WHEN SIR WILLIAM HOWE SAILED FROM New York on 23 July he had left Sir Henry Clinton with 7,000 men—4,000 regulars and 3,000 Tories—to defend the main British base in the colonies. Clinton had not received orders from Howe to move to support Burgoyne, only such vague council as, "If you can make any *diversion* in favor of General Burgoyne's approaching Albany, I need not point out the utility of such a measure" (italics mine).

For at least six weeks after Howe's departure, Sir Henry was so concerned that "Mr. Washington" and others might move against New York that he apparently gave no thought to Howe's suggestion. However, when he wrote the 12 September dispatch received by Burgoyne on the twenty-first, he was expecting reinforcements from England.

Clinton did receive reinforcements on 24 September, bringing his force of regulars up to a strength of nearly 7,000. He now felt confident enough to lead an operation northward, despite the fact that he had not yet received a reply from Burgoyne. On 3 October he moved up the Hudson with 3,000 men organized in three divisions. His twin objectives were Fort Clinton and Fort Montgomery, both on the west side of the river.

On 5 October he made a deceptive move against Major General Israel Putnam which took Putnam right out of the operational area. He landed 1,000 men at Verplanck's Point, leading Putnam to believe that his force

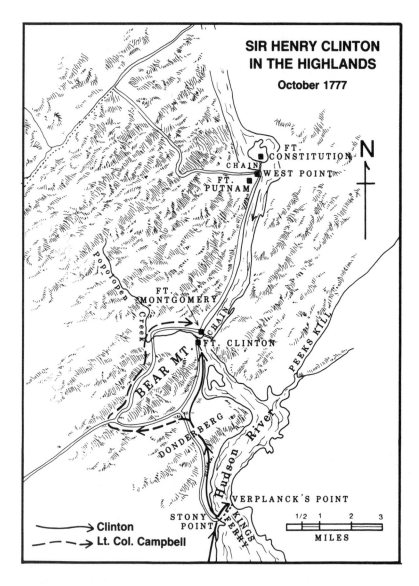

**SIR HENRY CLINTON
IN THE HIGHLANDS**

October 1777

FT.
CONSTITUTION

CHAIN

WEST POINT

FT.
PUTNAM

N

FT.
MONTGOMERY

Popotopen Creek

CHAIN

FT. CLINTON

BEAR MT.

PEEKS KILL

DONDERBERG

Hudson River

VERPLANCK'S POINT

STONY
POINT

KINGS FERRY

1/2   1   2   3

MILES

→ Clinton

— — → Lt. Col. Campbell

of 1,500 men was the objective of Clinton's army. Putnam obligingly took
to the hills, calling for reinforcements. Clinton was then free to move
unhindered against the two forts.

Now began what could be called the "campaign of the Clintons." Sir
Henry was opposed by an American Clinton, Major General George

Clinton, who was also governor of New York. The governor had a brother, Brigadier General James Clinton. George commanded Fort Montgomery; James commanded Fort Clinton.

Sir Henry left 1,000 men at Verplanck's Point and with the remaining 2,000 moved up the west side of the Hudson, sending 900 men under Lieutenant Colonel Campbell against Fort Montgomery, while Sir Henry himself led the remainder to Fort Clinton. The British successfully stormed both forts, though suffering a combined loss of over 300 killed and wounded. The 600 Americans in the two forts took an even heavier proportion of losses: 250 killed, wounded, or missing.

On the next day, 7 October, the British broke the boom-and-chain barrier that blocked the Hudson from Fort Montgomery to the east bank. On the same day they captured Fort Constitution. Sir Henry then sent an expedition under General Vaughan, with 1,700 and a flotilla, to "feel his way to General Burgoyne." On 16 October Vaughan burned Esopus (now Kingston), the New York capital, but never came closer than forty-five miles to Albany. On 22 October he was ordered to withdraw down the Hudson. Meanwhile, Sir Henry sat down on 8 October at Fort Montgomery, and wrote Burgoyne: "*Nous y voici* and nothing now between us and Gates; I sincerely hope this little success of ours may facilitate your operations. In answer to your letter of 28 September [carried by] Captain Campbell, I shall only say I cannot order you or even advise you for reasons obvious.* I heartily wish you success."

Sir Henry's note was carried by Daniel Taylor, who carried the message encased in a silver bullet. He was captured and was observed to have swallowed something. George Clinton, whose men had grabbed Taylor, ordered a strong emetic administered which made the unfortunate "spy" give up the bullet. The bullet was opened and found to contain Sir Henry's message. At this stage of the game, the mishap was just a sample of the bad luck that was running Burgoyne's way.

Clinton had gone as far as he dared go in what he had considered, from start to finish, a diversion. As it happened, his journey up the Hudson did cause Gates no end of worry, but never to the point where he would move even a detachment to oppose Clinton's operation. On the British side, the northward thrust had raised Burgoyne's hopes, all for nothing, for on the day before Sir Henry's bullet message was written, Burgoyne was already fighting his last battle at Saratoga.

---

*Meaning that only Sir William Howe, as theater commander, could give orders to Burgoyne.

DURING LATE SEPTEMBER GATES'S FORTUNES CONTINUED to rise, even while Burgoyne's were continuing to run out. The murder and scalping of Jane McCrae on July 27 had fed fuel to the fires of rebel passion that were flaming throughout the countryside. That one event did more to arouse the Patriots and raise volunteers for Gates's army than all of the depredations of Tories and Indians in New York could possibly have caused. Volunteers were on the march in the form of newly raised militia, who continued to swarm into the camps on Bemis Heights and those of General Lincoln in Vermont. They came in their civilian clothes, each with the family musket or fowling piece—some in odd groups, some in companies, but all armed, and many with their own ammunition. By the end of September Lincoln had joined Gates at Bemis Heights, bringing his militia strength up to 4,300. At the end of the first week of October Gates's strength reached 11,000, of which 2,700 were Continentals, the rest militia.

Gates had no such luck in dealing with another problem—Benedict Arnold. Two more divergent personalities seldom clashed than these two did after Freeman's Farm. John R. Elting has observed that "the two men were utterly different personalities, but their quarrel undoubtedly had its beginning somewhere in Gates' enigmatic character. A man who could display the 'frowsy manners of an ill-bred boor' on relieving Schuyler . . . would not be likely to tolerate an aggressive, independent subordinate such as Arnold" (*The Battle of Saratoga*).

Arnold's righteous anger at Gates for refusing to support him at Freeman's Farm was followed by other incidents. First, Gates transferred Morgan and Dearborn from Arnold's to his own personal command. There was also the case of the "misassignment" of three New York militia regiments which Arnold had been assured would go to Poor's brigade in his division, but instead went to another.

The real rift between the two came when Gates's letter to Congress reporting on the battle of 19 September failed to mention Arnold or even Morgan or Dearborn. Always supersensitive to slights, Arnold was enraged. When Arnold protested, Gates's response was to bait the furious Arnold by expressing doubt that Arnold really held a commission in the Continental army. Gates also hinted that the command of the left wing— until then nominally Arnold's—was to be given to General Lincoln. Gates finally went even further. In a general order of 25 September, he appointed Lincoln to command the *right* wing while Gates assumed personal command of the left, leaving Arnold with no command at all.

Throughout the whole affair there had been "an exchange of foolish, quibbling letters" that had only served to build up rancor on both sides. In Isaac N. Arnold's words, "Gates was irritating, arrogant and vulgar; Arnold indiscreet, haughty and passionate" (*The Life of Benedict Arnold*). After the issuance of the order of 25 September, Arnold stayed in his erstwhile command post, a general without command or any other function, a latter-day Achilles sulking in his tent before Troy.

WHILE GATES WAS ALTERNATELY ORGANIZING HIS reinforcements and quarreling with Arnold, Burgoyne was throwing up entrenchments across his front from the Hudson to the high ground northwest of Freeman's Farm. A system of redoubts with extended trenches covered the army's two-and-a-half-mile front. The so-called great redoubt anchored the left (east) rear. A little over a half mile to its front, other entrenchments, outposts, were constructed near the river and south of the Great Ravine, protecting the stores and bateaux, as well as securing the army's left. Farther west, the Balcarres redoubt had been built just south of Freeman's Farm. Still farther west, the extreme right of the British line curved back around a low hill northwest of the Balcarres redoubt. There a U-shaped fortification called the Breymann redoubt, facing generally southwestward, secured the army's right. The gap between the two redoubts was covered only by some Canadians occupying two fortified cabins in a clearing.

On the American side there had been only one significant addition to Gates's fortifications. The high ground west of Fort Neilson, Burgoyne's main objective in his advance on 19 September, was entrenched and occupied. Thus a potential threat from the direction of that terrain had been eliminated.

WHEN BURGOYNE CALLED A COUNCIL OF WAR on 4 October, certain conditions needed no discussion, as they were by now common knowledge. The only food for some time had been flour and salt pork; only the day before, the commander had been forced to cut even those rations in half. Horses were dying for lack of forage. Desertions added to battle losses had reduced the army's effectives from 8,000 to 5,000. And to keep the general morale at low ebb, the Americans were giving Burgoyne's troops little time for rest. In Burgoyne's own record, "not a night passed without firing, and sometimes concerted attacks, at our advanced picquets . . . it was the plan of the enemy to harass the army by constant alarms and their superiority of number enabled them to attempt it without fatigue to themselves."

If Burgoyne had been discouraged by all this, he was not letting it show. He had a bold plan to lay before Phillips, Riedesel, and Fraser. He would leave 800 men to defend the army's boats and supplies, and with the rest of the army he would move to turn the American left and attack it in flank and rear. To the three generals the plan seemed more than bold: it was desperation, without assurance of success. Because of the dense woods and the enemy's impenetrable security, they had no adequate intelligence of the American positions. Moreover, to risk the army's last stores to destuction or capture by an American threat while Burgoyne's columns were entangled in the forest was unacceptable. Riedesel proposed as an alternative a retreat to their former positions at Fort Miller, where they could maintain a line of communication with Canada and at the same time be in position to act in conjunction with an advance by Clinton. Burgoyne rejected the idea of a retreat while they could still fight.

When Burgoyne reconvened the council he presented a new plan, this time for a large-scale reconnaissance in force. His plan resembled his advance of 19 September—moving in three columns—but this time he would employ fewer than half the army's rank and file: 1,500 regulars and some 600 auxiliaries. The main objective was that same magnet, the high ground to the American left, which would be "felt out" to determine whether a major attack could still be made from that direction. Apparently the thwarted British intelligence efforts had also failed to reveal that the Americans had by then occupied and fortified that high ground.

Burgoyne's intention was first to determine whether the Americans' left was still assailable, and if so to seize the high ground. Then he could launch a main attack, preceded by heavy artillery fires, and break through or around the American left. Conversely, if the reconnaissance revealed that a major attack was unfeasible, Burgoyne would order a withdrawal of the army northeastward to the Batten Kill.

The new plan was adopted, and on the morning of 7 October the columns were forming up. Although the scarlet coats of the British line were faded and torn, and the dark blues of the Brunswickers were decidedly worn, the overall turnout was soldierly. Musket barrels and bayonets reflected the bright sun of "a very pleasant morning" as ranks were dressed before wheeling into column. Sometime after 10:00 A.M. three

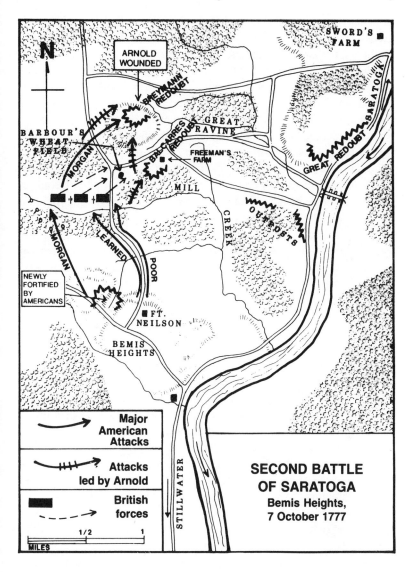

**SECOND BATTLE
OF SARATOGA**
Bemis Heights,
7 October 1777

Major
American
Attacks

Attacks
led by Arnold

British
forces

columns marched out of the Balcarres redoubt near Freeman's Farm, advancing three quarters of a mile to the southwest. The right column, led by Major Balcarres, was made up of the light infantry companies. The center column, commanded by Riedesel, contained picked detachments of Brunswickers as well as Breymann's jägers and the British 24th

Regiment. On the right of Riedesel's column marched Major Acland's grenadiers. The force was followed by ten artillery pieces: six six-pounders, two twelve-pounders, and two howitzers.

When the columns reached the edge of Barbour's wheatfield, they deployed into line on the gently sloping ground north of the main branch of Mill Creek. The infantry was then allowed to sit down in ranks, resting their muskets between their knees. The artillery went into positions which commanded the open ground in front of the infantry, and the gunners were at ease along with their infantry comrades. The line was about a thousand yards long, with excellent fields of fire to the front and both flanks resting on thick woods—ideal flank coverage under European battle conditions, but also ideal for the approach and open-order fighting so favorable to the Americans. While infantrymen and artillerymen rested, they watched foragers out to their front busily cutting wheat for the starving horses. The senior officers were also watching, their attention devoted to focusing field glasses in efforts to make out the distant American positions. The trees and distance prevented their seeing anything. So the British and Germans waited and rested.

THIS INACTIVITY WAS WHAT AMERICAN MAJOR James Wilkinson, Gates's aide-de-camp, observed when he was directed to check out the reports of outposts along Mill Creek. When Wilkinson reported the British situation, Gates was willing to listen to Morgan's recommendation that his riflemen and light infantry attack the British right (west) flank. Gates directed Morgan "to begin the game." He also saw the opportunity to catch his enemy on both flanks, and ordered Poor to coordinate his brigade's attack against the British left with Morgan's. The overall plan called for both forces to slip through the woods and fall upon both British flanks at the same time. Morgan started first, since he would have to make a wide turning movement through the thick woods to get into his attack position.

Poor's brigade, about 800 strong, consisted of the New Hampshire Continentals of Cilley, Hale, and Scammel, the militiamen of Livingston and Van Cortlandt, and Cook's and Lattimer's Connecticut militia. The brigade's numbers included many veterans, for whom the shorter march and quiet deployment were easy going. At 2:30 P.M. Poor attacked, attaining complete surprise. His men had to attack uphill in the open, but they swept up the slope without firing. Major Acland's grenadiers loosed off a hurried volley, which was followed by an artillery volley with grapeshot. Both British volleys swished over the heads of Poor's men, who came on without hesitating. Acland ordered his men to "fix bayonets and charge the damned rebels," but before they could move out, the astounded grenadiers were on the receiving end of an American volley. Poor's men had held their fire until its effects were murderous at short range. Swathes of redcoats were mowed down, among them Acland, with bullets through both legs. The whooping Americans, carried away with their success, were unstoppable. Infantrymen surrounded a twelve-pounder, whipped it around, and turned it on the fleeing British. Acland, lying helpless, was taken prisoner.

As Poor's attack went in, Morgan unleashed his riflemen on Major Balcarres's flank and rear. Morgan had made a wide sweep through the wood and had dealt first with Captain Fraser's Canadians and Indians, who had manned the outposts on the British right. The riflemen sent these auxiliaries packing in short order, then moved on to come upon Balcarres's right flank, which had deployed behind a fence. Morgan's attack, coming on with a suddenness that unnerved the British, delivered a crushing blow that was beautifully timed to strike in conjunction with Poor's assault. Major Balcarres was in the act of shifting light infantry companies to refuse his threatened flank when Dearborn came up in time to deliver a smashing volley at such close range that the British light infantry fell back, their formations shattered. The gallant Balcarres rallied enough of his men to deploy them along a second fence, but in a matter of minutes Morgan's and Dearborn's men were sweeping around both flanks and coming over the fence. The British infantry broke and fled in confused disarray back to the Balcarres redoubt, and the artillerymen joined the flight, abandoning their guns to the Americans.

Now it was Riedesel's turn. His stolid grenadiers and jägers were standing like the remains of a dam whose center still held even though its sides had been swept away by floodwaters. The unshaken little German general looked around him and saw that no British support was coming from flank or rear. Well, he'd had no orders to withdraw; he would hold his ground.*

To his immediate front Riedesel could see an American force advancing to the attack. When it came closer the German general saw that an American general on a tall brown horse was leading them, shouting and waving his sword to encourage them.

---

*When both the British right and left had been broken, Burgoyne had sent Sir Francis Clarke with orders for a general withdrawal back to entrenched lines, but Clarke was seriously wounded and captured before he could deliver the orders.

It was no other than Major General Benedict Arnold, late commander of the American left wing and now a fighting spirit very much on his own. He had suffered long enough, though certainly not in silence, and had been left in disgrace and alone, but now nothing could have kept him in camp. Here was a battle and no force commander on the field. He galloped off to find action that needed his direction. Gates sent Major Armstrong with an order for Arnold to return, but all that Armstrong ever saw of Arnold's whereabouts was a flurry of dust and the rear of a big brown horse.

Arnold galloped past cheering Connecticut regiments, then passed the flank columns of Learned's brigade. When he came to the head of the brigade, Arnold placed himself in the front of the foremost regiment and called out, "Follow me!" They followed him, across Mill Creek, up the facing slope, to run head-on into Colonel Specht's waiting Brunswickers. The steady German regulars, reinforced in the nick of time by units of the Rhetz and Hesse-Hanau regiments, stood fast, firing disciplined volleys until the Americans broke and fell back. The Germans continued to hold their position against renewed American attacks spurred on by Arnold. His presence among the cheering troops was increasing the pressure on the Germans, and it became evident that they would be cut off. Fortunately for them, the order finally came for a withdrawal, and they fell back to the cover of entrenchments.

Arnold, riding back and forth to observe the action, caught sight of General Fraser doing the same on the British side. Arnold soon saw that Fraser was the heart of a stiffening British defense. Fraser led the 24th Regiment up to reinforce the light infantry companies he had rallied, and with them he was reforming a new line. Arnold called on his old friend Morgan: "That man on the gray horse is a host in himself and must be disposed of." Morgan called up Tim Murphy, one of his best marksmen.

Murphy was a noted Indian fighter and was known along the frontier for his famous double-barreled rifle. He climbed a tree and sighted down on the British general. His first two shots were near misses, both almost grazing Fraser's horse. One of his aides saw that his general was a target and suggested that he move out of range. Fraser, a rugged Scot and veteran of a dozen battles, disagreed. His presence had already proved its worth at this critical place and time, and he knew where he was most needed. Murphy's third shot felled Fraser; the bullet passed through his body, mortally wounding him. When the word of Fraser's fall spread through the British infantry, the line that Fraser had tried so gallantly to restore collapsed, and the British ran to take cover behind their entrenchments.

At this point a lesser general would have been content for his troops to pull back, reorganize, and remain masters of the field. If Horatio Gates had commanded on the field, things would probably have ended with the withdrawal of the last British units to the safety of their field fortifications. Fortunately for the Americans, Gates was not there, nor did he ever show himself outside his headquarters. Benedict Arnold *was* there, and that fact turned the next phase of Bemis Heights into a decisive battle. Arnold possessed the aggressiveness needed to drive his men on from mere tactical success to smashing victory. As Sir John Fortescue observed: "With true military instinct [Arnold] seized the opportunity to order a general attack upon the British entrenchments" (*A History of the British Army*).

Arnold then personally led the assault on the Balcarres redoubt. The Americans were met with such a fierce fire that at first it seemed they would be stopped in their tracks. Arnold got the leading ranks into and almost through the tangled abatis, but they took such severe losses that they were forced to pull back. When he had time to survey the situation, Arnold saw that nothing was to be gained in mounting another bloody assault on the front of that strongly held redoubt. While he was looking around in preparation for his next move, the answer appeared in the rear of his reforming regiments. It was Learned's brigade, heading northwest toward the British right.

Arnold mounted and rode directly across the field of fire, and with the luck that seems to stick with the bold, came out unscathed to take command, for the second time, of Learned's troops.

Arnold's quick eye saw the objective of his next attack. He led them clear of the Balcarres redoubt, passing beyond its right to spring upon the two stockaded cabins between the Balcarres and Breymann redoubts. In one fierce rush the attacking Americans cleared the cabins and the area of the Canadians, and the way was clear for a breakthrough on the British right. First, however, Arnold saw the chance to destroy Breymann redoubt, at the extreme right of the British position. He found that Morgan had gotten his men around the British right and was ready to attack again. Arnold directed Morgan, reinforced by the regiments of Wesson and Livingston, to attack the redoubt in flank and rear, while he would personally lead an assault against the right rear of the redoubt. His assault force was already at hand, in the form of Brooks's Massachusetts regiment. He led them around the redoubt and forced his horse through a sallyport. As he made his entrance, his horse went down from a bullet wound, and Arnold took a bullet himself, one that fractured the thigh bone of the same leg wounded at Quebec.

As Arnold was carried to safety, there was a scene that would have done justice to the fifth act of a Shakespearean history. Major Armstrong had finally caught up with Arnold and could deliver Gates's order for him to return to camp. There is a sort of Homeric irony in Arnold's being borne off the field, the hero triumphant at last, going, as Ward saw it, "with the glory of that mad afternoon coruscating about him."

In the heat of the action the German commander Breymann fell, mortally wounded by one of his own men after using his sword on four others to drive them back into the fight. With Breymann's death, the remainder of his small command, reduced from 500 to 200 by detachments to other commands, gave up the redoubt to the Americans.

The way was open to the British right rear, and the rupture of Burgoyne's line that Arnold had foreseen was now possible. But there was no Arnold to organize and lead that final strike. Consequently there was no continuation of the attack. It was getting dark, and the only action that ended the day was a minor counterattack led by Colonel Specht at the head of some Germans in an effort to retake the Breymann redoubt. Instead, Specht was taken prisoner and the attackers withdrew. So ended the Battle of Bemis Heights. British casualties for the afternoon totaled 600; the American losses came to about 150.

It was obvious even to Burgoyne that his whole fortified line was no longer tenable. That night, the night of 7–8 October, he pulled his entire force back, in a well-controlled move, to positions north of the Great Ravine. There on the heights, behind well-fortified lines, he could reorganize while simultaneously protecting his supplies on the ground, his artillery train, and the boats. On the following day the Americans moved forward to occupy the low ground along the river as well as the abandoned British campgrounds.

While Burgoyne appeared to be offering battle in his new position, that was also becoming untenable. American forces were moving up the east side of the river. What followed has been summarized by Fortescue:

> [Burgoyne] found himself compelled to retire up the river to Saratoga, abandoning some five hundred sick and wounded men to the enemy. The retreat itself was accomplished without hindrance; but so heavy was the rain and so severe the weather, that the men on

coming into camp had not strength to cut wood or make fires, but threw themselves down, old soldiers though they were, on the sodden ground to sleep. When the light came on the morning of the 9th, it revealed the Americans in the act of entrenching the heights on the opposite side of the river, so as to prevent the British from crossing. Burgoyne therefore decided on the following day to abandon his artillery and baggage and to withdraw by a forced march to Fort Edward. Scouts, however, came in to report that the whole of the fords on the road were beset, and that the Americans were strongly entrenched, with cannon, between Fort George and Fort Edward. The British were in fact surrounded. Gates had by this time from eighteen to twenty thousand [?] men; and there was no escape. For yet a few days Burgoyne waited in the vain hope of news from Clinton; but the message in the silver bullet had been intercepted and the messenger hanged. The army was not only surrounded but starving, and on the 14th Burgoyne made overtures for a capitulation, which was finally concluded on the 17th. It was agreed that Burgoyne's troops should march out with the honours of war, pile their arms, and be conducted at once to Boston for shipment to England, on the understanding that they should serve no more in America during the continuance of hostilities. (*A History of the British Army*)

THE MILITARY EFFECTS OF THE SURRENDER AT Saratoga were immediate. An entire British army of 5,721 men, including seven generals, had been taken out of the war, not to overlook 27 cannon, some 5,000 stand of arms, and all the army's other matériel and ammunition. The British evacuated Forts Ticonderoga and Crown Point, and their garrisons returned to Canada. Sir Henry Clinton recalled General Vaughan's force as well as the garrison he had left in Fort Clinton. By November 1777 the only ground occupied by British forces in the north was around New York and Philadelphia, and in Rhode Island.

The strategic-political effects were so far-reaching in 1777 as to be almost inconceivable. As every American history student knows, France could now openly declare itself an ally of the Americans—which it did in the treaty signed on 6 February 1778. France and England were now at war, and even Spain and Holland declared themselves for the Americans. French arms and munitions, arriving in great quantities, sustained the Patriots until the French navy and army were able to take part in joint operations with American forces.

SEVEN

Kings Mountain

WHEN BURGOYNE'S ARMY PILED ITS ARMS on the surrender field at Saratoga, the event could have been rightly celebrated by the Americans as their greatest victory of the war. Some thirty months later, and hundreds of miles to the south, the British were entitled to claim *their* greatest success of the war. On 12 May 1780 General Benjamin Lincoln, the same Lincoln who commanded a wing of Gates's army at Saratoga, surrendered the city of Charleston, South Carolina, and its garrison to Sir Henry Clinton. The loss of the South's largest city and seaport was serious enough, but what went with it was staggering—one of the major catastrophes suffered by the colonials during the whole war. The forty-four-day siege yielded to the British over 5,000 prisoners of war, 6,000 muskets, 391 cannon, and immense stores of ammunition and other supplies. The cost to the British: 76 killed and 189 wounded.

What had brought Sir Henry Clinton to Charleston and this surprising success? Clinton had succeeded Howe as commander in chief of His Majesty's forces in America in March 1778. He assumed actual command in May upon Howe's departure. After undergoing several setbacks in the North, Clinton found himself on the strategic defensive, though he had never given up his grand plan to take the offensive in the South. When the combined forces of American and French failed to take Savannah by siege and storm, French Admiral d'Estaing reembarked his troops and sailed back to France in October 1779. The small American force withdrew to Charleston, amid hard feelings toward the French by the Patriots and no end of jubilation among southern Loyalists, who renewed their call for a British invasion of the Carolinas.

All this good news, along with the assurance of a firm British hold on

SOUTHERN THEATER

Miles

25   0   50   100

Georgia, led Clinton to decide that the time was right for undertaking his southern campaign. His plan was a bold one, and clear enough on the map. His first objective was Charleston, and following its seizure he would make that seaport his base of operations in the South. From then on it would be mainly a land campaign, with its major thrust northward across South Carolina, through North Carolina, and up into eastern Virginia. A major purpose behind all the thrusting was that steadfast aspiration that so influenced British strategic planning throughout the war: the belief that the Loyalists would come forward to reinforce British regular forces in large numbers. That illusion, as Page Smith saw it, was "that the great majority of the people of the South were loyal to the Crown and would with a little encouragement, avow that loyalty and take up arms, if necessary, to vindicate it" (*A New Age Now Begins*). When British commanders became disillusioned enough to see the real world, it was obvious that the Crown's law and order could be maintained only in the areas occupied by His Majesty's forces. When British troops passed on or were withdrawn from an area, either that quarter reverted to Patriot control or guerrilla warfare broke out anew.

Sir Henry Clinton was able to carry out the initial phase of his southern offensive without a hitch. Accompanied by Cornwallis as his second in command, Clinton sailed from New York in December 1779 with a fleet of ninety transports carrying 8,500 troops. In spite of a near-disastrous storm—the fleet was dispersed over a great expanse of the Atlantic for nearly a month and lost one transport full of Hessians, which was driven clear across the ocean to the English coast—the ships were finally reassembled and repaired at Savannah. Clinton then sailed for Charleston and began land operations in mid-February 1780. Although the operation was conducted at such a snail's pace that the city was actually under siege only by the end of March, on 12 May Charleston was surrendered to Clinton, at tremendous cost to the Patriot cause in the South.

Clinton's next step was the subjection of large interior regions of the Carolinas. His method was, insofar as practicable, to employ sizable detachments of Tories to do the job. Those operations resulted in raising Tory hopes and recruits, but also served to enflame what Christopher Ward describes as no less than "a civil war within the war against England" that was "marked by bitterness, violence and malevolence such as only civil wars can engender" (*The War of the Revolution*). The effects of the civil war on the operations of regular forces will be seen presently.

By the end of May Clinton was satisfied that things were going well enough for him to turn over operational control to Cornwallis. He sailed for New York on 5 June, leaving Cornwallis with some 8,300 men to carry on. Clinton's concept of carrying on was to hold on to Georgia, South Carolina, and New York, and not to venture further in the immediate future. Cornwallis, however, had ideas of his own. He was to make his own broad interpretation of offensive operations that "did not jeopardize his primary mission of holding the large region of Georgia and South Carolina left . . . in British control when Clinton ventured to New York" (Boatner, *Encyclopedia of the American Revolution*). In effect, Cornwallis was going to embrace the old maxim that an offense is also the best defense. He envisioned, in fact, that an invasion of North Carolina would rally enough Loyalists to his banner so that he could eventually carry his offensive into Virginia, where he could link up with British forces from the North.

Cornwallis's first moves to implement his own strategy included securing the subdued regions of Georgia and South Carolina by strengthening the critical posts at Savannah, Augusta, and Ninety-Six. Leaving his main force at Charleston, he then established a forward base at Camden, with outposts as far out as Georgetown, Cheraw, Hanging Rock, and Rocky Mount. Thus the solidly held territory of South Carolina was ringed by posts extending from Savannah in the south, northward through Augusta and Ninety-Six, and northeastward to Cheraw. The forward base at Camden was held by Lord Rawdon with 2,500 British regulars and Tory units.

The area to be secured was immense, comprising some fifteen thousand square miles, yet it had been subdued and occupied with ease. After the fall of Charleston only one Continental regiment remained in South Carolina, and what happened as it retreated northward clearly marked the end of Patriot resistance in South Carolina.

IN MID-MAY 1780 COLONEL ABRAHAM BUFORD had marched his regiment, the 3rd Virginia Continentals, within forty miles of Charleston when he received news of the surrender; he then got orders to retreat to Hillsboro, North Carolina. Cornwallis dispatched Lieutenant Colonel Banastre Tarleton in pursuit. With a task force of 270 men, Tarleton caught up with Buford's rear guard on the twenty-ninth at a place called Waxhaws, about ten miles east of present-day Lancaster, S.C. The American commander deployed into line on open ground, and his officers ordered their men to hold their fire until the charging cavalry came within ten yards of their line. The Continentals' single volley was too late to break the momentum of Tarleton's charge. The American line was shattered, and simultaneously the Tory cavalry swept around both flanks. The Continentals were encircled and soon became a helpless mass, most men throwing down their arms. Buford had Ensign Cruit raise a white flag; when Tarleton himself charged at the flag, his horse was killed. Seeing him downed, a fury swept through his troopers with the word that their leader had been shot down in front of a flag of truce. Tarleton could not or would not hold back his men. They were out of control, sabering right and left, ignoring any cries for quarter. In moments the Tory infantry of the legion were into the Americans with their bayonets. The Americans by now were completely helpless, since they had grounded their muskets when the white flag was raised. In Robert Bass's version of the affair, "the infantrymen continued to sweep over the ground, plunging their bayonets into any living American. Where several had fallen together, they used their bayonets to untangle them, in order to finish off those on the bottom" (*The Green Dragoon*).

In this massacre was born the American battle cry of "Tarleton's quarter!" The "Waxhaws massacre" and "Tarleton's quarter" flamed across the Carolinas and Georgia to become household words, and Tarleton became the hated symbol of the Crown and Tory oppression, and henceforth was known as Bloody Tarleton.

American casualties were 113 killed and 203 prisoners, but 150 of those were too badly wounded to be moved. Buford escaped on horseback, losing all six pieces of his artillery and his entire supply train. Tarleton counted his casualties at 19 killed or wounded and a loss of 31 horses. Buford's losses, however, became more symbolic than material; they symbolized the end of organized Patriot military power in South Carolina.

THE WAXHAWS AFFAIR ALSO SIGNALED THE SPREAD of civil war. Although there were too many skirmishes to recount, at least four actions took place after Waxhaws that could be called battles. They were notable not only for blood and bitterness but further for the absence of British regular troops.

On 20 June 400 Patriots under Colonel Francis Locke attacked some 700 Tories at Ramsour's Mill in North Carolina. Each side lost about 150 men, losses which speak clearly for the fierceness of the encounter.

At Williamson's Plantation on 12 July a hastily organized band of Patriots surprised a Tory raiding party by attacking its camp at dawn. Out of 115 Tories in the camp only 24 escaped; of the remainder, 30 to 40 were killed and 50 wounded. The attacking Patriots lost one man killed out of about 250 who actually made the attack.

The victory at Williamson's Plantation encouraged many of the rebels to rally to the side of famed Thomas Sumter, the "Carolina Gamecock," who was building up a force in Mecklenburg County, North Carolina. Sumter decided to move against the fortified post at Rocky Mount, South Carolina, held by the Tory Lieutenant Colonel Turnbull with some 150 New York Volunteers and a detachment of South Carolina Tories. Turnbull had been warned of Sumter's approach and was prepared. Three successive assaults were beaten back by the heavy fire of the defenders. After unsuccessful attempts to burn out the Tories, Sumter had to call it quits and withdraw to Land's Ford on the Catawba River. Losses were equally light on both sides, each losing about fourteen killed or wounded.

Sumter had not earned the title of Gamecock by sitting around camp fires; four days after Rocky Mount, he left Land's Ford to attack the heavily garrisoned outpost at Hanging Rock, about twelve miles east of Rocky Mount. Sumter had mustered 500 North Carolina militia and about 300 South Carolinians; all could be considered mounted infantry. Sumter divided his force into three columns, each with the mission of attacking one of the Tory camps. Their guides went astray, and all three divisions ended up on the front and flank of the North Carolinians on the Tory left. Sumter's men drove on but were stopped by heavy fire from the legionaries and rangers of the enemy center. The Tory force commander, Major Carden, seeing his chance, took a detachment and fell upon Sumter's flank. The surprised Americans rallied and, with amazing fierceness for militia, retaliated with such firepower that Tory casualties mounted to the point where Carden's men fled or surrendered.

The main Tory camp and supply center were now wide open, and the triumphant victors went hog wild. Stores of rum were uncovered and gulped down, and while Sumter's disorganized men were getting drunk and out of control, Carden formed some rallied men into a hollow square with two cannon on its corners and prepared to continue the fight. Carden was opposed by Major William Davie, a noted partisan leader. Davie had kept his "dragoons" under control and away from the looting. In the meantime Sumter had succeeded in drawing about 200 of his men from the looted camp. While so engaged he was threatened by two companies of legion cavalry who had come to join the fight. Davie led a charge against the new threat and drove the Tory cavalry out of sight. At this point, with the enemy square still standing fast, Sumter decided that further offensive action was out of the question and offered a general withdrawal. Outside of the fiasco in the looted camp, the battle had been fought with firmness and courage on both sides. The Tory losses were especially heavy: nearly 200 killed and wounded. The Patriots claimed to have suffered casualties of only 12 killed and 41 wounded, which is unlikely.

The Battle of Hanging Rock was the largest and last of the civil war actions after the fall of Charleston. Now, in early August 1780, new Patriot forces were entering the arena, forces not composed of partisans or irregulars.

WHEN SIR HENRY CLINTON WAS MAKING UP HIS MIND whether to stay on in Charleston or leave and turn the southern command over to Cornwallis, his decision was hastened by a bit of news: Comte de Rochambeau had left France for America carrying a large force of French troops bound for New England. The news prompted Sir Henry's departure for New York on 5 June 1780. What was bad news for Clinton was, of course, good news for Congress and Washington. The latter had already sent a small force south under Major General Baron de Kalb in April 1780 to give "further succor to the Southern States." De Kalb's little army consisted of two brigades: the first comprising four regiments of Maryland Continentals; the second, three Maryland regiments and the Delaware regiment, all Continentals. The 1st Continental Artillery Regiment of eighteen guns marched in support. The force totaled 1,400 rank and file.

De Kalb was marching into North Carolina when he learned of Charleston's surrender; the news had traveled with unaccountable slowness and reached de Kalb five weeks after the fact. Tough professional that he was, de Kalb refused to be disheartened. After several forward moves southward, he set up camp at Buffalo Ford, and from this base tried to raise reinforcements of militia, which should have become available. The hoped-for volunteers did not show up. Militia Major General Caswell, with a strong force of North Carolina militia, preferred to chase Tories elsewhere. Virginia militia led by Stevens and Porterfield also made themselves unavailable. While at Buffalo Ford, de Kalb got word of

Horatio Gates's appointment to command of the Southern Department. Washington's man for the job had been Nathanael Greene; but Congress, with characteristic perversity, preferred the hero of Saratoga. The hero arrived at de Kalb's new camp on Deep River on 25 July and assumed command of an army short of clothing as well as discipline. Through no fault of de Kalb's, the army was exhausted and in bad need of all sorts of necessities, including rations and rum.

Gates immediately went on the offensive, his objective no less than the seizure of that tantalizing forward base of Cornwallis's at Camden, with all its promise of life-restoring stores. Rejecting the route of advance proposed by de Kalb and his commanders, which would have taken the army through a relatively fertile region where most of the locals favored the Patriot cause, Gates ordered a more direct march through a desolate area dominated by swamps, pine barrens, and Tory sympathizers. Gates also turned down the request of Colonels William Washington and Anthony White for aid in recruiting horsemen, aid which would have been repaid handsomely if the two colonels had joined Gates's army and furnished him with a reconnaissance and security force.

The army marched on 27 July, only two days after Gates's arrival, and without the rations and rum which the soldiers had been promised. The hungry troops made 120 miles in two weeks, setting no records at an average of less than 9 miles a day. The promised rations never did catch up, so Gates promised them corn when they reached the Pee Dee River. "He was right, but the corn was still green, and soldiers who had been getting sick on green peaches now got sick on green corn instead" (Boatner, *Encyclopedia of the American Revolution*). Across the Pee Dee, Gates was joined on 3 August by Lieutenant Colonel Charles Porterfield with a small band of militia, and the yet-to-be-famous Colonel Francis Marion with twenty of his men.

Two days later Gates got a message from General Richard Caswell that he was about to attack a British outpost at Lynches Creek. When Caswell, with an estimated 2,100 men, advanced against the outpost, his "army" was thrown into disorder by a British surprise attack. The attack was actually a feint made by Lord Rawdon, commanding Cornwallis's forces based on Camden. After his successful feint, Rawdon withdrew his detachment to Little Lynches Creek, where he occupied a strong position blocking the route to Camden.

On 6 August Gates was finally joined by Caswell, "adding 2,100 to his grand army, but greatly weakening it as the event proved" (Ward, *War of the American Revolution*). The combined forces moved forward toward Little Lynches Creek, bumping into Rawdon's blocking force there on 11 August. De Kalb proposed to march up Little Lynches Creek at night, cross it, and turn the British out of their position while continuing to advance on Camden. Gates rejected the plan and instead tried a clumsy envelopment of the British left in broad daylight. Rawdon threw out a screening force of Tarleton's legion and quietly pulled back to Camden.

Rawdon was met in Camden by Cornwallis on 13 August. What Cornwallis found was anything but cheering. His enemy's estimated strength was 7,000, which Mark Boatner says was "an understandable error inasmuch as Gates himself was under the same misapprehension." Cornwallis's own strength was reported to him at 2,117 rank and file present for duty, with a dismaying 800 sick in the Camden field hospital. Of the effective 2,117, about 1,500 were regulars and the rest were dependable Tory units such as Tarleton's legion, the Volunteers of Ireland, and two North Carolina regiments. Considering the estimated adverse odds of more than three to one, a lesser general would have fallen back on Charleston. Not so Charles Cornwallis; he would not abandon his sick in Camden. But even if they had not been there, he would still have taken the initiative and attacked his enemy. This he proceeded to do, and advanced northward to meet the Hero of Saratoga.

ON 14 AUGUST 1780, THE DAY AFTER CORNWALLIS'S ARRIVAL at Camden, Gates's army at Rugeley's Mill received its last reinforcement, the 700 Virginia militia of General Edward Stevens. On that date Gates's strength returns included de Kalb's 900 Maryland and Delaware Continentals,* Caswell's 1,800 North Carolina militia, Armand's command (formerly Pulaski's legion) of 120, Porterfield's 100 Virginia light infantry, about 70 volunteer cavalry, and 106 guns in Colonel Harrison's Virginia artillery. In all, counting some "miscellaneous" attachments, Gates's total would have come to about 4,100. Yet when Otho Williams, Gates's adjutant general, showed him the morning report strength of 3,052 fit for duty, Gates, still believing he had over twice that many men, didn't want to be confused with facts. He brushed off Williams with "there are enough for our purpose."

With his "purpose" in mind, Gates, in a command conference on 15 August, read his operation order for an attack that night to his com-

---

* After detaching 100 Maryland Continentals to support Sumter's operation against British supply routes.

manders. It would require them to maneuver over wooded sand hills and scattered swamps with an army of which over two-thirds were green militia and whose major elements had never operated together.

Before the troops fell in for the march, a full ration of meat and corn meal was to be issued. There was, however, no rum, a customary stimulant before going into action. In its stead, Gates had a gill of molasses from the hospital supplies issued to each soldier. "The men ate voraciously of half-cooked meat and half-baked bread with a dessert of corn meal mush mixed with the molasses." A sergeant-major described the results of the solution: "Instead of enlivening our spirits . . . it served to purge us . . . [and, Colonel Otho Williams added] the men were of necessity breaking the ranks all night and were certainly much debilitated before the action commenced in the morning" (Ward, *War of the American Revolution*).

WITH THESE UNHAPPY AUGURIES GATES'S TROOPS began their march as scheduled, at 10:00 P.M. on 15 August. The axis of advance was southward on the main road from Rugeley's Mill to Camden. Colonel Armand's horsemen preceded the advance, despite his warning to Gates that a cavalry unit was not right for the mission because it would be too noisy on the march and could not operate effectively in the woods. It was followed by Armstrong's and Porterfield's militia, who were followed by the advance guard of the Continentals. There was only starlight to see by; it was of no help to either the files slogging through sand and swamps or the column on the main road hemmed in by the dark pine woods.

About 2:30 A.M. on the sixteenth the march was brought to an abrupt halt by the sound of firing up ahead around Armand's troops. They had run smack into the cavalry and infantry of Tarleton's legion. Although the British advance party had only twenty cavalrymen and an equal number of legion infantry, Tarleton acted so quickly in attacking Armand's troops that they wheeled away, spreading confusion among the Continentals' advance guard. There was a firefight of sorts, which broke off in about fifteen minutes, since neither side had anything to gain by blazing away in the dark.

Cornwallis had marched north from Camden at 10:00 P.M. to carry out his decision to attack Gates. The opposing forces had met on the Rugeley's Mill–Camden road, bounded in this area by open pine forest, which in turn was flanked on each side by extensive swamps. Although the Americans had the minor advantage of some slightly higher ground, the open forest to their rear widened out so that their flanks would be

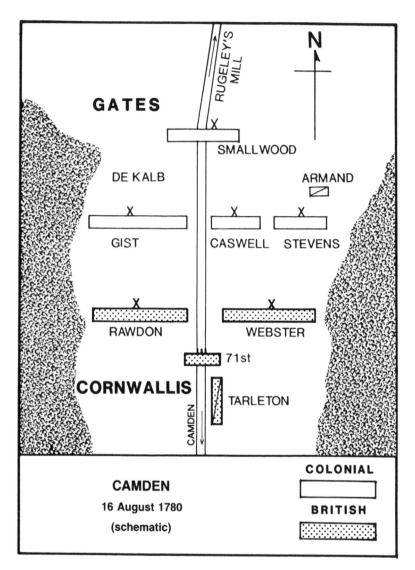

CAMDEN
16 August 1780
(schematic)

COLONIAL

BRITISH

exposed if they were driven back. Both sides deployed with their fronts parallel, in line perpendicular to the road. On the British side, Lieutenant Colonel Webster led Cornwallis's right wing, that is, all the units on the east side of the road. Lord Rawdon commanded the left wing, west of the road. Cornwallis's second line, support or reserve as the situation called for, was composed of the 71st Highlanders astride the road. Behind them Tarleton's legion was held in reserve, in column because of the terrain. The British artillery had only four guns—two six-pounders and two three-pounders—positioned in front of the center.

Gates's army was also in two lines. Gist's brigade of Continentals was on the right, Caswell's North Carolina militia was in the center, and Stevens's Virginia militia was on the left, backed up by Armand's legion. The reserve was Smallwood's brigade of Maryland Continentals. The American artillery was also positioned in front of the army's center. De Kalb commanded the right wing, that is, the troops west of the road. Gates took up his own position about 600 yards behind the front line.

When artillery Captain Anthony Singleton told Otho Williams, Gates's adjutant general, that he saw enemy infantry advancing in line of columns at several hundred yards distance, Williams told him to open fire. The adjutant general then rode back to report to Gates. When Gates appeared to be in no hurry to take any action, Williams recommended that Stevens advance and attack the enemy when they would be most vulnerable, in the act of deploying from columns into lines. According to Christopher Ward, Gates answered: "Sir, that's right. Let it be done." It was the last order he gave in that battle or in any other to the end of the war.

Williams had skirmishers thrown out to cover the advance of Stevens's Virginians. Just before the Virginia militia were ready to advance, Cornwallis ordered Webster to attack the American left. The sight of ordered ranks coming at them with field music playing, drums beating the charge, regimental colors flying, and lines of glittering bayonets leveled at charge bayonet was all too much for the Virginia militia. Before the first British assault reached them, Stevens's units broke and fled, throwing aside their muskets as they ran. Caswell's North Carolina militia needed no prompting to follow their Virginia comrades and also took off smartly for the rear. Gates and Caswell tried to rally the fleeing men, but "they ran like a torrent, dashing past the officers and . . . spread through the woods in every direction."

While the American left was breaking, Rawdon advanced with his wing. On the east side of the road Gist's Continentals stood their ground, along with some North Carolina militia who had stayed to fight. By now there was so much smoke and dust obscuring the battlefield that de Kalb and his wing didn't yet know that they were having to fight the whole battle. De Kalb went back to bring up Smallwood's Maryland brigade in person, its commander having been carried away by the fugitives.

Cornwallis was as firmly in command of his battle as Gates was not. The British commander's quick eye saw the opportunity to turn Webster's regulars against the reserve brigade. The Marylanders fought back, were twice driven back and twice rallied, then were finally overcome and driven from the field.

It was Gist's Maryland and Delaware Continentals who fought the rest of the battle—and fought it well indeed. They took on the whole of Rawdon's wing, 1,000 to the American 600, and threw them back. Counterattacks followed each British thrust for almost an hour; at one point they broke through attacking British units to snatch 50 prisoners at bayonet point. In the midst of this fierce action de Kalb and Gist kept up the fight, still unaware that their wing was doing all the fighting. They had received no orders from Gates, and so saw no reason to save their men by falling back.

Even after de Kalb's horse had been shot under him and his head laid open with a saber cut, he refused to quit. But "Cornwallis, as vigilant as Gates was not, had now thrown his entire force on these last remaining foemen, 2,000 men [by this time] no more than 600. Overwhelmed by numbers that almost surrounded him, de Kalb called for the bayonet again. . . . But ball after ball had struck their heroic leader . . . yet the old lion had it in him to cut down a British soldier, whose bayonet was at his breast. That was his last stroke. Bleeding from eleven wounds, he fell" (Ward, *War of the American Revolution*).*

With de Kalb's fall and the breakup of Gist's command, the Battle of Camden was over. A handful of Maryland and Delaware officers rounded up about sixty men; this was the only organized group in the retreat. Gates's entire army—those who were not casualties or captured—had scattered and fled, most into the swamps, others dashing madly toward Rugeley's Mill. Cornwallis unleashed Tarleton, whose pursuit lasted for more than twenty miles and came to a halt only because the horses gave out. On his way he picked off Gates's entire baggage train, which was being looted by American fugitives.

CAMDEN WAS SOON BEING PROCLAIMED PUBLICLY as the worst defeat ever to be suffered by an American army. After such a debacle it is not surprising that American losses were not accurately reported and that estimates vary. Carrington estimates 1,000 killed and wounded; the fig-

---

*De Kalb was later rescued from looters by no other than Tarleton, who got him attended to by British doctors, but he died from his wounds three days later.

ure does not include captured or missing. Otho Williams also estimated that 2,000 out of the army's 3,000, or two-thirds of the force, fled without firing a shot. Ward's conservative total come to 650 Americans killed or captured, and leaves the total wounded to be included among the captured. Matériel losses included 150 wagons loaded with ammunition and supplies, most regimental colors, and seven cannons. Much more significant, however, is the fact that Gates's army was completely dispersed, never to be reformed as such again. Cornwallis's losses were 69 killed, 285 wounded, and 11 missing.

So much for numbers; one still must account for the American army's commanding general. Horatio Gates, along with Smallwood and Caswell, had been swept from the field by the torrent of fugitives as far as Rugeley's Mill. Apparently it was in that vicinity that he began his famous ride. By nightfall he had reached Charlotte, a distance of almost 60 miles. In Page Smith's words, "The bubble [of Saratoga fame] was pricked. The flight made him an object of almost universal scorn and ridicule. Had he escaped with Gist, or taken refuge at Hanging Rock . . . or found his way to join Sumter's force across the Wateree River, he might have survived the defeat and been given another opportunity to display his ineptness as a military leader. But it was the sixty-mile flight that finished him" (*A New Age Now Begins*).

Continuing his northward hegira, mounted on a relay of horses, Gates reached Hillsboro, North Carolina, on 19 August, a total ride of 180 miles, leading Alexander Hamilton to comment in a letter to James Duane: "But was there ever an instance of a general running away, as Gates has done, from his whole army? And was there ever so precipitous a flight? One hundred and eighty miles in three days and a half. It does admirable credit to the activity of a man at his time of life [age fifty-two]. But it disgraces the general and the soldier."

AFTER CLINTON HAD TAKEN LEAVE OF CORNWALLIS, the difference in their strategical concepts was beginning to show. In order to put his basic strategy into action, Cornwallis secured permission to communicate directly with the London officials who could authorize his strategy. Clinton agreed to the arrangement, which left Cornwallis free to operate as he wished. First, he would consolidate his hold on the coastal and interior regions of South Carolina and eastern Georgia in order to maintain secure bases from which to operate. Then he would thrust to the north and northeast through North Carolina, gathering Loyalist support and recruits as he advanced. After that he planned to move into Virginia to link up with British forces from the North and thus complete his inferred mission of bringing the South, from Georgia to Maryland, solidly under the Crown.

Following his triumph at Camden, Cornwallis planned to advance his main force up the Camden-Charlotte-Salisbury axis. By so doing he expected to crush rebel resistance along that line while his regular forces provided the bases to which Loyalist elements would rally. The rallying was expected to come mainly from two separate regions where the Loyalists were, actually or potentially, the strongest: in the east an area centered around Cross Creek (present-day Fayetteville), about 125 miles east of Charlotte; and in the west a much larger area lying roughly between the Broad and Little Catawba rivers. Cornwallis reasoned that once the two regions were under his control, the task of subduing North Carolina would be fait accompli.

The British establishment of a system of bases and outposts in Georgia and South Carolina has already been described. In support of the system Cornwallis sent out several detachments with the mission of rallying Loyalist recruits to his banner. By far the most active and successful were the Tory forces raised and trained by Major Patrick Ferguson. Shortly after the fall of Charleston, that promising professional had been appointed by Sir Henry Clinton to the post of inspector of militia in the southern provinces. The imposing title belied the real nature of the job: the raising and transforming of Loyalist recruits into trained units capable of subjugating and controlling provincial regions and fighting alongside British regular forces as dependable troops.

While Cornwallis was still in Charleston, Ferguson had set up a rallying post at his camp on Little River, a few miles east of Lieutenant Colonel Balfour's post at Ninety-Six, and raised a force of 4,000 Tories, which he organized into seven regiments. By the end of June Ferguson had already begun to move into the up-country north of Ninety-Six, sending out detachments in all directions to rally more Tories to the Crown. Rallying and pacification were closer to Ferguson's nature than the bloodshed and terror that accompanied Tarleton's raids. Many of Ferguson's recruits, however, were Loyalists who were fiercely antagonistic to any Patriots and would stop at nothing when they were on their own and riding roughshod over their former neighbors. This kind of Tory raiding party, operating beyond Ferguson's personal control, became known for their plundering of "cattle, horses, beds, wearing apparel, bee-gums, and vegetables of all kinds—even wresting the rings from the fingers of the females" (Dykeman, *With Fire and Sword*). When foraging parties were through plundering, it was not uncommon to turn the horses into grain fields to complete the depredation. Hence it was not surprising that Carolinians were aroused to firmer and firmer resistance, as Ferguson was to learn the hard way.

By no means was the subjugation of the up-country, or any other area within a radius of seventy-five miles from Ninety-Six, an unopposed effort. While the Patriot partisans of the low-country had their leaders—Francis Marion, Thomas Sumter, Andrew Pickens—the up-country didn't lack its own. Colonel Charles McDowell was the most noted leader of North Carolina Patriot militia at the time. After Charleston's surrender and the beginning of Ferguson's forays, McDowell needed reinforcements to carry out his raids against the Tories and British outposts. He sent a message requesting help to Colonel Isaac Shelby, one of the two famed leaders of the "over-mountain" men. Shelby responded by leading 200 mounted riflemen to join McDowell on the Broad River. They were joined by Colonel Elijah Clarke with a force of Georgia militia. During the three-month interval between Charleston's fall and the Battle of Camden, these three leaders and their mounted men combined at various times to attack Tory and British posts in three major actions. At Thicketty Fort on 30 July, Shelby and Clarke succeeded in forcing the surrender of the fort's garrison without firing a shot. Exhilarated by their easy victory, they went after foragers from one of Ferguson's forces. On 8 August, at Cedar Spring, the British won the field but were unable to recapture prisoners the Patriots had taken at the beginning of the fight.

Ten days later, on 18 August, Shelby and Clarke teamed up with Colonel James Williams to make a surprise attack on the Tories at Musgrove's Mill, far to the rear of Ferguson's main force. The surprise failed, and the attackers had to take up a defensive position of their own. They repulsed the Tory counterattack, and dealt the Tories severe losses, to the tune of sixty-three killed, ninety wounded, and seventy prisoners. The Patriots lost only four killed and eight wounded. It was a stunning little victory, and such a morale builder that the leaders planned a really daring coup: an all-out attack on Ninety-Six, about thirty miles away. The men were already mounting up for the ride when the news came of Gates's disaster at Camden two days before.

They stayed mounted and headed north for the hills. Ferguson, who had swift news of the Patriot retreat, set out in hot pursuit. At one time he was only thirty minutes behind the tail riders when he was halted near Fair Forest by a message from Cornwallis ordering him to report to his commander at Camden.

At British headquarters Ferguson was briefed on Cornwallis's strategy for advancing into North Carolina, and how he expected to raise Tory forces from east to west to rally around his central axis—Charlotte to Salisbury—and use them to control the rest of the state. Ferguson was then given his mission: to act independently in making a western sweep, in other words, to serve as Cornwallis's left wing in the subjection of rebels and the raising of Tory troops. Since Ferguson was already pursuing the most dangerous Patriot force in the area, his mission further authorized him to proceed as far north as Gilbert Town (present-day Rutherfordton) to raise sufficient Tory forces to control the region. Upon completion of his mission, when British control was ensured and large numbers of recruits had rallied to Ferguson, he was to rejoin Cornwallis's army with his force in the vicinity of Charlotte.

Cornwallis had chosen Ferguson for the job because he needed a keen professional who could act in independent command. Ferguson was born to a family of landed gentry in Aberdeenshire in 1744. The life of the soldier attracted him from childhood. He attended a London military academy, and at age fourteen had a commission purchased for him as a cornet in the Scots Greys (then the Royal North Irish Dragoons). In 1768 he bought a captaincy and served with the 70th Foot in the West Indies during the subjugation of a slave rising.

Back in England Ferguson became obsessed with the idea of a breech-loading rifle that would not only be as accurate as the famed American frontier rifle but would have a far greater rate of fire than that muzzle-loading flintlock. The Ferguson rifle was years ahead of its time. Its inventor demonstrated its capabilities in tests where he fired it six times a minute, reloading from the prone position (it was necessary to stand to load the muzzle-loading flintlock). Yet, like so many inventions that have been too far in advance of their time, Ferguson's failed to impress generals like Sir William Howe, and only about 200 were ever manufactured.

Ferguson arrived in America with permission to raise a detachment of rangers. It was his rangers that were scouting in advance of Knyphausen's march to Chadd's Ford before the Battle of Brandywine in September 1777. Ferguson took a bad wound in that battle; a bullet shattered his elbow, permanently crippling his right arm. Captain Ferguson was next heard from a year later when he led a successful raid on Little Egg Harbor, New Jersey, in October 1778. In October 1779 he was appointed major in the 71st Highlanders, and he accompanied Clinton's expedition to Charleston in 1780. He took part with Tarleton in his victory over the Americans at Monck's Corner on 14 April 1780. After that operation

Ferguson was glad to be separated from Tarleton, for he disapproved strongly of that cavalryman's ruthless methods against both civilians and the military.

While Cornwallis had not hesitated in assigning Ferguson his mission of making the western sweep, he had some reservations. Cornwallis probably felt, as Henry Lumpkin observed, that "he clearly was highly intelligent and a fine combat officer, but his commander feared Ferguson's willful, impulsive, and somewhat erratic personality. He was soft spoken, with a personal magnetism that drew people to him. Oddly enough, he got along well with frontier Americans, even though he considered them his social inferiors. He would sit down and talk for hours with farmers whose loyalty to the Crown had begun to waver and argue his case with humor, comprehension, and sympathy" (*From Savannah to Yorktown*). Yet, as we will see, the image he finally projected to the Patriots of the frontier through his proclamations and the acts of his Tory troops was that of a monster in human form who would not hesitate to burn and slay at will.

ISAAC SHELBY'S AND CHARLES MCDOWELL'S MEN had been in the field for months, raiding and fighting actions such as those at Cedar Spring and Musgrove's Mill. Now they were exhausted and hungry, and it was time to go home and get some rest. They scattered and faded into the hills, many disappearing over the Blue Ridge Mountains. Such a dispersal after a series of forays was not at all uncommon, but it served to deceive Ferguson into believing that his pacification operations were beginning to succeed.

On 7 September Ferguson invaded North Carolina and occupied Gilbert Town. Many of the locals appeared to rally to him and came to take the oath of allegiance to the Crown. It may not have occurred to Ferguson that most of them took the oath only to protect their property from his Tory raiders. Three days later, on 10 September, Ferguson left with his troops in the hope of intercepting Elijah Clarke, who was supposed to be withdrawing northward after an unsuccessful attempt to capture Augusta. He failed to find Clarke and returned to encamp at Old Fort, twenty-two miles northwest of Gilbert Town. Things appeared to be quiet throughout the area. Beyond the Blue Ridge, however, and unknown to Ferguson, things were stirring.

Ferguson himself was the unwitting cause of the activity. Just before leaving on 10 September he had paroled Samuel Phillips, one of the prisoners taken at Musgrove's Mill, and sent him with a message to

Colonel Shelby. The message was in effect an ultimatum stating that if Shelby and other rebels of his ilk did not "desist from their opposition to the British arms and take protection under his standard, he would march his army over the mountains, hang their leader, and lay their country waste with fire and sword" (Dykeman, *With Fire and Sword*). Seldom did a message have a more opposite effect from that intended. Far from being cowed by Ferguson's threats, the "fire and sword proclamation" was circulated rapidly and widely among the over-mountain men, who had already decided that the best way to protect their homes and families was to get Ferguson before he could get them. To transform that decision into action, the partisan leaders had sent out the call for volunteers on both sides of the Blue Ridge. Ferguson's ultimatum now served to turn that call into action.

No doubt carrying Ferguson's message in his pocket, Isaac Shelby rode to meet with Colonel John Sevier, known across the frontier as "Nolichucky Jack," the Indian fighter whose home was on the Nolichucky River, west of the mountains. The two completed their plans to raise a powerful "posse" to go after Ferguson. To cover the expenses involved, the two pledged themselves to make good the money taken out of the public treasury. Their final call for armed men went out to famous leaders such as Colonel William Campbell of Virginia and Colonels Charles McDowell and Benjamin Cleveland, whose men rode on both sides of the Carolinas' border. The call named the rendezvous point as Sycamore Shoals on the Watauga River, near present-day Elizabethton, Tennessee.

What kind of men did they expect to answer the call? The term *over-mountain men* was applied loosely to the colonists who had settled on the western side of the Blue Ridge in what is now eastern Tennessee. They were mostly North Carolinians of Scotch-Irish descent who were moving westward "in the same way that the Virginians who followed Boone crossed the mountain into Kentucky" (Fisher, *The Struggle for American Independence*). They were also called back water men—a term used by Ferguson—because they chose to settle along the upper waters of the Watauga, Holston, and Nolichucky rivers. The over-mountain men were by no means the only, or even the principal, source of the frontier manpower that rode against Ferguson. Out of the 1,800 who joined up, Shelby's and Sevier's men counted as only the initial 480. What the over-mountain men should be given credit for is forming the nucleus of the volunteer force that fought at Kings Mountain.

Over-mountain men or not, all of the Patriot fighters were a tough lot. In his *Memoirs of the War in the Southern Department of the United States,* Light-Horse Harry Lee later referred to them as "a hardy race of men, who were familiar with the horse and rifle, were stout, active, patient under privation, and brave. Irregular in their movements [as opposed to the marches and maneuvers of regular units], and unaccustomed to restraint, they delighted in the fury of action, but pined under the servitude and inactivity of camp."

They came to Sycamore Shoals, many with their families, but each with horse and rifle. That weapon was one of the most prized possessions of the frontiersman. Most of them carried the so-called Kentucky, or long rifle, of the type made by Jacob Dickert of Lancaster County, Pennsylvania.* The caliber was usually .50, but could vary from .35 to .60, and it had a barrel from thirty-six to forty-eight inches long with a rifling twist of about one turn in forty-eight. It was called a long rifle because its overall length varied between fifty and sixty inches. It was a muzzle-loading flintlock with surprising accuracy up to about 300 yards. It fired a round lead ball which was rammed home with a greased patch, thus making the ball fit tightly against the rifling, which gave the ball its spin; the spin in turn gave the ball its velocity and accuracy. The rifle had the disadvantage of slowness in loading—a trained soldier with his musket could fire from three to five rounds while the rifleman was firing one—and the fact that it could not be fitted with a bayonet. Those disadvantages, however, meant little to the backwoodsman, because the rifle was ideal for its purposes: hunting and Indian fighting. For hand-to-hand combat the frontiersman had learned from the Indians to carry tomahawk or knife.

Of the more than 1,000 mounted riflemen who assembled at Sycamore Shoals on 25 September, Shelby and Sevier brought 240 each. Colonel William Campbell, a towering, red-haired Scot carrying the family's Highland broadsword, came in with 400 Virginians. Colonel Charles McDowell arrived with 160 of his North Carolinians. The majority of those present brought their womenfolk and children, who came to see fathers, sons, or brothers off to the war. The gathering had a gala

---

*"Of the type" because many historians have implied that all the Americans at Kings Mountain were armed with the Dickert rifle. Since that rifle—and most like it—was a masterpiece of hand craftsmanship, good Jacob Dickert (1740–1822) could not possibly, by 1780, have turned out the 940 rifles carried by the Patriots into that battle.

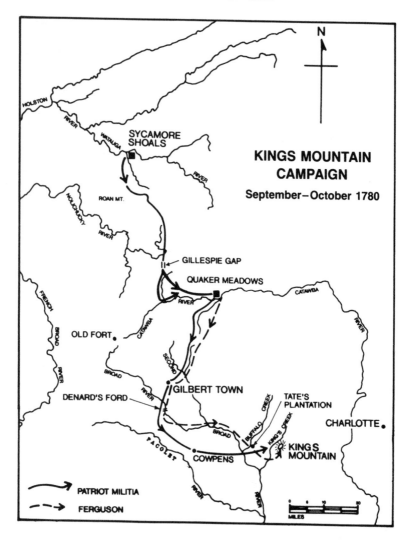

air. As Wilma Dykeman recounts: "The men talked and planned and prepared. And the women cooked, made last-minute patches or polishings on clothing or equipment, and they talked and worried over the dangers" (*With Fire and Sword*). Finally, on the early morning of 26 September, these deeply religious people heard the Reverend Samuel Doak say the prayer for the departing expedition. He compared their cause to that of Gideon's men in the Bible going forth to fight the Midianites. Doak ended with a ringing battle cry, "The sword of the Lord and of Gideon." It was fitting, and it was remembered.

The long column that rode out of Sycamore Shoals was, in Dykeman's words, "an army without uniforms. Many of their hunting shirts were of fringed buckskin while others were of homespun linsey-woolsey, 'clumsily made, blouse fashion, reaching to the knees and gathered up, tied around the waist.' Their breeches and gaiters were of rough, home-dyed cloth. Long hair was tied back in a queue beneath their wide-brimmed hats. They were an army little encumbered with baggage, unaccompanied by a supply train. Each man had a blanket, a cup, and 'a wallet of provisions'. . . principally of parched corn." There were, of course, rifles, powder horns, and "possible bags" with hunting necessaries.

The little army had to make a ninety-mile march to reach its next rendezvous at Quaker Meadows, near present-day Morganton, N.C. There were delays—some expected, some not. Slowed down at first by the cattle they were driving as meat on the hoof, they made only twenty miles the first day. On the second they had trouble with a stampede, which was irksome enough to cause the men to slaughter a few cattle for a portable supply of beef, then abandon the remainder to valley farmers. The column went on to climb the gap between Yellow and Roan mountains, where they encountered snow "shoe-top deep." When they encamped on the plateau beyond the gap, they found that two of Sevier's men were missing—probably deserters who had gone to alert Ferguson of the frontiersmen's approach.

The deserters raised another problem: in order to attack Ferguson before he could get reinforcements from Cornwallis, they would have to speed up their march. Yet they couldn't use the trail the deserters knew, so they must select another that would still give them time to pick up the back-country militia en route to join them. They decided on one that would allow a faster march, and Nolichucky Jack Sevier and Shelby led off. They crossed the Blue Ridge at Gillespie's Gap and rode on to arrive at Quaker Meadows on 30 September. There, at McDowell's Plantation, their numbers were increased to 1,400 by North and South Carolina reinforcements.

Here were the leaders who would march to catch up with and attack Ferguson. Besides Shelby and Sevier, the expedition had already been joined by Colonel William Campbell, the six-foot-six giant who was an Indian fighter and a born leader. He had fought in Lord Dunmore's War (1774), and had married Patrick Henry's sister. In Hank Messick's summation,

Other leaders who gathered on this venture were Joseph McDowell, a Virginian who had forsaken the easy life to move to the Carolina Piedmont, and Benjamin Cleveland, another Virginian, who had moved west and built his reputation as an Indian fighter. These would soon be joined by other outstanding fighters: James Williams, a longtime Tory hater who had served as a delegate to the provincial legislature of South Carolina; William Chronicle, a veteran of the 1780 skirmishes and a resident of the south fork of the Catawba; Joseph Winston, a leather-tough frontiersman who had been fighting Indians since he was 17; and Edward Lacey, a one-time Pennsylvanian who at the age of 13 had served with Edward Braddock's army in the Indian campaigns. (*King's Mountain*)

The senior officer, Colonel Charles McDowell, brother of Joseph McDowell, was a respected fighter who had served in Rutherford's campaign against the Cherokees.

The leaders were of the opinion that a force the size of theirs needed a general—or at least a commander of reputation who, coming from outside, would not arouse jealousies among the men from different localities. They sent Charles McDowell to General Gates to ask him to assign someone like Daniel Morgan or William Davidson to the job. Gates didn't answer the request, so they elected William Campbell commander of their combined forces. That done, the army marched again, and on 2 October camped sixteen miles north of Gilbert Town, where they hoped to find Ferguson.

But their quarry was no longer in Gilbert Town. Ferguson had already learned of the expedition seeking him out, and had started withdrawing to the south on 27 September. He was hastened in his decision to march toward Ninety-Six when he learned that Elijah Clarke's forces might be moving to join the rebel army. On 30 September the deserters from Sevier's men caught up with Ferguson. The two of them, James Crawford and Samuel Chambers, were able to give Ferguson detailed information about the expedition: its numbers, composition, and leaders. The news was disturbing enough for Ferguson to dispatch riders to Cornwallis, now at Charlotte with his main body, and Lieutenant Colonel John Cruger, the commander of the Ninety-Six garrison, asking for reinforcements posthaste.

The next day Ferguson issued a proclamation to the countryside, a strange declaration which smacked of bravado and betrayed a sense of growing frustration. "I say, if you wish to be pinioned, robbed, and murdered, and see your wives and daughters, in four days, abused by the dregs of mankind—in short, if you wish and deserve to live and bear the name of men, grasp your arms in a moment and run to camp." As Messick said, "The Backwater men have crossed the mountains, Ferguson warned; McDowell, Hampton, Shelby and Cleveland are at their head, so you know what you have to depend upon. If you choose to be pissed upon forever and ever by a set of mongrels, say so at once and let your women turn their backs upon you, and look out for real men to protect them" (*King's Mountain*).

At heart he was a bold fighter, however, so some of the twists and turns of his marches may have been deliberate ruses to keep his pursuers confused and off the track. On 2 August, after seeing his proclamation distributed, Ferguson turned his column eastward toward Charlotte, anticipating that the rebels would keep on going south, in the direction of his apparent march toward Ninety-Six. The Patriot army was indeed confused by Ferguson's turning east, but only temporarily. It marched through Gilbert Town on 3 October; then its leaders lost Ferguson's trail at Denard's Ford on 4 October, at the very place he had turned to the east. In the meantime Ferguson had forded the Second Broad River, Sandy Run, and Buffalo Creek, and marched on to the plantation of a Tory named Tate, about ten miles west of Kings Mountain. There he lingered, awaiting reinforcements and resting his men for two days, 4–5 October.

Frustrated at losing Ferguson's turn at Denard's Ford, the Patriot leaders were using all their means to scout out his trail. Finally they camped for the night of October 5. Campbell and his colonels then decided on a bold measure to make a fast move to catch Ferguson. They picked men with the best horses—some 700 in all—to make a dash for Cowpens, twenty-one miles to the southeast. If the advance column did not intercept Ferguson en route, it would still be in position to swing to the northeast to find Ferguson or his trail. Moreover, at Cowpens, a well-known cattle-herding center, the leaders would be in an area likely to yield the information they were so urgently seeking.

Their column arrived at Cowpens on Friday, 6 October. It was early evening and they found the principal landowner in the area, a well-to-do Tory farmer named Hiram Saunders. The first men to arrive hauled Saunders out of bed to question him. He said he knew nothing of Ferguson's troops or their whereabouts; apparently he was telling the truth. By the time they had finished questioning Saunders, the main body arrived and began to help their hungry selves to Saunders's bounty.

There was more than food to bolster morale. Soon Colonel James Williams came riding in with 400 of his men. While the greetings were going around, another piece of good luck, undoubtedly the most important event of the day, fell the way of the Patriots. Joseph Kerr arrived to confirm reports of Ferguson's location. A cripple who served the cause by acting as a spy, Kerr used his lameness to gain access to Tory formations under the guise of seeking shelter. He had been among Ferguson's troops when they halted that same day for their noon meal about six or seven miles from Kings Mountain. Kerr had found out that they were headed for the mountain and would encamp there.

There was no time to lose. The leaders quickly made a new culling to pick 940 of their number: the best men with the best horses. "These included 200 picked riflemen from Campbell's command, 120 under Shelby, 120 led by Sevier, 100 men following Cleveland, 90 with Joseph McDowell, and 60 under Winston. Edward Lacey and William Hill commanded their 100 South Carolinians, Hambright and Chronicle led 50 picked soldiers, and Candler's 30 Georgians formed part of James Williams' unit of 90 selected riflemen" (Lumpkin, *From Savannah to Yorktown*). They left at 8:00 P.M. on Friday, 6 October, their destination Kings Mountain.

KERR'S REPORT WAS ACCURATE. FERGUSON HAD LEFT Tate's Plantation about 4:00 A.M. on 6 October. His troops followed him along the old Cherokee Road that ran between Buffalo Creek and King's Creek. They forded King's Creek and passed through Stony Gap heading toward the northeast. By then they knew their destination was not to be Charlotte, which lay about thirty-five miles farther east. Instead, Ferguson had chosen to make camp and take up a position on top of the ridge known as Kings Mountain.

While his units were filing off to occupy campsites atop the ridge, Ferguson wrote Cornwallis what was to be his final report: "I arrived to day at Kings Mountain & have taken a post where I do not think I can be forced by a stronger enemy than that against us." The dispatch was given to a lad named John Ponder, who was to carry it to Cornwallis.

All indications are that Ferguson was taking up his mountaintop location not like the fox brought to bay by the hounds but so as to command a formidable defensive position while awaiting reinforcements from Cornwallis. He had already received the answer to his request for reinforcements from Cruger at Ninety-Six, who had replied that he did not have enough men to hold that post, much less to send men anywhere else. So

Ferguson knew that he would get no help from the south. What he did not know, however, was that help would not be forthcoming from Cornwallis, either. His commander would not send Tarleton, the most mobile force left to him, because his legion needed a rest, and moreover, Tarleton was incapacitated with malaria, as was Major Hanger, his second in command. Cornwallis himself was down with a "feverish cold" and of no mind to dispatch any of his main force on a chase to the west of Charlotte.

KINGS MOUNTAIN IS ACTUALLY A LONG RIDGE rising independently from a low range running from the northeast in North Carolina to the southwest in South Carolina. The ridge itself is in York County, S.C., about a mile and a half south of the present border between the Carolinas. It is shaped somewhat like a canoe paddle with a short handle, with the crest of the ridge running from the broad "paddle end" on the northeast to the narrower "handle end" on the southwest extremity. The crest is about 600 yards long, varying in width from 120 yards at the paddle end to 60 yards on the handle. In 1780 the crest was practically treeless, but all of its slopes were, and are today, heavily wooded, with occasional ravines and great boulders strewn everywhere. There was no natural cover on the summit of the ridge, which rises some sixty feet above the surrounding terrain, whereas the trees and boulders on the steep slopes would provide ideal protection for riflemen in scattered skirmish order.

Because he had sent out a foraging detachment on the morning of 7 October, Ferguson's total strength on Kings Mountain was about 900 men. Of those, 100 were "regular" Tories who had come south with Ferguson from the King's American Rangers, the Queen's Rangers, and the New Jersey Volunteers, and 800 were Tory militia from North and South Carolina. Ferguson's second in command, Captain Abraham de Peyster, was an aristocratic New Yorker of Huguenot descent, an able and efficient officer. The adjutant was Lieutenant Anthony Allaire, also a New Yorker of Huguenot descent.

All of Ferguson's men were well trained under British army drill regulations. They were armed with the Brown Bess musket equipped with a socket bayonet, and the men were well trained in its use. Some few of the newly joined Tories were equipped with a crude, makeshift "plug" bayonet with a wooden hilt that could be inserted in the muzzle for close combat, though it rendered the musket useless as a firearm.

The Tory militiamen were drilled to fight like the British regulars, in close-ordered ranks which, once engaged in battle, could move only forward or rearward on command. If, however, their enemy did not stand

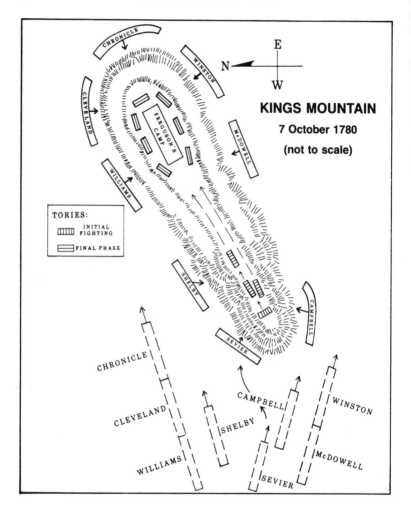

and fight—as the Patriot riflemen could not because they had no bayonets, nor was it in their style to stand when they could fade away and fire
from cover—the attackers could hold only the ground they stood on or
else fall back to reform a rearward line. And the rugged terrain they
would be fighting in was not conducive to maneuvering in close-ordered
ranks.

Another disadvantage of the position on Kings Mountain was one that
Ferguson could have overcome but did not. He had sufficient time to

protect his position with field fortifications such as abatis, breastworks, or earthworks, but he seems to have been content to rely on the slopes' boulders and trees as natural obstacles. It was possible, too, that he had underestimated his enemy's strength and capabilities, in particular the frontiersman's skill at fighting in wooded cover; the "barbarians" and "mongrels" cited in his proclamation were truly beneath contempt. There was the same arrogance in his pronouncement after he had established his position on the ridge: that "he defied God Almighty and all the rebels out of hell to overcome him."

THE NIGHT MARCH OF THE 900 PATRIOTS WAS ANYTHING but easy. They left Cowpens in pitch dark, and the black night closed in on them, with no moonlight or even starlight to guide their way. Their march was along rough backcountry roads, and to make things even more miserable a steady drizzle set in that lasted through the night. The drizzle caused every rifleman to sacrifice the comfort that would have been provided by hunting shirt and blanket. Those articles had to be used to cover the precious rifle from the wet, and above all to ensure that the muzzle and gunlock were kept dry.

Short halts were made to wolf down a few handfuls of parched corn or whatever else the marchers had in wallets or saddlebags. Just after sunrise on Saturday, 7 October, the column forded the Broad River at Cherokee Ford, below the point where it was joined by Buffalo Creek. The weather had not improved. The drizzle had changed to a steady rain that made it all the more difficult to keep the rifles dry, but being used to all kinds of weather, the men managed. By mid-morning the men were cursing and grumbling about their tired horses, and Colonels Campbell, Sevier, and Cleveland agreed that a rest was in order. However, when they approached Shelby with the idea they met with a flat refusal: "I will not stop until night, if I follow Ferguson into Cornwallis' lines." The column pushed on.

About six miles farther, one of the scouts reported that he had come upon a Tory girl who admitted that she had been in Ferguson's camp that very morning. She pointed out the ridge where Ferguson was encamped. A little farther on, the scouts brought in a prisoner, the Tory John Ponder, with Ferguson's last message to Cornwallis. When he was asked if Ferguson could be identified by his uniform, Ponder said that "while that officer was the best uniformed man on the mountain, they could not see his military suit, as he wore a checked shirt, or duster over it." They would also recognize that officer because he would be the only one who carried his sword in his left hand.

By noon the rain had stopped, and the column halted about a mile from the base of Kings Mountain. They dismounted, tied up their horses, and each followed his leader's orders to "throw the priming out of his pan, pick his touchhole, prime anew, examine bullets and see that everything was in readiness for battle."

Having cursed the rain throughout the march, the men were now beginning to realize that it could also be a blessing. The packed leaves that carpeted the approaches to the mountain and its slopes were soaked through, so there would be no telltale rustling as the columns of riflemen, all of them hunters and stalkers, made their stealthy approach.

As the men checked their weapons, the countersign was passed around —"Buford," for the man whose command had received no quarter from Tarleton's Tories at Waxhaws. Then it was time to make their final advance on foot. They formed into four columns for their approach march, heading initially to the northeast to reach the narrow end of the ridge first. The battle plan was for the columns to split up and move to assigned positions which, when movements were completed, would completely encircle Kings Mountain. The column on the extreme right was made up of the units of Winston, McDowell, and Sevier. Campbell led the next column to the left, and Shelby the column in the left center. The left-most column was composed of the commands of Chronicle, Cleveland, and Williams.

The plan was simple, and it was going to be executed rapidly and skillfully. The signal for launching coordinated attacks was "that when the center columns [Campbell's and Shelby's] were ready for the attack, they were to give the signal by raising a regular frontier war whoop, after the Indian style, and rush forward, doing the enemy all the injury possible."

The columns moved out and headed for their assigned positions. Tory security was so slack that Shelby's command was only a quarter of a mile from their position at the foot of the ridge before the first Tory sentries fired on them. Shelby's leadership was showing: he made sure that no one returned the fire. There would be plenty of action after they had started up the ridge.

On the opposite slope of the paddle handle Campbell's men were already creeping toward the top. When the first shots were fired, Campbell stripped off his coat and shouted: "Here they are; shoot like hell and fight like devils." They raised the war whoop, the so-called Tennessee yell that the over-mountain men had picked up from the Indians in the

Cherokee War, said to be the forerunner of the famous Rebel yell of the Civil War. The war whoop was a high-pitched, keening scream that would set a man's hair stiffening. The cries were taken up by Shelby's men and those of the other forces as they came into action.

In the Tory camp the drums beat the call to arms while Ferguson and his second in command, Captain de Peyster, were getting set to move the units into battle formations. De Peyster recognized the whooping that he had heard before in action. He told Ferguson, "These are the same yelling devils that were at Musgrove's Mill."

Ferguson's reply was to direct his units into line toward the paddle-handle end of the ridge, where they formed a three-sided square facing the riflemen coming up the slopes. The Tory units delivered a series of disciplined volleys that made their enemies duck for cover. But the riflemen continued to advance, taking cover, Indian fashion, behind trees, rocks, logs, and in ravines, and keeping up a deadly fire that was taking an increasing toll on the exposed Tory formations on the crest of the ridge.

It was these losses that caused Ferguson to order the first bayonet charge. The counterattack appeared successful—at first. The Patriots could not stand up to the bayonet, and they ran back down the slopes. Most of Campbell's men scattered as far as the bottom of the ridge and even up the slope behind them. Here was a real challenge to Campbell's leadership. The red-headed Scot responded at once. He was all over the place, calling his men to rally and return to the attack. He succeeded in getting them to reload and take up the fire against their enemy, whose ragged lines were retreating back up Kings Mountain. The Virginians returned, resuming their dodging attack from cover to cover, reloading and firing from behind the rocks and trees they had used before. Shelby rallied his men every bit as effectively as had Campbell, and they too renewed a fire that thinned the withdrawing Tory ranks. In the meantime Sevier's force had joined the battle.

The fighting around the southeastern end of the ridge now took up a pattern that was to characterize the whole battle. Three times the skirmishing riflemen attacked, and each time they were driven back by bayonet charges. Each time, the Tory formations had to halt and withdraw up the slopes, whereupon the Patriots returned to the attack, their accurate rifle fire making the Tories pay a stiff penalty for each counterattack.

It was also becoming obvious that Ferguson was paying the price for his failure to fortify his position on the ridge and his reliance on the trees and boulders as obstacles. For the "obstacles" had become ideal cover for his enemies' skirmishing tactics. Furthermore, the volleys that returned the riflemen's fire were consistently ineffective. In the hands of trained troops the Brown Bess musket could deliver deadly volleys under the ideal conditions it was designed for: firing platoon volleys at ranges up to fifty to seventy-five yards between close-ordered opposing formations facing each other on open, level terrain. At Kings Mountain, however, the conditions were anything but ideal for the musket, and matters were made worse by the Tory units having to fire downhill. Troops firing downhill will, unless specifically trained to avoid it, fail to compensate by sighting low, and consequently will fire over the heads of their targets. That is what happened to the Tory volleys at Kings Mountain; and to compound their loss in firepower, their own ranks were silhouetted against the skyline, thus making ideal targets for rifles that could kill at two or three hundred yards. The words of Light-Horse Harry Lee about Kings Mountain, that "it was more assailable by the rifle than defended with the bayonet," were no doubt true.

A less significant feature of the battle is the popular misconception that Ferguson's troops were dressed in the traditional scarlet coats and white breeches of the British regular soldier. While it is true that some of Ferguson's men—the "provincials" from the north, such as the King's American Rangers or the Queen's Rangers—were so clad, by far the greater number were wearing the civilian clothes in which they had enlisted. The only difference in dress between Tory and Patriot was brought out in recollections like that of Thomas Young, a sixteen-year-old private who fought under Colonel James Williams, and who got left in the middle of a firefight where "I found myself apparently between my own regiment and the enemy, as I judged from seeing the paper the Whigs wore in their hats, and the pine twigs the Tories wore in theirs, these being the badges of distinction."

THE BATTLE SURGED UP AND DOWN THE SLOPES of the paddle-handle end. The riflemen of Shelby's, Campbell's and Sevier's commands attacked again and again with ever deadlier effect. Meanwhile, other forces had launched their attacks against the broader expanse of the ridge on its northeast end. William Chronicle led his men forward from their position at the foot of the ridge, waving his hat and shouting, "Face to the hill." Struck down by a musket ball as he shouted, the twenty-five-year-old major died instantly. German-born Colonel Hambright continued the assault, which was met by a bayonet charge led by Captain de Peyster. Hambright's men were driven down the slopes, just as had been Shelby's and Campbell's, and were rallied by him in no less courageous fashion. Though wounded in the thigh, with blood filling his boot, Hambright called out in his German accent, "Fight on, my brave poys, a few minutes more and the battle will be over."

Cleveland, delayed by his 250-pound bulk and a swampy area, was late, but he came up in time to throw his men into the battle alongside Hambright's attack. Williams and Lacey came in next, filling the gap between Cleveland and Shelby on the north side of the ridge. In like manner Joseph McDowell's and Winston's men attacked to complete the encirclement on the south side of the ridge. All this pressure on the Tories atop the broad end of Kings Mountain was felt by Ferguson as he led the defense on the southeast end. The shrill call of his silver whistle was heard constantly above the roar of battle as he rallied one formation after another to bolster the defense all along the crest. It was soon apparent that his efforts were becoming futile at the southeast end, however, and he managed to withdraw his troops back along the crest of the ridge to the broad end of the mountain. As the Tories withdrew, Sevier's men came over the crest, and in conjunction with Shelby's and Campbell's forces were now masters of the whole paddle-handle portion of the ridge.

By this time all of the Patriot forces had been engaged. The net thrown around Ferguson's force was being tightened as the riflemen came pushing up the slopes from all directions. The smoke from rifles and muskets covered the mountain, obscuring some Tory units from time to time and drifting down the ravines and woods of the slopes. Now and then Ferguson could be seen through the smoke as he rode from unit to unit, rallying his men around the formal tent camp on the broad end of the ridge. He had been wounded in the hand of his useless right arm but continued to carry his sword in his good left hand. He got some units lined up to defend the camp, but those he had formed into a square soon deteriorated into a shrinking circle of beaten men. In one Tory unit a white flag fluttered for a moment, but Ferguson towered over it on horseback and cut it down with his sword. Another went up on the other side of the camp; Ferguson galloped over and cut it down with another stroke. When Captain de Peyster counseled surrender, Ferguson shouted back that "never would he yield to such damned banditti." And he made it clear that he meant it. He charged at the rebels at the head of a few volunteers ready to follow him in his desperate assault, and tried to break out through Sevier's men. Brandishing his sword in his left hand, he spurred directly at the rebels on his white horse. It was an attempt as futile as it was desperate. At least fifty rifles were aimed at Ferguson and his party. Every man in Ferguson's band went down, either killed or mortally wounded. It is said that six or seven bullets ripped into Ferguson's body; both arms were broken, and he fell from his horse to die after he had been carried away from the firing.

With Ferguson's fall and the overrunning of the ridge by the combined forces of the Patriots, organized resistance crumbled away. Captain de Peyster took command of the masses huddled around the camp and the wagon park, but any attempt at counterattack or breakout was clearly impossible. The fight had gone out of the force. White flags in the form of handkerchiefs or shirts appeared among the milling defenders, but they were ignored and their bearers were shot down.

The aftermath of Kings Mountain is neither pleasant in the telling nor does it do credit to the Patriot forces. De Peyster, riding out on his gray horse, carried a white flag which was acknowledged by Campbell, yet the shooting of the now-defenseless Tories went on. De Peyster protested to Campbell, "It's damned unfair, damned unfair." Campbell strode through his men, knocking down rifles and ordering, "For God's sake don't shoot. It is murder to kill them now, for they have raised the flag." He then directed de Peyster to have the officers separate themselves, and for the men to lay down their arms, sit down, and remove their hats.

In other parts of the ridgetop Tories cried out for quarter and got "Buford's quarter" or "Tarleton's quarter" instead—in the form of rifle bullets. Shelby, enraged at both sides, came forward and shouted to the Tories, "Damn you, if you want quarter, throw down your arms!" All within earshot obeyed, but elsewhere the firing into the defenders went on. Finally, more of the responsible Patriot militia officers tried to stop the slaughter, knocking aside rifles or pleading with their owners by name to stop shooting. Yet even after the shooting stopped and the prisoners were seated on the ground, an alarm was raised when one of Ferguson's foraging parties returned. Some of them saw the situation and fired a parting shot before fleeing. One of the shots presumably struck down Colonel James Williams, who died later.

The cry went up of a Tory attack, and Campbell ordered the rifleman nearest him to shoot into the prisoners to subdue any attempt to break for freedom. The order was obeyed, and, according to Lieutenant Hughes, "We killed near a hundred of them and hardly could be restrained from killing the whole."

Shelby himself had this to say about the aftermath of the battle: "It was some time before a complete cessation of the firing on our part could be effected. Our men who had been scattered in the battle were continually coming up and continued to fire, without comprehending in the heat of the moment what had happened; and some who had heard that at Buford's defeat, the British had refused quarter . . . were willing to follow that bad example."

When the "bad examples" had been quelled and all the shooting stopped, the victors rounded up the prisoners and looked to their own wounded and dead. The Patriots had lost 28 killed and 64 wounded out of over 900 in the battle. Their enemies lost 157 killed, 163 wounded too badly to be moved, and 698 prisoners. On the following day, Sunday, 8 October, the partisans pulled their prisoners' wagons across the camp fires and left them burning as they marched the prisoners away. Near Gilbert Town, thirty were convicted in some sort of drum-head trial; twelve were condemned to die, and nine were actually hanged. The odyssey of the remaining prisoners went on as far as Hillsboro, where they were left by Cleveland's men. Eventually most of them escaped through the carelessness or the disregard of their warders.

Ferguson's body was defiled by some of the less compassionate of the frontiersmen, who urinated on it after it was stripped of belongings and clothing. Others, more humane, gave the fallen Scot a "decent" burial by wrapping his body in a raw beef hide and interring it in a shallow ravine near the crest of the ridge. On the 150th anniversary of the battle, a simple stone monument to Ferguson was erected by American citizens. It is dedicated to: "A soldier of military distinction and of honor."

THE FRONTIERSMEN HAD RIDDEN HARD AND LONG for vengeance, and they had tasted deeply of it. Now they dispersed, going their separate ways to homesteads and settlements in the backcountry and beyond the Blue Ridge. Though their accomplishment would be retold around firesides for generations, it is doubtful that any participant in the Kings Mountain campaign could have realized the far-reaching effects of the victory.

To the British and their Tory allies the impact of Kings Mountain was as appalling as it was immediate. Imagine the reaction of Cornwallis when the confirmation of Ferguson's disaster reached him at Charlotte. Ferguson dead and his entire force wiped out in one day—actually in one hour—and the western frontier exposed to a Patriot uprising. Rumor had the Patriot frontiersmen's numbers at 3,000 with their next objective Charlotte. Instead of the rebels of North Carolina being subjugated, the western half of the province had been lost, and the loss of the central area was now a looming possibility, especially without organized Loyalist forces to hold the countryside. Clearly, in Mark Boatner's summation, Kings Mountain had "tipped the balance of Whig-Tory armed support in favor of the rebel cause" (*Encyclopedia of the American Revolution*).

However reluctantly, Cornwallis decided to give up North Carolina and retreat back into South Carolina. On 14 October the dreary retrograde march began. The fall rains set in and beat down on the sodden British while the red-clay roads became quagmires; yet because of flooded swamps and dense forests, the roads could not be bypassed. Some twenty supply wagons were wrecked or abandoned; others were captured by Patriot militia that had turned out to harass the unhappy British. Cornwallis himself had to be carried in one of the wagons, having come down with a "bilious fever." After fifteen days of miserable marching, the commander in chief and his famished army pulled into Winnsboro, where they were immobilized in camp until December. Cornwallis's offensive into North Carolina had been stopped cold, and it could not be resumed without considerable reinforcement and change of plan. Kings Mountain had altered the whole course of the war in the South.

Although the long-range consequences of Cornwallis's failure were yet to be seen, there were ominous signals flashing beyond the horizon, not the least of which were Gates's replacement by Nathanael Greene and renewed offensive operations against the British in the South by partisan, Continental, and militia forces. The partisan victory caused Sir Henry Clinton to view Kings Mountain in retrospect as the check that "so encouraged the spirit of rebellion in the Carolinas that it could never afterward be humbled." With historic hindsight, he recognized the battle to be "the first link in a chain of evils that followed each other in regular succession until they at last ended in the total loss of America."

KINGS MOUNTAIN STANDS ON ITS OWN as a one-of-a-kind battle. With the sole exception of Ferguson himself, it was fought entirely by Americans against Americans, ending in a decisive Patriot victory. A force of Patriot irregulars, reaching a total of nearly 1,800, armed principally with the frontier rifle, had annihilated a trained body of the enemy armed mainly with the musket. The Patriot force had emerged on call, organized itself into units with competent leaders, marched on campaign as a controlled and highly mobile corps, and utterly destroyed its enemy. It was a force that was logistically independent and self-disciplined; Shelby said to his men before the battle: "When we encounter the enemy, don't wait for the word of command. Let each one of you be your own officer, and do the very best you can." It was led by veterans who had proved themselves in frontier warfare. The melding of those leaders with their riflemen resulted in skillfully coordinated combinations of tactical movement and firepower.

Kings Mountain appeared to mark the beginning of the end of Cornwallis's offensive in the South. The next encounter between organized forces would confirm that beginning.

EIGHT

Cowpens

TWO DAYS BEFORE THE BATTLE OF KINGS MOUNTAIN was fought, the South was beginning to get a well-deserved break. On 5 October 1780 the Continental Congress passed a resolution declaring "that the Commander-in-Chief be and is hereby directed to appoint an officer to command the southern army, in the room of Major General Gates." George Washington thereupon appointed Major General Nathanael Greene. On 2 December Greene arrived at Charlotte and assumed command of the "Grand Army" of the Southern Department.

History shows more than a few examples of armies in wretched condition taken over and revivified by able commanders. Although Greene's command had a strength of nearly 2,500 on paper, 1,000 fewer than that were actually present for duty, and of these, fewer than 800 were properly clothed and equipped. The army's soldiers had, in Greene's words, "lost all discipline," and had become "so addicted to plundering that they were a terror to the inhabitants."

To Greene's clear vision the immediate material needs were obvious: the scanty reserve rations had to be replenished; horses and wagons must be found to haul provisions and other supplies. Once these material needs were being filled, discipline must be restored. Nothing could be accomplished in the army's present location, however, so Greene's first priority was to establish a "camp of repose" in an area where there was enough food and forage to sustain the army while it was being equipped and readied to take the field against Cornwallis.

Still, not all of Greene's legacy was on the minus side. From Gates he had inherited superb leaders such as Brigadier General Daniel Morgan and Lieutenant Colonel John Eager Howard, as well as an able engineer in the person of the Polish volunteer Thaddeus Kosciuszko.

Greene sent Kosciuszko on a reconnaissance mission to find his camp of repose. The engineer reported back with a recommended area centered on Cheraw near the Pee Dee River, some sixty miles southeast of Charlotte. Marching his army to the Cheraw area, unopposed by Cornwallis, would present no problem to Greene. What did pose a problem was that such a move would uncover Cornwallis's central advance route of Camden-Charlotte-Salisbury, and, equally discomforting, would also present to the people of the region the appearance of retreating at a time when he wished to encourage the Patriots whose confidence and support he needed so much. In short, his dilemma was to get his army to Cheraw while still carrying on operations that would not only encourage the people but would further his support of partisan operations.

The last was a prime consideration because of his need to exploit his opponent's vulnerability. Although Cornwallis had his refitted main body at Winnsboro, the British leader had to continue to maintain his ring of outposts stretching from Augusta to Ninety-Six, to Camden, and to Georgetown on the coast. That widespread net of regional control required extensive lines of communication, and cutting those supply lines and raiding their security posts was the tour de force of the partisans Marion, Sumter, and Pickens. Until he could risk his army in offensive operations, these were the only cards Greene could play.

Greene's solution for employing his organized forces seemed as out of character as it was daring; he decided to divide his army in the face of a formidable opponent. In M. F. Treacy's appraisal: "He did it himself, on his own responsibility. He called no council of war. He simply issued the orders, knowing full well that he was violating all the classic rules of warfare. . . . Greene knew the rules and the penalties for breaking them, but he was also a realist" (*Prelude to Yorktown*).

Greene's reasoning for the decision to split his army between himself and Dan Morgan, with Morgan operating over 100 miles to the west, can be seen in its five elegant facets: (1) if Cornwallis struck in force against Greene at Cheraw, Morgan could at once attack Ninety-Six or Augusta; (2) conversely, if Cornwallis moved in strength against Morgan, Greene could move to threaten Charleston and the British main supply line; (3) if Cornwallis chose to resume his advance into North Carolina along the Camden-Charlotte-Salisbury axis, Morgan and Greene could move to threaten both British flanks or the main force's rear; (4) Greene and Morgan could rely on the superior mobility of their small forces to avoid pitched battle with the slower-moving main force of Cornwallis; (5) in the unlikely event of Cornwallis's remaining inactive at Winnsboro,

Greene could use that valuable time in rehabilitating his army while increasing his support of partisan forays.

On 20 December 1780 Greene's own wing of the army, nominally commanded by General Isaac Huger of South Carolina, marched to Cheraw in order to establish the camp of repose. Greene took with him about 1,100 men: 650 Continentals, 157 Maryland militia, and 303 Virginia militia. He then reconfirmed Morgan as commander of the light infantry and reinforced him, so that his total strength of 600 included 320 Maryland and Delaware Continentals, 200 Virginia militia, and 80 dragoons under Lieutenant Colonel William Washington. Morgan placed his infantry under the command of Lieutenant Colonel John Eager Howard of Maryland. If Greene was fortunate in having Morgan in his army, Morgan was equally lucky in getting two subordinates like Washington and Howard, as events were to prove.

After the Quebec expedition and the two battles at Saratoga, Congress had not done right by Daniel Morgan. Forced to see junior officers promoted over him time after time, in understandable disgust he had resigned his colonel's commission in July 1779 and returned to his farm in Frederick County, Virginia. In June of the following year Morgan received orders from that same Congress to report to General Gates and be "employed in the southern army." Since there was no mention of appointing him a brigadier general or even to his former rank, Morgan chose to ignore the order. When he heard about the Camden disaster, however, he set aside his injured pride and went straight to Hillsboro to report to Gates, who assigned Morgan to the command of his newly formed corps of light infantry.

Congress finally made Morgan a brigadier general, effective 13 October 1780. Greene then appointed Brigadier General Morgan to command of a force that would operate independently under Greene's "instructions." Morgan was to proceed to the west side of the Catawba River, where he would be joined by a body of volunteer militia units from General Davidson's and General Sumter's forces. He would operate against the enemy on the west side of the river, either offensively or defensively, "as your prudence and discretion may direct." An essential part of Morgan's mission would be to "give protection to that part of the country and spirit up the people, to annoy the enemy in that quarter, collect the provisions and forage." If the enemy moved after Greene's force, Morgan was to "move in such direction as will enable you to join me if necessary, or to fall back upon the flank or into the rear of the enemy, as occasion may require. You will spare no pains to get good intelligence of the enemy's situation, and keep me constantly advised of both your and their movements."

Morgan's orders were dated 16 December. Four days later, Greene and Huger were on the way. Heavy rains turned the roads to rivers of mud, and the weak horses and men found it tough going, but on 26 December they came to Cheraw Hill and established their base camp.

Morgan left Charlotte on the twenty-first, the day after Greene's departure, made the fifty-eight miles to the Pacolet River, and on Christmas Day set up his camp near Grindall's Shoals. The miserable weather and hard march were soon forgotten with the arrival of Major Joseph McDowell, of Kings Mountain fame, with his 190 North Carolina riflemen, bringing Morgan's strength to nearly 800 men. While planning his operations Morgan had not forgotten his instructions to "give protection to the people" and to "annoy the enemy in that quarter." Seeing an opportunity to do both, on 27 December he dispatched William Washington with his 80 dragoons and 200 mounted militia to intercept and destroy a Tory raiding party of 250 riders who had been raiding the Patriot settlements near Fair Forest Creek. Washington rode hard and struck with a vengeance. After covering forty miles on his second day, he attacked the Tories at Hammond's Store, about thirty miles northeast of Ninety-Six. Washington destroyed his enemy, killing or wounding 150 and capturing 40. Before returning to base, he sent Colonel Joseph Hayes fifteen miles closer to Ninety-Six with 40 dragoons to take a small Tory stockade called Fort Williams. Although Hayes did not linger in the area, a frantic message reached Cornwallis on New Year's Day 1781 that the rebels were mounting a massive raid and had already neared Ninety-Six.

OVER IN WINNSBORO, CORNWALLIS WAS PUZZLED. Why had the new rebel general split an army that was already inferior in numbers and quality to his own? In regard to the division and size of Greene's army, Cornwallis's intelligence was accurate. The latest reports that he had received by the evening of 1 January had to be exaggerated. Morgan advancing on Ninety-Six with 3,000 men? Nonsense! He went back to his map and began to discern what Greene had done. Although it defied all the rules, the American general's move made sense. Cornwallis saw what would happen if he struck out in force to his left at Morgan, toward his right at Huger (Greene), or up the center into North Carolina.

Very well then, perhaps this boldness of Greene's could be catching—and Cornwallis's personal military history had never revealed any lack of audacity. He would not divide his own army into two forces; instead, he would undertake a *three*-pronged offensive. A mobile force under Lord Rawdon at Camden would operate to fend off Huger should he advance from Cheraw. A second force under Tarleton would move at once to catch and destroy Morgan. Cornwallis himself, with the main body, would move north on or about 7 January to operate in conjunction with Tarleton in mopping up any of Morgan's force that should attempt to escape. Then, with Morgan out of the way, the next and final phase would be to turn on Greene and Huger with his main force, which would be aided by Rawdon and Tarleton.

Tarleton had, in the meantime, disposed of the chimera of Morgan moving on Ninety-Six with 3,000 men; the British cavalry leader's reconnaissance elements had confirmed that Washington's strikes at Hammond's Store and Fort Williams were made by raiders who had since withdrawn. In a letter to his chief dated 4 January Tarleton proposed that he be sent to destroy Morgan's corps, or push it over Broad River, toward Kings Mountain.

Cornwallis replied on 5 January that "you have exactly done what I wished you to do [pushing on in pursuit of Morgan], and understood my intentions perfectly. . . . I propose marching on Sunday [7 January]." Cornwallis actually left Winnsboro on 8 January, preceded by Tarleton, who had started after Morgan two days earlier. The hunt was on.

WE HAVE SEEN SOMETHING OF TARLETON and his modus operandi at Waxhaws some months before. The cocky redhead and his black dragoon helmet stand out in Reynolds's portrait in about as dashing a pose as a cavalryman could wish: undisturbed by rearing horses, he is reaching for the saber that would make him famous—or infamous, depending on whose side one was on—in a score of battles and skirmishes. Short, stocky, physically strong, handsome in a sensual way, he was as impetuous as he was ruthless; we have seen a sample of the ruthlessness that made "Tarleton's quarter" a term familiar to all southerners. He had been placed in command of the British Legion, a combined force of green-jacketed dragoons and light infantry, sometimes mounted, recruited from Tories in New York and New Jersey. He and his legion had come to South Carolina with Clinton and Cornwallis, and by January 1781 he had three victories to his credit there: Monck's Corner, Lenud's

Ferry, and Waxhaws. During the Kings Mountain campaign he had been desperately ill with a fever, but he was now completely recovered and itching for action. His force moving after Morgan consisted of his legion of 300 dragoons and 250 infantry; a battalion of the 71st Highlanders, 200 men; the 7th Regiment, whose 200 men had yet to see action; 50 troopers of the 17th Light Dragoons; a detachment of Royal Artillery with two "grasshoppers";* and a small party of Tory militia; in all a total of 1,100 rank and file.

Tarleton's northward advance, however, got off to anything but a flying start. Again the rains set in to slow down operations. Tarleton moved only as far as Duggin's Plantation on Indian Creek. There he was stuck, halted by rains and swollen streams, from 6 to 9 January. In the meantime, Cornwallis was having his own troubles. It took him eight days to cover the forty miles from Winnsboro to Hillhouse Plantation on Turkey Creek, where he encamped on 16 January. During the period 9–16 January Cornwallis received only one message from Tarleton, and as a result did not know that on the fourteenth Tarleton had crossed the Enoree and the Tyger rivers and was in hot pursuit of Morgan. Neither did Tarleton know that Cornwallis had slowed his own advance at Turkey Creek on the assumption that Tarleton was still being delayed by swollen rivers.

FROM HIS CAMP AT GRINDALL SHOALS ON THE Pacolet, Morgan had written Greene a gloomy letter on 4 January wherein, in uncharacteristic fashion, he set down a whole catalog of woes. Greene, however, was cheerful in both his knowledge of the enemy's troubles and his reply on 13 January: "It is my wish also that you should hold your ground if possible, for I foresee the disagreeable consequences that will result from a retreat. . . . Col. Tarleton is said to be on his way to pay you a visit. I doubt not but he will have a decent reception and a proper dismission." Prophetic words indeed.

Morgan no doubt intended to "hold his ground," but he wanted the ground to be that of his choosing, not Tarleton's. Consequently, when he learned of his enemy's crossing of the Enoree and Tyger rivers with a force of over a thousand men, Morgan moved on 15 January to block the fords across the Pacolet. His scouts then informed him that Tarleton had

---

*Light three-pounder guns carried on horseback and mounted on legs in the firing position. The legs and the fact that the gun bounced when fired (it had no way to recoil) apparently account for the name "grasshopper."

moved up the Pacolet to Old Iron Works. Morgan saw at once that if Tarleton got his force across the river above him, he would be poised to turn him out of his main position at Grindall Shoals, or, by moving eastward, get between Morgan and Greene. So Morgan moved his force upriver and bivouacked on the north side at Old Iron Works.

For once Morgan underestimated his opponent's maneuvering skill. Tarleton did indeed move to Old Iron Works and bivouacked across the river from Morgan. In the darkness of the early morning, however, Tarleton quietly broke camp and slipped away downriver to cross the Pacolet at Easterwood Shoals, only six miles below Morgan. Morgan learned of Tarleton's crossing about 6:00 A.M. on 16 January and wasted no time in falling back toward Thicketty Creek. His retreat was followed by Tarleton's patrols, one of which discovered that the Americans had moved again, and so hurriedly that their breakfast had been left half-cooked on their camp fires. Tarleton let his light troops finish off the breakfast while he wrote to Cornwallis that "*Morgan is in force and gone for Cherokee Ford.* I am now on my march. I wish he could be stopped." Tarleton was now expecting Cornwallis to move toward Kings Mountain in order to prevent Morgan from proceeding eastward toward Greene. Perhaps they could entrap the rebel between the two British forces. Unfortunately for Tarleton, Cornwallis was not close enough to threaten Morgan. Equally unfortunate for the British cause was Tarleton's assumption that Morgan would not stand and fight.

MORGAN HAD GIVEN TARLETON GOOD REASON for believing that the American force was in full retreat—for indeed it was. In Kenneth Roberts's words: "There was no question about it: Morgan and his army were running for dear life, and the one certain thing that Morgan couldn't risk was having Tarleton's cavalry catch him in the running" (*The Battle of Cowpens*).

There were plenty of things to be weighed in Morgan's mind while he was making that forced march on the sixteenth. John Eager Howard's mixed force of Continentals and veteran Virginian militia constituted no problem. They were superbly led, and the Virginians were mostly old Continental soldiers who had served their terms of enlistment and re-joined as volunteers. It was the other militia that bothered Dan Morgan. If he positioned them near swamps to protect his flanks or rear from Tarleton's dragoons, he might as well wave them a goodbye; militia were attracted to swamps like moths to candles, and they could disappear in them like magic. He had to find a field where he could put his militia of

Carolinians and Georgians in battle array where they would be fighting in front of Howard's men, the hard core of his little army.

Morgan was bold to stay and fight. Only two days before, he had learned that his enemy's force consisted mainly of regular and veteran units, and those units probably outnumbered his own hard core by three to one. Nevertheless, he was sick and tired of running, and moreover, if he kept on running he would soon face the problem of getting his force across the swollen Broad River with Tarleton closing in on his tail.

Dan Morgan was not dismayed, however; all indications are that he was more annoyed than anything. He was well aware of Tarleton's impetuous charges, his hell-for-leather tactics that could destroy an enemy caught by surprise. Morgan talked with a number of officers who could give him their personal experience of his foe's tactics. "Tarleton never brings on the attack himself," said Colonel Winn, who had commanded Sumter's reserve at the battle at Blackstock's Plantation. "His mode of fighting is surprise. By doing this he sends two or three troops of horse, and if he can throw the party in confusion, with the reserve he falls on and cuts them to pieces."

Sometime toward mid-afternoon a messenger from Andrew Pickens reached Morgan. Pickens had crossed the Broad River with about 150 mounted militia. Other groups of militia were also coming, by different routes, to join him. The question, of course, was where? Since Morgan and all the joiners were in motion, there had to be a designated place where all could converge—and it had to be nearby.

One of the most trusted officers Morgan could ask for expert advice was Major Joseph McDowell. The Patriots' last assembly area before the battle had been at Saunders's place at Cowpens. McDowell described Cowpens. It consisted mainly of rolling or flat ground, with some stands of hickory, pines, or red oaks, he said. There was no underbrush, and the long grass made fine pasturing for cattle that were turned loose to forage through the open forest. The center of the area, marked by the Green River Road, was about five miles from the Broad River and from Morgan's present location.

Morgan made his decision. He sent messages to Pickens and the other oncoming militia leaders to meet him at Cowpens. Then he rode ahead to reconnoiter, taking with him Howard and the senior militia leaders. They approached the Cowpens area from the south, coming up the red-clay trail known as the Green River Road, because Morgan wanted to familiarize his officers with the road that Tarleton's force would have to use to come into Cowpens.

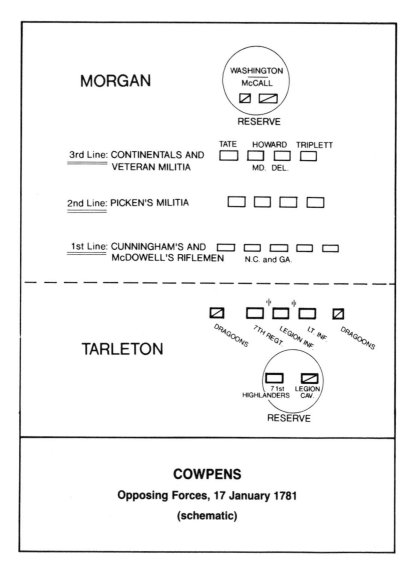

COWPENS

Opposing Forces, 17 January 1781

(schematic)

When he led his party out of the woods at the south end of Cowpens, Morgan halted to survey the ground in front of him to the northwest. The ground—meadowlike, as described by McDowell—sloped gradually upward to a low crest about 400 yards ahead. Beyond that was what appeared to be a ridge formed by two small hills. Morgan would later find that behind the nearer crest was a swale or extended dip running about 80 yards to the far, or more northern, crest. Taken in all, the terrain was indeed very gently rolling, with the higher ground never more than 25 yards higher than the plain.

The rolling open terrain was ideal for the movements of cavalry, and there were no obstacles such as thick woods, swamps, or underbrush, which could have served to cover Morgan's flanks. In addition, the Broad River, about five miles distant, curved around the rear of the position, cutting off a retreat in that direction. But Morgan had more on his mind. As he wrote later: "I would not have had a swamp in view of my militia on any consideration; they would have made for it. . . . And, as to covering my wings, I knew my adversary, and was perfectly sure I should have nothing but downright fighting. As to retreat, it was the very thing I wished to cut off all hope of. . . . Had I crossed the river [on 16 January], one half of my militia would immediately have abandoned me."

Morgan positioned his infantry in three battle lines, using the Green River Road to mark the center of the positions. The first line to encounter Tarleton's advance would be made up of 150 picked riflemen: North Carolinians under Major McDowell and Georgians under Major John Cunningham. The riflemen were to take cover—no need to instruct *them* in that regard—and wait until their targets were within fifty yards. Then they were to pick off "the men with the epaulets," getting at least two hits before they fell back to take their places in the second line of militia.

The second line of militia, about 300 men, would be commanded by Andrew Pickens and would be posted astride the road 150 yards to the rear of the first line. Morgan instructed the second line to get off at least two aimed volleys at a killing distance of fifty paces and then withdraw—*but not to the rear.* Instead, the whole force—the riflemen and militia of both lines—was to file off to the left, pass around the left flank of the third line, and reassemble in the rear, under cover as part of the army's reserve. In so ordering their fire and movement, Morgan had anticipated the militia not standing to fight. He knew they would not, and he made their withdrawal a basic part of his battle plan.

The third line, the main battle line, was to be positioned 150 yards behind the second line, just below the topographical crest of the first ridge. It would consist of the Maryland and Delaware Continentals in the center astride the road, flanked on the right by Tate's Virginians and a company of Georgians. On the left of the Continentals would be Triplett's Virginians. The whole was to be commanded by Lieutenant Colonel Howard. Morgan's main battle line was composed of as good a veteran infantry as would ever be found in an American army—battle-hardened men under one of the outstanding leaders of the war. John Eager Howard was a Marylander who had already served with distinction at White Plains, Germantown, Monmouth, and Camden. He would fight under Greene at Guilford Courthouse, Hobkirk's Hill, and Eutaw Springs, and would later be referred to by that commander as "as good an officer as the world affords. . . . He deserves a statue of gold no less than Roman and Grecian heroes."

Finally, in reserve under another formidable leader would be Colonel William Washington's eighty dragoons, reinforced by a provisional battalion of forty-five mounted militiamen from North Carolina and Georgia under Lieutenant Colonel James McCall. McCall's men were to be armed with sabers issued from a supply wagon. The cavalry were to be posted to the rear of the second ridge, about a half mile behind Howard's line. In Morgan's summation one can imagine him ending with something like this: "The whole idea is to lead Benny* into a trap, so we can blast his cavalry and infantry as they come up these slopes. When they've been cut down to size by our fire, we'll attack *them*."

MORGAN DID MORE THAN LAY OUT HIS PLAN TO his senior officers. Not only were junior officers and sergeants informed, but Morgan would not rest until every soldier understood what part he was to play in the battle. That was one reason why he could be found going from camp fire to camp fire throughout the night before the battle. Another reason was to check on and build morale, and still another was the twinges of rheumatism and sciatica that had plagued him for weeks and wouldn't let him sleep.

The Old Wagoner took every advantage of his reputation and the fact that he spoke the language of his men. He knew how to tell a dirty story and how to play on their hatred of the British and the Tories. And he knew how to stir up rivalry by intimating that he had heard much talk about Carolinians being such expert riflemen—but could they prove it, etc.

As he limped around the campfires Morgan was also seeing to a score of details. He made sure that rations had been issued for supper and that corn cakes were cooked for breakfast, that the troops had gotten their twenty-four rounds of ammunition per man, that the baggage wagons were ready to pull out as soon as the men had loaded their blanket rolls in

---

*Morgan liked to refer to Tarleton as "Ben" or "Benny."

the morning. He greeted Pickens and his 150 mounted men as they came in, as well as other groups. He made sure that the arrivals knew his battle plan. As the youthful Thomas Young, of Major Jolly's company of South Carolina militia, remembered:

> It was upon this occasion that I was more perfectly convinced of General Morgan's qualifications to command militia than I had ever before been. . . . Long after I had laid down, he was going among the soldiers, encouraging them and telling them that the "Old Wagoner" would crack his whip over Ben (Tarleton) in the morning, as sure as he lived. "Just hold up your heads boys," he would say, "three fires, and you are free! And then, when you return to your homes, how the old folks will bless you, and the girls kiss you, for your gallant conduct." I don't think that he slept a wink that night.

Morgan made his final round of the camp before first light, ignoring his rheumatism. There was still time left to make the most important inspection of all. He rode the lines. He joked with McDowell's and Cunningham's forward-line riflemen as he rode past, but his oft-repeated reminders to aim for the epaulet men had deadly meaning.

When he reached Howard's line of Continentals and veteran militia, he ceased his exhortations. Stirring speeches or instructions as to how to do their duty would have been insulting to the veterans. So Morgan took up his post behind his final line. His men were as ready as they could get. They had been rested and fed well, posted properly and quietly, and drilled in what was expected of them. As for his enemy, Morgan could only hope that Tarleton's men had been turned out to march in the cold darkness across creeks, ravines, and rough trails, and always with the knowledge that they were moving in unknown and hostile terrain.

TARLETON HAD INDEED TURNED HIS MEN OUT long before daylight. He had reveille beaten at 2:00 A.M., and within the hour his column was on the march. During the night Tarleton had gotten reports that the rebels "had struck into byways" that led toward Thicketty Creek. That same evening some of his Tory scouts brought in a prisoner, a rebel militia colonel who had apparently lost his unit. Tarleton questioned him, and the information he got confirmed that of his Tory scouts: he was within striking distance of Morgan's force, and it was imperative that the Americans be prevented from crossing the Broad.

Accordingly Tarleton took up a tactical order of march appropriate to a mobile column of pursuit prepared for a swift strike against its enemy.

He stripped his force of its baggage and wagons, which were left to follow at daybreak. Three companies of light infantry, supported by the legion infantry, made up the British advance guard. The 7th Regiment (with the two three-pounder grasshoppers), and the 1st battalion of the 71st composed the army's center, and the cavalry and mounted infantry brought up the rear. An advance guard of light infantry and the cavalry in the rear was a sensible arrangement for moving through broken terrain much intersected by creeks and ravines. The march proceeded even more slowly because of the need to scout out the front and flanks. Thicketty Creek was crossed before dawn, when an advance guard of cavalry was ordered forward.

Part of the advance cavalry ran into an American patrol of Georgia Rangers led by Captain Inman. The British captured two Americans, but Inman and the rest got away to report the encounter to Morgan. When questioned, the prisoners revealed that the Americans had encamped only five miles further on, at Cowpens. Tarleton at once sent forward Captain Ogilvie of the legion with two companies of dragoons. About 6:45 A.M., fifteen minutes before full sunrise, Ogilvie rode up the Green River Road and came out of the woods into Cowpens. He had a few troopers advance cautiously into the open. They drew scattered shots from overeager riflemen and galloped back into the woods. Ogilvie sent a messenger flying to Tarleton: Morgan had not only halted, but his army had formed for battle.

Tarleton took time to call in Tory guides, who gave him a hasty but accurate description of the ground General Morgan occupied and the country in his rear. An exultant Tarleton was sure that at last he had got Morgan where he wanted him, pinned down with a swollen river at his rear.

Tarleton took no time out to rest his troops, who had just made a four-hour night march through rugged terrain, nor did he even consider a halt. He rode forward with his command party to reconnoiter the American position while his column continued to advance up the Green River Road. According to Christopher Ward, "a sight of the first line of riflemen checked him before he was near enough to observe satisfactorily the main battle line. He at once ordered his Legion cavalry forward to dislodge the sharpshooters" (*War of the American Revolution*). They broke from a walk into a trot, an advance calculated to drive in the American forward line. A sudden rattle of rifle fire, however, pulled the dragoons up short. The lucky ones wheeled and made it back to the woods—with fifteen out of fifty saddles emptied.

Undismayed, Tarleton ordered his column to debouch into the open, some 400 yards in front of the American front line, and deploy in battle formation. He put his light infantry on the right with one grasshopper on its left. In the center the legion infantry was deployed with the other grasshopper on its left. The 7th Regiment formed on the left of the legion infantry. A detachment of fifty dragoons covered each force flank, with the 71st Highlanders and 200 legion cavalry in reserve.

Seen from Morgan's vantage point, Tarleton's army was a brilliant panoply displayed before the dark green of the forest background:

A company of British dragoons led off to the British right, followed by the scarlet coats and white breeches of infantry companies wheeling into line with drill ground precision. A small blue-coated section followed the infantry, then there was a second column of infantry in green jackets. Behind it another scarlet and white column debouched from the forest and came up into precise line to the left of the green jackets. Another dark blue section moved up alongside the scarlet infantry, and finally another company of green dragoons took post on the British left flank. Sergeants dressed the ranks into rigid lines that became a brilliant array of scarlet, green, blue, and white. The colorful line was topped with a glittering line of bayonets as the British infantry shouldered arms, and the long line came marching forward, drums rolling and regimental colors rippling in the wind. (Wood, *Leaders and Battles*)

Tarleton could not restrain his eagerness. He issued the order to attack before all of his commanders were ready to advance. He had the grasshoppers open fire as the infantry marched forward. The first line of American riflemen fell back, firing as they withdrew, still taking their toll of British casualties. They then found places in Pickens's line, which was standing steadily in place, ready to deliver the first volley.

The second line of militia had not long to wait. Undeterred by the fire of the skirmishes, the long ranks of British soldiery were coming on. When those ranks were at a sure killing distance—less than a hundred paces—the first volley tore into the British line. The effect was a shock that was quickly followed by the second volley. The overall effect was to smash the British into a stunned halt; more than 40 percent of the marksmen's victims were officers, just as Morgan had urged.

Even so, the British reformed and, bayonets at the ready, their realigned line came on. Now was the moment of decision. If Andrew Pickens's militia panicked and fled, all would be lost for the Americans. But

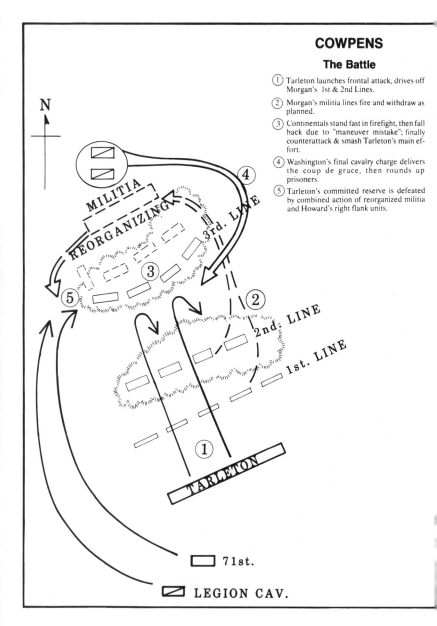

COWPENS

The Battle

1. Tarleton launches frontal attack, drives off Morgan's 1st & 2nd Lines.

2. Morgan's militia lines fire and withdraw as planned.

3. Continentals stand fast in firefight, then fall back due to "maneuver mistake"; finally counterattack & smash Tarleton's main effort.

4. Washington's final cavalry charge delivers the coup de grace, then rounds up prisoners.

5. Tarleton's committed reserve is defeated by combined action of reorganized militia and Howard's right flank units.

N

MILITIA

REORGANIZING

3rd. LINE

2nd. LINE

1st. LINE

TARLETON

☐ 71st.

▨ LEGION CAV.

the militia proceeded to carry out Morgan's order to take off to the left—though not without a hitch. The "filing off to the left" became a racing river of men which flowed around Howard's left but didn't slow down to rally or reorganize. Instead, many were heading for their horses tethered to trees far to the rear. Eventually, however, their officers, no doubt with some encouragement from Pickens and Morgan, stemmed the flood and reformed the men into their companies and battalions.

To Tarleton, the running retreat of Pickens's militia presented a golden opportunity for a cavalry charge. He ordered Ogilvie to take the fifty dragoons on the right and charge into the "fleeing" Americans. Ogilvie's dragoons charged, sabers poised. Then they were hit, first by the fire of Triplett's Virginia riflemen, then by a countercharge by Washington and his dragoons. Coming down on Ogilvie's right flank, Washington's dragoons, with McCall's mounted men, sent the British dragoons flying for the rear. Now Pickens's militia could complete their retreat in safety.

All those actions took place in less than twenty minutes, and by 7:15 A.M. Tarleton was readying a renewed frontal attack. His infantry, with the American militia out of the way, could now advance triumphantly and finish up the job on Morgan's third line. A cheering British infantry advanced up the slopes, only to be stopped abruptly by a volley from Howard. The red-and-green line staggered, but recovered. British discipline prevailed over shock, and Tarleton's infantry returned the American volley. For nearly half an hour a vicious firefight continued with neither side giving ground. Seeing the opposing forces apparently equally balanced, Tarleton decided to throw his infantry reserve, the 71st Highlanders, against the American right flank while his cavalry encircled it.

About 7:30 A.M. Tarleton gave Major McArthur of the 71st the order to move out. Spotting the movement of the Highlanders, Morgan looked down to his right front and saw Howard riding toward his right flank. Well beyond the right of Howard's line he could see the Highlanders marching in column and swinging wide around the British left flank. As Morgan watched, however, mere observation must have changed to something like shock, something that called for immediate and personal action. Howard's right flank company, Wallace's Virginians, had faced about and were marching to the rear, backs to the enemy with whom they had just been exchanging fire. Whereupon all down the right side of Howard's line other unit commanders were facing their units about and had begun marching them rearward, aligning on Wallace's company!

Unknown to Morgan, Howard had decided to draw back his right flank to oppose the oncoming Highlanders, and to do so he had ordered

Wallace to change front by ninety degrees. The company should have been given the command to face about, followed by the command to wheel to the left and halt. Instead of wheeling left, however, through some error or misunderstanding the company had marched straight ahead after facing about—that is, to the rear. Then adjacent units followed suit, though, it should be noted, all in good order. Seeing that so far nothing had been lost, Howard evidently decided to let the rearward movement continue until he could halt the entire line in a new position. About that time Morgan had ridden over and demanded an explanation from Howard.

"Why are your men retreating?" Morgan demanded.

"I am trying to save my right flank," Howard replied.

"Are you beaten?"

"Do men who march like that look as though they are beaten?"

"I'll choose you a second position," Morgan said. "When you reach it, face about and fire!"

Soon the British infantry renewed the attack, rushing forward for the kill. This time their spirited and hasty advance was disorganized and out of control. The situation was exactly what Howard wanted. When his line had moved far enough up the slope of the second ridge, he was ready for Morgan's order to face about and fire. As the unruly mess of redcoats and legion infantry came pouring down the reverse slope of the first ridge, the closest only fifty paces away, Howard's men faced about and delivered their most destructive volley yet, at point-blank range. This time the shock was overwhelming, and Howard ordered a bayonet charge into the reeling mass of stunned survivors.

Howard's charge, enough in itself to have finished off Tarleton's infantry, was capped by another blow. While Howard's line had been marching to the rear, Washington had sent a galloper to Morgan with the message: "They're coming on like a mob. Give them one fire, and I'll charge them." Morgan ordered Washington to do just that. Washington's and McCall's horsemen thrust aside Ogilvie's dragoons on the British right and smashed into the flank and rear of the shaken British infantry, sabering down fugitives right and left. The first mass surrender was made by Major Newmarsh's recruits of the 7th Regiment, who threw themselves on the ground and bellowed for quarter. They might have had a taste of "Tarleton's quarter," but American officers stopped it before it got started and called on the beaten British to "throw down your arms, and we'll give you good quarter."

Other British troops on the far right—light infantry and legionaries—now tried to get away by fleeing to the right rear, but McCall led his horsemen in pursuit and rounded up some 200 fugitives. By this time Tarleton was seeing his right and center dissolving before his eyes. On his left the Highlanders were still hotly engaged with the right of Howard's line. The fighting Scots, however, were a doomed lot. Pickens's re-formed units had by this time made a three-quarter circle of the battle, and had formed into a firing line on the Highlander's left rear. Tarleton sent forward a company of legion cavalry to relieve the pressure on McArthur's men, but the dragoons, taken under fire by Pickens's rifle-men, broke and fled the field. Even then, the Highlanders, surrounded now on three sides by the incessant fire of Pickens's and Howard's men, continued to fight on. Major McArthur tried to lead them in a breakout, but after losing nine of sixteen officers, and with his men reduced to hand-to-hand fighting, the gallant Scot had to surrender his battalion.

The only reserve that Tarleton now had left was the 200 legion dra-goons. But when he gave the order to advance, the dragoons, the men he had led to victory in a dozen actions, in Tarleton's own words, "foresook their leader, and left the field of battle."

Even then, Tarleton was not through fighting. He rallied "fourteen officers and forty horsemen" and made a dash to save the guns. But this last desperate effort was too late. The blue-coated Royal Artillery gun crews had fought their guns to the last. Patriots under Captains Ander-son and Kirkwood, on Howard's orders, took the guns in a swift charge. The British artillerymen continued to defend their guns until the last of the gunners had been cut down.

Tarleton could now save only himself and a handful of followers. He led their retreat from the field; when he looked over his shoulder he saw Washington following in hot pursuit, doubtless intending to make Tarle-ton the finest trophy of the American victory. What followed was pure drama, a fitting Shakespearean ending to a battle piece. Tarleton and his horsemen turned, and Washington slashed at the officer on Tarleton's right, only to have his sword break near the hilt. Before the British offi-cer could saber him, however, he was shot through the shoulder of his sword arm. Next the officer on Tarleton's left slashed at Washington, but Sergeant Major Perry deflected the blow. Now Tarleton himself, his saber upraised, charged at Washington, who parried the slash with his broken sword. Tarleton then fired his pistol at Washington, missing his target but wounding Washington's horse. In Robert Bass's words, "having fired the last shot at Cowpens, Banastre Tarleton galloped after his fleeing Green Horse" (*The Green Dragoon*).

It is said that Morgan, in his exuberance over his dazzling victory, picked up a nine-year-old drummer boy and kissed him on both cheeks. But there was much to be done, and little time in which to do it. He placed Pickens in charge of mopping up the battlefield: taking care of wounded, dead, and prisoners while supervising the loading up of the captured matériel and supplies. Morgan marched off at noon, followed by his wagon train, to cross the Broad River and camp on its far side that same day.

The comparative losses at Cowpens are startling. Tarleton had, in effect, lost his entire force: 110 killed, 830 captured (including 200 wounded), 2 regimental colors, 2 grasshoppers,* 800 muskets, 35 baggage wagons, 60 Negro slaves, 100 cavalry horses, and large stores of ammunition. Morgan's losses were 12 killed and 61 wounded. In one hour he had cost Cornwallis his entire left striking arm and brought the opening strategy of his campaign down in ruin.

The news of Cowpens was a boost to American morale that spread across the colonies from south to north. In contrast to Kings Mountain, which was regarded as an affair between backwoodsmen and Tories, Cowpens was seen as a victory of an American combination of regulars and militia over veteran British regulars in a stand-up fight. The news so electrified Congress that it voted Brigadier General Morgan, who was usually passed over for honors, a gold medal. Washington and Howard were honored with silver medals, and Pickens was awarded a sword.

---

*The two three-pounder fieldpieces were accumulating a history of their own. They had been captured from the British at Saratoga, lost to the British at Camden, only to be retaken by the Americans at Cowpens.

Battle of Bennington.—*from Henry Cabot Lodge,* The Story of the Revolution *(1898)*

Surrender of Burgoyne at Saratoga.—*from Henry Cabot Lodge,* The Story of the Revolution *(1898)*

General John Burgoyne, portrait by Thomas Hudson.—*from Henry William Elson,* History of the United States *(1906)*

General Daniel Morgan, drawn from the original in the Capitol Rotunda, Washington.—*from James Graham,* Life of Daniel Morgan *(1856)*

"The Gathering of the Mountain Men," by Lloyd Branson.—*courtesy Tennessee State Museum*

Battle of King's Mountain—Ferguson's Death Charge.—*from Lyman C. Draper,* King's Mountain and Its Heros *(1881)*

Colonel Isaac Shelby.—*from* The National Portrait Gallery of Distinguished Americans *(1834)*

Colonel John Eager Howard.—*from* The National Portrait Gallery of Distinguished Americans *(1834)*

General Nathanael Greene.—*from* The National Portrait Gallery of Distinguished Americans *(1853)*

Colonel Henry Lee.—*from Henry Lee*, Memoirs of the War in The Southern Department of the United States *(1869)*

Left: The Fight Between colonels William Washington and Banastré Tarleton at Cowpens.—*from Henry Cabot Lodge, The Story of the Revolution (1898)*
Bottom: Battle of Guilford Courthouse.—*U.S. Army Center of Military History*

Colonel Banastré Tarleton, portrait by Joshua Reynolds.—*from Henry P. Johnston,* The Yorktown Campaign and the Surrender of Cornwallis, 1781 *(1881)*

General Charles, Marquis Cornwallis, portrait by Thomas Gainsborough.—*from Henry William Elston,* History of the United States *(1906)*

General Comte de Rochambeau.—*from* Les Combattants Français de la Guerre Américaine, 1778–1783 *(1903)*

Admiral Comte de Grasse.—*from* Les Combattants Français de la Guerre Américaine, 1778–1783 *(1903)*

Admiral Thomas Graves.—*from* European Magazine *(1795)*

Admiral Sir Samuel Hood.—*from* European Magazine *(1782)*

"Battle off Virginia Capes," painting by V. Zveg.—*courtesy Naval Historical Center*

"Battle of the Capes," painting by Jack Woodson.—*courtesy U.S. Historical Society*

NINE

Guilford Courthouse

HAVING WON HIS BATTLE, DANIEL MORGAN found himself, ironically, in considerable peril. Cornwallis's army was still between him and Greene. After Pickens rejoined him the day after Cowpens, on 18 January, Morgan and his whole command marched together until they reached Gilbert Town. There Pickens was detached with the major share of the militia and Washington's cavalry to march the prisoners captured at Cowpens to Island Ford on the upper Catawba, where they could be turned over to other escorts and moved to Virginia. Morgan then continued his march via Ramsour's Mills to the main Catawba, which he crossed at Sherrill's Ford on 23 January, and encamped on the north side—safely, for the time being.

Meanwhile, Cornwallis remained at Turkey Creek, readying his force to move out. He was now irrevocably committed to moving north because all his troops and material for campaigning were concentrated with him, and by his order the far-away fortifications of Charleston had been razed.

With 3,000 excellent troops at hand, Cornwallis did not leave Turkey Creek until 19 January, and then in the wrong direction. Underestimating Morgan's marching capability as well as his anxiety to be reunited with Greene, the earl marched to the northwest toward the Little Broad River, intending to cut off Morgan. En route Cornwallis learned from Tarleton's search of the area that he was in error, and he changed his direction toward Ramsour's Mills, where he arrived early on 25 January, only to learn that Morgan had passed there two days before.

Cornwallis now had to reevaluate his estimate of Morgan's capabilities and make a painful decision. In less than five marching days Morgan had covered over a hundred miles and had placed two rivers between the two armies. The British commander's decision—no doubt arrived at only with difficulty—was to strip down his army and convert it into a mobile force able to march fast enough to catch the Americans. To do so he took two days to destroy all his superfluous impedimenta. Into the fires went the tents and all the provisions that could not be carried in knapsacks. Then the wagons and their loads were burned, saving out only the essential ones for hauling ammunitions, salt, and hospital stores, and four others for the transport of the sick and wounded. Cornwallis set the example for his officers by watching most of his personal belongings go up in smoke, and his officers followed his example (the latter must have been a tremendous lightening of encumbrance, considering the typical British officer's "campaign comforts"). But Cornwallis didn't stop there; what followed was—as any old soldier could attest—no less than a tragic end to a harrowing scene. All the rum casks were smashed, "and the precious liquor was poured out on the ground."

After two days of holocaust, Cornwallis set out to catch up with Morgan. A rapid march from Ramsour's Mills eastward toward Beattie's Ford ended in pure frustration, however, because the Catawba was impassable due to heavy rains. Cornwallis halted four miles short of the ford and was held up there for two days, through 30 January.

NATHANAEL GREENE, IN HIS CAMP AT CHERAW, didn't get word of the victory at Cowpens until 23 January, but with it came the realization of Morgan's danger if he were caught by Cornwallis's main force. Greene was not without resources; with typical foresight, when he had made his decision to divide his army, he sent "Lieutenant Colonel Carrington, his quartermaster, to explore and map the Dan River, and Edward Stevens, Major General of Virginia militia, and General Kosciuszko to the Yadkin and the Catawba for the same purpose. They were also to collect or build flatboats to be carried on wheels or in wagons from one river to another" (Ward, *The War of the Revolution*). Consequently Greene was able, after 23 January, to give orders to set things in motion. He dispatched Carrington back to the Dan River to assemble enough boats on the south side to transport his whole force. He then directed General Huger to march his wing of the army to Salisbury, North Carolina, where he could anticipate joining Morgan's force. Huger started his 125-mile march on 28 January, the same day that Greene, escorted only by a guide, one aide, and a sergeant's guard of dragoons, left Cheraw to ride to Morgan's camp east of the Catawba. That he made it through Tory country in only two days, across a rough stretch of some 120 miles, makes it seem that luck played an important part in getting him safely to Morgan's camp on 30 January.

As soon as Greene and Morgan began comparing notes, it became apparent that the latter was more concerned with the safety of the army than its raison d'être. Morgan thought that only a fast, strategic withdrawal westward into the mountains could save the army. Greene, with his strategic objectives uppermost in mind, took an opposite—and prevailing—view. When Morgan told him of Cornwallis's baggage burning and his obvious intent of driving north at all costs, Greene is said to have exclaimed, "Then, he is ours!"

It was then that Greene added another bold concept to his strategy: If Cornwallis were to carry out his "mad scheme of pushing through the country," Greene would do no less than accommodate him. In so doing, the American commander would retreat to the north, where Cornwallis would be sure to take the bait and follow. Then Greene would entice his opponent farther and farther north, stretching the British supply lines to the breaking point while the Americans were drawing closer to supplies in Virginia. And during the retreat Greene would keep his forces just out of reach of his enemy's advance elements, keeping alive in Cornwallis the hope that he would bring the Americans to battle. Finally, when Greene had gathered enough strength and the right opportunity was presented, he would turn and strike his enemy. Morgan apparently was shocked at the dangers inherent in such a bold plan, and declared he could not be held responsible if it met with disaster. Greene, never shying away from responsibility, replied that Morgan should have no such worries, "for I shall take the measure upon myself."

Accordingly Greene sent a letter to Huger informing him of his plan and urging him to make haste in his march to join Morgan's main body at Salisbury. He also dispatched orders for Light-Horse Harry Lee's legion to break off operations with Marion, then somewhere along the lower Pee Dee River, and rejoin Greene at once. By then the floodwaters of the Catawba had begun to recede, so Greene was able to direct Morgan to continue his main body's march to Salisbury. With those matters taken care of, Greene, accompanied by Morgan, met William Washington and General William Davidson near Beattie's Ford to plan the defense of the fords of the Catawba in the area. Afterward Morgan and Washington rode off to rejoin their commands, and Davidson was left to deploy his militia to defend the fords.

Cornwallis meanwhile had kept a close eye on the Catawba's waters

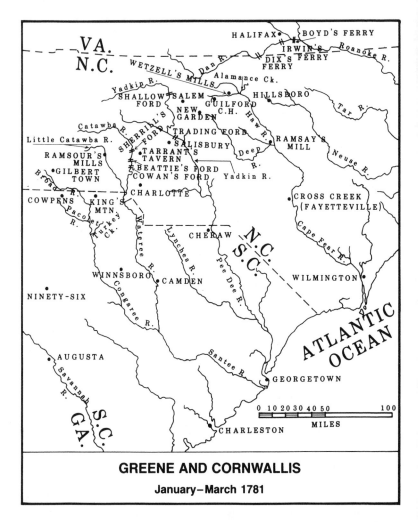

GREENE AND CORNWALLIS

January–March 1781

while formulating his crossing plan. Believing that Morgan's main force
was still near Beattie's Ford, the earl planned to entrap him by executing
two crossings of the river. The first was to be a feint at Beattie's Ford by a
division under Lieutenant Colonel Webster, who would keep Morgan
occupied, starting with an artillery preparation. Cornwallis would take
the main body across at Cowan's Ford, about five miles downstream from
Beattie's, then swing north to encircle Morgan.

Morgan, however, had marched away from his camp on the evening of
31 January, headed toward Salisbury and Trading Ford, while Corn-

wallis's forces had begun moving only by early morning of 1 February. At Cowan's Ford the British ran into real difficulties. The ford was 500 yards wide, and the water three to four feet deep and still running fast. Halfway across the river, the ford split into two parts. The wagon ford ran straight ahead through deeper water, while the so-called horse ford split off at a forty-five-degree angle to the south and ran through shallower water. Led by Dick Beal, their Tory guide, the British troops plunged ahead in waist-deep water. About a hundred yards into the river they were taken under fire by the small party at the wagon ford. About halfway across, Beal lost his nerve and disappeared, without telling the officer leading the advance that he should break off to the right and take the horse ford to its landing below. As a result, the column pushed on, straight ahead through the deeper wagon ford, where it suffered considerable losses. Even the three generals' horses became casualties: Cornwallis's horse was wounded but didn't collapse until it reached the far bank; Generals Leslie and O'Hara were thrown when their horses were swept down by the current.

Discipline and plain raw courage carried the British through, and the leading ranks stormed the bank, loaded their muskets, and drove off the defenders. General Davidson heard the firing and led a detachment from the horse ford up to reinforce the wagon ford. When he got there he took a bullet from a Tory rifleman and fell dead from his horse. With that his men broke and fled before the British volleys.

Cornwallis was across at Cowan's Ford, and later that day Webster crossed unopposed at Beattie's. The British commander rapidly reorganized to resume the chase after Morgan, who was already well on his way to the Yadkin River. Tarleton meanwhile was screening the British front and simultaneously reconnoitering for rebels in the direction of advance. About ten miles from the river he found and attacked, in his usual hell-for-leather style, a group of Davidson's militia at Tarrant's Tavern. Two or three hundred rebels were dispersed for good, Tarleton reporting that he had routed 500 and killed 50, with a loss of only 7 of his own men. His concluding statement summarized the real results of Tarrant's Tavern: "This exertion of the cavalry succeeding the gallant action of the guards in the morning, diffused such a terror among the inhabitants, that the King's troops passed through the most hostile part of North Carolina without a shot from the militia."

Tarleton's cavalry also came close to capturing Greene, who had gone alone to a prearranged place to meet the militia withdrawing from the fords. At midnight a messenger came with the news of Davidson's death, the dispersal of the militia, and the crossing of Cornwallis's force. Greene then rode on to Salisbury. In Christopher Ward's description, "At Steele's Tavern in that village he dismounted stiff and sore to be greeted by a friend. 'What? Alone, Greene?' 'Yes,' he answered, 'alone, tired, hungry and penniless.' Mrs. Steele heard him. After getting him a breakfast she brought two little bags of hard money and gave them to him. 'You need them more than I do,' she said. The contents of those two little bags constituted the entire military chest of the Grand Army of the Southern department of the United States of America."

In the next nine days, beginning on 2 February, Greene and Morgan carried out the series of marches that have become famous as the Retreat to the Dan. The Dan River was the final objective of Greene's strategic moves. He was keenly aware that only after he had gotten his army across that river could he rest his troops, replenish stores, and, most important, gather in reinforcements from Virginia. Both of the opposing armies were now across the Catawba, but there remained three major rivers to cross: the Yadkin, the Haw, and the Dan. And if the rains of midwinter should set in and render fords impassable, only boats could ensure timely river crossings. We have seen that Greene's foresight, plus the efforts of Carrington and Kosciuszko, had made the boats available, but they had to be at the right place at the right time. Greene could leave the execution of that part of his plan to those two capable officers, but the Dan River crossings posed another problem, for Cornwallis would probably close on his trail at crossing time. The upper river had usable fords; the lower river could be crossed only by boats at three ferry sites: in order from upper to lower, Dix's Ferry, Irwin's Ferry, and Boyd's Ferry. Greene's plan was to deceive his enemy into thinking that the American main body was headed for the fords of the upper Dan, when in reality it would make a last-minute switch of direction to cross at a ferry site on the lower Dan.

WHILE HE WAS STILL AT STEELE'S TAVERN, Greene sent a message to Huger to change his direction of march to the northeast and meet up with Morgan at Guilford Courthouse. He then rode to join Morgan's column.

Cornwallis, following Tarleton's action at Tarrant's Tavern, had reunited the two divisions of his army at a point on the road to Salisbury. There he formed a mobile advance force to move ahead and catch Greene and Morgan before they could cross the Yadkin. The force, under General O'Hara, was made up of the cavalry and O'Hara's mounted infantry. It set out at once, while Cornwallis remained with his main body to supervise a second baggage burning. This time he reduced the number of wagons, gaining more teams to pull the others through the soft red clay.

O'Hara, pushing on, was well aware that the rain-swollen Yadkin was above fording depth. Here, if ever, was the time and place to catch Morgan. When his advance party came in sight of the Yadkin's west bank, it came upon some wagons guarded by militia. The vanguard quickly dispersed the militia, only to discover that the American army and all its boats were on the other side of the river. Greene's careful planning and Kosciuszko's execution had made possible the first major boat crossing on 2 and 3 February.

Marching through rain and over miserable roads, Cornwallis made it into Salisbury by mid-afternoon of 3 February. The Americans had all the available boats, and the Yadkin River was too high even for fording by horses. Cornwallis sent forward a few artillery pieces, with which O'Hara attempted to bombard Greene's camp across the river. Because the American position was protected by a high ridge, no damage was done "except to knock the roof off a cabin in which he [Greene] was busy with correspondence."

While at Salisbury, Cornwallis received reports that there were insufficient boats on the lower Dan to enable Greene to use the ferries. This false—or misconstrued—information was to prove costly indeed in Cornwallis's future moves, since it added to the earl's deception that Greene would have to use the fords of the upper Dan. Cornwallis saw that he could operate on interior lines by interposing his army between what he thought were the still-divided forces of Greene and Huger and defeat them in detail. His plan was to head northwest from Salisbury, cross the Yadkin at Shallow Ford, which was still passable in spite of the rain, get to Salem, and from there strike out at the separated American forces. Accordingly he sent Tarleton up the Yadkin, which he crossed at Shallow Ford on 6 February. Cornwallis followed, leaving Salisbury on the seventh and reaching Salem on the ninth.

WHAT WERE GREENE'S FORCES DOING AFTER Morgan had crossed the Yadkin on 3 February? On the evening of the following day Greene and Morgan marched north out of their camp at Trading Ford. Their initial direction must have added to Cornwallis's misconceived idea of the objective of the march. On the way, the Americans halted at Abbott's Creek, not far from Salem, long enough to confirm reports of Cornwallis's whereabouts. They then switched direction to the east to make an incredible march to Guilford Courthouse, covering forty-seven miles in forty-eight hours despite unceasing rain, terrible roads, and hungry men who marched on short rations for two days. Reaching Guilford on 6 February, they encamped and waited for Huger to join them. The next day Huger's scarecrow force arrived "in a most dismal condition for the want of clothing, especially shoes" but without the loss of a man!

While at Guilford Courthouse, Greene seems to have wavered momentarily in his purpose. His forces were concentrated, Lee's legion had arrived with Huger, and he hoped his still-scanty force of 2,000 would be joined by local militia as well as reinforcements from Virginia. Moreover, he could hope to build up provisions and receive ammunition along with the hoped-for Virginia troops. Greene studied the terrain and considered it suitable for a good position to confront Cornwallis. He laid his considerations before a council of war, which decided against such a stand. The American commander then wasted no time in reorganizing his units for continuing the march to the lower Dan. He sent Pickens back to recruit militia, arouse the countryside, and raise havoc in general with British supply lines and foraging parties.

Next Greene organized a light, mobile force designed to act both as rear guard and decoy force for Cornwallis's advance elements. The force totaled 700 men and was composed of William Washington's cavalry, with Lee's legion cavalry attached as well as John Eager Howard's infantry, which included his 280 Continentals, the 120 infantrymen of Lee's legion, and 60 Virginia riflemen. Specifically, the mission of the light force was to keep between Greene's main body and the British, delaying the enemy wherever possible while keeping him deceived in regard to the army's true objective: the ferries on the lower Dan.

Command of the force was offered to Morgan, but he declined, because, as he told Greene in writing on 5 February, "I can scarcely sit upon my horse." The curse of hemorrhoids had been added to his rheumatism and sciatica, making him unfit to campaign further. A reluctant Greene accepted the loss of Morgan: "Camp at Guilford C.H. Feb. 10th, 1781. Gen. Morgan, of the Virginia line, has leave of absence until he recovers his health, so as to be able to take the field again." It was to be Morgan's last campaign with regular forces.

The command then went to Colonel Otho Williams of Maryland, a happy selection indeed; he was an officer with a record of distinguished service and destined to add brilliant accomplishments to his record in the near future. While Williams was organizing his light force, Greene, according to Lee's *Memoirs,* was listening to Lieutenant Colonel Carrington's suggestions for crossing the lower Dan "at Irwin's Ferry, 17 [should read 70] miles from Guilford Courthouse, and 20 miles below Dix's. Boyd's Ferry was four miles below Irwin's; and the boats might be easily brought down from Dix's to assist in transporting the army at these and lower ferries. The plan of Lt. Col. Carrington was adopted, and that officer charged with the requisite preparations."

Williams left Guilford Courthouse on 10 February, turning west toward Salem to take a road which would put him between Cornwallis and Greene's main body. On the same day, Greene left, taking the main body on the most direct route to Carrington's ferry sites.

Cornwallis had at first thought to threaten Greene by feinting eastward, but when he learned of the march of Williams's force coming swiftly across his front, the earl took the bait and headed for the fords of the upper Dan, thus, as he thought, keeping Greene from his objective.

The subsequent pursuit of Greene by Cornwallis has been referred to as the "race to the Dan." The conditions under which the two armies marched, however, were anything but conducive to a race. It was still midwinter, and when it wasn't raining in northern North Carolina, it was snowing. The oft-mentioned red-clay roads would freeze at night and soften into sticky mud in the "warmth" of the day. To top it off, the Americans had to exist on short rations, and the clothing of most soldiers was in tatters. The British soldiers were not a great deal better off, for their uniforms were wearing out and usually wet through. There were no tents on either side: the Americans didn't have time to erect or strike them, and the British soldiers' tents had been the first things thrown on the fires of Cornwallis's baggage burnings.

Soon after heading out in pursuit of Williams, Cornwallis found that they were marching on parallel roads. His own column had become strung out over a distance of four miles, so he halted long enough to close it up, then drove his troops on, pushing them to the limit. They made up to thirty miles a day, a nearly unbelievable march rate under the conditions. Williams, if he were to keep ahead of his enemy's van, had to move even faster. His other and constant anxiety was maintaining a continuous surveillance of the roads to his right and rear to ensure that the British did not get between him and Greene. This meant patrolling and picketing on a twenty-four-hour basis, with half of his troops screening his own force at night to avoid being surprised. Hence his men got only six hours rest out of forty-eight, and started each day's march at 3:00 A.M. A hasty halt for breakfast provided the only meal of the day. The British may have marched on better rations, but they too were driven constantly in their dogged pursuit.

A picture of the opposing forces at this time would show three parallel columns heading generally northward. They were echeloned, with Greene's main body on the left and leading. Williams was in the center, and to his right and rear were the pursuing British. On 13 February the picture began to change between the forces of Williams and Cornwallis. Before dawn Tarleton reported to Cornwallis that the enemy's main body was actually moving toward the lower Dan. The earl decided to create a deception of his own by directing his vanguard to continue following the same route parallel to Williams while he and the main body made a forced march over a causeway that would bring him onto Williams's rear. He came very close to catching up to the American rear, and might have caught the light troops at breakfast had it not been for a farmer who warned the Americans that the British were coming on fast and were only four miles away. Williams sent Harry Lee back to check on the farmer's information, and the result was a sharp little action with Tarleton's cavalry, which lost eighteen men in the fight. Just before Lee and his cavalry detachment engaged the enemy, some of Tarleton's dragoons cut down Lee's bugler, a fourteen-year-old, and killed him as he lay defenseless on the ground. After the engagement Lee was going to hang in reprisal the captured leader of the dragoon detachment, Captain Miller, who argued that he had tried to save the bugler's life but had not succeeded. Miller's life was spared, not only due to his defense but also because of the approach of Cornwallis's advance guard. Lee had no choice but to gallop away and rejoin the rear guard.

While the cavalry clash was going on, Williams decided that he had gone as far as he could in leading Cornwallis toward Dix's Ferry. Now, in order to save his own command while continuing to cover Greene's rear, it was time for him to change to a road that would take him more directly to Irwin's Ferry, where he could get across the Dan behind Greene's main body. Since Lee had caught up with him, Williams told him of his plan to change to the new route and ordered him to continue screening the light force's rear. Williams then moved to Irwin's Ferry.

Cornwallis was not fooled for long, however, and for a second time his advance party came close to catching Lee's men at a delayed breakfast. The American troopers had gone up a side road to a farmhouse and were just getting into their meal when shots were heard from the direction of an outpost. At once Lee got his infantry on the way, then went back to support his outpost in checking the enemy's advance party. The Americans escaped by the skin of their teeth, Lee's cavalry being hotly pursued by the British dragoons and saved only by having better horses.

By now Cornwallis was convinced that a final, all-out effort would enable him to catch the Americans before they could cross the Dan. All through the day of the thirteenth and into the night the weary British were pushed on by their commander. Several times the British vanguard was within a musket shot of the American rear guard, and it seemed likely that the light troops would have to make a stand. Each time Lee's troops got away. Just before dusk Lee's men caught up with Williams. It soon became evident that Cornwallis was not to be halted by darkness, however, so Williams had to keep going, his men stumbling along in the dark over the rough road.

Williams now sent part of Lee's cavalry ahead to try and connect with Greene's rear. It was not long before they saw, ahead of them, a distant line of campfires. They were as dismayed as they had been surprised. Greene hadn't gotten away after all, and here they all were, with the British closing in on them. "All their struggles, all their hardships had been for naught. Now there was only one thing to do; they must face their pursuer and fight." However, when Williams came up and led them forward, they found that the campfires were indeed Greene's, but he had moved on two days before. The fires had been kept burning by the locals, who knew that the light troops were coming.

Williams, however, could allow no halt. He had gotten a message from Greene which told him that the main body's baggage and stores had been sent on to "cross as fast as they got to the river." Finally word came to Williams from the rear guard that the British had halted, so he could halt too—but only for a couple of hours. By midnight the light troops were pounding on again, their feet breaking the half-frozen ruts and sinking into the soggy red clay beneath. Even though their pursuers were having the same troubles, at times they seemed to be gaining on Williams's weary troops. Both sides pushed on, and during the whole morning of 14 February neither force made a rest halt of more than an hour.

Then, sometime before noon of the fourteenth, another of Greene's couriers met Williams with a message dated 5:12 P.M. of the day before: "All our troops are over and the stage is clear . . . I am ready to receive you and give you a hearty welcome." Williams passed the word down the columns, and the roll of American cheers was so loud that General O'Hara's advance party could hear them and must have realized that the race might be won by the Americans.

There were still fourteen long miles to go before reaching the river.

The news of Greene's dispatch had so lifted the American spirits that Williams's troops, like a runner getting his second wind, were giving it their all in this final stretch.

As for O'Hara, for all the adverse sounds of rebel cheers, he was more determined than ever to catch up to and trap his enemy with his back to the river. Equally determined to cross before O'Hara could intervene, Williams sent Lee back in mid-afternoon again to cover the rear and delay the British. Meanwhile, the light infantry pressed forward, having gained on O'Hara's van: the British had marched forty miles in twenty-four hours, but the Americans had covered those same miles in sixteen hours.

At last, just before the end of daylight, Williams's leading troops reached the ferry site and loaded up on the boats to be ferried across. The boat transports kept moving the infantry until the last of them reached the other side after dark. By 8:00 P.M. on 14 February Lee's horsemen arrived and began crossing on the boats that had finished transporting the infantry. Carrington was directing the crossing in person, and it was he who had Lee's horses "unsaddled and driven into the water to swim across, while their weary riders clutching their saddles and bridles, crowded into the boats." Lee then recorded that "in the last boat the quartermaster-general attended by Lt. Colonel Lee and the rear troops, reached the friendly shore." Less than an hour later, O'Hara arrived at the river to find his enemies all safe on the far side. Page Smith summed up O'Hara's sense of bitter letdown: "All the weary miles, the burned baggage and wagons, the destroyed tents, the short rations had gone for nothing" (*A New Age Now Begins*). Cornwallis learned of the failure a little later, and with it the not-surprising news that the river was too high to ford and all the boats were gone with the Americans.

Obviously the boats were the key to Greene's getting his army to safety. The fact that they were where they were needed, when they were needed, is ample testimony to Greene's genius and the skill and energy of Carrington and Kosciuszko.

Greene had now been driven out of the Carolinas, and no longer was there an organized Patriot force located south of Virginia capable of fighting a British army. Yet, by retreating north of the Dan, the American general had not only saved his army but was still capable of preventing Cornwallis from marching into Virginia and linking up with British forces there to subdue the rest of the South.

CORNWALLIS AND THE BRITISH NOW FACED a critical operational problem. To get into Virginia he had to cross the Dan and the Roanoke, and there were no boats to make the crossings. If he tried to use the fords on the upper stretches of river, Greene would know of his moves in time to move his army to hold any crossing site. And even if he should out-maneuver Greene, an unlikely outcome in view of the painful experiences of the past weeks, the American could fall back and be reinforced by the troops that Baron von Steuben was raising in Virginia, and would be the stronger in numbers. So there was no way for the British at this time to drive to the north.

The earl's other problems were formidable as well. In pursuing Greene he had left his main base over 230 miles behind, and there was no way to replace all the stores and matériel destroyed back at Ramsour's Mills. His army had swept the nearby countryside clean of provisions and forage, and Pickens had reportedly raised some 700 militia with which he could attack British foraging parties or supply trains. Obviously Cornwallis could not stay where he was, either.

He took the only way out left to him. He would make a safe march back to Hillsboro, where the Tory population would surely rally to him now that Greene had been driven out of North Carolina. His mind made up, Cornwallis marched to Hillsboro, set up the royal standard, and issued a proclamation: "Whereas it has pleased the Divine Providence to prosper the operations of His Majesty's arms, in driving the rebel army out of this province, and whereas it is His Majesty's most gracious wish to rescue his faithful and loyal subjects from the cruel tyranny under which they have groaned for many years [all were invited to repair] with their arms and ten days provisions to the royal standard."

Some forty miles away, on the north side of the Dan, there were causes for rejoicing and "enjoying wholesome and abundant supplies of food in the rich and friendly county of Halifax." There Greene rested his men while gathering stores and intelligence of both friendly and enemy forces. In Greene's way of thinking, the crossing of the Dan had ended one campaign; now it was time to start another. In spite of his urgent need for reinforcement, he would not hold up operations waiting for them. The high waters of the Dan were subsiding, and Cornwallis might seize the initiative to try new maneuvers against him. Moreover, Steuben's Continental recruits might be weeks away from joining him. Uppermost in his consideration was the nagging realization that the climax of all his retrograde operations had not yet been reached—his turning back to strike the enemy he had enticed so far from his base, and who now would be weakened enough to be vulnerable to Greene's masterstroke. In Greene's mind that time had come. He must now reenter North Carolina and move against Cornwallis with the forces he had at hand.

In short order Greene transformed decisions into actions. On 18 February he sent Lee with his legion and two companies of Maryland Continentals to reinforce Pickens in harassing British communications and foraging parties, as well as keeping down Tory uprisings. Greene's next move was to send ahead Colonel Otho Williams with the same light infantry force that he led so brilliantly during the retreat. Williams crossed the Dan on 20 February, two days after Lee. About the same time, escorted by a detachment of Washington's dragoons, Greene rode to meet with Pickens and Lee near the road running from Hillsboro to the Haw River. There he told them of his plans to cross the Dan with the rest of his army and move in the general direction of Guilford Courthouse. Greene then returned to the main army.

Sometime later, Pickens and Lee set out to act on a piece of hot intelligence that told them that Tarleton had been sent to escort a force of several hundred Tory militia to Hillsboro to join Cornwallis. The Tories, a force of Royal Militia that had been raised between the Haw and Deep rivers, were presently en route to join Tarleton.

On their way to locate the enemy, Lee's troopers picked up two Tory countrymen, who were duped into thinking that Lee's men were Tarleton's, an understandable mistake since the cavalrymen of both legions wore green jackets and similar black helmets. They sent one of the Tories ahead to Colonel John Pyle, who commanded the 300-man Tory force, asking him if he would form his men in a line facing the road so that "Colonel Tarleton" and his troops could pass on to their bivouac area for the night. Completely taken in, Pyle not only formed his line on the right side of the road but also took post on the right of the line where he could greet the British cavalry leader when he passed.

In the meantime the Maryland light infantry and some of Pickens's militia were following Lee's dragoons, the infantry concealed by the woods through which the road ran. Lee rode down the road at the head of his men, in his own words, passing along the line at the head of the column "with a smiling countenance, dropping, occasionally, expressions complimentary to the good looks and commendable conduct of his loyal friends." Lee went on to say that his only intention was to reveal himself and his men to Colonel Pyle and suggest that he surrender and disband his men, and send them home in order to avoid harm coming to them.

According to American accounts, Lee was about to deliver his surrender demand—having first grasped Pyle's hand in his role as Tarleton—when firing broke out at the rear of Lee's column. Evidently some of the Tories at the opposite end of the line had spotted the American infantry in the woods and fired on them.

Lee's troopers fell upon the surprised enemy with slashing sabres. The Tories were caught like rounded-up rabbits, and the rest of the action, known as Pyle's Defeat, or Haw River, was nothing less than a massacre. Of the 300 or more Tory militia, 90 were killed on the spot and 150 who could not get away were left "slashed and bleeding." Lee's loss was one horse wounded. If Pyle's Defeat was not a massacre, it would be hard indeed to accept the American assertion to the contrary, since the casualties with their wounds spoke for themselves.

Moral issues aside, the results of Haw River were unmistakable. The Tory populace throughout the region was thoroughly subdued by the news of the action, and few Tories rallied to the royal standard in North Carolina.

GREENE KEPT HIS WORD WITH LEE AND PICKENS, crossing the Dan to join them on 23 February after his main body had been reinforced by 600 Virginia militia under General Edward Stevens. Greene's immediate operations were directed toward backing up Pickens with the support of Williams's light troops while the main army was building up its strength. The buildup was going to take time, but eventually reinforcements would be forthcoming in the form of Steuben's recruited Continentals and more Virginia and North Carolina militia. In the interim Greene directed his next marches toward Hillsboro.

Cornwallis, at the same time, was arriving at a decision to leave that place—not because of Greene's latest move but because of the area's decreasing means of supporting the British forces encamped there. Provisions were running critically short, and Cornwallis's commissaries were hard put to force more out of a disgruntled people. These were the same people who, after Pyle's Defeat, had suddenly ceased to provide recruits. Thus it was to Cornwallis's advantage to move to greener pastures. Consequently, on 27 February he moved to an encampment south of Alamance Creek. This placed him near a junction of roads that permitted moving east to Hillsboro, west to Guilford Courthouse, or downriver to Cross Creek and Wilmington.

On the day that Cornwallis departed from Hillsboro, Otho Williams

crossed the Haw River and took up a position on the north side of Alamance Creek, several miles from Cornwallis's camp on the south side.
Williams now led a formidable force, his light troops having been reinforced by Pickens's command, which included Lee's legion, Washington's cavalry, and about 300 Virginia riflemen under Colonel William
Preston. Williams's force closed in its position on the night of 27–28
February, and the next morning Greene moved the main army to a position about fifteen miles above the British camp.

The American commander had no intention, however, of remaining
there. He planned to keep his forces in motion and thus keep Cornwallis
off balance while the Americans controlled the countryside and continued to gather in reinforcements. At the same time Williams would also
be on the move for the same general purpose, and in addition would act
as a screening force for Greene's main army. On the British side Tarleton began to carry out his screening mission in much the same way.

All this shuttling back and forth served the Americans' purpose in at
least one way—they had begun to annoy Cornwallis. He decided on a
surprise move of his own, and marched at 3:00 A.M. on 6 March in the
hope of surprising Williams. In so doing he anticipated drawing Greene
to the support of Williams, and thereby into a general engagement. In the
earl's view, the American commander could not afford to stand off and
see his invaluable covering force destroyed.

As usual, the American intelligence was more timely and accurate than
British intelligence. A scouting party of Williams's on another mission on
the night of 5–6 March learned that Cornwallis's army was on the move.
When Williams got the report, Tarleton's cavalry and Cornwallis's van of
light infantry under Lieutenant Colonel Webster were already within two
miles of Colonel William Campbell's (the same red-headed Scot of Kings
Mountain) Virginia militia, which was outposting Williams's left. Williams
dispatched Lee's and Washington's cavalry to support Campbell while he
hurried the rest of his force toward Wetzell's Mills, a ford across Reedy
Fork. Williams got across the ford first, and the swift arrival of the British van brought on the engagement known as Wetzell's Mills, in which
some twenty casualties were taken on each side. Greene was not pulled
into the action, but he did move from his last position near Reedy Fork
and camped at the ironworks on Troublesome Creek.

After that affair both armies remained inactive for the next eight days.
During the period Greene's most anxious hopes were beginning to be
fulfilled. Steuben's Continentals arrived at long last, 400 of them, under
Colonel Richard Campbell. About the same time the long-awaited Vir-

ginia militia joined Greene: almost 1,700 men organized into two brigades under Brigadier Generals Edward Stevens and Robert Lawson. Then came two brigades of North Carolina militia, totaling 1,060 men, commanded, respectively, by Brigadier General John Butler and Colonel Pinketham Eaton. While overseeing the reorganization of his army, Greene decided to disband Williams's force and return its units to their parent regiments, with the exception of Captain Kirkwood's famed Delaware company of Continentals and Colonel Charles Lynch's Virginia riflemen, who were attached to Washington's cavalry to form a legion similar to Lee's.

Greene now had 4,400 effectives that he could count on to do battle with Cornwallis. The latter's intelligence, to Greene's undoubted advantage, had succeeded in magnifying the American numbers to 9,000 or 10,000. If Cornwallis believed the figures, and there is no evidence that he did not, he was undismayed. His 1,900 regulars were all of them seasoned veterans, who doubtless would prove to be worth more than twice their number in battle with American militia.

Greene had drawn his opponent northward, stretching Cornwallis's supply lines to the breaking point. If he did not strike before the enemy was reinforced, his strength would dwindle away once the militia had served out their six-week commitment. Moreover, both he and his enemy had stripped the area of food and forage, and neither force could sustain itself in the region for more than a few days. Greene knew that his enemy, just recently moved to New Garden a few miles away, would not refuse the challenge to fight a pitched battle once the Americans had taken up a fixed position.

No doubt Greene had in mind just the locale that would favor his battle. He had studied the terrain when he had first stopped at Guilford Courthouse, when his council of war had talked him out of fighting. Now there was no need for a council. Greene moved on 14 March to take up a defensive position at Guilford Courthouse.

IT HAS BEEN COMMONLY ACCEPTED THAT Greene deployed his army for battle using the same tactics that had worked so brilliantly for Morgan at Cowpens. The point, I think, has been very much overstated. It is true that Morgan advised Greene, in a letter dated 20 February, in regard to deploying his forces when confronting Cornwallis in battle, but there is no evidence to show that Greene unthinkingly adopted Morgan's every suggestion, even though his three-line-deep deployment might appear on the surface to be a carbon copy of Morgan's. The terrain on which

Greene made his dispositions was markedly different in character from Cowpens. Morgan had been successful in South Carolina because he fitted his firepower to the terrain in such a manner that he could observe and control his troops throughout the action. The terrain of Cowpens, with its excellent all-around fields of fire, allowed Morgan to do just that.

The terrain at Guilford Courthouse denied Greene any such freedom of action. Its most striking feature was the dense forest that dominated the area, with the exception of the few clearings that offered fields of fire, usually limited to the immediate front. If the Americans were to adopt Morgan's three-line deployment, the terrain dictated that there could be no mutual support between the lines. Nor could the commander or his senior leaders even see the first two lines, because the troops would be out of sight in the woods.

For all that, Greene proceeded to deploy as indicated on the map. The road from Guilford Courthouse to New Garden bisected the positions of the two forward lines. The front line was composed of the two North Carolina militia brigades of 500 men each: Butler's on the right of the road, Eaton's on the left. The right flank of the line was covered by Washington's legion, with his cavalry on the extreme right. His infantry, composed of Kirkwood's light infantry company and Lynch's Virginia riflemen, was formed in a line that was angled inward in order to provide enfilading fires against the attacker. On the left flank Lee's legion was deployed in the same manner as Washington's. The cavalry covered the end of the flank, with the legion infantry and Campbell's riflemen formed in line facing obliquely to enfilade the main line from their position. Captain Anthony Singleton, with two of Greene's four six-pounder guns, was in the center, with his guns positioned on the road and laid to fire across the clearings to their front.

The second line, about 300 yards behind the first, comprised the two Virginia militia brigades of 600 men each: Stevens's on the right of the road, Lawson's on the left. The second line was deployed entirely in the woods, with connecting files posted in the rear to facilitate contact with the third line.

Greene's main line of resistance was his third line, 550 yards to the right rear of the second line. In order to take advantage of the high ground west of the courthouse, this line had to be displaced westward, with only about half of it directly in the rear of Stevens's brigade. Two brigades of Continentals made up the line. On the right was Huger's brigade of Virginia Continentals, 778 men: Colonel Green's 4th Virginia on the brigade's right, and Hawes's 5th Virginia on its left. The other bri-

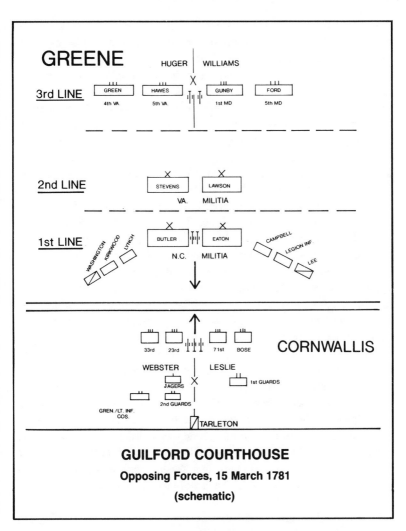

GUILFORD COURTHOUSE

Opposing Forces, 15 March 1781

(schematic)

gade was the Maryland Continentals, 630 men under Otho Williams: Gunby's 1st Maryland on the brigade's right, and Ford's 5th Maryland on the left. Captain Samuel Finley's two six-pounders, the other half of Greene's artillery, were positioned in the center, in the interval between the two brigades. Greene remained with the Continentals throughout the battle.

Along with the terrain and the disposition of the troops, several other factors are noteworthy. Greene had put his entire army in the three lines.

There was no provision for an army reserve of any kind, whereas the terrain of Cowpens had permitted Morgan to hold all of his cavalry in reserve. The question of Greene's lack of a reserve has been well addressed by Boatner: "It would appear that he should have been able, however, to set himself up a general reserve, either from the flanking units of his first line, or by eliminating the second line and using these flanking units as a delaying force between the first and last lines" (*Encyclopedia of the American Revolution*).

The quality of Greene's troops was decidedly uneven. At opposite ends of the spectrum were the battle-hardened veterans such as Kirkwood's Delaware company and Gunby's 1st Maryland Continentals; on the other end was the North Carolina militia, which could not be depended upon at all to stand up to British bayonets. Two units, the 5th Maryland and some of the Virginia Continentals, were getting their first taste of combat.

Greene was well aware that his front line, much like Morgan's second-line militia at Cowpens, would vacate the premises shortly after the shooting started. That is why he walked the line of his North Carolina militia, exhorting them as best he could and reminding them of his basic instruction: Get off at least "two rounds, my boys, and then you may fall back." In that exhortation lay another case of the difference in the terrain of Morgan's and Greene's battles. Morgan's militia could file off around the left of the Continental line behind them and reform to reconstitute a reserve. Greene's militia had no place to go except the woods around and behind them, so when they "fell back" they would vanish off the earth, as far as their further participation in the battle was concerned. Consequently, the only recourse left to Greene was to order, ahead of time, the Virginians in the second line to open their ranks and let the Carolinians pass through. He also made sure that Washington's and Lee's flanking units knew that they should fall back and take up positions on the flanks of the second line.

His instructions given and his inspections made, Greene rode back to his command post behind the third line. The morning was clear and cold under a cloudless sky. It only remained now to sit tight and await Cornwallis's advance.

TWELVE MILES TO THE SOUTHWEST, Cornwallis, in his camp at New Garden, had begun his preparations to advance on 14 March. Late in the day he sent his sick and wounded, in the wagons that remained to him, back to Bell's Mills on Deep River under a small escort of infantry and cavalry. Then, in the hope of catching Greene off guard, the earl had his troops fall in and start the twelve-mile march to Guilford at 5:00 A.M., without taking time for breakfast. The main body was preceded by an advance guard under Tarleton of about 450 men: his legion cavalry and infantry (272), 84 jägers, and some 100 light infantry of the guards.

About 7:15 A.M., seven miles down the road, Tarleton's dragoons were fired on by a detachment of Lee's legion. Greene had sent Lee, with the infantry and horse of his legion reinforced by Campbell's riflemen, as a covering force, and it was Lieutenant Heard's squad of the legion cavalry that had fired on the British. When Heard galloped back to inform Lee of the British approach, Lee pulled back, looking for an advantageous place to delay his enemy, and Tarleton pressed forward.

Lee found the spot he was looking for, "a long lane with high curved fences on either side of the road." He waited until Tarleton's dragoons poured into it, then ordered a charge that resulted in the whole of the enemy's advance being dismounted, and many of the horses downed. Some of the British dragoons were killed and the rest made prisoner; not a single American soldier or horse was injured. Tarleton thereupon retired, and Lee's horsemen pursued until they ran into the infantry of the enemy's advance guard near New Garden Meetinghouse. The British infantry deployed and fired on the American cavalry, driving them back, Lee being momentarily unhorsed during the confusion. Lee's infantry came up, and a smart little skirmish ensued in which Tarleton lost about thirty killed or wounded. Lee claimed much lighter losses. Tarleton took a musket ball in his right hand, causing him to lose his middle and index fingers.

Lee then withdrew his force and fell back toward the American defensive position. There were more exchanges of fire, which by then could be heard by Greene's troops three miles away. Finally, when the skirmishing grew to a firefight, Lee could see that he had checked the British advance long enough. He withdrew again and warned Greene of the approach of the enemy's main force. Lee's men closed into their positions in the first defensive line not long before noon.

WHEN CORNWALLIS RODE UP THE NEW GARDEN ROAD and came up the low rise on the south side of Little Horsepen Creek, he was able to observe the ground in front of the American position. Before him the road sloped downward to the creek, a small stream beyond which the terrain began to rise. There were open fields on each side, but at the top of the rise the road entered a dense wood, and in front of it, behind rail fences, the North Carolina militia waited. In order to get at them, Cornwallis's troops would have to advance for some 500 to 600 yards uphill across a quarter-mile-wide expanse of muddy fields, exposed all the while to enemy fire.

The leading troops of the British main body emerged from the north end of the defile above Little Horsepen Creek and began deploying from column into line. Cornwallis had divided his attack force into two "wings" (provisional brigades). The right wing, under Major General Leslie, had on its right the Hessian Regiment von Bose, and on the left the 71st (Fraser's) Highlanders. The left wing, under Lieutenant Colonel Webster, had on its right, lining up with the 71st Highlanders, the 23rd Regiment of Royal Fusiliers, and on its left the 33rd Regiment. Unlike Greene, the British commander had retained a strong reserve. The 1st Guards Battalion was behind General Leslie's wing. Behind Webster's wing were the jägers, the 2nd Guards Battalion, and the grenadier and light infantry companies. Also in reserve was Tarleton's cavalry, held back in column, to the rear on the New Garden Road. The reserve was commanded by General O'Hara. The Royal Artillery detachment, three three-pounders under Lieutenant MacLeod, would first occupy positions in the center along the road.

LOOKING SOUTHWARD ACROSS THE STUBBLE FIELDS, the North Carolina militiamen were no doubt impressed by the display, as intended, of the British forming into line of battle. Companies came up from the defile in compact columns, turned at right angles to the road, and wheeled smartly into long scarlet lines. Polished musket barrels glittered in the noonday sun, while the roll of the drums and the keening of the fifes were carried to the Americans in the clear March air.

When the first body of British infantry came within range, Captain Singleton opened up with his two six-pounders. Within minutes Lieutenant MacLeod's Royal Artillery guns were answering the American fire. The cannonade lasted for less than half an hour, with negligible effect on either side. About 1:30 P.M. the British attack came on, straight ahead across the quarter mile of open fields. When the first British ranks were within about 150 yards, the thousand muskets and rifles of the Americans opened fire. It was not a crashing volley like the Continentals would have delivered; instead it was a rolling fire, at too great a range for maximum effect. Nevertheless, gaps were opened in the red-coated line, which continued to come on steadily. When the British line came within its own musket range, it snapped to a halt and fired its first volley. At

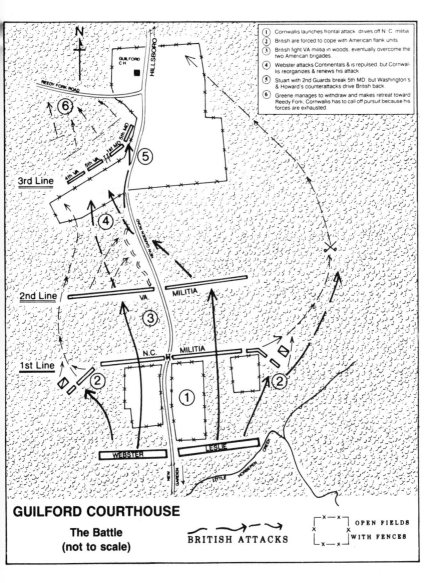

1. Cornwallis launches frontal attack, drives off N.C. militia
2. British are forced to cope with American flank units
3. British fight VA militia in woods, eventually overcome the two American brigades
4. Webster attacks Continentals & is repulsed, but Cornwallis reorganizes & renews his attack
5. Stuart with 2nd Guards break 5th MD, but Washington's & Howard's counterattacks drive British back
6. Greene manages to withdraw and makes retreat toward Reedy Fork. Cornwallis has to call off pursuit because his forces are exhausted.

GUILFORD COURTHOUSE
The Battle
(not to scale)

BRITISH ATTACKS

OPEN FIELDS WITH FENCES

Colonel Webster's command, his lines advanced with muskets lowered at charge bayonet. About 40 yards from the rail fence the advance came to an abrupt halt. British Sergeant Lamb, of the 23rd Regiment (Royal Welsh Fusiliers), recounted in his journal that "their whole force had their arms presented and resting on a rail fence . . . they were taking aim with nice precision. . . . At this awful period a general pause took place; both parties surveyed each other for a moment with the most awful suspense. Colonel Webster then rode forward in front of the 23rd Regiment and said, with more than his usual commanding voice . . . 'Come on, my brave Fusiliers.' These words operated like an inspiring voice. Dreadful was the havoc on both sides. At last the Americans gave way."

With the exception of the flank units of Lee and Washington, the American line broke across its whole length. The militia, having delivered its fires per Greene's instructions, turned and fled, disappearing into the woods. According to Lee, "Every effort was made by the Generals Butler and Eaton . . . with many officers of every grade to stop this unaccountable panic for not a man of the corps had been killed or even wounded." (It appears that Lee was unaware of Greene's permission for the Carolinians to leave the field.) At this point there appears to have been a great deal of difference between Lee's observations and Sergeant Lamb's picture of dreadful havoc in front of and behind the rail fence. Lee goes on to say that he "joined in the attempt to rally the fugitives, threatening to fall upon them with his cavalry. All was vain, so thoroughly confounded were these unhappy men, that throwing away arms, knapsacks, and even canteens, they rushed like a torrent headlong through the woods" (*Memoirs*).

The action in the first American line was not over when the militia had taken off into the woods. Although Webster's and Leslie's line had reached the fences on the north end of the clearings, both the British and Hessian regiments were suffering severe casualties from enfilading fire on both flanks. On the British left the deadly fire was coming from Kirkwood's Delaware company and Lynch's riflemen; on the right the same deadly fire was being thrown at them by Campbell's riflemen and Lee's legion infantry. Before the British could advance upon the line of Virginians waiting 300 yards back in the woods, these twin threats would have to be dealt with.

The problem was handled on the British left when Webster directed the 33rd Regiment to divert its attack obliquely against Kirkwood and Lynch, while jägers and light infantry available on the left were brought up to augment the 33rd. At the same time General Leslie, in similar fashion, swung the Regiment von Bose and the 71st to face Campbell's and Lee's units. These maneuvers on both flanks of the British line left a wide gap in the center, which O'Hara plugged by bringing up the 2nd Guard Battalion and the grenadiers. The line was also extended in Leslie's wing by advancing the 1st Guard Battalion to the extreme right.

When the British attack was resumed, the first heavy fighting took place on the flanks. Washington, on the American right, kept Kirkwood's and Lynch's infantry forward as long as he could, but soon they were thrown back by the weight of the British 33rd, reinforced by the light infantry and jägers. Seeing that his infantry's position was becoming untenable, Washington covered their withdrawal with his cavalry until Kirkwood and Lynch could take up new positions on the right of the second line.

On the American left, things took a different turn. Although Lee's infantry had been augmented by Captain Forbes's company of North Carolina militia, which had stayed to fight on, Campbell's riflemen were assailed by the British 1st Guard Battalion. This action, along with a co-ordinated attack by the Regiment von Bose, prevented Lee from falling back to the second line, as Washington had done on the other flank. As Lee was driven back, he found his infantry being pushed farther and farther toward the left, separating them completely from the American main body. Lee's force thus had to fight its own separate battle, engaged continuously with the guards and von Bose. This private affair was to be continued throughout the battle, with the result that both Cornwallis and Greene were deprived of troops that were sorely needed in the main actions.

The British now advanced through the woods to attack the American line, only to find that the real battle had just begun. No longer could the redcoats advance in firm lines and deliver controlled volleys against their enemy. That enemy was now shielded by trees and undergrowth that broke up the battle into a series of small-unit actions. Stedman, who was at the battle, reported that the Americans were "posted in the woods and covering themselves with trees, [from which] they kept up for a consider-able time a galling fire, which did great execution." All across the second line the Virginians, fighting to hold their positions, were beginning to feel the whole force of Cornwallis's attack. The heavier weight of Webster's and O'Hara's troops was thrown against Stevens's brigade on the Ameri-can right: the 33rd, the grenadiers, the guards' 2nd Battalion, the jägers, the light infantry were all directing their main effort against Stevens. The pressure was too much, and the brigade was forced back on its right.

Like the opening of a huge door, the left of the brigade held like the hinges while its right was swung back, until it finally broke. The rest of the Virginia line fought on stubbornly, fighting off three bayonet attacks and holding up for a time the advance of the 23rd, the Royal Welsh Fusiliers, and the 71st.

While the British 23rd and 71st Highlanders were being held up by the left of the American line, Colonel Webster took stock of the situation. With the driving off of the American right, the way was open to him to continue the advance and attack Greene's third line. He led forward the 33rd Regiment, the light infantry, and the jägers. Emerging from the woods, they came up against the best of Greene's troops, the Continentals of the 1st Maryland and the 5th Virginia, supported by Captain Finley's two six-pounders. Waiting along the forward slope of the high ground south of the Reedy Fork Road, the Continentals had been listening to the growing sounds of battle in the woods ahead: the banging of muskets and the crack of rifles swelled to a continuous roll. As the firing below them seemed to diminish, they began to see little groups of Virginians trotting out of the woods headed toward the rear. Then the groups grew to a steady stream, and the Continentals could be sure that the second line had broken. Over on the right, two columns were coming back, one in Continental uniforms, the other, larger column in brown hunting shirts and gray homespun. They were Kirkwood's Delaware Continentals and Lynch's Virginia riflemen, filing back to fall in on the right of Colonel Green's 4th Virginia.

In a few minutes groups of redcoats appeared on the near edge of the woods and began to form into line. Then the British line came on, led by Webster: on the right the 33rd was headed directly toward the 1st Maryland; on the left the light infantry and jägers were coming on toward Hawes's 5th Virginia. The Continentals stood, rock-firm, awaiting the command to fire. Their officers held back until the British line was within thirty paces, then the command came: "Fire!" The volley crashed into the red-coated formations, which disintegrated under the blow. Falling back in disorder, the British infantry left a swathe of dead and wounded. But the Continentals were not through. Colonel John Gunby of the 1st Maryland called for a bayonet attack. The Maryland and Virginia regulars slashed through the knots of their disorganized enemy and drove the fugitives down into a ravine and up its other side. With that the British fled into the woods. Webster was carried back with them, his knee shattered by a musket ball.

Now victory seemed held in balance for either side. On the British far right the guards and Hessians were out of the main battle, held up by Lee's men on a wooded height far to the south. In the center, the left of the American second line was still entangled with the British 23rd and 71st regiments. And the center of the third line had just repulsed and shattered Webster's too-bold attack.

Accordingly, at this critical moment, historical "what ifs" begin to pop up: What if Greene had thrown his cavalry against the disorganized British? What if Greene had attacked the British center with the whole of his Continental line? Yet Greene could not have known that a critical moment had arrived, for the simple reason that he could not see the battlefield that involved his first and second lines, nor Lee's separate, faraway battle. Also, Greene had no reserve to commit, and in any event he would not have thrown his third line into the fray, because he had entered into this battle—indeed into the whole campaign after Cowpens—with the firm resolve not to risk the hard core of his army in any way that might hazard its destruction. The loss of his veterans, he was certain, would surely leave the South in British hands.

WHILE WEBSTER WAS MOVING THROUGH THE WOODS and delivering his disastrous attack against Greene's third line, the resistance of the Virginians in the second line was weakening. When General Leslie became aware of the fact, he disengaged the 23rd and 71st regiments and sent them to take part in the attack against the American third line. During the lull that followed, Cornwallis was restoring his forward line to launch his main attack against Greene's Continentals. As part of this reorganization of force, General O'Hara, who had been wounded, turned over command of the 2nd Guard Battalion and the grenadiers to Lieutenant Colonel James Stuart. That officer didn't wait for the other three units— the 23rd, 71st, and grenadiers—to come up into line. He led the 2nd Guards, "glowing with impatience to signalize themselves," toward that part of the American line to their front, Ford's 5th Maryland Continentals and Captain Singleton's two six-pounders.

The 5th Maryland was not made of the stuff that had enabled Continentals to stand and exchange volleys with British regulars. Mostly recruits in a newly reorganized unit that was facing battle for the first time, the raw Marylanders gaped at the hedge of British steel coming up the hill directly at them. They got off a ragged volley, and to a man turned and ran. The guards dashed ahead and seized Singleton's two guns.

Then, as Stuart continued to drive on through the penetration his guards had made, his battalion was struck on both flanks by two charging counter-attacks, both made on the initiative of local commanders. The close-in combat that followed was out of Greene's control; he was already consid-ering saving his invaluable Continentals, having observed that it would soon be "most advisable to order a retreat," and had ordered Colonel Green to pull back his 4th Virginia to cover a general disengagement.

William Washington, observing from the American left on the hill, saw the 5th Maryland collapse and the subsequent British breakthrough. Seizing the chance to restore the situation, he led his entire cavalry force in a pell-mell charge that smashed into the right rear of Stuart's guards, sabering right and left as they broke through the British formation. Among Washington's troopers was the famed Sergeant Peter Francisco, a six-foot-eight giant who wielded an awesome five-foot sword said to have been given him by General Washington. It was said, too, that he had the reputation of being the strongest man in Virginia. According to his com-rades, Francisco cut down eleven British soldiers "with his brawny arms and terrible broadsword." Not only did Francisco ride through the guards, he wheeled around and went back through them, sabering as he went.

In the meantime Colonel Gunby, having returned the 1st Maryland to its original position, was informed by his second in command, Lieuten-ant Colonel John Eager Howard, that the guards had broken through the 5th Maryland and were pushing on through the breached American line. At once Gunby wheeled the 1st Maryland and charged into the guards; when the Americans continued to drive into the British, the encounter turned into a melee. During the hand-to-hand fighting that followed, Stuart himself was killed, cut down by a sword blow from Captain Smith of the Marylanders when he and the British leader engaged in personal combat. In Franklin and Mary Wickwire's account of the close combat:

> Even the Guards' experience and discipline could not forever stand proof against such an onslaught. They had plainly begun to get the worst of it and had begun to fall back when Cornwallis . . . resorted to a desperate measure . . . Lieutenant MacLeod had brought two 3-pounders along the road to a small eminence just beside it on the south side . . . Cornwallis ordered MacLeod to load his guns with grapeshot and direct his fire into the middle of the human melange. O'Hara who lay bleeding nearby in the road, supposedly 'remon-strated and begged' his commander to spare the Guards, but Corn-wallis repeated the order. . . . The carnage upon friend and foe

alike was frightening, but it did serve the purpose. When the smoke cleared away, the surviving Guards had regained the safety of their own guns [lines?] and those of Washington's and Howard's men [Howard having relieved Gunby when the latter was pinned down by his wounded horse] who could still move had abandoned their pursuit and retired to their own lines. (*Cornwallis: The American Adventure*)

With both sides retiring, there was a new lull in the action during which Cornwallis again restored his front line, this time in preparation for a final assault by the 23rd and 71st regiments. Webster had reorganized his former attacking force, and returned to renew the attack against the American right.

Greene was now faced with a restored British line which was about to launch an all-out attack. At 3:30 P.M. he decided on a general retreat. The only fighting units left intact to confront the enemy were the 1st Maryland, Hawes's 5th Virginia, and Washington's cavalry; the 4th Virginia had already been pulled back to aid in covering the retreat. Howard retired the 1st Maryland in good order, while Washington and Green's 4th Virginia got in position to cover the withdrawal. On the left, Hawes's 5th Virginia repulsed Webster's new attack with enough volleys to end the battle.

The retreat was "conducted with order and regularity," even though Greene's four guns all had to be abandoned because most of the artillery horses had been killed. For a short time Cornwallis pushed a pursuit, using the 23rd, the 71st, and a part of Tarleton's cavalry, but those worn-out men were too fatigued to be effective and the earl had to call it off.

Greene's retreating force moved out in a driving rain and crossed Reedy Fork, about three miles west of Guilford Courthouse, where he halted long enough to close up his column and collect stragglers. He then pushed on, making an all-night march to his former camp at the Ironworks on Troublesome Creek.

As for Lee's semi-independent battle, he and Campbell had fought the Hessians and the 1st Guards through the woods and over hills, trying to hold their enemy while maneuvering to get back to Greene's third line. When Lieutenant Colonel Norton, commanding the 1st Guards, disengaged to take his battalion and link up with the 71st, Lee and Campbell seized the opportunity to force the Hessians back. Lee then left Campbell to hold the enemy while he took his infantry back to rejoin his legion cavalry near the courthouse. A charge by Tarleton's cavalry finally released the pressure on the Hessians, and with that Campbell got his men clear and away.

GUILFORD COURTHOUSE PROVED TO BE ONE OF the bloodiest battles of the war, and most of the blood that was shed was British. Greene's casualty count was 78 killed and 183 wounded out of a force of 4,444. Out of a force of 1,900, Cornwallis lost 532 officers and men, 93 of whom were killed and 50 dead of wounds before they could be evacuated. The guards took the heaviest casualties: 11 of 19 officers and 206 of 462 men.

Shortly after Greene had broken off the battle, a continuing rain set in. It was an unusually black night, and it was still cold there in late winter. The search for the British wounded had to go on all night over a large area, much of it wooded. The last time Cornwallis's soldiers had eaten was at supper on the evening of 14 March. They then had been forced to march twelve miles the next day, fight one of the fiercest battles of the war, and sink down on wet ground that night, hungry and without tents. After forty-eight hours they were finally rewarded with a repast of four ounces of flour and four ounces of lean beef.

Cornwallis had won the battle, but he had lost his campaign. Greene had withdrawn intact, and as events were to show conclusively, his fighting force would be capable of moving and fighting almost anywhere in the Carolinas. Cornwallis could not. As Page Smith observed: "For Cornwallis, the possession of the Guilford Courthouse battlefield had no meaning if Greene's army survived to fight another day." After the battle had been fought, it was impossible for the British general to resume his pursuit of Greene. In Smith's words, "His shattered army could not sustain another battle. Instead of following Greene he issued a proclamation, claiming a glorious victory for British arms and urging all loyalists to come to his support. Then he turned toward Wilmington, North Carolina, the country of the Scottish Highlanders, where he hoped to rest and equip his battered army" (*A New Age Now Begins*).

TEN

The Chesapeake Capes

On the afternoon of September 5th, 1781, off the Capes of Virginia, two and a half hours of cannonade between warships of the British and French navies determined the outcome of the American Revolution.

—Harold A. Larrabee, *Decision at the Chesapeake*

AS WE HAVE SEEN, CORNWALLIS'S RUINOUS VICTORY at Guilford Court-house left him with no realistic alternative but retreat to his nearest strategic base at Wilmington, North Carolina. After some consulting with his senior officers, he turned to rationalizing new strategies that would get things moving—moving in his own way and under his direction.

Virginia, it seemed, was the great and indispensable link between the British in the North and the British in the Carolinas and Georgia. Virginia had not been subjected to the mass depredations of conflicting armies and so remained a rich and fertile region to be taken and held by His Majesty's forces. Moreover, Greene, in departing from North Carolina, had left the back door to Virginia wide open. By marching north through that door, Cornwallis could link up with General Phillips's now considerable force in Virginia, take command of the combined forces, and bring Virginia under British rule. With that done, British forces could block the movement of American armies from north to south as well as furthering British expansion along the Chesapeake.

THE BRITISH HAD BEEN DRAWN TO VIRGINIA since early 1779 because that province was wealthy and productive enough to make continuing contributions of vital supplies to the rebel cause. Virginia ports and coastal areas became magnets that drew British raids in increasing size. In May 1779 a British expedition under Major General Edward Matthews (a force of 1,800 transported by the Royal Navy ships of Admiral Sir John Collier) made an unopposed foray that seized Portsmouth, Norfolk, and Suffolk.

In January 1781 Benedict Arnold, now holding a brigadier general's commission in the British army, led a force of 1,200 on a massive raid into eastern Virginia. Washington had been well informed of Arnold's operations in Virginia. He was eager to bring Arnold to justice for his betrayal of the revolutionary cause, and so was bent upon capturing the traitor while relieving the people of eastern Virginia from his depredation. The commander in chief's initial plan called for a joint land and sea operation with a small force of 1,200 under the Marquis de Lafayette, now a major general in the Continental army, cooperating with a French force based on Newport, Rhode Island.

Lieutenant General de Rochambeau, commanding the French army in America, had agreed to send 1,200 French troops with the French fleet under Admiral Destouches to operate with Lafayette, who had arrived at Head of Elk, Maryland, on 3 March. Destouches sailed on 8 March from Newport, and two days later his troubles began. His fleet (eight ships of the line and three frigates) encountered a British fleet under Admiral Arbuthnot on 16 March while both fleets were heading toward the entrance to Chesapeake Bay. The two fleets had an equal number of ships of the line, but heavier weight of armament and British gunnery tipped the scales in Arbuthnot's favor. Destouches turned back and returned to Newport, having, in real terms, been chased away from the Chesapeake, leaving Lafayette without the reinforcements that would have doubled his strength to 2,400. As a consequence, when Lafayette was marching south he was already outnumbered before he arrived in the field: his 1,200 Continentals would be opposed by the combined forces of Phillips and Arnold, numbering nearly 4,000 regulars.

As might be expected, Phillips continued to carry out raiding expeditions of the kind that Benedict Arnold had managed with consistent success. He sent Arnold with 2,500 men north from Portsmouth, leaving there on 18 April by ship, bound for the James River. On 27 April Phillips took Chesterfield Courthouse, where he burned a great range of barracks and 300 barrels of flour, with other stores. At the same time Arnold marched to Osborne, where he attacked and routed the Americans manning a small flotilla on the James River. He then burned or sank nine ships and several smaller vessels which had been assembled to cooperate with the French fleet in upcoming operations. The British general then withdrew downriver to Jamestown Island.

Cornwallis had written Phillips of his decision to march with his whole force to join the latter at Petersburg. Cornwallis arrived there on 20 May, to learn to his sorrow that Phillips had died of typhoid fever only a week before. The next phase of operations in Virginia has been aptly called "Cornwallis versus Lafayette"; if such is the case, it would be helpful to compare their strengths and strategies as the two opponents were squaring off. Cornwallis had arrived in Petersburg with a strength of 1,500, mostly British and Hessian regulars plus Tarleton's legion and Hamilton's Tories. In a few days a new reinforcement reported to him. It had been sent by Clinton and was composed of the 17th and 43rd British regiments and two German (Anspach) battalions, totaling 1,500 men. Thus, Cornwallis's army, after combining with Phillips's force and absorbing the newly arrived reinforcement, totaled an impressive 7,200 professional rank and file.

Lafayette had marched south with 1,200 Continentals, a force made up of three regiments of light infantry from the New England and New Jersey regiments of Vose, de Gimat, and Barber. As he marched through Virginia, Lafayette was joined by some 2,000 Virginia militia and 40 dragoons from Armand's legion, bringing his total strength to 3,240—a less than formidable force with which to oppose Cornwallis.

Being well aware of his opponent's strength and purpose, Lafayette had to adopt a strategy that would be the converse of that of Cornwallis. It was made plain in a letter to Washington: "Were I to fight a battle, I would be cut to pieces, the militia dispersed and the arms lost. Were I to decline fighting, the country would think itself given up. I am therefore determined to skirmish, but not to engage too far, and particularly to take care against their immense and excellent body of horse, whom the militia fear as they would so many wild beasts" (Ward, *War of the Revolution*).

CORNWALLIS MADE THE FIRST MOVE. He left Petersburg on 24 May, crossed the James at Westover, and reached Hanover Junction by 1 June. Using his camp at that place as a forward base, he sent out mobile detachments under Tarleton and Simcoe to find Lafayette, whose last known position had been at Winston's Bridge about eight miles north of Richmond.

Lafayette kept falling back northward until he reached Ely's Ford on the Rapidan on 4 June. At that point he was, for the time being, out of reach of Cornwallis's main army but in no position to protect any part of the region from the raids of mobile forces like Tarleton's and Simcoe's. One of the more successful flying raids—from Cornwallis's viewpoint—was Simcoe's advance toward Point of Fork, where Steuben was guarding Lafayette's main supply depot with about 500 newly enlisted Continentals.

Lieutenant Colonel John Simcoe's nominal command was the Queen's Rangers, but he had frequently been given command of mobile task forces. He was a veteran of numerous cavalry battles and forays in both the northern and southern theaters of war and undoubtedly the most experienced leader (with the possible exception of Tarleton) of light cavalry and rangers in the British army. Cornwallis dispatched him with his rangers and the 2nd Battalion, 71st Foot on 1 June, with the mission of capturing Lafayette's stores and destroying Steuben's force. About the same time Tarleton with 250 mounted men was leading a raid against Charlottesville where Governor Jefferson and the state legislature were doing business. Although the legislators had been warned of his coming, Tarleton rounded up a few and almost captured Jefferson, who escaped only by skedaddling into the mountains. Before Tarleton returned to rejoin Cornwallis, he had destroyed a supply train of uniforms intended for Greene's army as well as a thousand muskets and stores of gunpowder and, of course, many hogsheads of tobacco.

Lafayette remained relatively helpless until he was finally joined by Wayne's brigade of Pennsylvania Continentals, a force of three regiments and the 4th Continental Artillery. Three days later he was reinforced by a force of 600 riflemen under the redoubtable William Campbell, now a brigadier general of Virginia militia. In addition Lafayette had gained 425 Virginia Continentals now commanded by the respected veteran Colonel Christian Febiger. The Virginia militia, totaling 2,100, was organized into three brigades under Generals Campbell, Edward Stevens, and Robert Lawson. The Continental 2nd and 4th artillery could now count ten guns, and the cavalry numbered 120 dragoons. Thus Lafayette's army now totaled nearly 5,000 men, a respectable force.

Although considerably strengthened, Lafayette even so was not about to cross swords with Cornwallis in a general engagement. Wisely the young marquis held to the strategy he had confided to Washington. On 16 June Cornwallis entered Richmond, then left on the twentieth to continue his march back toward Williamsburg on the peninsula. Lafayette followed warily, keeping his distance, often as much as twenty miles from the British columns of march. The next major move was directed by neither Cornwallis nor Lafayette. It was caused by Clinton, who had become increasingly fearful of the combined armies of Washington and

Rochambeau threatening New York. Hence he had directed Cornwallis to send 3,000 of his men to New York. The earl complied willingly enough, but to do so he had to move his army to Portsmouth to embark the 3,000 on Royal Navy transports. This meant crossing the James and undertaking another retrograde march to the south. Cornwallis set out on 4 July, followed by Lafayette, keeping closer this time in the hope of striking his enemy's rear guard. The marquis soon saw that a lovely opportunity would be presented if he could attack Cornwallis while his army was in the act of crossing the James.

Unfortunately for Lafayette, the wily Cornwallis also saw an opportunity. He tricked Lafayette into thinking he was encountering only the British rear guard, then fell upon Anthony Wayne's detachment of 900 men at Green Spring Farm. Wayne counterattacked instead of pulling back, stopping the enemy in his tracks. Lafayette otherwise might have lost a sizable portion of his army. Even so, the real savior of the American force had been nightfall. In Cornwallis's words in a letter to Clinton, another half-hour of daylight "would probably have given us the greatest part of the [American] corps." The Battle of Green Spring Farm cost the British 75 casualties. Lafayette's losses were 133 killed or wounded and 12 missing.

Cornwallis continued his march southward until he encamped at Suffolk, while Lafayette concentrated his army at Malvern Hill. In the meantime, Cornwallis received the latest of a confusing series of dispatches from Clinton. On 20 July he read Clinton's order countermanding the sending of the 3,000 troops to New York and directing Cornwallis to establish a base at Old Point Comfort, from which he could conduct joint operations with the Royal Navy. Clinton also authorized the occupation of Yorktown if necessary. When Cornwallis made a reconnaissance with his engineers, he learned that the Hampton Roads channel was too wide at Old Point Comfort to be covered by shore batteries, and thus that position could not provide a secure base for navy ships. Cornwallis therefore selected Yorktown and Gloucester, on opposite sides of the York River, and proceeded to occupy and fortify both places. For the immediate future his only enemy of any consequence was Lafayette, watching from his positions of surveillance. But, as yet inconceivable to Cornwallis, enemies of much greater consequence farther north were making plans that had him very much in mind.

In early May 1781 Admiral the Comte de Barras had arrived to take command of the French fleet at Newport. He brought orders authorizing Rochambeau, the general commanding French land forces, to undertake a campaign under Washington. Additionally, de Barras informed Rochambeau that Admiral de Grasse was on his way with a fleet which would reinforce the one at Newport and participate jointly in operations against New York or another reasonable objective. Washington then proposed a combined operation against Clinton in New York. Rochambeau agreed, adding the provision that de Barras could take his fleet to another base after Rochambeau had moved his troops from Newport to join Washington on the Hudson.

Washington began at once to call up all the militia he could muster, and in his camp at Peekskill began the reorganization of his army. In the first week of July, Rochambeau joined Washington on the Hudson, bringing the armies' combined strength up to 9,000—half American and half French. For the next five weeks after Rochambeau had joined Washington the two planned, reconnoitered, probed, and conferred, all leading to an inevitable conclusion—there were no vulnerable points in the British defenses.

Then, on 14 August—while Cornwallis was busily fortifying Yorktown and Gloucester—a letter arrived from de Grasse to Rochambeau, a dispatch that "cleared the air, resolved all doubts, and determined the course of the war" (Ward, *War of the Revolution*). In sum, de Grasse said that he would sail in August from Haiti to the Chesapeake bringing with him 3,000 French troops augmented with artillery and 100 cavalry in his fleet of twenty-eight warships. There was a catch to the dispatch: the troops were "borrowed" from the Haitian establishment, and therefore de Grasse could remain in Chesapeake waters only until 15 October, when he would have to return to the West Indies.

Washington was at first disappointed with the news, his heart still being set on an operation with the French against Clinton, but trapping Cornwallis in Virginia had always been in the back of his mind. On the following day, 15 August, he wrote Lafayette directing him to keep Cornwallis pinned down and not allow him to slip away and return to the Carolinas. Four days later he marched off, leaving Major General Heath, with 2,500 men, to cover the departure of Washington's and Rochambeau's troops when they passed out of New York on their march southward.

No one was more aware of the desperate character of his adventure than Washington himself. He proposed to lead to Virginia, with all possible speed, all the available strength of the allied armies, while leaving in his rear only the paltry 2,500 troops under Heath to cover his rear and distract Clinton's powerful force, which, if alerted and skillfully employed, could wreck the whole operation—and probably drown the hopes of any future allied operations as well as the outcome of the Revolution. Yet, with characteristic moral courage, he went full speed ahead with his preparations. Secrecy was, of course, of the utmost importance. False orders were allowed to fall into British hands; bread ovens were built as if to prepare for a permanent bivouac for the French.

On 21 August the allied armies began their march southward. Whether or not Clinton was completely taken in—at least at first—may be doubted. It seems certain that he was aware that de Grasse would be coming up from the West Indies, but he placed his confidence in the Royal Navy.

WHEN ADMIRAL COMTE DE GRASSE'S FLEET of 24 ships of the line appeared off Martinique on 28 April 1781, it posed a very real strategic threat to British sea power in the West Indies. De Grasse entered Fort Royal the next day to pick up the 4 ships there, bringing his line of battle to 28 ships reinforced by 3 frigates and 150 supply ships. De Grasse was being watched by Admiral Sir Samuel Hood's blockading squadron, so on 30 April de Grasse sailed out in force to attack Hood, but the British admiral, outnumbered, slipped away after his brush with de Grasse.

Hood was second in command in the theater to Admiral George Rodney. Both men fit the term "sea dog" in its best sense—though each was destined to make critical mistakes in the operations that led to Hood's going north to the Chesapeake. In April 1781 Rodney had put little stock in reports that a large French fleet was bound for the West Indies, and as a consequence failed to reinforce Hood off Martinique. Instead, he was content—after Hood was driven off his blockade of Fort Royal—to leave his station at Saint Eustatius (newly taken from the Dutch) and join Hood at Antigua on 9 May, where several of his ships were to be repaired.

Their opponent, François Joseph Paul, Comte de Grasse, was born in 1722 of a noble family in their chateau at Bar-sur-Loup in the Maritime Alps. In October 1779 de Grasse had the misfortune of serving under Admiral d'Estaing in the stinging defeat the combined French and American forces were handed by the British at Savannah. After his return to the Antilles, de Grasse commanded a division of the French fleet in a series of engagements with Rodney's fleet, as Harold A. Larrabee writes, "with much the same result in shattered English ships but no territorial gains for the French." In the fall of 1780 de Grasse was taken ill and invalided to France, where he soon recuperated. In April 1781, as we have seen, he led a formidable fleet to the West Indies, where he assumed command of all French naval forces.

AFTER RODNEY AND HOOD HAD JOINED FORCES at Antigua on 9 May, there followed a series of near engagements interspersed with amphibious attacks on island possessions. De Grasse tried to attack Saint Lucia on 10 May but found the English defenses too strong. He was luckier at Tobago, where he landed troops on 23 May, and by 2 June had taken the island. Two days later Rodney appeared and challenged the French fleet, but de Grasse had other plans and avoided an engagement.

On 26 July de Grasse anchored off Cap Haitien to find the *Concorde* waiting with the dispatches from Rochambeau requesting his support of operations against New York or in the Chesapeake. De Grasse sent the *Concorde* back with his affirmative reply, which was received by Rochambeau and Washington on 14 August. De Grasse's decision and subsequent actions speak for themselves of his strategic insight and moral courage.

While the French commander in chief in the West Indies was acting on his own with firmness and dispatch, the British were causing themselves no end of confusion and difficulties on all fronts. Rodney sent a dispatch on 7 July to Rear Admiral Graves, now commanding the English fleet at New York, to the effect that: (1) a French fleet of 28 ships of the line was at Martinique, *a part of which* would reportedly be sent to America; (2) if and when the French fleet sailed, British ships would reinforce the fleet in America; (3) such reinforcement should proceed to the Chesapeake Capes, thence to the Delaware Capes, and on to New York; and (4) Graves should order cruisers to look for Rodney's squadron off the capes. There are two events of importance regarding this dispatch. The sloop *Swallow* bearing the dispatch did not catch up to Graves because its captain yielded to the temptation of trying to capture a prize in the form of a Yankee privateer. However, instead of the *Swallow* doing the capturing, *it* was captured and destroyed by three privateers—as were the dispatches. As a result, Admiral Graves, who was out at sea with his squadron on some sort of operation designed to forestall French naval operations, did not learn of Rodney's dispatch until he had returned to New York on 16 August.

Of greater importance was Rodney's conviction that *only a part* of de Grasse's fleet would be sent to America. This idée fixe of Rodney's was to prove a fateful factor in reducing the contribution of the British West

Indies fleet to reinforce Graves in America. On the same day that Rodney sent the *Swallow* off with his dispatch, he also sent an order to Hood "to proceed without loss of time to send seven ships to Antigua to refit them for a foreign voyage," because he had intelligence that "a very considerable squadron of the enemy's line of battle ships are intended to reinforce the French squadron in America."

Even as he wrote—and for the next three weeks—Rodney's health was getting worse, finally to the point where he had decided that he could only survive his gout and prostate trouble with the care of British doctors and the waters at Bath. After much remonstrance from the First Lord of the Admiralty and others, Rodney sailed homeward from the West Indies on 1 August. He left Hood in command, after instructing him to take fifteen ships of the line and five frigates and escort the Jamaica trade fleet through the Windward Passage and then "to make his way toward the coast of North America."

On 6 August Hood sent the *Active* back to Graves, informing him of his prospective departure but without any updated intelligence regarding the whereabouts of any of de Grasse's fleet. The *Active* commander was every bit as unlucky as the captain of the *Swallow*; on his way to New York his ship was captured and taken to Philadelphia.

British misfortunes were not limited to the loss of dispatch ships. Lord Sandwich, First Lord of the Admiralty (known to his critics as "Old Jemmy Twitcher"), contributed his inimitable share to the distorted intelligence picture. He believed that the West Indies and New York squadrons combined with a reinforcement under Rear Admiral Digby (then on its way across the North Atlantic) would give the British thirty-one ships of the line. Even more damaging, he was convinced that de Grasse would use part of his fleet to convoy the summer trade fleet to France and would send no more than half his fleet (fourteen ships of the line or less) to America.

Hood, however, as the man on the scene, took a dim view of the actual British strength in warships. Rodney had taken three line ships home with him. Three other line ships had been sent on 1 July to convoy trade ships to Jamaica. Two more were held back by Sir Peter Parker on the Jamaica station in spite of Rodney's instruction "not to detain them a single moment." Add to those losses the ships laid up for emergency repairs, and Hood could count on a force of only fourteen ships of the line out of the original twenty-one in the West Indies—a reduction of one-third of his force! And those fourteen were all that he had when he sailed north from Antigua on 10 August.

WHILE HOOD WAS GATHERING HIS FLEET AND preparing it for the voyage northward, de Grasse had already sailed from Cap Haitien, Haiti, on 5 August with twenty-six ships of the line and five frigates. His fleet carried the 3,200 French troops de Grasse had promised in the dispatch received by Rochambeau and Washington on 14 August. De Grasse had no intention of setting a direct course for the Chesapeake, for two reasons. He needed to rendezvous near Havana with his frigate *Aigrette*, with its precious cargo of 1.2 million borrowed livres. Additionally, he wished to follow a course that would confuse British intelligence, and to do so he sailed through the Old Bahama Channel between Cuba and the Bahamas. The fleet made it through the channel without incident, being joined en route by the *Bourgogne* and the *Hector*, which brought the total of ships of the line up to twenty-eight. On 17 August de Grasse was met by the *Aigrette* off Matanzas, Cuba, where he dropped his Spanish coastal pilots and headed northward into the channel between Florida and the Bahamas. By 22 August the French fleet was through the channel, and on the following day its faster ships chased and captured three small British ships: the *Corp Morrant* (24 guns), the *Queen Charlotte* (18 guns), and a yacht. A couple of days later, the French captured the frigate *Sandwich* (34 guns), which had been headed for Charleston to repair a dangerous leak. Thus, according to Charles L. Lewis: "the French seemed to have succeeded in capturing all the enemy vessels that were sighted. This concealed from the British all knowledge of the movements of De Grasse's fleet" (*Admiral de Grasse and American Independence*).

BECAUSE HOOD HAD SAILED FROM ANTIGUA five days after de Grasse's departure from Haiti, it might be thought that he would be losing the "race for the Chesapeake."* Such was not the case. In the first place, Hood sailed a direct course for the Chesapeake. Second, he had the benefit of good winds prevailing in the season. Finally, Hood's ships were copper bottomed, a process that prevented the leaks and loss of speed caused by worms and barnacles that were curses to sea captains.

Though not consciously in a race, Hood was a man in a hurry. Writing later he said, "Lest the enemy should get to America before me . . . I pushed on as fast as possible." As a result of all the factors in his favor,

---

*Not a race in the sense of the two opponents being aware of it. Neither Hood nor de Grasse had knowledge of the other's course or real destination.

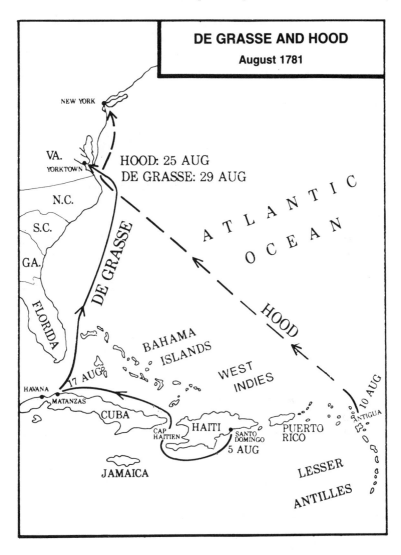

DE GRASSE AND HOOD

August 1781

NEW YORK

VA.
YORKTOWN

HOOD: 25 AUG
DE GRASSE: 29 AUG

N.C.

S.C.

GA.

FLORIDA

A T L A N T I C

O C E A N

DE GRASSE

HOOD

BAHAMA
ISLANDS

WEST
INDIES

10 AUG

17 AUG

HAVANA
MATANZAS

CUBA

CAP
HAITIEN

HAITI

SANTO
DOMINGO

5 AUG

PUERTO
RICO

ANTIGUA

JAMAICA

LESSER

ANTILLES

Hood made landfall a little to the south of Cape Henry on 25 August. He had arrived first at the entrance to Chesapeake Bay. Yet what seems to have been his good fortune was, in reality, another piece of the bad luck that dogged the British from the time they had first opposed de Grasse. Hood looked around and, finding neither a French fleet nor the cruisers that Graves had posted to meet him, sailed on northward to the Delaware Capes. The same result there—no sightings of French or British ships—sent him on to New York, and he arrived off Sandy Hook on 28 August when, in his words: "I got in my boat and met Mr. Graves and Sir Henry Clinton on Long Island." In the ensuing conference Hood urged the other two: "You have no time to lose; every moment is precious. My arguments prevailed, and he [Graves] promised to be over the bar the next day." A startling piece of news arriving that same evening added an exclamation mark to Hood's urgings: Comte de Barras had left Newport with his fleet three days before on 25 August.

In spite of the obvious urgency, Graves delayed—or was delayed, depending upon the viewpoint—for three days (29–31 August) in getting organized and waiting for favorable winds. Finally, on 1 September, Graves brought his squadron "over the bar" to join Hood off Sandy Hook, and "salutes of fifteen guns were exchanged between the two admirals, and without coming to anchor the combined fleet of nineteen warships put out to sea at 7:00 P.M. under Graves' command" (Larrabee, *Decision at the Chesapeake*). It is worth noting that the only intelligence Graves had of his enemies as he sailed southward was that de Grasse and de Barras were at sea—their destinations unknown. He must have felt sure, however, that somewhere in or around Chesapeake Bay the two French admirals would try to effect a rendezvous.

WHILE THE BRITISH AND FRENCH FLEETS WERE converging on fateful courses, the long columns of Washington's and Rochambeau's armies were snaking southward through the late summer countryside of New Jersey and Pennsylvania. The head of Washington's army reached Princeton on 30 August. By 2 September the American troops had passed through Philadelphia, followed by Rochambeau's troops on 3–4 September. The Americans reached Head of Elk on 6 September, and the French troops marched in two days later. There the two armies encamped and waited for the French transports. In the meantime Washington had left Philadelphia on 5 September with his staff, and that afternoon arrived at Chester on the Delaware River where he was to meet the French army commander. As Rochambeau was arriving at Chester, "he was perplexed to see the normally taciturn and dignified General Washington dancing around on the dock and waving his hat. His confusion turned to amazement when he stepped ashore and Washington grabbed him in a bear hug and whirled him around the pier. He had good cause for joy" (Symonds and Clipson, *A Battlefield Atlas of the American Revolution*). De Grasse had reached the Chesapeake!

The good news, however reassuring, could not end the commander in chief's concerns. There was still the problem of de Barras: when would he arrive with his fleet and the vital train of siege artillery? And could Lafayette, even when reinforced by the three thousand troops that de Grasse would be disembarking, keep Cornwallis pinned down long enough for the American and French forces to arrive and catch him on the peninsula?

ON 30 AUGUST DE GRASSE SAILED UNOPPOSED into the Chesapeake and anchored his fleet in three lines in Lynnhaven Bay. Soon a staff officer of Lafayette's came on board de Grasse's flagship to brief the admiral on the situation on the peninsula. The next day de Grasse sent four ships of the line to block the York and James rivers. He then ordered the debarkation of the 3,300 troops under the command of the Marquis de Saint-Simon. On 1 September the boats of the fleet, manned by 1,500 sailors and carrying the troops, were convoyed by frigates up the James River to reinforce Lafayette. During the next three days the French fleet's efforts were dedicated to the support of the land forces. The lighter ships were being readied to move up to the head of the Chesapeake to embark the waiting American and French troops and transport them down the bay to link up with Lafayette on the peninsula. In addition to the logistical support of the allied armies, some 1,800 sailors and 90 officers were engaged ashore in the routine tasks of taking on wood and water.

On the morning of 5 September, as the French scouting frigate *Aigrette* was patrolling the mouth of the Chesapeake between Capes Henry and Charles, at 8:00 A.M. she signaled to de Grasse's flagship, the *Ville de Paris*, the approach of a fleet from the northeast, reporting the sighting of ten sails.* The word spread from ship to ship amid much rejoicing—it must be de Barras's ships coming to join them! Then, as the *Aigrette* retreated back within the capes, the count of approaching ships rose from ten to twenty, far too many to be de Barras's fleet. Finally British ensigns were identified, and de Grasse ordered urgent signals to recall the boats of the fleet—a vain effort, as it turned out, because only a few of the boats were close enough to see the signals. At the same time boatswains' pipes sounded and the drums beat the order to clear for action. Gun crews sprang to prepare for action while other details cleared the decks.

---

*The time has been variously reported as 9:30 A.M. and 10:00 A.M. I have used the time in Mahan's *Major Operations of the Navies*.

Battle nets were spread to catch men or debris that could fall from aloft in combat, and sand was spread on the decks to help barefoot crews keep their footing when blood would make the decks slippery. There was an ironic twist in the absence of the ships' boats: "It was reported that 'every vessel had a hundred men in the boats,' which meant also that the French warships were virtually boatless in getting to sea. In an action, however, that was not wholly a drawback, since 'boats lumber the decks,' and splinters from them, when smashed by enemy cannonballs, were notorious sources of battle wounds" (Larrabee, *Decision at the Chesapeake*).

The shortage in seamen was felt immediately as ships cleared for action. The case of the ship of the line *Citoyen* (74 guns) was typical. She was short five officers and two hundred sailors, making her captain draft the marines for gun crews, and even then the upper-deck batteries were still unmanned. Nevertheless de Grasse made ready to sail; at 11:30 A.M. he gave orders for ships to slip their cables (to cut cables and attach anchors to buoys) in order to put to sea on a moment's notice. But after that de Grasse was forced to proceed slowly, because the tide was still coming into the Chesapeake. A half hour later, just about noon, the tide began to ebb, and de Grasse's *Ville de Paris* began signaling to sail and prepare to form battle line. Further signals ordered captains of the twenty-four ships of the line to form battle line without regard to regular stations. The order resulted in a reversal that placed Commodore de Bougainville's squadron—normally in the rear—in the van of the line of battle. Yet that was only the start of the French fleet's delay in getting out to sea. Ships' captains had to maneuver to avoid the shoals and the headland of Lynnhaven Bay, calling for some tacking back and forth to avoid those obstacles as well as other ships. Yet the fleet made it out of the bay and around Cape Henry, albeit in ragged order and with many captains striving for a place in the forward part of the line in order to be one of the first to engage the enemy.

De Grasse's apparent haste after the tide had turned is understandable, since he had two overriding reasons for getting out of Chesapeake Bay and into the Atlantic Ocean. He could ensure the French retention of the Chesapeake only by taking on the British in a general engagement. And that engagement should take place as far as possible from the entrance to the bay, in order to ensure that de Barras could slip into the bay if he arrived in the meantime.

As the two fleets maneuvered to approach each other, their commanders shared common concerns that would determine their tactical dispositions. The weather was described as moderate and fair in the log of the British admiral's flagship. The prevailing wind was light and from the north-northeast, which gave the British fleet the advantage of the "weather-gage." The lay of the land and sea, as described by Mahan, was also of importance: "The mouth of the Chesapeake is about ten miles wide, from Cape Charles in the north to Cape Henry on the south. The main channel is between [the] latter and a shoal, three miles to the northward, called the Middle Ground." Mahan accounted for the strength of the forces now about to be opposed: "nineteen British sail of the line to twenty-four French, constituted as follows: *British,* two 98's (three-deckers), twelve 74's, five 64's, beside frigates; *French,* one 104 (three-decker), three 80's, seventeen 74's, and three 64's [plus frigates]." Thus the British were outnumbered by five ships of the line and in firepower on the order of three to four—the French having close to 2,000 guns against the British 1,500 (*Major Operations of the Navies*).

GRAVES AND HOOD HAD TAKEN ABOUT three and a half days to sail from New York to Chesapeake Bay. As the British fleet passed the Delaware Capes, Graves encountered the cruisers he had stationed there, but no enemy. At dawn on 5 September Graves was within sight of the Chesapeake Capes, with still no sign of French ships. At about 9:30 A.M. the lookout on the scouting frigate *Solebay* called out a sighting of ships at anchor in Lynnhaven Bay, about ten miles away. *Solebay*'s Captain Everitt, skeptical, climbed to the masthead to make certain. Once he had counted eight ships, he scrambled down to signal Graves's flagship. At first the British took the ships at anchor to be de Barras's squadron. At the same time, de Grasse was taking Graves's ships to be those of de Barras, too. As the day wore on, however, each was to see the count of his enemy's strength grow.

By 10:00 A.M. the *Bedford* had reported sighting at least fifteen French ships in the Lynnhaven anchorage. At 10:05 Graves signaled his captains to prepare to clear for action. What followed was the British counterpart of what was already going on in the French fleet. Gun crews manned their guns, battle nets were rigged on the top decks, carpenters and their helpers made ready the wadding and plugs needed to repair holes in hulls, sand was spread on the decks, ammunition handlers began running up powder from the magazines—in short, all preparations were made to turn the great sailing ships into deadly war machines.

While the preparations for battle were under way, the British fleet was coming on in column out of the northeast under foresails and topgallants. The column, five miles in length, was composed of three divisions: the van under Rear Admiral Sir Thomas Hood in his ship *Barfleur*; the center under Graves in the *London*; and the rear division under Rear Admiral Sir Francis Drake in the *Princessa*. The fleet was running before a wind out of the north-northeast and had "a small sea running." All the conditions favored a rapid British advance, since they held the weather-gage, meaning that they had the advantage of the wind by being in the windward (upwind) of their enemy. A ship or a fleet was said to hold the weather-gage when, in Mahan's words, "the wind allowed her [or a fleet] to steer for her opponent, and did not let the latter head straight for her. . . . The distinguishing feature of the weather-gage was that it conferred the power of giving or refusing battle at will, which in turn carries the usual advantage of an offensive attitude in the choice of the method of attack" (*Major Operations of the Navies*).

The other side of the picture was being presented as the French fleet got under way and struggled to form their battle line after rounding Cape Henry. Due to the wind direction, de Grasse was forced to accept battle holding the lee-gage, that is, on the defensive. Consequently, when de Grasse accepted battle with his fleet on the lee-gage he was able to avoid all the risks of advancing to engage while in the act of forming his line of battle. In addition, the French admiral could make his approaching enemy suffer by subjecting him to enfilading fire to which—for a critical period of time—he could not reply effectively. As it turned out, de Grasse was able to form only a partially effective line of battle, and even that was in great part made possible only by one of his opponent's tactical errors. Hence the crippling effect of his ships' initial fires was reduced simply because of the limited number of French ships that actually engaged.

WE HAVE ALREADY SEEN THE DIFFICULTIES the French fleet encountered in getting out of Lynnhaven Bay and out to sea. The van was led by Commodore Louis Antoine de Bougainville, the epitome of French élan so admired by the French military on land or sea. As his division got out to sea—recall that de Grasse had to reverse his usual order of battle, thus putting de Bougainville in the *Auguste* (80 guns) in command of the van—it was far in advance of the rest of the French fleet, thanks to its commander's zeal. This forward echelon was made up of the *Pluton* (74 guns), the *Bourgoyne* (80 guns), the *Marseillais* (74 guns), and the *Diademe* (74 guns). Next, a mile and a half astern, came the *Reflechi* (64 guns) and the *Caton* (64 guns).

By 12:45 P.M. de Grasse's flagship, the *Ville de Paris*, twelfth in line, was rounding Cape Henry. She was now in the approximate center of the future line of battle. At about the same time Graves signaled the order to form line head at one cable's length (120 fathoms, or 720 feet, between ships). A few minutes later, at 1:00 P.M. he modified the order by signaling for an east-west line at the same interval. In addition, he ordered a reef in the topsails because the wind was threatening "to be squally." There were more signals at 1:25 P.M., 1:30 P.M., and 1:39 P.M.—mostly to keep laggards in line or to close up, prompting a French officer to comment that "they made an immense number of signals to each other before engaging us."

Thus for about an hour the two fleets were on approaching courses, the British sailing in an inland direction, the French coming into line as they headed out to sea. At this point it is difficult to resist wondering what a Nelson would have done under the conditions: his British fleet well in hand with the weather-gage in his favor, his enemy's fleet in disorder, its van split off from its center and its rear struggling to get free of its anchorage. Yet it is profitless to think about another Nile or Copenhagen, for the British admiral at the Chesapeake Capes was anything but a Nelson; instead, he was the embodiment of the Royal Navy's "Fighting Instructions"—and an unlucky one at that.

A large shoal called the Middle Ground lay north of the ship channel in the Chesapeake. At 2:05 P.M. Graves became aware that Hood's leading ship, the *Alfred*, was heading toward the Middle Ground. Not wanting to endanger his fleet's progress, and hoping to maintain an orderly line of battle, Graves signaled for all of his ships to "wear," that is, for each ship to bring its stern through the wind, which kept each ship in its place in line but reversed its course by 180 degrees. The result—due to an orderly, well-executed maneuver by each ship captain—was the British fleet heading out to sea on a port tack and still about four or five miles from the enemy. The wearing further resulted in a British reversal of the order in line of battle: Hood's squadron, which had been the van, now became the rear, while Drake's squadron now became the van.

About the same time Graves had become aware of the dismaying total of French ships. His understandable concern was that de Grasse could use his superiority of five ships to "double," or overlap, the British line, meaning that the rearmost French ships could envelop the rear of his line and attack from both sides at the same time.

What went on in the mind of the British commander will, of course, never be known. We can be certain, however, of the alternatives open to him as the two fleets, still miles apart, were sailing away from the Chesa-

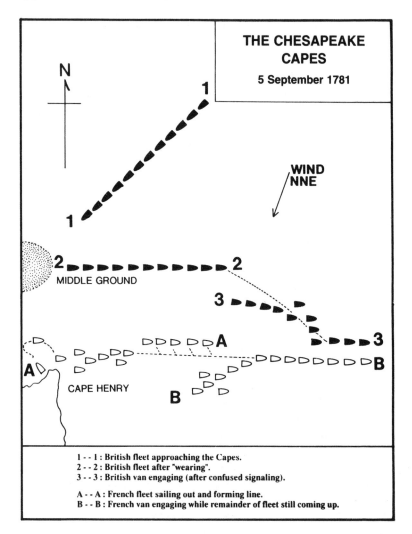

THE CHESAPEAKE CAPES

5 September 1781

N

WIND NNE

1

1

2   2
MIDDLE GROUND

3   3

A

A

B

CAPE HENRY

B

1 - - 1 : British fleet approaching the Capes.
2 - - 2 : British fleet after "wearing".
3 - - 3 : British van engaging (after confused signaling).

A - - A : French fleet sailing out and forming line.
B - - B : French van engaging while remainder of fleet still coming up.

peake. He could have chosen to bear down and attack while the French fleet's van was separated from its center. Instead, Graves chose to let the French line close up so that, in his reasoning, the two lines of battle could engage in the conventional manner. Hence, "to the astonishment of his own officers as well as the French, he dropped sails and waited until the French had closed the gap in their line. The *London*'s log recorded the maneuver: 'Brought to [hove-to or relatively dead in the water] in order to let the Center of the Enemy's ships come a Brest of us.'

Hood was incredulous that Graves should allow the enemy so long to recover; from the deck of the *Barfleur* he timed the respite at an hour and a half" (Davis, *The Campaign that Won America*). Again, we can wonder what de Grasse might have been turning over in his mind upon receiving this precious gift of time. In any case, he took advantage of it by putting on all possible sail, endeavoring to bring order to his still-forming line. The van, however, was still far ahead of the center; at 3:45 P.M. de Grasse signaled de Bougainville to "bear two points large," in effect, an order to slow down so that the rest of the fleet could catch up.

IN ALLOWING THE FRENCH TO COME INTO LINE, Graves could now take on the enemy in conventional combat, that is, with the two fleets battling it out in two parallel lines of battle. But now he was faced with the next tactical problem: How was he to bring his ships, still miles away from the nearest French, within engagement range of some 50 to 150 yards? The problem was anything but academic, for the solution could determine the outcome of the battle.

According to the naval tactics of the day, because Graves had the weather-gage he could adopt one of three methods of coming down-wind to attack the French line of battle. The first was to order all ships to engage, that is, to turn simultaneously toward the enemy and approach him bows-on. A second, called "lasking," was to have each ship turn obliquely, each keeping its place in line, with the wind in this case on the port quarter, and sail down on the enemy until within engagement range, and then come back into "line ahead" as they engaged the enemy. The third method was to maintain the line ahead—the formation the British fleet was now in—and come down with the leading ship approaching at an oblique angle until engagement range was reached, after which all ships would come into line parallel to the enemy's, and the fleet would engage.

It is only fair to emphasize the great weight that the day's tactical doctrine, the rigid "Fighting Instructions," laid upon British admirals and captains, especially when the rules applied to maintaining the line ahead when engaging the enemy.* At least two horrible examples of failure to

---

*Graves could well have had in mind Article 19 of the "Fighting Instructions" in force in 1781–83: "How to engage the enemy when the fleet has the wind of them [the enemy]. If the admiral and his fleet have the wind of the enemy, and they have stretched themselves in a line of battle, the van of the admiral's fleet is to steer with the van of the enemy and there to engage them" (Robison, *A History of Naval Tactics from 1530 to 1930* [Annapolis: U.S. Naval Institute, 1942], 359).

conform surely weighed on Graves's mind, because that mind was undoubtedly of the old school. In February 1744 Admiral Matthews, in
an action off Toulon, under conditions hauntingly similar to those now
facing Graves, broke the line ahead with his flagship to attack the enemy's flagship. Matthews was court-martialed and cashiered from the
service. An even worse fate was dealt to Admiral Byng in 1757 when he
was condemned to be shot by a firing squad on the quarterdeck of his
own ship; his offense—taking severe losses in an indecisive battle in
which he had employed, or misemployed, a lasking approach.

Graves chose the third method, and at 3:45 P.M. ordered the signal for
line ahead—a white pennant at the masthead—to be hoisted. By this
time the opposing vans and centers were becoming parallel, with the vans
being much closer than the centers, as shown on the map. Both rear divisions were still miles from each other. By 4:00 P.M. Graves's van was
bearing down on de Bougainville's squadron, but neither side had yet
fired a shot—after nearly six and a half hours of maneuvering.

At 4:03 P.M. Graves ran up another signal on the *London*'s masthead, a
blue-and-white-checkered flag which was the order for ships to bear
down and engage close, meaning that each captain should attack the
French ship opposite him. The new signal was hoisted *underneath* the
white pennant, and the sight caused consternation among the rear admirals of the fleet. The two signals were contradictory: ships could not
maintain line ahead and at the same time bear down and engage close.
The two signals flew together for eight long minutes—or until 4:11 P.M.—
at which time the *London*'s log recorded that the order had been given
to haul down the signal for the line-ahead so that it would not inter-
fere with the signal to engage close. However, in the eight minutes the
two signals had flown together the harm done was irreparable, despite
Graves's later efforts to signal his way out of the mess. Graves's subsequent move to take the *London* into action from his place in the center of
the line served to add to the confusion. The once-orderly British formation fell into disarray as the opposing vans collided at "musket range,"
and at 4:15 P.M. the battle was finally joined.

Under full sail and with all guns run out, ship engaged ship as the captains maneuvered to deliver their broadsides. When two opposing ships
came around to face each other, that terrifying moment must have seemed
like hours as the classic prayer was muttered among the waiting crews:
"For what we are about to receive, God deliver us." The ideal broadside
was one in which all the guns (thirty to fifty, depending upon the ship's
size and armament) on one side of the ship fired simultaneously, thereby

delivering the most smashing punch of the action. The ideal was seldom attained, however, because the ship's batteries had to follow the standard fire order to "fire as your guns bear." Even so, the effect at a range of a hundred yards was appalling. A broadside from a seventy-four-gun ship of the line could deliver as many as thirty-five iron round shot (cannonballs), each weighing from nine to thirty-two pounds. When such a volley tore into a wooden ship, the carnage and damage, inflicted in seconds, produced scenes like hell itself, scenes that were inescapable to the crews literally locked in combat, for the hatches were closed and guarded by marines. Yet it was not the cannonball itself that was most feared; the splinters flying from smashed shipsides or other wooden objects caused the most fearful wounds.

After the first volley, gun crews reloaded and fired independently, as fast as trained crews could function. In this battle, as in all others between British and French ships, the differences in gunnery soon showed in the type of damage sustained. The French gun captains were trained to fire, usually on the up-roll of their ship, at the masts and rigging of the enemy. British gunners tried to fire at the enemy's hull, in the expectation of sinking the ship. The French gunnery technique was probably the more effective in this battle. According to Admiral F. E. Chadwick, "It would seem that one had but to fire a gun and a mast went by the board. . . . The battle pictures of a sea covered with floating masts and debris of yards and sails are in no degree, as a rule, overdrawn" (*The Graves Papers*).

Commodore de Bougainville stood on his quarterdeck and watched the leading ships of the British line bearing down upon his waiting squadron. His leading ships were cruising eastward in a regular line a half mile long. Their decks had been cleared for action hours ago, and now gun crews were staring through the open ports, eager to get off that first round. The commodore put his glass to his eye for the last time to scan the approaching ships. Although he could make out the yellow hulls under the spread of white sails, now less than a half mile away, de Bougainville had cause to feel more than an aesthetic appreciation of the sight: the British were having to bear down bows on. It was everything he could hope for. In a matter of minutes the French ships could deliver deadly raking fires to enfilade each British ship when its sides were presented while rounding up to engage.

The British *Shrewsbury* (74 guns) was the first to take the shattering impact of the French gunners' opening volley. She was the leading ship of Drake's van and came into action "in a very gallant and spirited manner." But her opponent, the *Pluton*, was throwing the full weight of her port batteries into the *Shrewsbury*, wreaking havoc with her enemy's masts and rigging. In the same broadside the British Captain Mark Robinson had his left leg torn off, while his first lieutenant fell dead beside him. Thirteen of the *Shrewsbury*'s crew were killed in the same exchange of fire. In the ensuing action the ship was to lose twelve more men killed and forty-eight wounded. Her damage was so severe, as related in after-action reports, that "all her masts, yards and sails were cut to pieces," causing her to pull out of action.

The next ship in Drake's line, the *Intrepid* under Captain Molloy, came flying up to shield the *Shrewsbury*, and in so doing placed herself at once under the guns of the *Marseillais*, which gave her such a battering that she was soon "much disabled in every respect," taking sixty-five shot holes in the starboard side, which caused her to lose her place in the battle order.

The fearful initial casualties were by no means restricted to the British. On the French side the *Reflechi* was broadsided by Drake's flagship, the *Princessa*, whose fire was so fierce that Captain de Boades and another officer were killed. At this time the *Pluton* and the *Reflechi* had to withdraw; they had been so severely pounded that they could not remain in line. Soon they were followed by the *Caton*, which had been reduced to the same damaged state.

De Bougainville had engaged while the center of de Grasse's fleet was still out of supporting distance. A French officer who was a witness to de Bougainville's unequal fight wrote that "the four ships found themselves engaged with seven or eight vessels at close quarters. The *Diademe* was near Rear Admiral Drake [the *Princessa*], who set fire to her at every shot, the wadding entering her side. The English could not cut off our van . . . they contented themselves simply with cutting up that part of our fleet which kept up a distant fight." As a result of her pounding by the *Princessa*, the *Diademe*, in the same officer's account, "was utterly unable to keep up the battle, having only four thirty-six pounders and nine eighteen pounders fit for use, and all on board killed, wounded, or burnt." Captain de Chabert of the *Esprit* witnessed the *Diademe*'s distress, and in spite of the wound he had just suffered in the action ordered on full sail and came across the *Diademe*'s stern to drive off her attackers. The *Esprit* delivered such a constant fire "that the gentlemen of Albion could not stand, and had to haul their wind."

While the *Esprit* was rescuing the stricken *Diademe*, de Bougainville, not to be outdone by any of his captains, laid his flagship, the eighty-gun *Auguste*, so close alongside Drake's *Princessa* that their hulls almost scraped. In Page Smith's words, "the expressions of the sailors and marines were plainly visible and the shouts and orders on both ships could be easily heard" (*A New Age Now Begins*). Drake bore off to avoid being boarded, then pulled away under the covering fire of nearby frigates. De Bougainville did not follow; instead, that high-spirited commander wore about and turned all his guns that would bear upon the unlucky *Terrible*, which by this time was so in name only.* Two rounds of de Bougainville's broadside tore through her foremast, and among her other injuries she received "several shot between wind and water."

In the meantime de Bougainville's *Auguste* had been taking her share of pounding. She had already lost ten killed and fifty-eight wounded. Part of the damage sustained was the loss of her foretop bowline, which was essential to the trim of the mainsail. Two foretopmen in succession went aloft to repair the line, but each was shot down by musket fire from the *Princessa*. What followed was described by the Swedish naval officer Karl Gustaf Tornquist in his account of the French side of the action: "When he [Bougainville] observed that no one would make a third attempt, wherefor he, with his usual kindness, offered his purse to the person who would put the bowline in shape. A common sailor immediately went out on the yard and called back: 'My General, we do not go there for money,' whereupon he tackled the work and fortunately carried it through" (*The Naval Campaigns of Count de Grasse*).

Finally, about an hour after the vans had become engaged, the two main fleets came within battle range. The delay was due to the wide angle between the main battle lines, an angle so great that the rear divisions never became seriously embattled. Harold Larrabee explains the final result of Graves's strange approach: "Each time he [Graves] gave the order to his leading ship to bear more to starboard, the angle of approach of his whole column became steeper, and the ships in the rear had less and less chance of making contact with the French. Meanwhile the latter . . . delivered their broadsides and wheeled away, uniformly inflicting more damage than they received" (*Decision at the Chesapeake*).

---

*As a leaking and partially disabled ship (even before the battle) the *Terrible* had been in the rear division before Graves had ordered his fleet to wear and reverse direction. The reversal of vans and rears that resulted placed the *Terrible* in the van, where she was when the engagement started. The ship was in such bad shape that Captain Clement Finch had tried to fall out of line as the fleets approached each other, but Drake had three shots fired across *Terrible*'s bow to force her back into line.

The battle between the two vans is considered to have been the only real close-quarters action of the Battle of the Chesapeake Capes. The casualties suffered by two ships at the head of Drake's van constituted one-half of all the British killed and about one-third of the wounded. However, the two leading ships of Graves's center, the *Europe* and the *Montagu*, also took their share of battering as they came into action. "The masts and rigging of the *Europe* were badly shattered, and her hull was holed dozens of times. The *Montagu* took heavy losses in her crew and dropped out of the line with her masts ready to topple at any moment" (Page Smith, *A New Age Now Begins*).

The rest of the British center—*Royal Oak, London, Bedford, Resolution, Centaur,* and *Monarch*—suffered relatively little loss. Graves's *London* had "one large shot through the mainmast and two in the foremast; a number of shot through the mainmast and two in the foremast; a number of shot in the side . . . sails and rigging much cut; four men killed and eighteen wounded." At 5:25 P.M. Graves hauled down the signal for line ahead. A disgusted Hood turned his division to bring it into contact, but the resulting encounter was hardly more than a skirmish. Captain d'Ethy of the French ship *Citoyen* described the incident: "At 5:45 P.M. the three-decked ship [Hood's flagship *Barfleur*] commanding the enemy rear came up, as well as the two ships ahead of her—they hove to and experimented to see whether their cannon balls would reach our ships. The enemy admiral began by firing several shots and the other ships . . . followed suit . . . their fire became general up as far as my ship, but it did not last long. . . . I had much the better of the exchange with the three-decker, for it appeared to me that nearly all of her cannon balls fell into the sea."

At 6:30 P.M., shortly before sunset, Graves hauled down his signal for engaging the enemy. The battle of 5 September was over. British casualties totaled 336 killed and wounded; the French lost 209 killed and wounded. The losses in men, on both sides, were relatively light if one considers them in terms of their relevance to each fleet as a whole. The real damage done in the battle was material. Six of Graves's ships were, for the time being, effectively out of action. *Shrewsbury, Montagu,* and *Intrepid* had long ago fallen out of action; *Princessa* was laboring along with her topmast about to topple; and *Terrible* was taking on so much water that it was doubtful that she could ever again be counted on for battle. *Ajax* was remaining afloat only with "double pumping."

French damages were severe enough, with four ships forced out of line: *Pluton, Diademe, Reflechi,* and *Caton.* De Bougainville's *Auguste* had taken terrific punishment, but was still under way. There was, however, a significant difference in the overall damage sustained by the opposing fleets: "The French vessels . . . had been less affected in their sailing capabilities than their British counterparts. The French strategy of directing fire at masts, riggings, and upper works of the enemy had proved successful. It was easier to patch a riddled hull than to replace the delicate and complicated rigging of a sailing ship" (Smith, *A New Age Now Begins*).

The French could claim another success: in de Bougainville they had a real hero. Before the battle he and de Grasse had treated each other with cool *politesse*, but now the usually aloof de Grasse warmly praised the commodore in front of his staff: "Now that is what I call 'combat'! For a while I thought you were going to board!" Later, de Grasse again praised de Bougainville, this time in a public statement to Washington and Rochambeau: "the laurels of the day belong to de Bougainville . . . for having led the van and having personally fought the *Terrible.*"

THE TENDENCY OF SOME HISTORIANS TO STYLE the action of 5 September a draw deserves scrutiny. The tendency apparently derives from taking the narrow view of comparing casualties and ship damage as a measure of tactical success or failure while failing to take a wider view of strategic results. The tactical results have already been enumerated above; but the true measure lies in the success or failure of the missions of the opposing admirals. After all, what were the two fleets doing when they came in contact? And why?

De Grasse's fleet was anchored in Lynnhaven Bay because he was carrying out a deduced mission that comprised a threefold purpose: (1) he had to prevent the British navy coming to Cornwallis's aid, and by the same token to keep that navy from interfering with land-sea operations in the Chesapeake; (2) he had to deliver the promised military aid to Washington and Rochambeau in the form of French troops and artillery; (3) finally, he had to unite with de Barras, or at least ensure that the latter got safely into the Chesapeake where he could deliver his precious cargo of siege artillery.

As we have seen, de Grasse had already accomplished the second part of his mission by delivering the goods and stationing ships to bottle up Cornwallis from the sea. All he had to do to accomplish the other, and more important, parts of his mission was to keep the British fleet out of Chesapeake Bay.

On the other side of the picture, Graves had, after uniting with Hood at New York, sailed down the coast toward the Chesapeake. His mission? He too could be said to have had a threefold purpose: (1) he had to intercept de Grasse and prevent him from getting into the Chesapeake, and in so doing keep him from uniting with de Barras; (2) he had to intercept de Barras or keep him from joining de Grasse; (3) finally, he had to keep open the sea lanes to Cornwallis. So it would scarcely be too much to say that de Grasse had thus far accomplished his mission most effectively, while Graves had so far failed in his, and, moreover, the only way he could salvage his operation was to reengage the French fleet and defeat it decisively.

On the French side, de Bougainville had fought a gallant and desperate action: desperate because his squadron in the van had gotten so far from the center division of the fleet that when attacked by the British van he had to fight it out on his own, which he did most gallantly. De Bougainville's squadron was not destroyed due to the same reasons that allowed de Grasse to get his fleet out to sea and take up the challenge to battle: the errors "committed by Graves and to a degree compounded by Hood" (Smith, *A New Age Now Begins*).

Graves's failure to attack the French fleet when it was most vulnerable—in the midst of its disordered effort to round Cape Henry and get out to sea—was pointed out by Hood in his bitter critique entitled "Sentiments upon the Truly Unfortunate Day," when he declared that "several of the enemies' ships must have been cut to pieces." Graves's most condemnable error was probably the heaving-to of his whole line and waiting for de Grasse to form his. Thus a second chance to attack and cut up the French fleet while it was still in a vulnerable state was thrown away.

The subsequent mixed-up signaling from Graves's flagship resulted in the British fleet bearing down in a diagonal fashion that committed the van and center ships to action piecemeal instead of in a coordinated attack. The simultaneous flying of the "line ahead" and "engage the enemy" signals permitted the other admirals to make their own interpretations of contradictory orders. Although the van and the center, following Graves's own example in the *London*, bore down and engaged the enemy, Hood chose to sail his squadron along in a rigid line ahead, thus it never got into any real action. Later, Graves became stone hard in his belief that it was Hood's dilatory conduct that had cost the British navy a victory. As Page Smith wrote about Hood's critique of the conduct of the battle, "The 'Sentiments' were extensive and explicit and, for the most part, correct. Of his own excessive scrupulosity in regard to the *London*'s signal, he had little to say."

ON THE MORNING OF 6 SEPTEMBER the sun rose over a calm sea, with very light winds and the British still holding the weather-gage. There was no attempt made on either side to take the initiative and renew the action. While lookouts kept the enemy ships under surveillance, the main efforts in both fleets were directed toward damage repair. Hands that could be spared were placed at the disposal of the carpenters, riggers, and sailmakers. During this period Captain d'Ethy of the *Citoyen* reported that at least five British ships were replacing topmasts, and one seemed to be rigging a new mainmast. The two fleets continued on a southeast course, content to keep each other under a watchful eye while busily engaged in jury-rigging everything that could be repaired for maneuver and combat. Late in the day, Graves dispatched Captain Duncan with his frigate *Medea* to scout out the Chesapeake and return with his findings.

The seventh dawned with a continuing calm sea and light air. About 10:30 A.M. a light breeze sprang up out of the southeast, indicating that the ridge line or spine of an anticyclone had moved past the meridian of the Virginia capes. Had he wanted to, de Grasse could have changed course enough to take advantage of the weather-gage, but he did not. By nightfall the two fleets were almost a hundred miles from the Chesapeake and some distance off Cape Hatteras, North Carolina. De Grasse was, for all practical purposes, continuing to carry out his mission. Graves, for his part, had yet to accomplish his purpose, for a numerically superior French fleet, as far as he could ascertain, was still ready to renew the battle.

On 8 September light wind conditions prevailed in the morning and afternoon. Late in the day, however, "it came on to blow pretty fresh," soon followed by "thunder and lightning enlivening the formerly placid scene." In the British fleet the rising winds and rougher sea were causing anxiety about the *Terrible*, which was now flying a distress signal. The *Intrepid* was in for her share of trouble, having lost her main-topmast and carrying a forearm that was about to give way. Graves wrote that "these repeated misfortunes in sight of a superior enemy who kept us all extended and in motion, filled the mind with anxiety and put us in a position not to be envied."

On the following day, 9 September, de Grasse was beginning to worry about how far his fleet had moved from the Chesapeake. He had not forgotten the ships and seamen he had left behind when he sailed out of Lynnhaven Bay, nor had he ceased to worry about the whereabouts of de Barras and what he had accomplished. The general anxiety preying upon de Grasse and his officers was expressed by de Bougainville in his journal: "I was very much afraid that the British might try to get to the Chesapeake . . . ahead of us. It is what we ought to have been doing since the battle: That is, our very best to get back into the bay, recover our ships, barges and boats. . . . Perhaps we would also find the squadron of M. de Barras." De Grasse reached the same conclusion late in the day, and that night, under cover of darkness, turned and headed for the Chesapeake under full sail.

In the early morning light of 10 September Hood ascertained that the French fleet had disappeared. He sent a message to Graves: "I flatter myself you will forgive the liberty I take in asking you whether you have any knowledge of where the French fleet is, as we can see nothing of it from the *Barfleur*. . . . I am inclined to think his aim is the Chesapeake . . . if he should enter the bay . . . will he not succeed in giving most effectual succour to the rebels?" In response, Graves called another conference aboard the *London*, where all concerned were dismayed to discover they were mutually ignorant as to where the French fleet was.

At this point one would imagine that mislaying a French fleet of twenty-four ships of the line would have sent British frigates flying and the main fleet hoisting all possible sail to head for Chesapeake Bay. But no matter; no hurry. Graves recorded in his report to the secretary of the admiralty: "It being determined in a council of war held on the 10th to evacuate the *Terrible* and destroy her, I took the first calm day to effect it, and at the same time distributed the water and provisions which were wanted . . . the wreck was set fire to, and I bore up for the Chesapeake about nine at night."

Meanwhile, de Grasse had made good time and by noon on 10 September was within sight of Cape Henry. At first he was astounded by sightings of the masts of about twenty ships behind the cape. Could it be that the British fleet had beaten him to the Chesapeake? He was relieved to learn that the masts were those of de Barras's squadron: eight warships and the rest supply ships and transports. Barras had made it via a wide circuit at sea, coming back along the North Carolina coast and thence north to the Chesapeake. With the two fleets united in the Chesapeake, de Grasse could count on the command of thirty-five ships of the line, without doubt the greatest naval force in North American waters.

While he prepared for his next operation, de Barras's supply and transport ships were sent up the James to land their precious cargoes of siege artillery and supplies.

On 13 September Graves was still sailing toward the Chesapeake when he encountered the *Medea* hurrying back to report the bad news: de Grasse's fleet was back in Lynnhaven Bay and had been joined by Barras. A superficially polite exchange with Sir Samuel Hood ended with, "Sir Samuel would be very glad to send an opinon, but he really knows not what to say in the truly lamentable state we have brought ourselves." Graves then did what came naturally to him; he called a council of war, which concluded with a resolution signed by the three admirals:

> At a Council of War held on board His Majesty's ship *London* the 13th September, 1781, upon a report from Captain Duncan of his majesty's ship *Medea,* that they had seen the evening before, the French fleet at anchor off the Horseshoe Shoal in the Chesapeake. . . . Upon this state of the position of the Enemy, the present condition of the British Fleet, the season of the year so near the Equinox, and the impracticability of giving any effectual succour to General Earl Cornwallis in the Chesapeake, It was resolved that the British Squadron under the command of Thomas Graves, Esqr. Rear Admiral of the Red . . . should proceed with all dispatch to New York, and there use every possible means for putting the Squadron into the very best state for service.

Graves put into New York on 19 September with ten of his ships in need of repair and at least four requiring major refitting.

WHILE GRAVES WAS CONTINUING ON HIS altered course toward New York, the allied armies were making good time on the long march to Virginia. By 14 September Washington and Rochambeau had joined Lafayette at his camp at Williamsburg to plan the next phases of their operations. Their immediate concern was Lafayette's ability to keep Cornwallis pinned down at Yorktown until the Allied armies could assemble near Williamsburg, since at least ten days would be required for completing that phase. Washington was assured that Lafayette could carry out his task, because the French reinforcements that de Grasse had landed on 5 September had brought his fighting strength up to 8,500. The combined forces were certain to outnumber Cornwallis's force in Yorktown, thought not to exceed 7,000 rank and file. Unknown to Washington, Cornwallis had decided against trying to break out of the peninsula and retreat to the Carolinas after several probes revealed that Lafayette had blocked all the usable routes. Also unknown to the American commander in chief was that Cornwallis's decision to stay put had been made easier by his confidence that Clinton's relief force was—or would soon be—on the way.

Three days after his arrival at Williamsburg, Washington was paying a visit to de Grasse on board the *Ville de Paris*, where he was greeted by the French admiral with kisses on both cheeks and affectionately addressed as "my dear little General," though Washington was the taller by an inch. The conference concluded with de Grasse agreeing to keep his fleet on station until the end of September. In the actual event, de Grasse was able—most fortunately for the Allied cause—to stay in the Chesapeake until the first week in November.

On 28 September the allied armies marched from Williamsburg to invest Yorktown. By nightfall all the major formations were encamping in their initial positions, most units within about a mile of the British outposts. On the left the French wing drove in the pickets of Abercromby's light infantry, while the Americans on the right forced the withdrawal of Tarleton's legion's outposts. The next morning the Allied commanders and their senior officers reconnoitered the terrain and the enemy positions while orders were sent to bring up the siege artillery from its parks on the James.

On Sunday morning, 30 September, the Allied commanders and staffs were presented with confirmed intelligence that British units had been withdrawn from the redoubts that commanded the approaches via the Goosley Road and the road that crossed Yorktown Creek halfway up—intelligence that was as astounding as it was welcome. This opening move of Cornwallis's aroused controversy then—Clinton had no kind words to say about it—and later. He had given up critical positions that might have held up the approaches in the French sector for weeks. However, Cornwallis had acted on a message received from Clinton on 29 September that read in part: "It is determined that above five thousand men, rank and file, shall be embarked on board the King's ships and the joint exertions of the navy and army made in a few days to relieve you." Moreover, the British commander was rightly concerned that the three positions in question could have been turned and overwhelmed by Allied forces. Accordingly, he withdrew the outposts within the perimeter of the inner defenses.

The Allied armies were deployed in a rough semicircle about six miles long: the French on the west, with their lines extending from the York

River to the marshes bordering Beaverdam Creek; the Americans to the south, from the marshes to Wormley Creek, which flowed into the York a couple of miles below Yorktown. Across the York, facing the British force occupying Gloucester Point—700 men under Lieutenant Colonel Dundas with Tarleton and his legion—Washington posted a force of 1,400 French soldiers and 1,500 Virginia militia under French General de Choisy. The allied armies totaled 16,650 men: 8,850 Americans and 7,800 French. Cornwallis's effectives in Yorktown numbered somewhere around 7,000.

YORKTOWN HAD BEEN BUILT ON A BLUFF on the south bank of the York opposite Gloucester Point where the river narrowed to about a half mile. To the west of Yorktown two creeks joined to form two deep ravines. The town itself consisted of some sixty houses and a few public buildings surviving from the early eighteenth century, when Yorktown had been considered for the provincial capital. The British defenses were as extensive as they were formidable. Their main trace followed a curve encircling the town and consisted of seven redoubts and six fortified battery positions, the whole being connected by a series of entrenchments. There were also battery positions commanding the narrows as well as the strong fusilier's redoubt along the river to the northwest. The fortifications were completed by three redoubts along the ravines as well as redoubts numbers 9 and 10 south of the town. Cornwallis was not without his "navy," since the frigates *Guadeloupe* and *Charon*, with forty-four guns each, and three transports were anchored, somewhat forlornly, close in to the town.

By 6 October the allies were closing in to commence conventional siege operations. The siege guns were at hand and ready to be emplaced, and that night the first siege parallel trench was begun by a force of 4,300 men, with 1,500 doing the pick-and-shovel work while protected by a security force of 2,800. The parallel trench site was chosen south of Yorktown because of the open terrain, which permitted starting within 600 yards of the enemy. By first light of 7 October a 2,000-yard-long trench had been completed, and it was soon supplemented by the construction of five redoubts and five battery positions within the parallel.

Two days later both the French and American siege artillerists were ready to open fire. Although an American battery had reported ready first, the honor of opening fire went to Marquis de Saint-Simon's artillery. The French bombardment began at 3:00 P.M. from positions opposite the fusilier's redoubt. The immediate effects drove the *Guadeloupe* from its anchorage to seek safety on the Gloucester side. On the southern side of Yorktown the first American round was fired by Washington himself, followed by volleys from six eighteen- and twenty-four-pounders, four mortars, and two howitzers. The next day, 10 October, four more Allied batteries—two American and two French—joined the action, bringing the total Allied pieces to forty-six. The first spectacular casualty was the remaining British frigate, the *Charon*, which took a red-hot French shot amidships. The frigate went up in flames, as did two transports near her. Less spectacular, but far more damaging to the British, were the effects of the overall bombardment, which reduced their return fire to only about six rounds per hour.

On the following day, 11 October, the Allied bombardment continued without letup. By now a total of fifty-two siege guns were battering the British so steadily that their artillery batteries' fires were reduced again. That afternoon Cornwallis was writing Clinton: "We have lost about seventy of our men and many of our works are considerably damaged . . . against so powerful an attack we cannot hope to make a very long resistance."

During the night of 11–12 October the second parallel was started, and, amazingly, over 750 yards were completed, making a trench three and a half feet deep and seven feet wide. At this point, however, it was evident to the Allied command that British redoubts 9 and 10 must be taken before the second parallel could be extended to the river. The infantry at last could see action, although it was necessary to share the preliminaries with the engineers, who laid out the extension of an outwork from the east end of the second parallel that would reach as far as possible toward the enemy redoubts. The digging went on for three nights. On the afternoon of 14 October Washington was convinced that assaults on the two redoubts should now be mounted.

Plans had already been laid for joint assaults. The American light infantry in Lafayette's sector, closest to the river, were to take redoubt 10. That force was led by Lieutenant Colonel Alexander Hamilton and was made up of 400 men from Hamilton's, Gimat's, and Laurens's battalions, coming from Massachusetts, Rhode Island, Connecticut, New York, and New Hampshire. The French assault force, also of 400, was composed of chasseurs and grenadiers from the regiments of Gatinais and Royal Deux-Ponts, and was commanded by Colonel Guillaume de Deux-Ponts, whose mission was to take redoubt 9. Both forces were to be backed up by reserves, and both were provided with detachments of sappers. Provisions had also been made for diversionary demonstrations by Saint-Simon against the fusilier redoubt and by Choisy against the Gloucester defenses.

Both the diversions and the main attacks went off right on schedule. At 8:00 P.M. the two assaulting forces moved out in darkness with fixed bayonets and unloaded muskets. The French, advancing in platoon columns, were challenged by a Hessian sentinel in redoubt 9: "Wer da?" (who goes there?). The French chasseurs moved on silently but were soon held up by abatis and covering fire from the redoubt. While pioneers chopped gaps in the abatis, the French charged forward, following their officers, who would not be held up waiting for support. They stormed over the parapets, overcoming the resistance of the 120 defenders who first tried to take cover within the redoubt. The French loaded and fired into the cowed Hessians and British, who were soon surrendered by their commander, Lieutenant Colonel McPherson. In the half hour of action in redoubt 9, the French losses were 15 killed and 77 wounded, while the defenders lost 18 killed and 50 wounded among the prisoners.

The American assault on redoubt 10 was even more successful, since it went faster and took fewer casualties. Led by a "forlorn hope"—what today would be termed a suicide squad—under Lieutenant John Mansfield of the 4th Connecticut, Hamilton's command stormed through the abatis, across the ditch, and through the palisade to force its way into the redoubt. At the same time two companies under Lieutenant Colonel John Laurens encircled the redoubt from the rear, cutting off any chance of escape for the seventy defenders. The brilliantly executed little operation cost the Americans only nine killed and thirty-one wounded. The American attack probably went faster because the assault teams did not wait for pioneers to clear gaps, thus accelerating the momentum of their rush; neither leaders nor soldiers were aware of the finer points of European siegecraft.

Deux-Ponts and Hamilton immediately consolidated their positions in preparation for the counterattack that never came. Cornwallis seemed content to mass all his available artillery against the captured redoubts, which didn't prevent the Allies' working parties from refortifying the positions and tying them into their second parallel. The sudden Allied success was dismaying to Cornwallis, who wrote to Clinton the next day that his situation had now become very critical: "We dare not show a gun to their old batteries, and I expect that their new ones will open tomorrow morning. . . . The safety of the place is, therefore, so precarious that I cannot recommend that the fleet and army should run great risque in endeavoring to save us."

Meanwhile, in New York, Clinton and Graves were preparing their relief expedition for embarkation. By 17 October Clinton's force of 7,149 soldiers, 2,000 in excess of the 5,000 promised Cornwallis, was loading into the transports, and the embarkation was completed the following day. The fleet that was to escort the transports was a formidable one: twenty-five ships of the line, three of them three-deckers, each with ninety guns. The chosen sailing date was 19 October.

THE CAPTURE OF THE TWO REDOUBTS, THE REFORTIFICATION of the allies' second parallel, and a renewed bombardment all posed threats that Cornwallis's officers would not allow him to ignore. By all the rules of siege warfare a sortie was demanded, one that would silence the new batteries and put an end to the threat. Accordingly, Cornwallis directed Lieutenant Colonel Abercromby to take 350 picked guards and grenadiers on a raid to spike the enemy's guns. At 4:30 A.M., 16 October, Abercromby's detachment struck the second parallel at a vulnerable point between the French and Americans, surprised a part of the slumbering Agenais Regiment, and spiked four guns. Continuing westward along the trench, the British spiked three more American guns before they were counterattacked by Count de Noailles. After a brief clash Abercromby's men withdrew, having lost eight killed and twelve captured. It had been a gallant stroke, but a futile one. The seven guns had been ineffectually spiked; they were back in action that same morning.

But Cornwallis would not be discouraged by an unsuccessful sortie. His mind was on a far greater effort, one that involved gambling selected elements of his army on a breakout through General de Choisy's Allied force holding the lines across the York River around Gloucester. The British commander's plan—bold, yet preferable to surrender—was to smash de Choisy's force, seize the 600 horses of Lauzun's legion, and make forced marches northward toward a linkup with Clinton's forces around New York. That night, 16–17 October, an advance force of 1,000 picked men was ferried to Gloucester. When the boats tried to return with follow-up elements, however, they encountered violent squalls that made further passage of the narrows impossible. So ended the last chance of a breakout.

That morning, 18 October, on the fourth anniversary of Burgoyne's surrender, the Allied guns opened up with a concerted bombardment that the British had no hope of answering. Their ammunition was exhausted. A short time after 9:00 A.M. the little figure of a scarlet-coated drummer boy appeared on the parapet of the British fieldwork on the Hampton Road and began to beat a parley. His tinny rattle couldn't be heard above the roar of the cannonade, but he was observed. The meaning of his presence was clear enough. The guns were silenced, and soon a British officer came out holding up a white handkerchief. He was blindfolded and led to Washington's headquarters, where he presented Cornwallis's request for an armistice and a meeting of commissioners to negotiate terms of surrender.

Cornwallis had hoped to get terms of capitulation similar to those granted Burgoyne by Gates; that is, to have his army placed on parole with an eventual return to England. His commissioners were soon disillusioned. Washington rejected the condition and specified that Cornwallis's army be surrendered as prisoners of war, with only the senior officers to be accepted on parole. Cornwallis had no choice but to agree.

At 2:00 P.M., 19 October, while Clinton's relief force was setting sail from New York, a British officer in dress uniform came forth at the head of the long column of the garrison. The British ranks marched down the Hampton Road, between lines of American and French units lined up facing each other across the road. The British rank and file were dressed in bright new uniforms, while the French were turned out in their white broadcloth uniforms. Not all the Americans had uniforms to wear, and their appearance was scarcely stylish, but their ranks were impeccably aligned. The British column, however, was not led by their commander; the earl had excused himself and had sent Brigadier O'Hara, of the guards, in his place. The British had to march "with colors cased, and drums beating a British or German march."

When General O'Hara reached the surrender field he "rode directly to Count Rochambeau at the head of the French troops. Clearly it was his intent to offer surrender to the Frenchman. But Rochambeau shook his head. We are subordinate to the Americans, he told O'Hara in French, and gestured to General Washington . . . O'Hara rode to face Washington. He offered an apology for the absence of Cornwallis. . . . If he was disappointed, Washington did not show it. He directed O'Hara to receive his instructions from General Lincoln" (Symonds and Clipson, *A Battlefield Atlas of the American Revolution*).

When it was all over, the surrendered army was marched away under militia guards to prison camps in Virginia and Maryland. The prisoner count totaled 7,247 of all ranks, plus 840 seamen. According to Christopher Ward, "Eighteen German regimental standards and six British were captured, as well as 244 pieces of artillery, thousands of small arms, and considerable quantities of military stores and equipment. The casualties on both sides were comparatively light, the Americans losing 20 killed and 56 wounded, the French 52 killed and 134 wounded, the British 156 killed 326 wounded" (*War of the Revolution*).

FIVE DAYS LATER, ON 24 OCTOBER, ADMIRAL GRAVES again sighted the Chesapeake, no doubt with thoughts of revenge as well as hopes of relieving Cornwallis. His thoughts must have been quickly tempered when sightings were confirmed of de Grasse's thirty-five ships of the line, deployed in a crescent from which they could block the Chesapeake or sail into battle. De Grasse had been able to do better than keep his promise to Washington; he was still there in late October to cover the closing of land operations around the Chesapeake.

Nevertheless, Graves must have felt obligated to put on a show of force. For two days, in his words, "we stood close in to the back of the sands [the shoals at the mouth of the bay], to offer them battle, for two successive days . . . but the French showed no disposition to come out." De Grasse did not need to come out. He had accomplished his mission. It remained for him only to face off the British fleet, which departed for a return voyage to New York on 27 October, since Graves had deemed that "nothing was so proper as to return with the fleet to New York." It was, as the young Comte de Revel summed it up in his diary, "too late. The hen had been eaten."

THE BRITISH SURRENDER AT YORKTOWN MARKED the end of any further major operations by either side on the continent of North America. It can be considered a decisive action simply for that reason, though today we tend to accept Yorktown not only in that light but as the end of the American War of Independence. At the time, however, leaders like Washington and Greene had to see events from a more realistic perspective. They were only too aware that the British were still firmly in control of New York and Charleston, as well as holding on to Wilmington in North Carolina and Savannah in Georgia. Strong British forces in those places were capable of carrying on operations should they be so directed from Lord North's ministry.

In Downing Street, however, the significance of Yorktown was fully appreciated. On 25 November, thirty-six days after Cornwallis's surrender, the news was delivered in person by Lord Germain to Lord

North, whose reaction was, in Germain's account, like that of a man who had "taken a ball in his breast"; he paced up and down the room, repeating, "O God! It is all over!" North, however, had to contend with the king and Parliament, a matter that dragged on for almost two years until the British government could bring itself to accept the finality of defeat. In the end, American independence was acknowledged in the terms of the Treaty of Paris in September 1783.

ESSAY ON SOURCES

GENERAL SOURCES

SOME GREAT WRITER, WHO SHOULD HAVE known better, let himself be quoted to the effect that an essential qualification for greatness was having an unhappy childhood. One of the many reasons that I have not qualified was having a father who had the uncanny knack of anticipating the next book I would want. Getting such a book was a double joy: I had gotten something I could treasure, and I was spared the gift of an Erector Set intended for boys who had a positive hatred for gadgetry designed to frustrate and embarrass them.

Now, many years later, I have found another way to ensure my happiness. I leave—very casually—a list lying about where a clever wife can pick it up, and seeing that it is indeed a wish list of wanted books, quietly leak copies to family and friends, thus making sure that I get for Christmas or birthday a *book*—instead of a tie or shirt that I wouldn't wear on a rattlesnake hunt.

Perhaps this is the reason that I want to leave my reader some sources that he can really use, especially if he is working in a field like my own. It is in that spirit that the following sources have been assembled.

The two richest and most dependable general sources are almost companion pieces which deserve to be within arm's reach when one is searching for an overall view of the war that can be further focused on specific campaigns and battles. The first, a classic, is Christopher Ward, *The War of the Revolution*, 2 vols. (New York: Macmillan, 1952), which is by no means restricted to the narration of military operations, but also includes personalities, background events, weapons, uniforms—the whole gamut of military interests, all presented in a never-dull narrative style. The second is Mark M. Boatner III, *Encyclopedia of the American Revolution* (New York: David McKay, 1976), which goes into every aspect of the American Revolution—social, political, economic, and biographical. Yet the depth of coverage of everything military—from Arnold's treason to Yorktown—is truly rewarding.

Another comprehensive work is Page Smith, *A New Age Now Begins*, 2 vols. (New York: McGraw-Hill, 1976). We are indeed fortunate that the bicentennial encouraged the writing of this work. Samuel Eliot Morison has called it "a great and magnificent work. . . . He [Smith] is equally good on political events and military history. . . . He has, so far as I can judge, left no source, printed or manuscript, unread, he has really absorbed them, eschewing footnotes, at which the public will rejoice."

For the operations that Washington directed there can be no better source than the monumental seven-volume work of Douglas Southall Freeman, *George Washington, A Biography*, 7 vols. (New York: Charles Scribner's Sons, 1951), with particular reference to the battles of Trenton, Princeton, and Brandywine. For seeing military operations from the British side, there is the highly respected Sir John Fortescue's *A History of the British Army*, 13 vols. (London: Macmillan, 1902), wherein one can draw on volume 3, 1763–1793, for Fortescue's insight in his analysis of a leader's tactics or strategy.

For a concise overview of the war, one that can provide guidance to more detailed studies, one can rely on the one-volume condensation of R. E. Dupuy and T. N. Dupuy, *An Outline History of the American Revolution* (New York: Harper and Row, 1975). Those who wish to explore events from a personal narrative viewpoint will find a wealth of material in the two-volume compendium of Henry Steele Commager and Richard B. Morris, *The Spirit of 'Seventy-Six: The Story of the American Revolution as Told by Participants* (Indianapolis: Bobbs-Merrill, 1958). And for those who care to do their own exploring of battlefields and campaign regions there is the excellent three-volume guide by Sol Stember, *The Bicentennial Guide to the American Revolution* (New York: E. P. Dutton, 1974), which can be relied on as a Baedeker and historical authority all in one.

AUTHOR'S INTRODUCTION

Because the Introduction opens with a brief look at the background of the war followed by the rationale for the book's focus on the selection of pertinent examples, I have depended on the general sources noted above for presenting the background of the war and the book's focus on strategy and tactics. Once past the opening portion, I turn to subjects that will provide the reader with enough orientation information to aid him in understanding the soldier and officer on both sides as well as their weapons and dress.

The evolution of tactics which guided the employment of the combat arms on both sides (the American leaders as well as the British they at first emulated) are best traced in two sources. The first is Archer Jones, *The Art of War in the Western World* (Urbana: University of Illinois Press, 1987), a recent work that is gaining recognition for its perception of the influences which bore upon the development of strategy and tactical systems. The other is David G. Chandler, *The Art of Warfare in the Age of Marlborough* (New York: Hippocrene Books, 1976), which, as its title indicates, examines the evolution of tactics and strategy that continued to govern the employment of British forces throughout the eighteenth century. Another source, J. F. C. Fuller's *British Light Infantry in the Eighteenth Century* (London: Hutchinson, 1925), gives more information on infantry tactics in general than the title would indicate. Another that belies its title by providing much more than it indicates is Edward E. Curtis, *The Organization of the British Army in the American Revolution* (New York: AMS Press, 1969), which goes into fine detail on many other factors such as administration, logistics, command, pay, recruiting, and the regimental system—down to the uniforms of individual regiments.

The following deal with the individual soldier: his life on campaign, his weapons (including their effectiveness in battle), and his dress. Charles K. Bolton, *The Private Soldier under Washington* (New York: Charles Scribner's Sons, 1902), looks into most of the aspects of the Continental and militia soldier's life in training and in the field. Joe D. Huddleston, *Colonial Riflemen in the American Revolution* (York, Pa.: George Shumway, 1978), does much the same for the rifleman. Harold L. Peterson concentrates on the American "regular" in *The Book of the Continental Soldier* (Harrisburg, Pa.: Stackpole, 1968). Getting into the weapons of both sides, a full coverage with excellent photographs and sketches can be found in George C. Neumann, *The History of Weapons of the American Revolution* (New York: Harper and Row, 1967). The description and development of weapons and their effectiveness on the battlefield are covered by an expert in the field, Major General B. P. Hughes of the British army, in *Firepower: Weapons Effectiveness on the Battlefield, 1630–1850* (London: Arms and Armour Press, 1974). The drill regulations for the American soldier and units, covering training and combat, have been presented in a simplified version of von Steuben's original manual, featuring excellent illustrations, in A. N. Schultz and Robert Coleman, *Illustrated Drill Manual and Regulations for the American Soldier of the Revolutionary War* (Charlotte, N.C.: Sugarcreek, 1976). The uniforms of the soldiers and officers of the various branches, both American and British, are discussed and shown in color in two publications: Philip Katcher, *Armies of the American Wars, 1753–1815* (New York: Hastings House, 1975); and Martin Windrow and Gerry Embleton, *Military Dress of North America, 1665–1970* (New York: Charles Scribner's Sons, 1973).

BUNKER HILL

There are no better leads into the military background of the siege of Boston than the host of problems that beset the British high command in 1775. John R. Alden presents the situation from the British viewpoint in *General Gage in America* (Baton Rouge: Louisiana State University Press, 1948). General Gage's case is broadened by Troyer S. Anderson, *The Command of the Howe Brothers during the American Revolution* (New York: Oxford University Press, 1936). The history of the siege, including the Battle of Bunker Hill, is contained in a classic source: Richard Frothingham, *History of the Siege of Boston* (1903; reprint, New York: Da Capo Press, 1970). An interesting picture of the Minutemen and their background before Lexington and Concord is offered in Robert A. Gross, *The Minutemen and Their World* (New York: Hill and Wang, 1976).

As one might expect, there are numerous books narrating and analyzing the Battle of Bunker Hill. Those I have found to be most useful fall into two categories: first, those that typify the formal nineteenth-century approach; second, modern works that combine stimulating description with critical perception. The following two fall into the first category. The title indicates the contents of Samuel A. Drake, *Bunker Hill: The Story Told in Letters from the Battlefield* (Boston: Nichols and Hall, 1875), bearing in mind that the letters were those of British officers. The second is in a more traditional style: George E. Ellis, *History of the Battle of Bunker's [Breed's] Hill* (Boston: Lockwood, Brooks, 1875).

In the second, or present-day, category, one work stands out as best fitting the above definition: John R. Elting, *The Battle of Bunker's Hill* (Monmouth Beach, N.J.: Philip Freneau Press, 1975), is narrated in a wryly realistic way, while the author at the same time displays military perception of a high order in analyzing the course of the action. Thomas J. Fleming, *Now We Are Enemies: The Story of Bunker Hill* (New York: St. Martin's Press, 1960), not only takes a good look into the background of the battle but tells its story in detail. The same may be said for the narrative by Richard M. Ketchum in *The Battle for Bunker Hill* (Garden

City: Doubleday, 1962), and is also excellent for his portrayal of personalities. Henry I. Kurtz, "Bunker Hill, 1775: A Dear Bought Victory," *American History Illustrated* 2 (1967), provides a concise summary of the battle.

QUEBEC

In no other action of the war does the recounting seem to center more on the leaders than the ill-fated siege and the assaults on Fortress Quebec at the end of 1775. Richard Montgomery, the overall commander, was killed while leading one assault, and Benedict Arnold, the secondary commander, was badly wounded while leading the other. For comprehensive coverage of background, the expeditionary forces' approaches, the siege, and the assaults, the following sources are noteworthy. Justin H. Smith, *Our Struggle for the Fourteenth Colony*, 2 vols. (New York: G. P. Putnam's Sons, 1907), remains a classic that retains its worth. George F. G. Stanley, *Canada Invaded, 1775–1776* (Toronto: A. M. Hakkert, 1973), is a modern study which presents events more from the British viewpoint. Other useful present-day studies are Harrison Bird, *Attack on Quebec* (New York: Oxford University Press, 1968); and Robert McConnell Hatch, *Thrust for Canada: The American Attempt on Quebec in 1775–1776* (Boston: Houghton Mifflin, 1979). An accurate account of the siege and assaults can be found in Michael Pearson, "The Siege of Quebec, 1775–1776," *American Heritage* 23, no. 2 (February 1972).

Arnold's march to Quebec, so famous for the incredible adversities and hardships endured by his men, is best seen through the journals of the participants. The most interesting and accurate accounts have been assembled by the novelist Kenneth Roberts, a scholar in his own right, in *March to Quebec: Journals of the Members of Arnold's Expedition* (New York: Doubleday, Doran, 1938). An excellent overall view of the expedition is found in the article by Robert G. Crist and Joseph P. Cullen, "Arnold's March to Quebec," *American History Illustrated* 3, no. 7 (November 1968).

TRENTON AND PRINCETON

The first sources given here are the more comprehensive studies of the background and conduct of the campaign (given that the battles of Trenton and Princeton were fought in one campaign, and not two) as well as that of the battles. Richard M. Ketchum, *The Winter Soldiers* (Garden

City: Doubleday, 1973), is that kind of book, written in a lively yet accurate fashion. Another comprehensive study in the broader context of the war in the east is Leonard Lundin, *Cockpit of the Revolution: The War for Independence in New Jersey* (Princeton: Princeton University Press, 1940). An older but still reliable source is William S. Stryker, *The Battles of Trenton and Princeton* (Boston: Houghton Mifflin, 1898). Howard Fast's *The Crossing* (New York: William Morrow, 1971), tells the story of Trenton with an absorbing style which gives one a fresh look at the personalities on the American side. Ray Thompson, *Washington along the Delaware* (Fort Washington, Pa.: Bicentennial Press, 1970), is interesting for a view of the locales around which the Trenton part of the campaign took place.

Additional works pertaining to the Princeton part of the campaign and the battle itself start with Samuel S. Smith, *The Battle of Princeton* (Monmouth Beach, N.J.: Philip Freneau Press, 1967). A second is Alfred Hoyt Bill, *The Campaign of Princeton, 1776–1777* (Princeton: Princeton University Press, 1946). An article which provides both a detailed account and excellent terrain sketches is Thomas J. Wertenbaker, "The Battle of Princeton," in *The Princeton Battle Monument* (Princeton: Princeton University Press, 1922).

Two supplementary works should not be overlooked. An exceptionally fine account of the artillery's role in both battles (really critical at Trenton) is Jac Weller, "Guns of Destiny: Field Artillery in the Trenton-Princeton Campaign," *Military Affairs* 20 (Spring 1956). Another critical aspect, the crossing of the Delaware, is covered in the article by George A. Billias, "Soldier in a Longboat," *American Heritage* 11, no. 2 (February 1960), which centers on Colonel John Glover and his Marblehead, Massachusetts, regiment of sailor-soldiers who did such a superb job of ferrying Washington's troops across the Delaware on that stormy Christmas night.

BRANDYWINE

There are no more accurate and militarily perceptive sources than my old reliables, Ward and Boatner, for this campaign and battle. Ward's *War of the Revolution* offers its usual penetrating treatment of events and personalities, and also contributes insight into the intelligence picture— or the obscuration of it on the American side. Ward is seconded, as almost always, by Boatner, *Encyclopedia of the American Revolution,* in the entries under PHILADELPHIA CAMPAIGN and BRANDYWINE, which contribute to intelligence as well as to operations. The above are well supported by Douglas Southall Freeman in volume 4 of his noted *George Washington, A Biography*. Freeman is particularly valuable for clarifying the reasons behind the confusing intelligence picture that so distressed Washington on the day of the battle.

The following three sources serve to round out, in varying detail, the works cited above. First is John F. Reed, *Campaign to Valley Forge, July 1, 1777–December 19, 1777* (Philadelphia: University of Pennsylvania Press, 1965; reprint, New York: Pioneer Press, 1980). Another is Troyer S. Anderson, *The Command of the Howe Brothers during the American Revolution*, which was also useful in the chapter on Bunker Hill. There is also the work of Edward S. Gifford, Jr., *The American Revolution in the Delaware Valley* (Philadelphia: Pennsylvania Society of Sons of the Revolution, 1976). A source that is particularly interesting because the author was born and raised in the Brandywine area and furnishes abundant detail of the terrain is Wilmer W. MacElree, *Along the Western Brandywine* (West Chester, Pa.: published by the author, 1909).

Eyewitness accounts which provide corroborative detail are, first, *Major John André's Journal* (Tarrytown, N.Y.: William Abbatt, 1930), the same André who was captured and hung as a spy in the Benedict Arnold–West Point affair in September 1777. André was serving as a staff officer with a fine opportunity to be in on British plans and operations. Another well-qualified observer was the Hessian officer Major Baurmeister, whose letters provide a good part of the picture: *Letters from Major Baurmeister to Colonel von Jungkenn, Written during the Philadelphia Campaign, 1777–1778* (Philadelphia: Historical Society of Philadelphia, 1937). A local civilian who was caught up in the action has left his impressions of the battle in "Some Account of the British Army under General Howe and of the Battle of Brandywine," *Bulletin of the Historical Society of Pennsylvania* 1, no. 7 (1846).

ORISKANY

As usual, both Christopher Ward and Mark Boatner provide the starting point for background as well as for narration and critical insight. In the case of Oriskany, however, I have leaned most heavily on John Albert Scott, *Fort Stanwix and Oriskany* (Rome, N.Y.: Rome Sentinel Company, 1927), for depth of detail and the exploration of local sources and terrain of both the region and the battlefield. Following Scott I have found most useful Hoffman Nickerson's enduring work in volume 1 of *The Turning*

Point of the Revolution, 2 vols. (Boston, 1928; reprint, Port Washington, N.Y.: Kennikat Press, 1967). Useful also for checking on recorded information is the *Orderly Book of Sir John Johnson: During the Oriskany Campaign, 1776–1777* (Albany, N.Y.: John Munsell's Sons, 1882). A wealth of detail regarding the Loyalists and the Indian allies is found in William L. Stone, *The Campaign of Lieut. Gen. John Burgoyne, and the Expedition of Lieut. Col. Barry St. Leger* (New York: Da Capo Press Reprint series, 1970). Another source, old but still of value, is Howard Swiggett, *War out of Niagara* (New York: Columbia University Press, 1933).

Several articles by scholars who have been interested in Oriskany must be included. Freeman H. Allen, "St. Leger's Invasion and the Battle of Oriskany," *Quarterly Journal of the New York State Historical Association* 1, no. 12 (1913), is based on solid research. Another is J. Watts DePeyster, "Oriskany," *The Magazine of American History (With Notes & Queries)*, vol. 2 (1878). A third is Gerard A. Patterson, "The Battle of Oriskany," *American History Illustrated* 11, no. 4 (July 1976).

SARATOGA

Whether reading for research or pleasure about Saratoga (or, more realistically, the *two* battles of Saratoga) it is helpful to approach the subject by heeding what J. F. C. Fuller had to say about Waterloo in volume 2 of *A Military History of the Western World:* "[It] has been so thoroughly investigated and criticized that the errors committed in it are apt to appear exceptional and glaring. They were not, they were the usual errors to be found in most campaigns." So true is that about Saratoga and the number of works written about it that it is small wonder that one is hard put to select those most helpful. My selective criterion has been, of necessity, made simple: I list those sources to which I would return if I were to do further research on the battle(s).

First, there is the venerable but enduring classic by Sir Edward S. Creasy, *The Fifteen Decisive Battles of the World* (1851; reprint, New York: George Macy Companies, 1969), for background of the battle's place in history. Next, and deservedly next to Creasy, is John R. Elting, *The Battles of Saratoga* (Monmouth Beach, N.J.: Philip Freneau Press, 1977), which does the same superb job that Elting did for Bunker Hill, that is, with a combination of an engaging style and critical insight. Another by an Englishman writing in America is Rupert Furneaux, *The Battle of Saratoga* (New York: Stein and Day, 1971), which has succeeded in putting a lot in a small space. Two other books are even better for their treatment of Saratoga than they were for Oriskany, in which they proved so valuable: Hoffman Nickerson, *The Turning Point of the Revolution;* and William L. Stone, *The Campaign of Lieut. Gen. John Burgoyne, and the Expedition of Lieut. Col. Barry St. Leger.*

General John Burgoyne presents his own case, as he laid it before the House of Commons three years after his surrender at Saratoga, in *A State of the Expedition from Canada* (1780; reprint, New York: Arno Press, 1969). Burgoyne's expedition and its trials and errors are narrated in a present-day work: Thomas Anburey, *With Burgoyne from Quebec* (Toronto: Macmillan of Canada, 1963). Burgoyne's life and his Saratoga campaign are well presented, first, in F. J. Hudleston, *Gentleman Johnny Burgoyne* (Indianapolis: Bobbs-Merrill, 1927), and, second, in James Lunt, *John Burgoyne of Saratoga* (New York: Harcourt Brace Jovanovich, 1975). Another official record of Burgoyne's has been edited by E. B. O'Callaghan in *Orderly Book of Lieut. Gen. John Burgoyne* (Albany, N.Y.: J. Munsell, 1860). More light is shed on Burgoyne's life and his various talents in Edward B. De Fonblanque, *Political and Military Episodes in the Latter Half of the Eighteenth Century Derived from the Life and Correspondence of the Right Hon. John Burgoyne, General, Statesman, Dramatist* (London: Macmillan, 1876).

Jane Clark has explored the complexities of the political/military factors which involved personages such as Lord Germain, Sir William Howe, and Burgoyne in "Responsibility for the Failure of the Burgoyne Campaign," *American Historical Review* 35, no. 3 (April 1930). The friction between Benedict Arnold and Horatio Gates that led to confrontation and Arnold's loss of command are examined in two articles: John F. Luzader, "The Arnold-Gates Controversy," *West Virginia History* 27, no. 2 (January 1966); and Paul D. Nelson, "The Gates-Arnold Quarrel, September 1777," *New York Historical Quarterly* 55, no. 3 (July 1971). Another article looks into the battle itself: Joseph P. Cullen's "Saratoga," *American History Illustrated* 10, no. 1 (April 1975). Yet another which provides background material on Daniel Morgan, his riflemen, and their parts in both battles of Saratoga is found in William W. Edwards, "Morgan and His Riflemen," *William and Mary Quarterly* 23, no. 2 (October 1914).

Key personalities are treated in the following biographies: James Graham, *The Life of General Daniel Morgan* (New York: Derby and Jackson, 1856); Samuel W. Patterson, *Horatio Gates* (New York: Columbia University Press, 1941); Charles C. Sellers, *Benedict Arnold: The Proud Warrior* (New York: Minton, Balch, 1930); Willard M. Wallace, *Trai-*

torous Hero: The Life and Fortunes of Benedict Arnold (New York: Harper and Brothers, 1954); William B. Willcox, *Portrait of a General: Sir Henry Clinton in the War of Independence* (New York: Alfred A. Knopf, 1964); and William L. Stone, *Memoirs and Letters and Journals of Major General Riedesel* (Albany, N.Y.: J. Munsell, 1868). Last, not a biography but rather the memoirs of a scoundrel whose accounts must be checked against those of other participants is James Wilkinson, *Memoirs of My Own Times*, 3 vols. (Philadelphia: Abraham Small, 1816), vol. 1.

KINGS MOUNTAIN

Turning to the war in the South, the first works recommended are the more general histories which furnish the background of the battle. First is John R. Alden, *The South in the Revolution, 1763–1789* (Baton Rouge: Louisiana State University Press, 1957). Another authoritative source is Sydney G. Fisher, *The Struggle for American Independence*, 2 vols. (1908; reprint, Freeport, N.Y.: Books For Libraries Press, 1971). A memoir by a famous participant is Henry Lee's *Memoirs of the War in the Southern Department of the United States* (New York: University Publishing, 1869). A recent study by the late Henry Lumpkin of the University of South Carolina, *From Savannah to Yorktown* (Columbia, S.C.: University of South Carolina Press, 1981), is excellent for both general history and detailed coverage of battles. For a close look into the North Carolina picture, see David Schenck, *North Carolina, 1780–81: Being a History of the Invasion of the Carolinas* (Raleigh, N.C.: Edwards and Broughton, 1889). Franklin and Mary Wickwire's work, while biographical in nature, gives an excellent narration of campaigns and battles: *Cornwallis: The American Adventure* (Boston: Houghton Mifflin, 1970).

The British Loyalist (Tory) background, including their conflicts with patriotic neighbors, is essential to the study of the war in the South; the following three sources provide an insight: North Callahan, *Royal Raiders: The Tories of the American Revolution* (Indianapolis: Bobbs-Merrill, 1963); Robert M. Calhoon, *The Royalists in Revolutionary America, 1760–1781* (New York: Harcourt Brace Jovanovich, 1965); and Robert O. DeMond, *The Loyalists in North Carolina during the Revolution* (Durham, N.C.: Duke University Press, 1940).

Getting into the campaign and battle, the following examine variously the precursors, the immediate events leading up to the battle, and the actions of participants. Robert D. Bass, *The Green Dragoon* (Columbia,

S.C.: Sandlapper Press, 1973), narrates events before the campaign from the viewpoint of the notorious Banastre Tarleton, the British cavalry leader. Wilma Dykeman, *With Fire and Sword: The Battle of Kings Mountain, 1780* (Washington: National Park Service, 1978), is outstanding for its depiction of the people of the region at the time, as well as the gathering of the over-mountain men and the events that followed. An official history that still furnishes interesting facets is George C. Mackenzie, *Kings Mountain National Military Park,* Historical Handbook Series no. 22 (Washington, D.C.: National Park Service, 1955). A source written by a journalist who was raised in the region is Hank Messick, *King's Mountain* (Boston: Little, Brown, 1976); it is excellent for the details of personalities in the battle. For more on personalities, see James Ferguson, *Two Scottish Soldiers* (Aberdeen, Scotland: D. Wyllie and Son, 1888), which includes a biography of Major Patrick Ferguson, the British commander at Kings Mountain, written by a descendant who knew how to bring out the details of Ferguson's life and follow up with detail on the battle from the Loyalist side. For the Patriots' side there are two obviously biased biographical accounts: Lyman C. Draper, *King's Mountain and Its Heroes* (Cincinnati: Peter G. Thompson, 1881); and Katherine K. White, *The King's Mountain Men* (Dayton, Va., 1924; reprint, Baltimore: Genealogical Publishing Company, 1970).

Because weapons, particularly the flintlock rifle, played an unusually important part in the battle, I recommend Ferguson, *Two Scottish Soldiers*; and Joe Kindig, Jr., *Thoughts on the Kentucky Rifle in Its Golden Age* (York, Pa.: George Shumway, 1960). Another source is Robert Lagemann and Albert C. Manucy, *The Long Rifle* (Eastern Acorn Press, Eastern National Park and Monument Association, 1980).

COWPENS

This American victory was an extraordinary engagement, and the strategy that led to it is of overriding importance. Accordingly, the following have been listed first. Theodore Thayer, *Nathanael Greene: Strategist of the American Revolution* (New York: Twayne, 1960), is the best source for Greene's strategy after taking command in the South. Next is an article which has thoroughly examined the strategy: George W. Kyte, "Victory in the South: An Appraisal of General Greene's Strategy in the Carolinas," *North Carolina Historical Review* 37, no. 3 (July 1960). Next, and very well laid out in regard to Greene's decisions, is M. F. Treacy, *Pre-*

lude to Yorktown: The Southern Campaign of Nathanael Greene 1780–1781 (Chapel Hill: University of North Carolina Press, 1963). Then there is Franklin and Mary Wickwire's *Cornwallis: The American Adventure.*

The following deal with events immediately before and during the battle. Robert D. Bass, *The Green Dragoon,* is an American biography of the British "villain" told in accurate detail after painstaking research. It is accompanied, appropriately, by Tarleton's own history, *A History of the Campaigns of 1780 and 1781 in the Southern Provinces of North America* (London, 1787). The next, invaluable for its excellent maps and detailed account, is Edwin C. Bearss, *The Battle of Cowpens: A Documented Narrative and Troop Movement Maps* (Washington, D.C.: National Park Service, 1967). Henry Lumpkin, *From Savannah to Yorktown,* is another work of scholarly worth. Kenneth Roberts does an outstanding job in portraying personalities in action as well as the course of battle in *The Battle of Cowpens* (Eastern Acorn Press, Eastern National Park and Monument Association, 1981). The last of this category is W. J. Wood, *Leaders and Battles* (Novato, Calif.: Presidio Press, 1984).

Sources about the key figure on the American side are few but valuable. North Callahan, *Daniel Morgan: Ranger of the Revolution* (New York: Holt, Rinehart, and Winston, 1961); and Don Higginbotham, *Daniel Morgan: Revolutionary Rifleman* (Chapel Hill: University of North Carolina Press, 1961), are both of biographical worth. James Graham, *The Life of General Daniel Morgan* (New York: Derby and Jackson, 1856), also presents Morgan's side of the battle.

GUILFORD COURTHOUSE

In this chapter the focus has been placed almost equally on the campaign and the battle which ended it. That is why most of the following sources are cited for their useful material on both. Again I used Ward and Boatner to advantage. Other sources include John R. Alden, *The South in the Revolution, 1763–1789,* followed by George W. Greene, *The Life of Nathanael Greene,* 3 vols. (Boston: Houghton Mifflin, 1890), and Henry Lee's *Memoirs of the War in the Southern Department of the United States.* Henry Lumpkin, *From Savannah to Yorktown,* is excellent for his observation of the battle from both sides. David Schenck, *North Carolina, 1780–81: Being a History of the Invasion of the Carolinas,* recounts the campaign from the regional viewpoint. Theodore Thayer, *Nathanael Greene, Strategist of the American Revolution,* lives up to its title in describing the race to the Dan by Greene and Cornwallis. The same strategic maneuvers and the battle that followed are seen from Cornwallis's viewpoint in Franklin and Mary Wickwire's *Cornwallis: The American Adventure.*

Three historians from the National Park Service and an affiliate have studied the battle, and their analyses offer an unbiased and accurate picture. First, there is Courtland T. Reid, *Guilford Courthouse National Military Park*, Historical Handbook Series, no. 30 (Washington, D.C.: National Park Service, 1959). Second, see Charles E. Hatch, Jr., *The Battle of Guilford Courthouse* (Washington, D.C.: National Park Service, 1971). Third is Thomas E. Baker, *Another Such Victory* (Eastern Acorn Press, Eastern National Park and Monument Association, 1981). Finally, there is Tarleton's view of the British side of the battle as told by his biographer, Robert D. Bass, in *The Green Dragoon.*

THE CHESAPEAKE CAPES

Because this chapter is devoted to the naval battle that may have decided the outcome of the Revolutionary War (although the question of any battle's decisiveness is outside the purpose and scope of this book), the first sources listed deal with naval strategy and naval matters. One could best start with the most noted scholar's works: Alfred Thayer Mahan, *The Influence of Seapower upon History, 1660–1805*, U.S. edition (Englewood Cliffs, N.J.: Prentice-Hall, 1980); and his *The Major Operations of the Navies in the War of American Independence* ([1913]; reprint, New York: Greenwood Press, 1969). Following Mahan is a source on which I relied heavily throughout my writing of this chapter for its splendid description and accuracy of content in general: Harold A. Larrabee, *Decision at the Chesapeake* (New York: Clarkson N. Potter, 1964). A documentary study, edited by F. E. Chadwick, is *The Graves Papers: and Other Documents Relating to the Naval Operations of the Yorktown Campaign* (New York: Naval History Society, 1916). Burke Davis devotes a goodly amount of his study to the naval battle in his *The Campaign that Won America: The Story of Yorktown* (New York: Dial Press, 1970). A documentary, brief but very useful, is Institut Français de Washington (eds.), *Correspondence of Washington and Comte de Grasse* (Washington, D.C.: U.S. Government Printing Office, 1931). A source valuable for background, though not the battle itself, is W. M. James, *The British Navy in Adversity: A Study of the War of American Independence* (London: Longmans, Green, 1926). A useful study is Charles Lee Lewis, *Admiral de Grasse and American Independence* (Annapolis: U.S. Naval Institute, 1945; reprint, New York: Arno Press, 1980). Fletcher Pratt, *The Battles that Changed History* (New York: Hanover House, 1956), is an interesting but very brief summary. By far the most absorbing and descriptive account of the battle is found in volume 2 of Page Smith's *A New Age Now Begins*. Karl Gustaf Tornquist's *The Naval Campaigns of Count de Grasse* (Philadelphia: Swedish Colonial Society, 1942) is useful for the views of an impartial foreign naval observer.

The following sources are useful in regard to naval history and tactics. Julian S. Corbett, *Fighting Instructions, 1580–1816* (Annapolis: U.S. Naval Institute, 1971), is important for the British naval doctrine (indicated in its title) which so influenced Admiral Graves's conduct of the Battle of the Chesapeake Capes. The next source, important for the same reason, covers much more about naval tactics: Rear Admiral Samuel Shelburne Robison and Mary L. Robison, *A History of Naval Tactics from 1530 to 1930* (Annapolis: U.S. Naval Institute, 1942). Directed more toward land operations leading to and at the siege of Yorktown are Henry P. Johnston, *The Yorktown Campaign and the Surrender of Cornwallis, 1781* (New York, 1881); the Marquis de Lafayette's *Memoirs, Correspondence and Manuscripts of General Lafayette*, vol. 1, 1777–1781 (New York: Saunders and Otley, 1837), and Henry Lumpkin, *From Savannah to Yorktown*. Also of value is Theodore Thayer, *Yorktown: Campaign of Strategic Options* (Philadelphia: Lippincott, 1975). One should also include William B. Willcox, *Portrait of a General: Sir Henry Clinton and the War of Independence* (New York: Alfred A. Knopf, 1964), and Franklin and Mary Wickwire, *Cornwallis: The American Adventure*, in order to appreciate the view of the whole from the standpoint of the British high command.

Finally, there are two studies of value in examining the British strategy—and its fatal shortcomings—that led to the end of major British operations in the war: George W. Kyte, "Strategic Blunder: Lord Cornwallis Abandons the Carolinas," *The Historian*, no. 22 (February 1960); and William B. Willcox, "The British Road to Yorktown: A Study in Divided Command," *American Historical Review* 52, no. 1 (October 1946).

INDEX